D1567285

b. 1832 5154

BURL
BF
318
I636
2007

IN ORDER TO LEARN

OXFORD SERIES ON COGNITIVE MODELS AND ARCHITECTURES

Series Editor
Frank E. Ritter

Series Board
Rich Carlson
Gary Cottrell
Pat Langley
Richard M. Young

Integrated Models of Cognitive Systems
Edited by Wayne Gray

In Order to Learn:
How the Sequence of Topics Influences Learning
Edited by Frank E. Ritter, Josef Nerb,
Erno Lehtinen, and Timothy M. O'Shea

How Can the Human Mind Occur
in the Physical Universe
John R. Anderson

IN ORDER TO LEARN

How the Sequence of Topics Influences Learning

Edited by

Frank E. Ritter
Josef Nerb
Erno Lehtinen
Timothy M. O'Shea

Faculty of Education

WITHDRAWN

APR 2 2 2008

Brock University

OXFORD

UNIVERSITY PRESS

2007

OXFORD
UNIVERSITY PRESS

Oxford University Press, Inc., publishes works that further
Oxford University's objective of excellence
in research, scholarship, and education.

Oxford   New York
Auckland   Cape Town   Dar es Salaam   Hong Kong   Karachi
Kuala Lumpur   Madrid   Melbourne   Mexico City   Nairobi
New Delhi   Shanghai   Taipei   Toronto

With offices in
Argentina   Austria   Brazil   Chile   Czech Republic   France   Greece
Guatemala   Hungary   Italy   Japan   Poland   Portugal   Singapore
South Korea   Switzerland   Thailand   Turkey   Ukraine   Vietnam

Copyright © 2007 by Frank E. Ritter, Josef Nerb, Erno Lehtinen,
and Timothy M. O'Shea

Published by Oxford University Press, Inc.
198 Madison Avenue, New York, New York 10016

www.oup.com

Oxford is a registered trademark of Oxford University Press

All rights reserved. No part of this publication may be reproduced,
stored in a retrieval system, or transmitted, in any form or by any means,
electronic, mechanical, photocopying, recording, or otherwise,
without the prior permission of Oxford University Press.

Library of Congress Cataloging-in-Publication Data
In order to learn : how the sequence of topics influences learning / edited by
Frank E. Ritter . . . [et al.].
p. cm. — (Oxford series on cognitive models and architectures ; bk. #2)
Includes bibliographical references and index.
ISBN 978-0-19-517884-5
1. Learning, Psychology of.   I. Ritter, Frank E.
BF318.I636 2007
153.1'53—dc22   2006024585

1 3 5 7 9 8 6 4 2
Printed in the United States of America
on acid-free paper

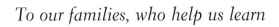
To our families, who help us learn

Foreword

David Wood

How can we explain our species' remarkable capacity to disseminate and propagate intellectual discoveries through generations and over time? For me, this is the most fundamental theoretical question that underpins and integrates the chapters offered in this volume. Deep divisions separate those theorists who have sought explanations in a selective, self-constructive, and self-evaluative learning process from theoretical positions that look to processes of spontaneous or intentional teaching as mediators of learning and rediscovery. Each of the two general positions is occupied by competing, special theories. These theories, in company with yet other approaches—ones that seek more integrated explanatory accounts of interactions between processes of learning and teaching—make for the complex conceptual and methodological landscape that this book explores.

The book's focus on the study of order effects in learning continues and advances a major methodological strategy for exploring this fundamental issue. Crudely, to the extent that the order and sequence of experience is crucial for learning and rediscovery (and to the extent that learners are unable to impose such ordering on their own learning environment), one is tempted to seek explanations in terms of an implicit or explicit pedagogy. Conversely, where order is irrelevant or of little account (or where learners are able to structure and evaluate their own environment to help optimize the learning process), one might take more seriously those theories that stress self-construction and autodidactics. Alternatively, of course, one might prefer to turn to learning theories that explain why sequential order is unimportant in the first place.

Added to the theoretical promise of research into order effects are potential educational applications afforded by a deeper understanding of sequential constraints on curriculum design. The book also contributes to this tradition with, for example, critical evaluations of and challenges to supposed "principles" of curricula organization found in contemporary educational settings.

Many chapters, the editors warn us, raise more questions than they answer. Some also generate empirical findings that either are less decisive or clear-cut than expected or seem impossible to reconcile with the hypotheses tested and theories advanced. Others generate unambiguous but intriguing and even counterintuitive outcomes that are worthy of future replication and extension into new learning contexts.

To give a flavor of these latter cases, I was struck by findings that, for me, gave rise to the following questions:

- How, when, and under what conditions is it possible for learners to learn from their own errors when they seem to lack the knowledge about how to be right?
- How can we explain a finding that implies that learning improves when learners impose their own order on the tasks to be learned—even when they change the order away from one found to benefit learning?
- How, why, and under what conditions can feedback to a learner that is actually based on a misconceived explanation of the phenomena they are attempting to understand enhance their learning more so than feedback based on a robust understanding of the phenomena?
- How should we conceptualize the nature of the relations between the processes underpinning original acts of discovery (such as the construction of a new and powerful theory) and those involved in subsequent learning (rediscovery?) by others about what has been discovered?
- Instructional support often seems to enhance learning best when it is contingent on learner problem solving, minimalist in content and offered in response to learner error or help request. This seems to apply not only to learning specific skills but also to learning strategies for regulating one's own learning. What kind of theory of learning can explain why learning should be enhanced by such attributes of instructional support?

- The idea that order effects might be optimized by sequences of tasks or assignments that become progressively harder has intuitive appeal. Under what conditions of learning might the idea prove false . . . and why?
- Why might the timing and spacing of learning activity that optimizes rapid learning be far from optimum in promoting the most enduring memorization of what has been learned?

I have drawn these questions from findings reported in this volume. These findings, when taken in company with other highlights found in the chapters that follow, do not exactly lend support to any one major theoretical position: In this sense, as the editors caution us, they spawn more questions than answers.

One has to ask whether and where the everyday connotations of natural language might mislead us to expect theoretical coherence across contexts that, though bound together under everyday uses of the verb "to learn" or "to discover," rest on quite different psychological processes, processes that might best be investigated using different empirical approaches. This book addresses such issues as an explicit part of its agenda and its rationale. The editors tell us that the volume has a self-conscious tutorial function. The inclusion of

- chapters that guide readers through the theoretical and empirical landscape
- efforts by the authors of each chapter to articulate questions, projects, or issues designed to support further thought and learning
- cross-referencing across chapters on key points

offer evidence of the authors' efforts toward these objectives. The result is a book that manages to explore the state of the art without trivializing the complexity of the challenges involved, one that also offers support to its intended readers as they try to meet the demands of such challenges.

Preface

The order that material, for acquiring both facts and skills, is presented or explored by a learner can strongly influence what is learned, how fast performance increases, and sometimes even whether the material is learned at all. This book proposes that these effects are more pervasive and important than we have previously believed. The chapters explore the foundational topics in this area at the intersection of psychology, of machine learning, of AI and cognitive modeling, and of instructional design. We inclued some case studies and numerous questions that should lead to further research projects and provide stimulation and encouragement for professionals working in areas such as education. In some ways, the chapters raise more questions than they answer.

This book will interest experimental psychology types, educational design folks, and machine learning aficionados, as well as cognitive scientists in general. The audience also inclueds graduates and practitioners of computer science (particularly AI and machine learning), psychology and cognitive science, and educational technology who are interested in order and learning. Readers may be potential researchers or informed consumers of future computing or instructional design products that support human learning or deploy machine learning techniques. This book is intended for those who are seriously interested in these issues and have some training or a strong interest in one of these fields.

Each chapter is self-contained and relatively short. They are directly accessible to at least one of the three types of readers that the book is designed for and should be useful for the others. We worked with the authors to help the book chapters integrate more like a textbook and to appear less like an edited conference collection. Many argue a surprising point of view on the importance or irrelevance of ordering or sequencing for instructional design domains and about human skill or machine learning mechanisms. Each chapter ends with clear conclusions, including generalizations, suggestions for action, and projects of various sizes. The book is also designed to be a source book for people at the early stages of their PhD. It has started to be used in this way.

HISTORY OF THE BOOK

This book arose out of a task force created as part of the Learning in Humans and Machines (LHM) project. Hans Spada was the leader of this European Science Foundation (ESF) initiative.

The research program was organized by means of five task forces on the following themes:

- representation changes in learning (Task Force 1, Kayser)
- learning with multiple goals and representations (Task Force 2, van Someren)
- learning strategies to cope with sequencing effects (Task Force 3, O'Shea and then Lehtinen)
- situated learning and transfer (Task Force 4, Bliss)
- collaborative learning (Task Force 5, Dillenbourg)

This book was discussed at several general meetings of the task force, including the first one in Milton Keynes, where Tim O'Shea put forward the idea of a highly edited, accessible book to serve as an introduction to order effects in learning. Over time, chapters were added by members of other task forces and by other prominent thinkers on learning. Thus, this book joins the other books produced by the other LHM task forces, including:

Learning in humans and machines: Towards an interdisciplinary learning science. Edited by P. Reimann and H. Spada. 1996. New York: Pergamon.

Modelling changes in understanding. Edited by D. Kayser and S. Vosniadou. 1999. New York: Pergamon.

Learning with multiple representations. Edited by M. W. van Someren, P. Reimann, H. P. A. Boshuizen, and T. de Jong. 1998. New York: Pergamon.

Learning sites: Social and technological resources for learning. Edited by J. Bliss, R. Säljö, and P. Light. 1999. New York: Pergamon.

Collaborative learning: Cognitive and computational approaches. Edited by P. Dillenbourg. 1998. New York: Pergamon.

PROGRAM STRUCTURE: THE TASK FORCES

Authors

The initial set of chapter authors were selected by the steering committee of the LHM special program to be members of a task force on the effects of task order on learning in humans and machines. Our task force's charge was to explore how the order in which learning tasks are performed affects the final outcome of learning. We were also to determine how each of the three areas of (a) psychology, (b) machine learning and cognitive modeling, and (c) instructional design can be fruitfully combined to understand and use order effects in learning tasks. Thus, cross-disciplinary results are common in the chapters. We invited members of other ESF task forces and other authors as appropriate who have a strong point of view on ordering and learning.

Other Acknowledgments

We would like to thank the members of the initial task force who were not able to contribute chapters but who contributed to our thinking and the design of the book: Eileen Scanlon, Nicolas Szilas, and Teresa del Soldato. Kurt VanLehn, Stellen Ohlsson, and Pat Langley supplied invaluable council on editing books, and Wally Feurzeig and Oliver Selfridge provided crucial support at the end of this process. Katharina Scheiter nudged us when we needed encouragement. Ying Guo offered valuable editorial assistance. We would also like to thank our senior editors, Tim O'Shea and Erno Lehtinen, for the guidance they gave us, as well as our editor at Oxford, Catharine Carlin, who was very supportive as we pulled this project together. We recommend her highly. Anonymous reviewers provided useful feedback on our book at the proposal stage, and Carlin helped us interpret and incorporate their suggestions. The graduate students in an advanced seminar on learning at Penn State (Mark Cohen, Joshua Gross, Sue Kase, Jong Kim, Andrew Reifers, and Bill Stevenson) made numerous useful suggestions on the first reading of the book as a whole. Final preparation of this book was performed with help from kind colleagues at TU/ Chemnitz and Tufts when Ritter was on a gratefully received sabbatical from Penn State. Finally, thanks to our families and friends who supported us in this endeavor. In particular, we would like to thank Josef Krems and Pat Langley for advice and comments and Nicole, Colleen, Robert, Paul, and David. Finally, *Alles in Ordnung!*

Contents

Foreword, *by David Wood* vii

Contributors xv

1. Call to Order: How Sequence
   Effects in Humans and Artificial
   Systems Illuminate Each Other 3
   Frank E. Ritter and Josef Nerb

Part I Introductory Chapters

2. Order, First Step to
   Mastery: An Introduction to
   Sequencing in Instructional
   Design 19
   Charles M. Reigeluth

3. The Necessity of Order in
   Machine Learning: Is Order
   in Order? 41
   A. Cornuéjols

4. Rules of Order: Process Models
   of Human Learning 57
   *Josef Nerb, Frank E. Ritter,
   and Pat Langley*

5. Order Out of Chaos: Order in
   Neural Networks 71
   Peter C. R. Lane

6. Getting Things in Order: Collecting
   and Analyzing Data on
   Learning 81
   *Frank E. Ritter, Josef Nerb,
   and Erno Lehtinen*

Part II Fundamental Explanations of Order: Example Models

7. An Example Order for Cognitive Skill Acquisition 95
   Alexander Renkl and Robert K. Atkinson

8. An Ordered Chaos: How Do Order Effects Arise in a Cognitive Model? 107
   Fernand Gobet and Peter C. R. Lane

9. Learning in Order: Steps of Acquiring the Concept of the Day/Night Cycle 119
   Katharina Morik and Martin Mühlenbrock

10. Timing Is in Order: Modeling Order Effects in the Learning of Information 137
    Philip I. Pavlik Jr.

11. The Effects of Order: A Constraint-Based Explanation 151
    Stellan Ohlsson

Part III Getting In and Out of Order: Techniques and Examples From Education and Instructional Design

12. Getting Out of Order: Avoiding Lesson Effects Through Instruction 169
    Kurt VanLehn

13. Order or No Order: System Versus Learner Control in Sequencing Simulation-Based Scientific Discovery Learning 181
    Janine Swaak and Ton de Jong

14. Making Your Own Order: Order Effects in System- and User-Controlled Settings for Learning and Problem Solving 195
    Katharina Scheiter and Peter Gerjets

Part IV Conclusions

15. All Is in Order 215
    John Sweller

Epilogue: Let's Educate 225
   Oliver G. Selfridge

Author Index 227
Subject Index 233

Contributors

Robert K. Atkinson
Arizona State University

A. Cornuéjols
Laboratoire de Recherche en Informatique (LRI)
Université Paris Sud

Ton de Jong
Faculty of Behavioral Sciences
University of Twente

Peter Gerjets
Knowledge Media Research Center
University of Tübingen

Fernand Gobet
Department of Human Sciences
Brunel University, London

Peter C. R. Lane
Department of Computer Science
University of Hertfordshire

Pat Langley
Computational Learning Laboratory
Center for the Study of Language and Information
Stanford University

Erno Lehtinen
Department of Educational Sciences
Turku University

Katharina Morik
University of Dortmund

Martin Mühlenbrock
German Research Center for Artificial Intelligence

Josef Nerb
Department of Psychology
University of Education, Freiburg

Stellan Ohlsson
Department of Psychology
University of Illinois at Chicago

Tim O'Shea
Old College
University of Edinburgh

Philip I. Pavlik Jr.
Human-Computer Interaction Institute
Carnegie Mellon University

Charles M. Reigeluth
School of Education
Indiana University

Alexander Renkl
Department of Psychology
University of Freiburg

Frank E. Ritter
College of Information Sciences and Technology
Pennsylvania State University

Oliver G. Selfridge
MIT Media Lab and BBN Technologies

Katharina Scheiter
Department of Applied Cognitive Psychology
and Media Psychology
University of Tübingen

Janine Swaak
BO 4 Business Consulting

John Sweller
School of Education
University of New South Wales

Kurt VanLehn
Computer Science Department and
the Learning Research and Development
Center
University of Pittsburgh

David Wood
School of Psychology
University of Nottingham

IN ORDER TO LEARN

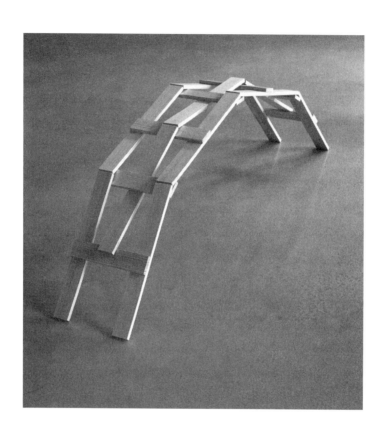

Chapter 1

Call to Order: How Sequence Effects in Humans and Artificial Systems Illuminate Each Other

Frank E. Ritter
Josef Nerb

We start by describing and defining order effects and how they can be further developed. We introduce the first five chapters that provide overviews of the relevant areas of instructional design, machine learning, cognitive models (symbolic and connectionist), and human data. The second group of five chapters presents information processing models that predict order effects and, in many cases, provide supporting data. The final group of three chapters illustrates order effects empirically obtained (or not obtained) in educational settings. A concluding chapter pulls together the results and calls for further, more detailed exploration of order effects by using techniques and data across, rather than simply within, the relevant areas. The chapters in this book show that the order in which material is presented can strongly influence what is learned in a variety of domains in both humans and theoretical models of learning. From these chapters we compile suggestions for improving learning through the development of better sequences of learning materials, and we highlight some of the numerous questions that the chapters raise.

In medieval Europe, as part of a performance, artists built a bridge similar to the one shown in Figure 1.1. Building this bridge without nails or glue was a spectacular beginning to the performance and indeed an artistic one, for the artists then used the bridge as a stage. Leonardo da Vinci first analyzed the bridge's construction and discovered the design principles behind it. In so doing he moved the bridge from the realm of art into the realm of science: The bridge was explained by means of scientific methods so that its construction principles could be reused and not just imitated. Through this process the bridge's construction moved from art to technique.

ORDER STARTS HERE: INSTRUCTION FROM ART TO TECHNIQUE

A similar process is being performed today in instructional science; we want to uncover basic principles of instruction and learning that can be reused in different settings, moving instructional ordering from art to technique. Taking again the bridge example, what matters for the construction of the bridge is the right sequence in putting the pieces together. The correct sequence leads to success—a bridge; an incorrect sequence leads to failure—a heap of sticks.

This is true for learning as well. The order in which material is presented can strongly influence what is

FIGURE 1.1. The nailless bridge.

learned, how fast performance increases, and sometimes even whether the material is learned at all. This is true for both skills and facts and remains true whether the material is presented by an instructor or explored alone by a learner. The analogy to the bridge continues to hold true: In the same way as da Vinci's analysis of the bridge's construction moved it from art to science, as we discover the underlying principles of the order effects in learning, we move instruction away from idiosyncratic expression and closer to a controlled and predictable science.

This book presents the case that order effects are more pervasive and important than they have previously been treated, and it explores how learning order affects the final outcome of learning and how methods and findings from the range of cognate disciplines that study learning can be fruitfully combined to understand and improve learners' performance. We also include case studies and numerous questions that should lead to further research projects. These case studies and questions provide food for thought for professionals working in these areas, including professionals in education.

Order effects in learning brings together foundational topics and research in psychology, machine learning, AI, cognitive modeling, and instructional design. As a result, cross-disciplinary combinations and impact are common features in this book's chapters. To paraphrase Stellan Ohlsson's thoughts (from Chapter 11) on the implications of this research for all areas relevant to learning:

Although several ordering principles for instruction are well established, such as the easy-before-hard principle, the existence of ordering effects in human learning poses more specific questions for research areas interested in learning. For example, in AI and machine learning, do different learning mechanisms make divergent predictions with respect to type and magnitude of ordering effects? If so, observations of such effects might turn out to be a hitherto underutilized source of empirical constraints on psychological learning theories and cognitive models. Is one combination of learning mechanisms more or less robust than another with respect to the sequencing of learning experiences? Better understanding of the relative strengths and weaknesses of different combinations of mechanisms might inform the design of machine learning systems. Finally, a deeper theory of ordering effects might allow us to go beyond the easy-before-hard principle for the sequencing of instruction.

In this chapter, after defining order effects and the intended audience for this book, we describe the chapters to introduce them, make some preliminary conclusions, and note open problems.

Definition of Order Effects

The definition this book uses when referring to order effects[1] is that they are differences in performance that arise from the same set of material being presented to learners in different orders (Langley, 1995). This strict definition of order effects explicitly excludes sets that are only nearly equivalent yet not equal. Multiple presentations of the same item are allowed, but both orders have to have the same number of presentations for them to be equivalent. This definition is consistent with its use in other areas (e.g., belief revision; see Hogarth & Einhorn, 1992).

Several chapters offer extensions to this basic definition of order. For example, Phil Pavlik Jr. reminds us in Chapter 10 that the times between presentations of stimuli are also important. Another extension is the exploration of near-order effects.

The Book's Intended Audience

Order effects are important to any field that explores learning, so we have this book to be accessible to a wide variety of readers. It should be directly accessible and of interest to researchers, practitioners, and students in the areas of cognitive science, machine learning and AI, and instructional design. It should also be useful for many related fields, including cognitive psychology, intelligent agents, and educational psychology. Teachers interested in learning theory should also find this book interesting and accessible. For example, many of these chapters and concepts speak to how to teach multiple-column subtraction and multiplication, including the multiple methods and sequences for teaching this early math skill currently in use in classrooms.

THE ORDER OF CHAPTERS

As this is a book about order, it should not surprise the reader that we had several discussions about how to order the chapters. We hope that the order we chose supports your reading. Several of the chapters show that high-knowledge learners will reorder material to suit their own needs, so we expect you will do so if necessary. To facilitate this adaptation process, the chapters begin with abstracts summarizing their contents. It is, however, important to keep in mind that many of the chapters interrelate and correlate, so you will also benefit from an exploratory reading process.

Orders of Order

One way to characterize and order the chapters is based on how they are tied to the various fields they address. This order is useful as a way to suggest how the fields are related. As a way to organize a book, however, it is does not work particularly well because it does not suggest where to begin or end. Research has also shown that the best way to organize instructional material is not necessarily the way it is organized in a learner's mental representation (McKendree, Reader, & Hammond, 1995).

We chose to organize the chapters into four groups: (a) introductory chapters that provide tutorial material, (b) chapters that describe models of learning that can provide explanations and predictions of order effects, (c) chapters that provide examples from educational settings, where students and teachers work to avoid bad orders and where order can be improved, and, finally, (d) a concluding chapter that summarizes the book.

The chapters are summarized in Table 1.1, which may help you with ordering your own reading. The third column, Fields, notes the most important fields that the chapter draws on, applies to, or both. Because most chapters have impact in several areas, in most cases these labels could have easily been shifted to similar fields such as educational psychology, artificial intelligence, and cognitive psychology, so they should be read somewhat broadly.

When a chapter speaks to a single task or uses several large examples, the Task column notes the tasks examined as an aide-mémoire; when a chapter reviews several tasks, it is noted in the Task column as "Review." While each chapter is based on at least one theory, the Model column indicates which chapters report computational models. Explicit instructional models for designing instructional sequences are noted as "IM." The Data column indicates where human data are presented in extended form. The Effect Size column indicates the largest effect size of different orders on learning reported in the chapter, from either theoretical predictions or empirical measurements as compared with the mean performance. This number may be one of several and may be approximate.

TABLE 1.1. The chapters, their authors, fields, approaches, and significant effect sizes (in percentages)

Title	Authors	Fields	Task	Model	Data	Effect Size
Introductory Chapters						
2. Order, first step to mastery	Reigeluth	InsDes	Review	No	No	NA
3. The necessity of order in machine learning	Cornuéjols	ML	Review	Several	No	NG
4. Rules of order	Nerb, Ritter, & Langley	CogSci	Review, choice reaction time	Simple Soar	No	25%
5. Order out of chaos	Lane	CogSci	Review, image recognition, and language learning	ART SRN	No	25% to ∞
6. Getting things in order	Ritter, Nerb, & Lehtinen	All	Review	No	No	NA
Models of Order						
7. An example order for cognitive skill acquisition	Renkl & Atkinson	InsDes	Instructional systems and InsDes	IM	Review	13%
8. An ordered chaos	Gobet & Lane	CogSci/ML	Grammar learning	EPAM	No	1,000%
9. Learning in order	Morik & Mühlenbrock	CogSci/ML	Learning the day/night cycle	Yes	Yes	30% to ∞
10. Timing is in order	Pavlik	CogSci	Word learning	ACT-R	Yes	11%
11. The effects of order	Ohlsson	CogSci/InsDes	Counting	HS	No	8%–223%
Empirical Studies						
12. Getting out of order	VanLehn	CogSci/InsDes	Multiplication	No	Yes	36%
13. Order or no order	Swaak & De Jong	InsDes	Electrical circuits	No	Yes	NS
14. Making your own order	Scheiter & Gerjets	InsDes/CogSci	Word problems (algebra)	IM	Yes	15%
Summary						
15. All is in order	Sweller	All	Review, paired associates	CLT	No	>70%

InsDes is instructional design. ML is machine learning. CogSci is Cognitive Science. NG indicates not given. NS is not significant. NA is not applicable.

Table 1.1 supports the conclusions that we draw below, for example, that order effects appear in many tasks. The table also shows that order effects are often large.

Section I. Introductory Chapters

There are five introductory chapters. They present the major concepts and areas, including instructional design, machine learning, cognitive science as represented by cognitive models, and empirical data gathering and preliminary analyses to study order effects. These chapters have been designed to be accessible to a wide range of readers.

2. *Order, First Step to Mastery*

Reigeluth's chapter provides an entry point for interested readers into the instructional design literature and introduces issues from this field. It shows how sequence effects relate to instruction and provides some introduction to an important context where order matters. Reigeluth reviews several of the major instructional design techniques for ordering instructional material, based on the nature of the content and their interrelationships. The chapter describes and discusses useful approaches to ordering material that fit the needs of instructional design in the field. These approaches support the development of new instructional methods beyond the ones presented here and help validate, illustrate, and teach these design principles.

The chapter gives special focus to the Elaboration Theory of Instruction, which was developed by Reigeluth in the last two decades. This theory provides holistic alternatives to the parts-to-whole sequencing that are quite typical of both education and training and synthesizes several recent ideas about sequencing instruction into a single coherent framework. The chapter closes with some general guidelines and principles for sequencing, organized by the order in which decisions need to be made.

3. The Necessity of Order in Machine Learning: Is Order in Order?

Cornuéjols provides a detailed introduction and overview of the theories from machine learning and introduces some of the basic theoretical concepts and models from computational studies of learning from the machine learning area of computer science. He presents ideas and directions of research that can answer questions that arise from order effects and shows that some of the results of how these models work may have significance for and counterparts in related disciplines that have an interest in learning and education.

Cornuéjols also notes some interesting new approaches in machine learning, including the concepts of helpful teachers and active learners. This chapter, like those that follow, concludes with a discussion of open research avenues, as well as questions designed to be used for class projects related to order effects in machine learning. A recent review (Selfridge, 2006) provides a related set of open questions in this area.

4. Rules of Order: Process Models of Human Learning

Nerb, Ritter, and Langley present the argument that, to understand sequential effects on learning in humans, we will have to have a rather complete theory of cognition—complete enough to perform a task like humans and to learn while doing so. Theories like this have typically been called *process models*. They are usually broken down into two components, architecture (the aspects of the model that do not change between tasks) and knowledge (the aspects that do change between tasks) (Newell, 1990). Where models have been used to understand sequential behavior

and sequence effects on learning, they have proved to be very powerful. This chapter describes a simple, abstract model of a simple task that shows how an optimal order can lead to significantly (25%) faster learning than a poor order. This chapter also presents a list of effects in models of cognition that can give rise to order effects.

Although powerful, using models to study order effects remains difficult to apply routinely. Nerb et al. report some history and results on making this approach more tractable for application by presenting the idea of abstracted models.

5. Order Out of Chaos: Order in Connectionist Models

Lane provides details about order effects in neural networks, a commonly used modeling approach. The chapter examines two networks in detail, the Adaptive Resonance Theory (ART) architecture and Jeff Elman's recurrent networks. The ART model shows that about a 25% difference in recognition rates can arise from using different orders. Elman's recurrent network shows that, with the wrong order, a task might not even be learnable. This chapter also discusses why these effects arise, which is important for understanding the impact and claims of computational models (VanLehn, Brown, & Greeno, 1984).

6. Getting Things in Order: Collecting and Analyzing Data on Learning

Ritter, Nerb, and Lehtinen provide a tutorial on the types of data that have been used to study sequence effects, some of the data collection methodologies that have been and will continue to be used because they are necessary to study order effects, and how to use model output as data. They start by introducing the basic measurements typically used in experimental psychology, such as reaction times and errors. This chapter also examines the feasibility of using protocol data that, although used infrequently, offer a rich record to study order effects. These types of data include sequential records of subjects' eye movements, subjects' thoughts spoken aloud as they solve problems (verbal protocols), and records of task actions.

Ritter et al. also look at how these data can be "cooked down" into theories, which can then be broken down into static and dynamic process models. Static descriptions, such as simple grammars and Markov models, depict the shape of the data. Process models perform the task that a person does in a manner that a person does and so provide a more dynamic description. Process models are inherently not only more powerful but also more difficult to use. The chapter concludes with a brief discussion on using model output as data.

Section II. Fundamental Explanations of Order: Example Models

The next section of the book describes five models that predict order effects in a variety of domains. We present the models before the data chapters: As theories, the models have primacy over data. As summaries of data, they may help interpret the later, more data-oriented chapters.

7. An Example Order for Cognitive Skill Acquisition

Renkl and Atkinson review several learning theories that address the stages of skill acquisition, offer a model of instruction ordering to foster cognitive skill acquisition, and suggest some ways to provide better support for learning based on their model. In five experiments that explicitly test fading and example-problem pairs (Atkinson, Renkl, & Merrill, 2003, experiment 1; Renkl, Atkinson, & Große, 2004, experiment 2; Renkl, Atkinson, Maier, & Staley, 2002, three experiments), they found on average 13% more correct answers with better instructional orders.

Their review is used to create an approach to teaching by example, which is related to the literature on learning from self-explanations with decreasing levels of support as learners become more expert. Renkl and Atkinson's model is based on initially providing worked-out examples and gradually increasing the amount of work the learner is expected to perform, moving the learner toward working independently.

8. An Ordered Chaos: How Do Order Effects Arise in a Cognitive Model?

Gobet and Lane describe the details of EPAM, a theory of learning that arose early in the development of AI and cognitive science and has continued to be developed. Since its creation in the early 1960s, EPAM has been applied to a wide range of problems. Gobet and Lane describe EPAM as a type of unsupervised learning; that is, it learns without feedback as to what to learn or what is correct. They examine the application of a current version of EPAM to language acquisition, which shows that rather large order effects are possible. Their detailed examination of this learning mechanism allows them to find some lessons for instructional design, including the desirability of highlighting salient features of the material.

9. Learning in Order: Steps of Acquiring the Concept of the Day/Night Cycle

Morik and Mühlenbrock present a detailed model of children's explanations of where the sun goes at night. Knowledge of the day/night cycle is one of the first relatively complex sets of knowledge that all people acquire. Their model shows how children progress through a lattice of possible explanations (a lattice is a partially but not completely ordered set).

The task and data modeled offer an excellent basis for the investigation of order effects, with implications for modeling scientific discovery and for learning in general. It shows that some transitions are particularly difficult, that some transitions require using incomplete or incorrect knowledge, and that not all transitions are possible. Their work also shows that the order of learning can make a large difference in the amount that has to be learned and, perhaps more important, unlearned. Better orders provide about a 30% reduction in facts that have to be learned. These findings make suggestions about the instructional complexity that children and, presumably, learners in general can handle and about the use and importance of intermediate stages of learning.

10. Timing Is in Order: Modeling Order Effects in the Learning of Information

Pavlik examines another aspect of learning sequences by presenting a model that accounts for the effects of different times between stimuli presentations across subjects. Pavlik's model is tested within a simple language tutor that adjusts the spacing of material based on how well the stimuli are learned. This system does not strictly maintain the number of presentations but works to maintain equivalent presentation strength. This system is interesting in its own right because it shows that performance can be improved by reordering sequences with multiple presentations to provide more optimal spacing of stimuli.

Pavlik's model predicts that more widely spaced presentations lead to better overall learning. Finding the optimal spacing allows the learner to approach maximum learning with minimal time cost, but at a higher total-time cost. The model's predictions were confirmed experimentally: The model predicts about 11% better learning with the tutor (66% correct for the widest spaced vs. 73% for optimized spacing). The tutorial system led to a 12% average increase in performance for the optimized spacing condition, depending upon condition and phase of the study.

11. The Effects of Order: A Constraint-Based Explanation

Ohlsson presents a computational model that shows how information migrates from declarative to procedural knowledge and provides a powerful new learning mechanism for machine-learning algorithms. Ohlsson uses his model to examine the effects of learning three different counting tasks. The model predicts order effects that vary in several dimensions, including the number of times the model has to revise its knowledge and how long it will take to learn. Although some of these effects are quite large within a subtask, the overall effect is muted by other aspects of the task, including interaction. This model suggests that the complexity of a task's constraints is important for computing transfer between similar tasks. The model's behavior has been compared to human performance, and a general summary is provided.

Section III. Getting In and Out of Order: Techniques and Examples From Education and Instructional Design

The three chapters in this section explore order effects from experiments that represent educational settings. These experiments use a variety of techniques to look at how learners and their teachers modify and take advantage of the order in which learning materials are presented.

12. Getting Out of Order: Avoiding Order Effects Through Instruction

VanLehn reports two experiments that test his felicity-conditions hypothesis that people learn best if a task is taught one subprocedure per lesson. In these experiments, children were taught multiplication skills by a human tutor. Although there was a slight trend that presenting one topic per lesson led to fewer errors than presenting two topics, the more important finding is that there is better transfer to new problems when teaching two subprocedures per lesson—about one-third fewer errors at test (0.309 vs. 0.197 mean confusion rate per problem at transfer).

These results suggest that it is crucial to learn when to apply a particular element of knowledge. Lessons that deliberately change the element of knowledge needed from problem to problem are more difficult for learners but can enhance the learner's ability to apply different types of knowledge and to transfer their learning. This effect also suggests why textbooks have evolved to use one disjunct per lesson and is also consistent with good practice in system documentation (Weiss, 1991). This study further suggests not only that teaching multiple items per lesson is safer if there is someone to help remove any confusion but also that some small amount of reordering by a teacher can help the learner to compensate for poor orders.

13. Order or No Order: System Versus Learner Control in Sequencing Simulation-Based Scientific Discovery Learning

Swaak and de Jong present an experiment that examines how students study with an electrical circuit tutoring system that allows them to examine the relationship between current and voltage sources. Some learners were constrained in how they ordered the instructional materials, while others were allowed to choose their own order.

No major differences were found between the two groups for a range of measures and analyses, suggesting that further studies should include additional measures about what is learned besides definitions. The results also suggest that presenting model progressions and assignments will allow learners to choose their own order.

14. Making Your Own Order: Order Effects in System- and User-Controlled Settings for Learning and Problem Solving

Scheiter and Gerjets explore how order influences learning and transfer in algebra word problems and how students reorder the problems. They present two experiments in which learners were given different orders; in the second experiment learners could also reorder their problems.

Sequences that varied the structure of problems helped students learn more than sequences that varied only the cover story, suggesting that forcing learners to differentiate the types of problems fostered learning (cf. VanLehn, Chapter 12, this volume). Learners who reordered their problems learned more, but only if they had sufficient domain knowledge, suggesting that allowing better learners to reorder their learning tasks might lead to deeper processing and thus more learning.

Section IV. Conclusions

15. All Is in Order

Sweller provides a useful overview and discussion of the chapters. He discusses and amplifies the results of each chapter using Cognitive Complexity Theory, a theory of how learning is constrained by the task's load on working memory capacity, and shows the effects that working memory load can have on learning with respect to order. The old maxim of ordering your reading of a text—that of first reading the introduction and then the conclusions—might be applied with some good effect in this case.

THEMES WITHIN ORDER

The chapters in this book provide lessons for work in cognitive science, education, and machine learning, including AI, and combining these areas to pursue theories of learning. Order effects occur in many places and ways, both predicted and observed, and also on a number of levels of analyses, from single problems and stimuli to larger structures, such as hour-long lessons. They occur in a wide range of theories, including machine learning (Cornuéjols) and connectionist theories (Lane), larger-scale learning theories like EPAM (Gobet & Lane), and constraint-based models (Ohlsson), and they do so for a variety of reasons. These effects have been established not only in the theories and data reported here but also in prior reports of research.

Order effects are useful phenomena that help us explore, understand, and choose between learning

mechanisms. Indeed, we can all imagine orders so bad that, as Morik and Mühlenbrock's and Gobet and Lane's models predict, the material cannot be learned at all because learners simply give up! Reordering thus offers a way to test and improve instructional design. We take up first the lessons and then the future research problems raised by these chapters.

Significant Order Effects Are Predicted

Models in this book predict that the order in which materials are presented has a considerable impact on learning. With the ART model, Lane demonstrated up to a 25% difference in error rate. Ohlsson found differences of about 25% on transfer between learning different ways to count. Using a model based on an early Soar model, Nerb, Ritter, and Langley showed that different orders could lead to a 25% difference in learning. With the EPAM model, Gobet and Lane have approximately a 25% difference in the percent correct between possible orders (approximately 30% correct for one order and less then 5% for the worst order), which represents almost an order of magnitude difference in performance. Their model also illustrates how different orders vary depending upon their use—retraining vs. learning for the first time. Morik and Mühlenbrock's model of learning the day/night cycle predicts differences of more than 30% on some measures between different orders, which suggests real differences in learning and time to learn.

Previous models have also found order effects. Ohlsson (1992) created a model of subtraction using HS (the same architecture reported in Chapter 11) to examine different methods of performing and learning subtraction. For subtraction, HS predicted that about 8% more procedural knowledge would be learned using one approach. Although this difference might not appear to be significant in an instructional setting, it is quite interesting that both approaches to learning subtraction were very sensitive to the training materials and their order. HS predicted that differences in learning and performance between combinations of approaches and training materials could be as great as 230%. Indeed, early work on modeling the instruction of subtraction focused on how to order tasks so that learners would always learn the correct rules rather than the buggy ones (Brown & Burton, 1980). Similar results would be shown by Selfridge's (2006) Count system.

Order Effects Are Found Empirically

Studies with people show similar effects of good and bad orders—order effects appear in a variety of materials and for a variety of subjects and tasks. As the effect-size column in Table 1.1 repeatedly shows, the order effects demonstrated in this volume are significant; they are large enough, in fact, to be important in most learning situations. Several of the chapters show how order effects can be tested and how one can find them in empirical data.

Pavlik (Chapter 10) found an 11% difference in percent correct at test in subjects trained with a better, dynamic schedule. VanLehn (Chapter 12) examined a wide range of measures for two orders that differed in several ways and showed errors on later transfer ranging from 15% to 52% across orders. Scheiter and Gerjets (Chapter 14) found differences in performance on a variety of measures, such as error rate, where the better order had 10–15% fewer errors.

While we examine order effects in educational and learning settings, order effects can also occur in other areas. To choose one example, reviews and models of order effects in belief updating (Baumann & Krems, 2002; Hogarth & Einhorn, 1992; Wang, Johnson, & Zhang, 2006) find effects similar to those presented in these chapters (i.e., 5–20% differences between orders).

Previous studies of order effects are consistent with the results presented in this volume and show that presentation order can have long-term effects. For example, Sweller (1976 and reviewed in his chapter) showed that the order for teaching word pairs could improve the rate of mastery to only 5.9 trials for each pair from 8.4. Moreover, when transferred to the alternate stimuli set, the group exposed to the better order learned the "bad" pairs in slightly more than one trial, whereas the group first exposed to the bad order needed almost three trials to learn the "good" pairs. Depending on the measure chosen (learning, transfer, total), the better order improved learning time by 31–71%.

Order Effects Can Help Test Theories

Because order effects are both significant and pervasive, they can provide insights into the architecture of cognition. For example, simple normative descriptions of belief updating, such as those based on Bayes's theorem, do not exhibit order effects. And yet order effects often occur. The chapters that present models (Cornuéjols; Nerb, Ritter, & Langley; Lane; Gobet & Lane; Morik and Mühlenbrock; Pavlik; Ohlsson) demonstrate how order effects can arise from cognitive architectures. Other models, for example, UECHO (Wang et al., in press), use order effects to test models as well. Confirming these order effects empirically will be important for building and testing cognitive architectures that learn.

Order Effects Have More Aspects, Including Timing

The models and studies presented here used many measures of learning and transfer. Examining the types of problems presented in more detail, as well as learners' performance on the component subtasks, will be important for understanding both learning and the effects of sequences.

We have seen that the concept of order effects in learning can be developed further in several ways. For example, Pavlik (Chapter 10) explores the pace at which items are presented, underscoring the importance of the temporal dimension. Further areas remain to be explored, including how different orders of presentation and variations in timing between items presented can cause both short- and long-term effects on particular types of learning and the relationship between stress and learning.

Several chapters approach the effects of order on learning by examining more details of the problems involved in problem-solving sequences. Scheiter and Gerjets (Chapter 14), for example, examine how varying the surface features of consecutive problems affects learning. In this way they are able to show how several orders of problems with the same surface features, but with different deep structures, have different effects on learning. Reigeluth (Chapter 2) examines scope and sequencing.

Gobet and Lane note how the learner's representation of information can influence predictions of order effects. Because EPAM has a hierarchical representation of knowledge, it appears to be more susceptible to order effects than systems with flat knowledge representations (like Kieras's CCT, explained below). Gobet and Lane also suggest that problem-solving tasks, such as many modeled by ACT-R, may be less susceptible to order effects.

Order Effects Can Be Mitigated

On the other hand, mitigation or avoidance of poor orders by learners and their instructors is both possible and important. Indeed, for some models and tasks, order effects are not even predicted and are not observed.

Several chapters found that both learners and instructors have ways to mitigate the effects of a bad stimuli order. Reigeluth (Chapter 2) suggests that, for short lessons, order can often be ignored. For longer lessons, Scheiter and Gerjets (Chapter 14) and Swaak and de Jong (Chapter 13) found that learners often reorder to improve learning. VanLehn (Chapter 12) found that instructors can help with reordering. Reordering might in the future be seen as a type of feedback to instructors: Sequences that learners prefer to reorder can be considered as a place for improvement. Even Pólya (1945) suggested reordering problem subtasks as a heuristic for solving difficult problems.

Scheiter and Gerjets (Chapter 14) also found that knowledge (expertise) mitigated bad orders. Indeed, the people with the most knowledge—the instructors setting the order—are the least effected by poor order; as a result, instructors may need advice about ordering if they are to overcome their own perspectives enough to benefit those they are instructing.

This finding that people with more expertise are less effected by order is consistent with several of the theories reported in this book. Cognitive load theory (Sweller, Chapter 15) and Morik and Mühlenbrock's theory (Chapter 9) both explain that order effects might be limited in relatively simple transitions from one state of knowledge to the next. For both of these theories, order effects occur only when the transition from one knowledge state to the next is particularly complex.

The lack of order effects can also be seen in previous models and show us where order effects may be avoided, for example, Cognitive Complexity Theory (CCT) and studies testing it (Bovair, Kieras, & Polson, 1990; Kieras & Bovair, 1986). In several studies users were taught to use text editors for several tasks in different orders (AB and BA), and the CCT model predicted transfer between the editors and the tasks based on how much knowledge the two task/editor combinations shared using production rules as the unit of measure. While CCT predicted that different tasks would take different amounts of time to perform and learn, it also predicted that there would be no order effects. That is, for any order of tasks, CCT predicted that the user would end up with the same knowledge. As it turned out, their data supported these predictions (with a high correlation); the users appeared to learn the same amount across orders. Thus, for text editing, the order of materials does not appear to influence learning.

Order Effects Can Be Applied to Improve Learning

As noted earlier, the order in which learning material is presented can have large effects both theoretically and experimentally. For the education of large populations, the savings are significant enough that it will often be worthwhile to compute the optimal order rather than to guess it. Where this computation is not possible, allowing or encouraging students to find their own order appears to lead to better performance, so in cases with high-knowledge learners, reordering should also be encouraged.

Table 1.2 provides an informal summary of the design rules arising from the material presented in this book. Many of the conclusions are tentative and so our rules are really heuristics and are neither final nor complete. This limitation is not surprising given the complexity of how and why order effects can arise.

Future Research: Questions Within the Core Areas

The work reported in this book allows us to identify some meta-issues related to order effects in each of these core areas of psychology, machine learning, and instructional design. We also note several topics for further research within these core areas.

There are many high-level questions in psychology, machine learning, and instructional design that can be kept in mind while reading this book. We introduce just a few of them here (and we thank Tim O'Shea for suggesting these meta-questions). For example, for psychology, can we discover new ordering effects in human learning? Can we understand when they occur and what factors influence human learners? How do humans vary with respect to order effects?

For machine meaning, can we develop flexible and powerful incremental learning algorithms that have benign or minimal ordering effects? How do algorithm complexity, speed, and space requirements influence order effects?

TABLE 1.2. Heuristics for Ordering Learning Materials

1. Be concerned about order only when there is a strong relationship among the topics with respect to the time to learn.
2. Consider the scope and context of what you are teaching.
3. Start with comprehensible but small items to learn (define the language).
4. Progress from smaller to larger items or examples, but learners also need to know about the big picture and to stay motivated.
5. Keep in mind the amount of novelty and the amount to learn, and attempt to maximize these without overwhelming the learners.
6. Avoid introducing so much new material such that the learners are overwhelmed or their motivation decreases.
7. Keep in mind both the time and/or repetitions it takes to learn an object or skill and the spacing of practice.
8. Switch between types of problems, or, if you want to encourage the learners to transfer and apply the knowledge later, make them choose which knowledge to apply.
9. Constrain novice learners more than more expert learners. Allow better learners to reorder where they think it is appropriate, and support them with information about the materials.

And finally, for instructional design, what is an optimal order for human learners? Can we determine that order experimentally or computationally, and how can we create tools to help compute that optimal order automatically and even tailor it to individual learners? What is the space of instructional-design activities in which ordering can be safely ignored?

There are also important areas where theories of learning will have to be extended. Each of these areas, and particularly psychology and instructional design, will need to consider the impact of motivation and emotion on learning. While this consideration is not directly addressed in the book, changes in emotion and in motivation can arise from different orders. It is important to remember that whereas most machine learning algorithms are quite content to continue to work on impossible problems, human learners can become demotivated or bored depending on the order of problems, even when these problems are solvable. Instructional design and psychology are both interested in these topics.

The relationship between stress and workload is also an important factor in learning. We know that, under stress (such as that brought about by high workload), the order of subtask performance changes (e.g., Kuk, Arnold, & Ritter, 1999). VanLehn (Chapter 12) and Swaak and de Jong (Chapter 13) suggest that, when faced with bad orders, learners will reorder their tasks. The changes seen in the order of subtask performance under stress and the changes that learners make when faced with bad orders may be related. It is important to keep in mind that learners who are af-

fected by external stressors (e.g., unsupportive educational environments) are likely to behave differently, and they may be more sensitive to order.

As briefly reviewed by Sweller (Chapter 15), working memory capacity influences learning, and we know that anxiety and worry can influence working memory capacity (e.g., Ashcraft, 2002; Beilock & Carr, 2005). As a result, orders that increase stress will be worse, and some orders may be less susceptible to the effects of stress. To optimize learning, perhaps we will also have to modify the order to support users who are inclined to rearrange subtasks, or we may have to encourage a finer-grained view of order to help learners order their subtasks within each problem.

Finally, we will have to examine long-term objectives and influences. The chapters here examine mostly direct and short-term effects and results. Different orders may also have longer-term and more subtle effects, including the quality of long-term performance, long-term learning, transfer to different problem types, short- and long-term motivation, and other qualities yet to be measured.

Back to the Bridge: Future Research Questions Linking These Areas

There remain at least three metaquestions that link the relevant disciplines studying learning, and each chapter addresses at least one of them. These questions help unify the chapters, so that readers interested in or knowledgeable about multiple relevant fields may find insights for their own use. These questions are:

(a) Can we develop machine-learning algorithms that model the effects of order on humans? Several chapters provide steps toward an answer to this question, showing how some cognitive architecture mechanisms give rise to order effects. (Similarly, these architectures must avoid effects where none exist.)

(b) Can we use theories from AI and data from cognitive psychology to develop approaches to instructional design that take advantage of human ordering effects? This is clearly one of the broadest possible practical applications of this research, if not the most important.

(c) How do interfaces and learning environments affect the individual's need to consider order when organizing attempts at learning? Or is the rapid progress in computing environments (and cheap access to them) going to make this issue moot through improved interfaces alone?

In her poem "Girder," Nan Cohen noted that bridges lead in two directions. We hope that this book serves as a bridge between these areas and in doing so helps knowledge move more effectively between these increasingly related fields.

PROBLEMS IN ORDER

Each chapter includes a short list of problems for the reader to pursue. These problems support the use of this book as a textbook and as a primer for someone preparing to do a PhD (or similarly sized research project) on the topic of order effects. We have attempted to make these lists uniform, but because of the subject matter they vary in size and approach, which is appropriate. Some of the problems are short and could be done within a small class project; others are large enough to be a class-length research project or even a springboard into a PhD project. Some are probably large enough to span a career. Many of the problems are novel and open ended and could lead to practical (and publishable) research. Some problems have already been used in this way, and indeed all of the chapters ask more interesting questions than can be answered currently, suggesting this will be an important area for further research. Here are our introductory problems:

1. How should these chapters be ordered? Come up with an order before you read the book. Compare this order to the one you create after you skim and then read the book.

2. What are important order effects in your area of study? As you read the book, summarize the chapters and their references with respect to your area of study.

3. Review the literature in your field with respect to one of the questions within the core areas or the metaquestions linking the areas mentioned earlier.

4. Design a pilot study to study one of the meta-issues noted earlier.

5. Explore one of the range of relevant issues not covered in this book, such as how order interacts with other factors (e.g., development, fatigue, individual differences in working memory capacity, gender, etc.). Prepare either a short review or small pilot study with humans or models to examine such differences. A computational pilot study might be fruitfully done by using an abstracted model rather than a computer program. That is, you might not have to run an ACT-R or a PDP program to understand its predictions.

6. Examine the results from Sweller's (1976) paper on pair-associate learning. Consider how they might have arisen, and come up with four possible mechanisms. Note three places in education where this effect and the possible mechanisms could be applied.

7. Design a software program you could teach something. Consider what representations would be required to start learning and which ones would be learned. As a larger project, consider implementing it (e.g., like the Count program referenced in Selfridge, 2006), or consider the application of such a program to teach teachers and learners about learning. (Many of the chapters provide additional insights into this question.)

How to Order a Bridge

The bridge shown on the cover of the book can be ordered from www.leobridge.com for approximately

US$25, plus shipping. It can also be easily made from most kinds of materials. The dimensions of this version of the bridge are 4 cm × 0.9 cm × 34 cm (11 pieces) and 4 cm × 0.9 cm × 20 cm (7 pieces). The building instructions are left as an exercise for the reader.

ACKNOWLEDGMENTS

Many of the ideas in this chapter were developed in task force meetings led by Tim O'Shea and Erno Lehtinen, who contributed several key ideas, as Stellan Ohlsson did later. Peter Reimann and Hans Spada were the principal investigators of the European Science Foundation grant—the process that brought us together. Partial support for the first author was provided by ONR grant N00014-03-1-0248. The IST 594 class in Spring 2005 helped outline this chapter and provided many of the insights brought out here; specifically, we thank Mark Cohen, Joshua Gross, Sue Kase, Jong Kim, Andrew Reifers, and William Stevenson. We also thank Susan Chipman, Peggy Cornelius, Joshua Gross, Peter Lane, Ying Guo, Georg Jahn, Katharina Morik, and Sue Phillips for comments that have helped improve this chapter.

References

Ashcraft, M. H. (2002). Math anxiety: Personal, educational, and cognitive consequences. *Current Directions in Psychological Science, 11*(5), 181–185.

Atkinson, R. K., Renkl, A., & Merrill, M. M. (2003). Transitioning from studying examples to solving problems: Combining fading with prompting fosters learning. *Journal of Educational Psychology, 95*, 774–783.

Baumann, M., & Krems, J. F. (2002). Frequency learning and order effects in belief updating. In P. Sedlmeier & T. Betsch (Eds.), *Etc.: Frequency processing and cognition* (pp. 221–237). New York: Oxford University Press.

Beilock, S. L., & Carr, T. H. (2005). When high-powered people fail: Working memory and "choking under pressure." *Psychological Science, 16*(2), 101–105.

Bovair, S., Kieras, D. E., & Polson, P. G. (1990). The acquisition and performance of text-editing skill: A cognitive complex analysis. *Human-Computer Interaction, 5*, 1–48.

Brown, J. S., & Burton, R. B. (1980). Diagnostic models for procedural bugs in basic mathematical skills. *Cognitive Science, 2*, 155–192.

Elman, J. L. (1993). Learning and development in neural networks: The importance of starting small. *Cognition, 48*, 71–99.

Hogarth, R. M., & Einhorn, H. J. (1992). Order effects in belief updating: The Belief-Adjustment Model. *Cognitive Psychology, 24*, 1–55.

Kieras, D. E., & Bovair, S. (1986). The acquisition of procedures from text: A production system model. *Journal of Memory and Language, 25*, 507–524.

Koubek, R. J., Clarkston, T. P., & Calvez, V. (1994). The training of knowledge structures for manufacturing tasks: An empirical study. *Ergonomics, 37*(4), 765–780.

Kuk, G., Arnold, M., & Ritter, F. E. (1999). Using event history analysis to model the impact of workload on an air traffic tactical controller's operations. *Ergonomics, 42*(9), 1133–1148.

Langley, P. (1995). Order effects in incremental learning. In P. Reimann & H. Spada (Eds.), *Learning in humans and machines: Towards an interdisciplinary learning science* (pp. 154–167). New York: Pergamon.

McKendree, J., Reader, W., & Hammond, N. (1995). The "Homeopathic Fallacy" in learning from hypertext. *Communications of the ACM, 2*(3), 74–82.

Newell, A. (1990). *Unified Theories of Cognition.* Cambridge, MA: Harvard University Press.

Ohlsson, S. (1992). Artificial instruction: A method for relating learning theory to instructional design. In M. Jones & P. H. Winne (Eds.), *Adaptive learning environments: Foundations and frontiers* (pp. 55–83). Berlin: Springer.

Pólya, G. (1945). *How to solve it: A new aspect of mathematical method.* Princeton, NJ: Princeton University Press.

Renkl, A., Atkinson, R. K., & Große, C. S. (2004). How fading worked solution steps works: A cognitive load perspective. *Instructional Science, 32*, 59–82.

Renkl, A., Atkinson, R. K., Maier, U. H., & Staley, R. (2002). From example study to problem solving: Smooth transitions help learning. *Journal of Experimental Education, 70*, 293–315.

Selfridge, O. (2006). Learning and education: A continuing frontier for AI. *IEEE Intelligent Systems Journal, 21*(3), 2–9.

Sweller, J. (1976). Asymmetrical transfer using a learning paradigm. *Australian Journal of Psychology, 28*(2), 91–96.

VanLehn, K., Brown, J. S., & Greeno, J. G. (1984). Competitive argumentation in computational theories of cognition. In W. Kintsch, J. R. Miller, & P. G. Polson (Eds.), *Methods and tactics in cognitive science* (pp. 235–262). Hillsdale, NJ: Erlbaum.

Wang, H., Johnson, T. R., & Zhang, J. (2006). The order effect in human abductive reasoning: An empirical and computational study. *Journal of Experimental and Theoretical Artificial Intelligence, 18*(2), 215–247.

Weiss, E. H. (1991). *Usable user documentation.* Phoenix: Oryx.

Part I

Introductory Chapters

Chapter 2

Order, First Step to Mastery: An Introduction to Sequencing in Instructional Design

Charles M. Reigeluth

To create quality instruction, you need to make two types of decisions well: what to teach and how to teach it. The purpose of this chapter is to describe an instructional design perspective on how to sequence instruction (a part of how to teach it). However, scope (a part of what to teach) is also included because it interacts greatly with ordering. This chapter provides an entry point for interested readers into the instructional design literature and introduces some of the issues from this field. It shows how sequence effects relate to instruction, and it provides some introduction to the context where order matters.

THE ROLE OF SCOPE AND SEQUENCE WITHIN INSTRUCTION

Where does the ordering of content fit within the broader process of creating quality instruction? In considering this question, we would do well to think of the instructional process as a series of decisions, which are shown as rows in Table 2.1. Each of those decisions requires that some analysis activities be conducted to collect the information required to make the decision, such as needs analysis for intervention decisions. Each also requires some synthesis activities and should be followed by formative evaluation activities to make sure the decision was a good one or to improve it before it becomes expensive to change. And each one should be accompanied by several decisions and activities on organizational change processes that will facilitate the implementation and effectiveness of the instruction.

Therefore, the process of creating quality instruction, called instructional systems design (ISD), can be viewed as a series of cycles—analysis, synthesis, eval-

uation, change (ASEC)—for each decision shown in Table 2.1. This view is taken from Reigeluth (2006).

This chapter provides a synthesis and evaluation of scope and sequence decisions for instruction. Table 2.1 shows how these decisions fit with other choices in ISD. They are explained in more detail in my forthcoming book, but I explain here a few of the most important ones for understanding the role and use of scope and order effects in instructional design.

Intervention Decisions [1]

Intervention decisions have to do with broader reasons for considering instruction at all. Intervention decisions can take a partial or a total systemic approach.

If you take a *partial systemic approach*, you identify one or more of the organization's performance problems, you analyze *all* the causes of, and potential solutions to, those problems, and you select the best set of solutions. These may include changes in the incentive systems, equipment, work processes, and/or

TABLE 2.1. Major Decisions in the Instructional Systems Design Process

Change	Analysis	Synthesis	Evaluation	Organizational Change
1. Intervention decisions	1.1	1.2	1.3	1.4

Instructional Design	Analysis	Synthesis	Evaluation	Organizational Change
2. Fuzzy vision of ends and means	2.1	2.2	2.3	2.4
3. Scope and sequence decisions	3.1	3.2	3.3	3.4
4. Decisions about what instruction to select and what to develop	4.1	4.2	4.3	4.4
5. Approach decisions	5.1	5.2	5.3	5.4
6. Tactical decisions	6.1	6.2	6.3	6.4
7. Media selection decisions	7.1	7.2	7.3	7.4
8. Media utilization decisions	8.1	8.2	8.3	8.4

Development	Plan	Do	Check	Organizational Change
9. Prototype development	9.1	9.2	9.3	9.4
10. Mass production of instruction	10.1	10.2	10.3	10.4

Evaluation and Change	Analysis	Design/ Development	Evaluation	Organizational Change
11. Evaluation of worth and value	11.1	11.2	11.3	11.4
12. Implementation, adoption, organizational change	12.1	12.2	12.3	12.4

management systems—as well as the knowledge and skills—of the learners (students or trainees). For Activity 1, you just *plan* the set of interventions that will best solve your problem. Implementation of those plans comes later.

If you take a *total systemic approach*, you will strive to be a "learning organization" (Senge, 1990), which means you will start by looking outside the organization to the relationships between the organization and its customers.[1] How well is the organization meeting its customers' needs? How are their needs changing? Do they (or other potential customers) have other needs that are not being met well and that you might be able to respond to? For Activity 1, you just *plan* the set of interventions that will best respond to those needs. Implementation of those plans comes later.

Regardless of which approach you take, you proceed with the ISD process only if one of your solutions is to advance knowledge or skills.

Scope Decisions and Sequence Decisions [3]

Scope decisions are choices about what to teach—the nature of the content.[2] They require decisions about what the learner needs and/or wants to learn. Sequence decisions are concerned with how to *group* and *order* the content. They entail decisions about how to break up the content into chunks that will not exceed the learners' cognitive load capacity (Sweller, this volume, Chapter 15), how to order those chunks, and how to sequence the content within each chunk. How to make these decisions is the focus of this chapter.

Decisions About What Instruction to Select and What to Develop [4]

Regardless of what you need to teach or learn, chances are that someone has already developed instruction

1. I use the term "customers" in the broader sense of all those the organization serves, including the learners.
2. I use the term "content" to refer to everything that comes under "what to teach." It therefore includes whatever tasks you might teach, as well as whatever knowledge, and the term "content analysis" includes "task analysis."

for it. You can often save yourself a lot of time and money by obtaining these existing materials. To do so, you first must identify the alternatives (existing instruction), evaluate their quality in relation to your needs and conditions, procure the most cost-effective alternative, and make whatever revisions are cost effective. The revision process entails making many of the remaining decisions (decisions 5–10 in Table 2.1). In most cases, you will need to develop some new instruction in addition to revising existing materials. The order of content can be important for revising and using existing resources.

Approach Decisions [5]

The systems concept of equifinality tells us that there is usually more than one way to accomplish any given end. Different teachers or trainers often use very different approaches to teach the same content, including various kinds of expository instruction (such as lectures, tutorials, drills, and activities), diverse kinds of inquiry or discovery instruction (such as problem-based learning and Socratic dialogue), and different types of experiential learning (such as problem-based learning, project-based learning, and simulation). A variety of approaches may also entail teaching individual students, small groups or teams, or large groups. Decisions about one's approach (5.1 in Table 2.1) will impact much of the rest of the design of the instruction and should therefore be made early in the ISD process.

Tactical Decisions [6]

As approaches are strategic decisions, their effective implementation requires tactical decisions. Different types of learning are fostered by different types of instructional tactics, regardless of the approach you use. For example, it is difficult to acquire a skill without practicing it and receiving feedback. Demonstrations (examples) and explanations (generalities) can be very helpful as well. On the other hand, understanding is best fostered by linking new knowledge with the learner's related prior knowledge. This may entail the use of tactics such as analogies, comparison and contrast, context, and relating to the learner's experiential knowledge. Memorization and higher-order thinking skills are other types of learning that require very different kinds of instructional tactics. (See Leshin, Pollock, & Reigeluth, 1992, for an in-depth treatment of instructional tactics.)

Evaluation of Worth and Value [11]

Summative evaluation is almost always worthwhile, as long as it addresses the impact on the overall mission or purpose of the organization. At the very least, it should indicate whether this particular ISD project was worthwhile. Ideally, it will also help the organization to decide whether to continue to invest in ISD projects. It may also yield information about how to increase the worth and value of this particular instructional system and of ISD projects in general for the organization.

Given this overview of the ISD process, this chapter focuses on the analysis and synthesis activities for decisions on scope and sequence of instruction (boxes 3.1 and 3.2 in Table 2.1). The following section explores definitions of scope and sequence, the reasons (or times) they are and are not important, and general issues relating to each. After that I review and explain some important sequencing strategies.

BASICS OF SCOPE AND SEQUENCE

Instructional design defines sequence effects slightly differently than the definition in Chapter 1, particularly because it examines the role and context of scope. This section presents a somewhat more contextualized definition of sequence effects.

Scope decisions are decisions about what to teach—the nature of the content, including tasks, skills, and higher-order thinking skills. They require us to make choices about what the learner needs and/or wants to learn. Sequence decisions are concerned with how to *group* and *order* the content. You cannot order the content without creating some kind of groupings to be ordered, and different kinds of sequences require different types of groupings. They require several types of decisions regarding size of groupings, contents of groupings, order within groupings, and the order of groupings (Figure 2.1). These all influence the quality of the instruction: its effectiveness, efficiency, and appeal.

Does Scope Make a Difference?

Setting the scope of instruction identifies the content that will be ordered. If you are in a training department for any of the three primary sectors (private, public, or nonprofit), the employees or customers need certain skills and knowledge to perform well. If you do

The size of each group of content (herein called a "learning episode" after Bruner, 1960)

The components of each learning episode

The order of components within each episode

The order of episodes

FIGURE 2.1. Types of decisions for sequencing content.

not teach what they need, it does not matter how good the remaining aspects of the instruction are.

However, a K–12 or higher education context is very different in that the needs are much less clear and depend largely on values. Furthermore, students have interests that may be unrelated to the values of the community and the parents. And the benefits of the instruction may not become apparent until many years later. All of these factors make it much more difficult to say whether scope makes a difference or, perhaps more accurately, what kinds of difference scope makes. Clearly, the differences scope makes vary from one student to another and from one "stakeholder" to another in the educational system. (Stakeholders are all those who have a stake in the particular educational system, such as parents, employers, taxpayers, students, and social service agencies). But ask any student or any stakeholder whether what is taught makes a difference to them, and you are almost certain to get a resounding

"Yes!" (Guidance for setting the scope of instruction is discussed later in this chapter.)

Technology is evolving to the point where we can create flexible, computer-based, learning tools that students can use—while they are learning—to create or modify their own instruction. This is one way that scope and sequence interact. Furthermore, with team-based learning, different teams can pursue different interests, with the teacher assuming the role of a coach or guide steering them to appropriate resources, many of which utilize advanced technologies. This means that students will be able to make decisions about what to learn (and even about how to learn it) while the instruction is in progress. Thus, sequencing decisions may need to be done on the fly. The later chapters by VanLehn, by Swaak and de Jong, and by Scheiter and Gerjets provide examples of learners and instructors doing this.

Just as the business world has been evolving from standardization to customization, a systemic content selection process is likely to reveal that students should not learn *all* the same things. Osin and Lesgold (1996) talk about "defining a required common curriculum and supporting additional student choices" (p. 642). The Indiana Curriculum Advisory Council (1991) came to a similar conclusion after much input from many stakeholder groups:

> The intent of 21st Century Schooling is to invent schools which give each child access to the conditions which make possible learning achievement to the limits of individual ability. . . . Required will be a 180 degree shift in Indiana's educational policy: from a narrow, rigid focus on covering isolated content, to a sensitive, responsive focus on each student. (p. 1)

Therefore, much of the content selection that is now done by a teacher (or curriculum committee) for a group of learners well ahead of the actual instruction could soon be done during the instruction as multimedia systems (and the teacher) continuously collect information from individual learners and/or small teams of learners and use that information to present an array of sound alternatives to the students, both about what to learn next and how to learn it. The learners' decisions will, in all likelihood, be tempered by collaborative input from the teacher and parents. Doing this well will be assisted by understanding order or sequence effects. However, I hasten to reemphasize that there will likely be some content that the stakeholders will believe all students should learn (or that students with certain interests should learn), and a stakeholder-based selection process, founded in the user-design approach (Banathy, 1996; Carr-Chellman & Savoy, 2003; Carr-Chellman, in press), should be created to help make that decision.

Does Sequencing Make a Difference?

This is a very common question, but it is the wrong one! The issue, as with most instructional strategies, is not *whether* it makes a difference but *when* it makes a difference and when it does not. The impact of sequencing depends upon two major factors: the strength of the relationships among the topics and the size of the course of instruction.

Sequencing is important only when there is a strong relationship among the topics of the course. If a course is composed of several unrelated topics, such as word processing, computer graphics, and electronic spreadsheets, the order for teaching the topics is not likely to make any difference because there are no important relationships among them. On the other hand, when there is a strong relationship, the sequence used will influence how well both the relationship and content are learned. For example, there is an important relationship between the analysis and design phases in the ISD process. Some sequences for teaching ISD take a fragmented approach that makes it difficult to learn the relationship and understand the content, whereas other sequences facilitate such learning.

Second, if a strong relationship exists among the topics, then as the size of the course increases, so does the importance of sequencing. When the content requires more than about an hour to learn, sequencing is likely to begin to make a significant difference, albeit a small one, in the learners' ability to master it because most learners will have a difficult time organizing so much content logically and meaningfully if it is poorly sequenced. However, when the content to be learned is minimal (e.g., less than about an hour), the human mind can compensate for weaknesses in the sequence. This type of compensation may be occurring in the studies reported in VanLehn's and in Swaak and de Jong's chapters.

Types of Sequencing Strategies: Relationships Are the Key

The importance of relationships in the content is twofold. As I have just mentioned, if no relationships

exist, then sequencing does not matter. But the second point is that each method of sequencing is based upon a single type of relationship. For instance, a historical sequence is based upon chronological relationships—a sequence is devised that follows the actual order of events. A procedural sequence, the most common pattern of sequencing in training, is based upon the relationship of the "order of performance" of the steps in the procedure. A hierarchical sequence is based upon the relationship of learning prerequisites among the various skills and subskills that compose a task. Moreover, the "simplifying conditions" sequence (described later) is based upon the relationship of the degree of complexity of different versions of a complex task.

Furthermore, when several topics need to be taught, two basic patterns of sequencing can be used that are fundamentally different: topical and spiral (see Figure 2.2).

Topical Sequencing

In topical sequencing, a topic (or task) is taught to whatever depth of understanding (or competence) is required before the next one is taught. There are both advantages and disadvantages of topical sequencing. Learners can concentrate on one topic or task for in-depth learning without frequently skipping to new ones. In addition, hands-on materials and other resources are all used in one block of time, rather than being used at different points scattered over several months or a year. However, once the class (or team or individual) moves on to a new topic or task, the first one can easily be forgotten. The learners do not gain a perception of what the whole subject domain is like

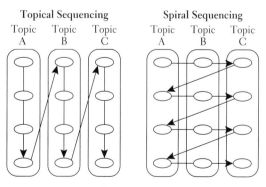

FIGURE 2.2. Topical and spiral sequencing (from Reigeluth & Kim, 1995.)

until they reach the end of the course or curriculum. The weaknesses of topical sequencing can be compensated for, to some extent, by incorporating tactics for overview, review, and synthesis.

Spiral Sequencing

In spiral sequencing, the learners master a topic or task gradually in several passes. They learn the basics of one topic or task, then another, and another, and so on before returning to learn each one in greater depth. They spiral back through all of the topics or tasks, learning each one in greater depth with each pass until the necessary depth is reached for all of them.

The main advantage of spiral sequencing is its built-in synthesis and review. The interrelationships among topics or tasks may be learned more easily using the spiral approach because it allows similar aspects of the various topics or tasks to be learned close in time to each other. Furthermore, cycling back to learn an earlier topic or task in greater depth provides a periodic review of the earlier one. On the other hand, the main disadvantage of spiral sequencing is disruption. Once a particular topic or task has been started, learners get into a particular frame of mind (schema). Frequently switching disrupts their thought development. In addition, switching may disrupt the efficient management of material resources needed as they progress from one topic or task to the next. The chapters exploring transfer (e.g., VanLehn, Scheiter, and Gerjets) point out some of the complexities.

Which One Is Best?

Again, this is a very common question, but, as before, it is the wrong one. The issue is not *which* pattern of sequencing is best but *when* each is best. Furthermore, in reality neither topical nor spiral sequencing exists in a pure form. In an extreme case, spiral sequencing could entail presenting only one sentence on each topic or task before spiraling back to make another pass on a deeper level. The real issue lies in how deep a slice a teacher or learner makes on one topic or task before going on to another. Rather than thinking of spiral and topical sequencing as two separate categories, it is useful to think of them as the two end points on a continuum. The instructional designer's (or the learner's) decision, then, is where on the continuum to be for any given training program or curriculum.

SOME MAJOR SEQUENCING STRATEGIES: UNDERSTANDING THE THEORIES

This section describes some of the major sequencing strategies: procedural, hierarchical, simplifying conditions, conceptual elaboration, and theoretical elaboration. The book (Reigeluth, in preparation) describes how to design and conduct analyses for each of these kinds of instructional sequences. I begin with the hierarchical sequence because it is used by all of the others. It is important to understand the procedural sequence before the Simplifying Conditions Method (SCM) sequence for the same reason.

Hierarchical Sequence

Robert Gagné developed the hierarchical sequence for teaching "intellectual skills" in the cognitive domain. Intellectual skills are domain-dependent skills (those that pertain to a single subject area, or domain) and are contrasted with "cognitive strategies," which are domain-independent skills (ones that can be applied across domains, such as critical thinking skills).

The hierarchical sequence is based on the observation that a skill is made up of simpler "component skills" that you must learn before you can learn the larger, more complex skill of which they are a part (the model in Chapter 5, for example, illustrates this). For example, you must learn to multiply and subtract whole numbers before you can learn how to do long division (see Figure 2.3). Thus the sequencing strategy is basically that, if one skill has to be learned before another can be learned, teach it first. It is that simple—in theory—but not so easy in practice.

How do you determine what the prerequisite skills are? This is the purpose of a hierarchical task analysis. To help with that task, Gagné has identified a variety of kinds of skills that are prerequisites for one another (Figure 2.4).

The skill for a discrimination is the ability to tell the difference between "stimuli that differ from one another along one or more physical dimensions" (Gagné, Briggs, & Wager, 1992, p. 56). For example, one particular discrimination is the ability to tell the difference between a triangle and a rectangle. It does not require being able to label either shape. It differs from memorization (or Gagné's "verbal information") in that it requires some degree of generalization, such

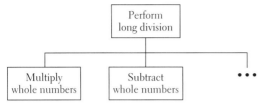

••• indicates other subskills not listed here

FIGURE 2.3. A learning hierarchy in which the lower skills must be learned before the higher skills can be learned. (The entire hierarchy is not shown.)

as being able to tell the difference between any triangle and any rectangle. The conclusion of the performance of this skill is usually saying whether two things are the same or different.

The skill for a concrete concept is the ability "to identify a stimulus as a member of a class having [an *observable* property] in common, even though such stimuli may otherwise differ from each other markedly" (Gagné, Briggs, & Wager, 1992, p. 57). For example, one particular such skill is the ability to identify any triangle as a triangle. Classifying a concrete concept differs from making a discrimination in that it requires naming or otherwise identifying a particular instance as belonging to a class, rather than just being

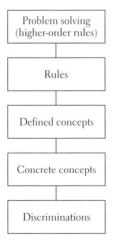

FIGURE 2.4. A hierarchy of intellectual skills (from Gagné, 1965). Reprinted with permission of Wadsworth, a division of Thompson Learning.

able to say that the instance is different from, or the same as, something else. The conclusion of the performance of this skill is usually indicating whether something belongs to a given class of things.

The skill for a defined concept is the ability to identify a stimulus as a member of a class having a *definable* property in common, even though such stimuli may otherwise differ markedly from each other. Defined concepts include objects (such as a "pen"), events (such as a "fight"), and ideas (such as "justice"). For example, one particular such skill is the ability to identify any polygon as a polygon. The differences between defined and concrete concepts are highlighted in the definition here. Defined concepts all have definitions, whereas many (but not all) concrete concepts do not (like the musical note C). All concrete concepts are tangible in some way (they can be touched, seen, heard, etc.). However, the distinction between defined and concrete concepts is not always easy to make. According to Gagné, Briggs, and Wager (1992),

> Some defined concepts have corresponding concrete concepts that carry the same name and possess certain features in common. For example, many young children learn the basic shape of a triangle as a concrete concept. Not until much later in studying geometry do they encounter the defined concept of triangle.... The concrete and defined meanings of *triangle* are not exactly the same, yet they overlap considerably. (p. 60)

It seems that the difference is "in the eye of the learner," as it were. If the skill is learned by generalizing from instances and the learner does not consciously use a definition to guide the performance of the skill, then it is a concrete concept for that learner. But if the learner uses a definition (either invented by, or given to, the learner) to guide the performance of the skill, then it is a defined concept for that person.[3] As with concrete concepts, the conclusion of the performance of this skill is usually indicating whether a specific instance belongs to a given class of instances. Most of the model chapters use rules (which are further explained in the chapter by Nerb, Ritter, and Langley), and several of the application chapters illustrate the learning of rules.

---

3. For instructional purposes, I do not see much value in the distinction between concrete and defined concepts, except that you cannot use a definition to help someone learn a concrete concept.

The skill for a rule is the ability to consciously or subconsciously apply the rule to new situations. A rule is "a *class* of relationships among *classes* of objects and events" (Gagné, Briggs, & Wager, 1992, p. 61). I find it useful to think in terms of two major kinds of rules: procedural rules and heuristic rules. A *procedural rule* is a set of steps for accomplishing a goal, such as the rule for multiplying fractions (first, multiply the numerators, then multiply the denominators, then . . .). A *heuristic rule* is a principle or a guideline, such as the law of supply and demand (an increase in price will cause a decrease in the quantity demanded and an increase in the quantity supplied, while a decrease in price . . .).

So what is the difference between a rule and a defined concept? As Gagné, Briggs, and Wager (1992) put it, "a defined concept is a particular type of rule whose purpose it is to classify objects and events; it is a *classifying rule*" (p. 62). A classifying rule may be either procedural (for well-defined concepts like "triangle") or heuristic (for "fuzzy" concepts like "justice"). Very often people are not consciously aware of the rules they use—they (particularly experts) cannot actually state the rules that govern their thinking and behavior. This is what Polanyi (1983) referred to as tacit, as opposed to explicit, knowledge. And this is why experts are often not the best teachers of novices. The conclusion of the performance of this skill is usually the attainment of a specific goal for a specific situation.

The skill for a higher-order rule is the ability to consciously or subconsciously apply a higher-order rule to new situations. A higher-order rule is "a complex combination of simpler rules" (Gagné, Briggs, & Wager, 1992, p. 63). Such rules may also be procedural or heuristic. The act of inventing a higher-order rule is called *problem solving*, but once it is invented by, or given to, the learner, then it becomes an act of rule using (or more accurately, higher-order rule using) rather than problem solving. The difference between a higher-order rule and a rule is simply one of complexity: A higher-order rule is a rule that combines several simpler rules. An example of problem solving is figuring out the area of an irregularly shaped figure for the first time. The conclusion of the performance of this skill is usually the attainment of a specific goal for a specific situation.

The hierarchical arrangement of these skills (shown in Figure 2.3) helps you to figure out what prerequisites any given skill might have, but it can also be misleading because it is not true that a skill on one level has prerequisites *only* on the next lower level. In fact, any given skill usually has many levels of prerequisites on the very same level of Gagné's hierarchy. For example, the skills on both levels 1 and 2 in Figure 2.3 are rules (or higher-order rules), and each of the rules on level 2 has its own prerequisite rules (e.g., "being able to carry a 10"), as well as its prerequisite concepts (e.g., "whole number"). It is fairly common to have 5–10 levels of rules in a hierarchical analysis of a complex skill and 2 or 3 levels of defined concepts. Thus, a typical learning hierarchy might look more like Figure 2.5, which is a minor modification of a hierarchy developed by Robert Gagné (1968, p. 184) himself. It is important to keep in mind that the accuracy of a learning hierarchy can be determined only by testing learners from the target population. If it turns out that learners were able to master one skill without acquiring one connected below it, then the lower one should be removed.

However, a hierarchical analysis could go on seemingly forever. How far down should you continue to break skills into subskills? The purpose of a hierarchical analysis is to identify the prerequisite skills that need to be taught (and the order of the prerequisite relationships among them). Therefore, you do not want to go down beyond the skills that need to be taught. Clearly, skills the learner has already mastered do not need to be taught. So you need to do your analysis only down to the learner's level of "entering knowledge" (at the beginning of instruction). Keep in mind that each individual skill becomes simpler the farther down you go in your analysis, even though each level down is a more complex description of the overall skill being analyzed. This is what I call the hierarchical paradox. Simpler is more complex.

A hierarchical sequence, then, is one that never teaches a skill before its prerequisites (ones immediately below it and connected to it by a line). You could take a spiral approach to hierarchical sequencing by teaching all of the skills on the bottom level of the hierarchy, then moving across the next level up, and so forth. Or you could take a topical approach by moving as far up a "leg" of the hierarchy as quickly as possible for one module of instruction and then moving on to other legs in other modules, always trying to get as high up as you can as soon as you can (these approaches are related to depth-first and breadth-first search techniques in artificial intelligence). Other options are possible, some of which we will look at when we explore the other sequencing strategies in this chapter.

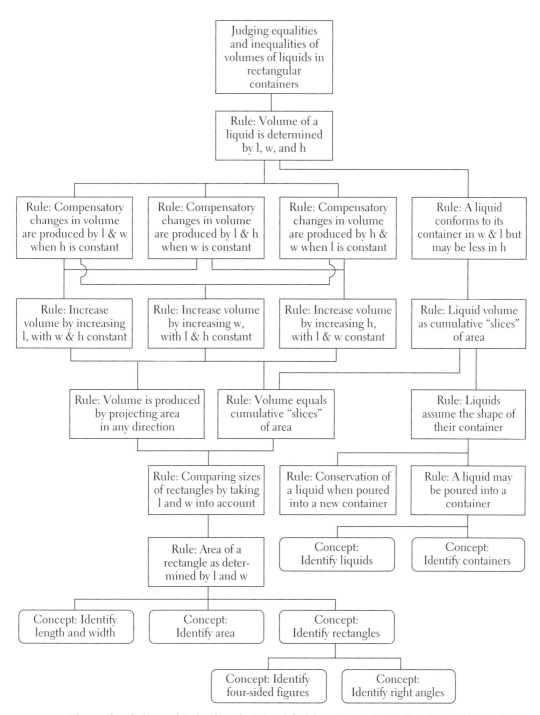

FIGURE 2.5. The results of a hierarchical task analysis (modified from Gagné, 1968). Reprinted with permission of Wadsworth, a division of Thompson Learning.

When and Why to Use Hierarchical Sequences

The strengths of the hierarchical sequence are these:

- In situations where one skill must be learned before another can be learned, it is extremely important to follow the requisite order, for any sequence that violates it is, by definition, doomed to failure (for a learning prerequisite is defined as a skill that must be mastered before it is possible to master a more complex skill of which it is a part).
- The hierarchical sequence is fairly broadly applicable because skills of one kind or another are a major component of most courses in both education and training contexts.
- The sequence is very easy to design once the analysis has been done, and the analysis is not difficult to do nor to learn to do.

The limitations of the hierarchical sequence are these:

- By breaking skills into simpler component parts, the instruction is fragmented, which can be demotivating for the learner and impede valuable schema formation.
- Because it applies to sequencing instruction for a single skill or set of prerequisite (or overlapping) skills, it offers no guidance as to how to sequence skills where one is not a part of the other and is therefore seldom useful for broader sequencing decisions in a large course or curriculum.
- Because it applies only when one skill must be learned before another can be learned, it does not provide any guidance as to how to handle "soft" prerequisites, that is, skills that facilitate learning another skill but are not absolutely necessary for learning it.
- Because it applies only to skills, it is not useful for courses in which skills play a minor role.

The net effect is that hierarchical sequencing is not something that can be violated, but it is seldom sufficient alone for sequencing a course or training program. It can, however, be combined with other sequencing strategies, including all of the remaining ones described in this chapter.

Procedural Sequence

As its name implies, the procedural sequence entails teaching the steps of a procedure in the order in which they are performed. Procedural sequences have probably been used (and fairly well understood) for millennia. They were systematically studied by the behaviorists in the late 1950s and the 1960s under therubric of "forward chaining" sequences (see, e.g., Mechner, 1967). Methodology was further developed by cognitivists in the 1970s under the rubric of "information-processing" sequences (see, e.g., Merrill, 1976, 1980; Resnick & Ford, 1980).

The procedural sequence is also based on a prerequisite relationship, only in this case it is a procedural prerequisite rather than a learning prerequisite. A procedural prerequisite is a step that must be *performed* before another step can be performed in the execution of a given task, whereas a learning prerequisite is a skill that must be *learned* before another skill can be learned.

To design a procedural sequence, therefore, you must first figure out the order in which the steps are performed (i.e., what the prerequisite steps are for each step). This is the purpose of a procedural task analysis, and it usually results in a flowchart of the steps that make up the procedure. Sounds pretty straightforward and easy, doesn't it? Well, not exactly. The problem relates to the hierarchical paradox. To teach someone how to fix cars, our procedural analysis could identify just two steps: (a) Find out what is wrong with the car, and (b) fix it. Clearly, more analysis is needed. We can describe the task at different levels of detail, just like in a hierarchical analysis—that is, we can break steps down into substeps, just as we can break skills down into subskills. But steps and substeps are always Gagné's higher-order rules or rules (specifically procedural or reproductive ones rather than heuristic or productive ones), never concepts or discriminations.

So, what we need to do is a hierarchical analysis in combination with the procedural analysis. We need to break each step down into substeps, and substeps into subsubsteps, and so on until we reach the entry level of the learner. As with the hierarchical analysis, each level of description describes the same procedure in its entirety, as the previous level did, only with more detail. Moreover, the more detailed the description of how to repair an automobile, the simpler each step is to do, even though the whole description seems more complex than our two-step procedure for fixing a car.

(Hence the hierarchical paradox is alive and well in a procedural analysis.) Furthermore, we need to keep in mind that almost every step contains at least one concept, so, once we reach the entry level of the description of the steps, we need to do a hierarchical analysis of those steps to identify any unmastered prerequisite concepts (and occasionally discriminations). Thus the result of a typical procedural analysis might look like Figure 2.6.

A procedural sequence, then, is one that teaches all of the steps in the order of their performance, after they have all been broken down to the learner's entry level. Naturally, it is important to teach prerequisite concepts before teaching the steps in which those concepts are used. Such concepts are often the inputs, the outputs, or the tools for the steps.

When and Why to Use a Procedural Sequence

The strengths of the procedural sequence are as follows:

- In both training and educational contexts, much instruction in the cognitive and motor domains focuses on procedures—learning to follow a set of steps to achieve a goal. For such situations, a procedural sequence is logical to the learner, and the order of learning the steps helps the learner to remember their order of performance.
- Both the analysis and design of the sequence are very quick and easy and do not require much training for the designer.

Because of these factors, the procedural sequence is one of the most common sequences for instruction.

The limitations of the procedural sequence are the following:

- The procedure must not be a very complex one, in the sense of having lots of decision steps and branches, because the methodology offers no guidance as to what to do when you come to a

branch—which one to follow first or even whether to teach all of one branch before teaching parts of others.
- The content must be primarily procedural (a set of steps) because the sequence cannot be applied to nonprocedural content.

The net effect is that the procedural sequence is simple and easy to use and quite effective for nonbranching procedures, but it is not sufficient for sequencing a complex branching procedure, nor is it appropriate for dealing with nonprocedural content. It can, however, be combined with other sequencing strategies, including the remaining ones described in this chapter.

Elaboration Theory and Elaboration Sequences

The Elaboration Theory of Instruction was developed to provide holistic alternatives to the parts-to-whole sequencing and superficial coverage of content that have been so typical of both education and training over the past five to ten decades. It has also attempted to synthesize several recent ideas about sequencing instruction into a single coherent framework. It currently deals only with the cognitive and psychomotor domains, and not the affective domain.[4] It is founded on the notions that different sequencing strategies are based on different kinds of relationships within the content and that different relationships are important for different kinds of expertise. So the kind of sequence that will most facilitate learning will vary depending on the kind of expertise you want to develop.

First, the Elaboration Theory makes a distinction between task expertise and subject-domain expertise (see Figure 2.7). Task expertise relates to the learner's becoming an expert in a specific task, such as managing a project, selling a product, or writing an annual plan. Domain expertise relates to the learner's becoming an expert in a subject not tied to any specific task, such as economics, electronics, or physics (but often relevant to many tasks). This is not the same as

---

4. However, there are strong indications that it can be and indeed is already being intuitively applied in the affective domain. For example, Mark Greenberg and associates (Greenberg, Kusche, Cook, & Quamma, 1995) have developed the PATHS curriculum (Promoting Alternative THinking Strategies), an emotional literacy program designed to help children avoid the road to violence and crime. According to Goleman (1995), "the PATHS curriculum has fifty lessons on different emotions, teaching the most basic, such as happiness and anger, to the youngest children, and later touching on more complicated feelings such as jealousy, pride, and guilt" (p. 278).

Steps at highest level of description

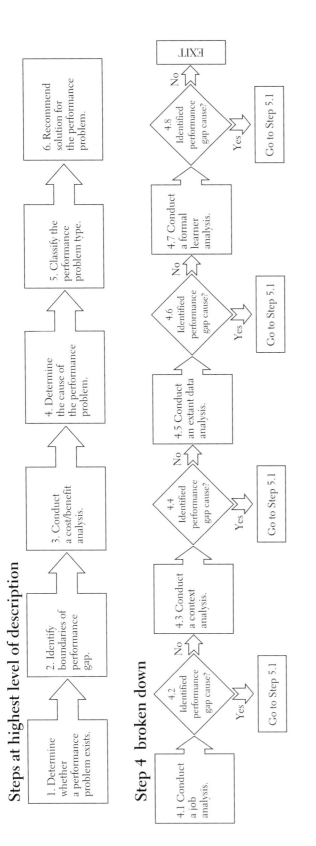

Step 4 broken down

Step 4.1 broken down

Identification of concepts for Step 4.1.3

Hierarchy, Subordinate, Coordinate, Superordinate

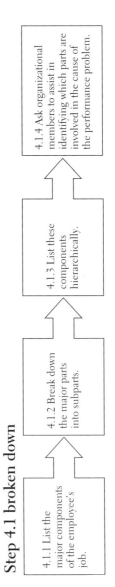

FIGURE 2.6. An example of a flowchart, based on a procedural task analysis for conducting a needs analysis by Terry M. Farmer.

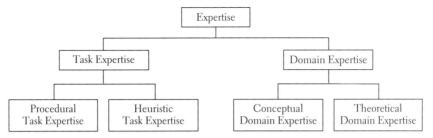

FIGURE 2.7. Kinds of expertise.

the distinction between procedural and declarative knowledge (J. R. Anderson, 1983), for task expertise includes much declarative knowledge, and domain expertise includes much "how to" knowledge.

Task Expertise

Tasks range from simple to complex. The Elaboration Theory is intended only for more complex tasks. It is based on the observation that complex cognitive tasks are done differently under various conditions, that each set of conditions defines a different version of the task, and that some of those versions are much more complex than others. For example, solving mathematical problems is easier when you are solving for one unknown rather than for two unknowns. The number of unknowns is a condition variable having two conditions: 1 unknown and 2 unknowns. Furthermore, skills and understandings of differing complexity are required for each condition. Thus, problems or projects that learners tackle should be ones that are within what Vygotskii (1986) called the "zone of proximal development"—close enough to the learner's competence for the learner to be able to deal with successfully with some help; in addition, the problems should gradually increase in complexity. Thus, the Elaboration Theory offers the Simplifying Conditions Method to design a holistic, simple-to-complex sequence by starting with the simplest real-world version of the task and progressing (by amounts appropriate for the learner) to ever more complex versions as each is mastered.

However, not all complex tasks are of the same nature. Some are primarily procedural, and some are chiefly heuristic. Procedural tasks are ones for which experts use a set of mental and/or physical steps to decide what to do when, such as a high school mathematics course or a corporate training program on installing a piece of equipment for a customer. Heuristic tasks are ones for which experts use causal models—

interrelated sets of principles and/or guidelines—to decide what to do when, such as a high school course on thinking skills or a corporate training program on management skills). Examples of causal models are found in many of the following chapters, including Chapter 9 by Morik and Mühlenbrock and Chapter 14 by Scheiter and Gerjets.

Domain Expertise

Domain expertise ranges not only from simple to complex but also from general to detailed. And it is the general-to-detailed nature of domain expertise that allows the design of a holistic sequence that goes from simple to complex. The Elaboration Theory's sequencing guidance for domain expertise was derived primarily from Bruner's (1960) "spiral curriculum" and Ausubel's (1968) "advance organizers" and "progressive differentiation," but it differs in several important ways from each and also provides greater guidance as to how to design such a sequence. A domain elaboration sequence starts with the broadest, most inclusive, most general ideas and gradually progresses to more complex, precise ideas. This makes an elaboration sequence ideal for discovery learning and other approaches to the construction of knowledge.

The Elaboration Theory recognizes two major kinds of domain expertise: conceptual (understanding what) and theoretical (understanding why). In their simplest form, these are concepts and principles, respectively, and in their more complex forms, they are conceptual knowledge structures (or concept maps) for "understanding what," as well as both causal models and "theoretical knowledge structures" (see Figure 2.8) for "understanding why." Although these two kinds of domain expertise are closely interrelated and are both involved to varying degrees in gaining expertise within every domain, the guidance for building a holistic, general-to-detailed sequence is different for

When light rays pass from one medium into another (of different optical density):

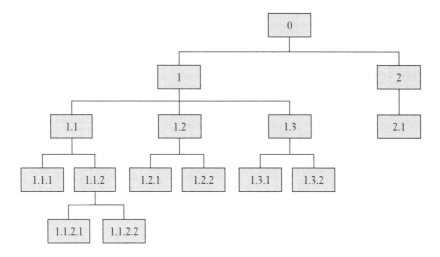

0   they behave unexpectedly.

1   they bend at the surface.

2   a straight object in both media looks bent at the surface.

1.1   the rays bend because they slow down in a denser medium or speed up in less dense medium (C).

1.2   rays bend and change their distance from each other but remain parallel to each other (A).

1.3   a portion of each ray is reflected off the surface, while the rest is refracted into the new medium (A).

2.1   the apparent position and size of an object usually change (A).

1.1.1   if they pass into a denser medium, the light rays bend toward the normal (B, D).

1.1.2   the greater the difference in optical density between two media, the more the light rays bend (D).

1.2.1   when rays bend toward the normal, they become farther apart (B, D).

1.2.2   the sharper the angle between a light ray and the surface, the more the ray bends (D).

1.3.1   the sharper the angle between a light ray and the surface, the more of each ray that is reflected and the less that is reflected (D).

1.3.2   if the angle is equal or sharper than the critical angle, all of the light ray is reflected (B, E).

1.1.2.1   the index of refraction (n) = c_i/c_r = (sin i)/(sin r) (D, E).

1.1.2.2   the relationship between the critical angle and the index of refraction is sin i_c = 1/n (D, E).

Codes:
    (A) What else happens?   (B) When?   (C) Why?   (D) Which way?   (D) How much?

FIGURE 2.8. An example of a theoretical structure.

each one. Thus, the Elaboration Theory offers guidance for sequencing for both kinds, and both types of elaboration sequences can be used simultaneously if there is considerable emphasis on both types of domain expertise in a course. This is referred to as *multiple-strand sequencing* (Beissner & Reigeluth, 1994).

What Is an Elaboration Sequence?

The Elaboration Theory has currently identified three types of sequences, one for each of the three types of expertise (see Table 2.2). However, I anticipate that additional ones remain to be identified. Each of these

TABLE 2.2. Types of Elaboration Sequences

Kind of Expertise	Task expertise (procedural and heuristic)	Conceptual domain expertise	Theoretical domain expertise
Kind of Sequence	SCM	Conceptual elaboration	Theoretical elaboration

three is discussed next, along with citations for additional information.

The Simplifying Conditions Method (SCM)

For building task expertise, the Simplifying Conditions Method is a relatively new approach that offers guidance for analyzing, selecting, and sequencing the "what to learn" (content). Briefly, the SCM provides practical guidelines for making a kind of simple-to-complex sequence that is very different from the hierarchical sequence, one that is holistic rather than fragmented. Given that any complex task has some conditions under which it is much easier to perform than under others, an SCM sequence begins with the simplest version of the task that is still fairly representative of the task as a whole. Then it moves to progressively more complex versions of the task until the desired level of complexity is reached, while ensuring that the learner is made explicitly aware of the relationship of each version to the other versions. Each version of the task is a class or group of complete, real-world performances of the task. This sequence contrasts sharply with the hierarchical sequence, which teaches all of the prerequisites first and usually does not teach a complete, real-world task until the end of the sequence. Figure 2.9 shows the differences between the hierarchical approach and the SCM approach.

The SCM (for both procedural and heuristic tasks) is composed of two parts: epitomizing and elaborating. Epitomizing is the process of identifying the simplest version of the task that is still fairly representative of the whole task. Elaborating is the process of identifying progressively more complex versions of the task.

The principles of epitomizing are based upon the notions of holistic learning and schema building. Therefore, epitomizing utilizes:

(a) a whole version of the task rather than a simpler component skill
(b) a simple version of the task
(c) a real-world version of the task (usually)

(d) a fairly representative (typical or common) version of the task

The epitome version of the task is performed by experts only under certain restricted conditions, referred to as the simplifying conditions, that are removed one by one to define each of the more complex versions of the task. Examples are provided in Reigeluth (2006).

The principles of elaborating are similarly based on the notions of holistic learning and assimilation-to-schema. Therefore, each subsequent elaboration should be:

(a) another whole version of the task
(b) a slightly more complex version of the task
(c) an equally (or more) authentic version of the task
(d) an equally or slightly less representative (typical or common) version of the whole task

While the principles of epitomizing and elaborating are the same for both procedural task expertise and heuristic task expertise, they are operationalized a bit differently for each.

The SCM sequence for procedural tasks (Reigeluth & Rodgers, 1980) was derived primarily from the work of Scandura (1973) and Merrill (1976, 1980) on the "path analysis" of a procedure. Every decision step in a complex procedure signals at least two different paths through the flowchart of the procedure (one of which is almost always simpler than the others), and it also represents at least two different conditions of performance. The SCM sequence starts with the simplest real-world version (or path) of the procedural task (a version or path is a set of performances that are done under the same conditions) and gradually progresses to ever more complex versions as each is mastered. The example cited earlier entailed progressing from one unknown to two unknowns in mathematical problems. Some different steps (meaning a different path, requiring different skills and knowledge) are required for each condition.

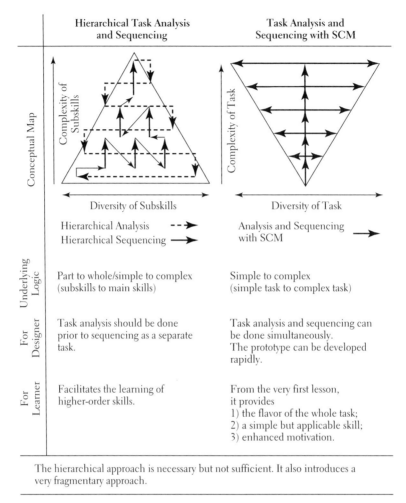

Hierarchical Task Analysis and Sequencing	Task Analysis and Sequencing with SCM

FIGURE 2.9. Hierarchical approach and the SCM approach (from Reigeluth & Kim, 1993).

In contrast, the SCM sequence for heuristic tasks (Reigeluth, 1992; Reigeluth & Kim, 1993) is based on the observation that heuristic tasks are characterized by great variations in the nature of an expert's performance, depending on the conditions of performance—so much so that experts do not think in terms of steps when they perform the task. This sequencing methodology was derived by Reigeluth primarily from the SCM sequence for procedural tasks. Like the procedural SCM sequence, this one also starts with the simplest real-world version of the task and gradually progresses to ever more complex versions as each is mastered. The major difference lies in the nature of the content that is analyzed and sequenced. Rather than a set of steps (with decisions, branches, and paths), you should attempt to identify the underlying tacit knowledge (principles or causal models that are hard to articulate) that

experts use to perform the task. Simpler versions require simpler causal models for expert performance. However, because most heuristic knowledge is tacit, for small populations of learners it may be uneconomical to identify all of the heuristics and teach them explicitly to the point of internalization (the solid arrows in Figure 2.10). It may be more appropriate to teach them indirectly by providing problem-based learning or simulations that help the learners to discover the principles through experience (the dotted arrow in Figure 2.10). However, if the learner population is sufficiently large or the efficiency of the instruction is sufficiently important (e.g., you are paying the learners' salaries while they are learning), a heuristic task analysis might be worth the expense. In either case, simplifying conditions should be identified and used to sequence the instruction.

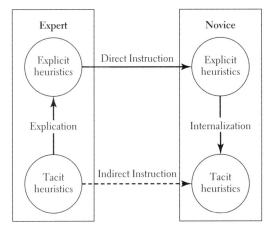

FIGURE 2.10. Two ways to teach heuristics (developed by Yun-Jo An).

Because most tasks entail a combination of both types of knowledge (procedural and heuristic), the SCM sequence is designed to be used simultaneously for both. Additionally, SCM and domain-elaboration sequences can be used concurrently as well. These are referred to as multiple-strand sequences (Beissner & Reigeluth, 1994).

For domain expertise, the conceptual elaboration sequence is described next, followed by the theoretical elaboration sequence.

The Conceptual Elaboration Sequence

For building domain expertise, the conceptual elaboration sequence is one of two sequencing strategies offered by the Elaboration Theory. Both types of elaboration sequences can be used simultaneously (multiple-strand sequencing) if there is considerable emphasis on both types of content in a course (Beissner & Reigeluth, 1994). The conceptual elaboration sequence (Reigeluth & Darwazeh, 1982) is intended for courses that focus on interrelated sets of concepts, which are usually kinds and/or parts of each other. Examples include a high school biology course that focuses on kinds and parts of animals and plants and a corporate training program that focuses on the kinds and parts of equipment the company sells. This sequencing methodology was derived primarily from Ausubel's (1968) "advance organizers" and "progressive differentiation" but provides greater guidance as to how to design that kind of sequence.

The sequence starts with the broadest, most inclusive and general concepts that have not yet been learned

and gradually progresses to their ever narrower, less inclusive, and more detailed parts and/or kinds, one level of detail at a time, until the desired level of detail is reached. This can be done in either a topical or spiral fashion (see Figure 2.2). You identify all of these concepts and their inclusivity relationships by conducting a conceptual analysis, which yields a conceptual structure (Reigeluth & Darwazeh, 1982), often referred to as a taxonomy. It is worth noting that the more detailed concepts are not necessarily more complex or more difficult to learn. For example, children usually learn what a dog is long before they learn what a mammal is. One point worth emphasizing is that the conceptual elaboration sequence does not violate the notion of learning prerequisites (hierarchical sequencing).

The Theoretical Elaboration Sequence

The theoretical elaboration sequence (Reigeluth, 1987) is the second of the two sequencing strategies currently offered by the Elaboration Theory for building domain expertise. As indicated earlier, it is intended for courses that focus on interrelated sets of principles at varying degrees of detail. Examples include a high school biology course that focuses on the principles of genetics, life cycles, and bodily functions and a corporate training program on how and why a piece of equipment works. This sequencing methodology was derived primarily from Bruner's (1960) spiral curriculum and Ausubel's advance organizers and progressive differentiation, but it differs in several important ways from each, and the Elaboration Theory also provides greater guidance on how to design the theoretical elaboration sequence than either Bruner or Ausubel provides for their sequences.

This sequence starts with the broadest, most inclusive, most general principles (which are also the simplest and generally the first to have been discovered) that have not yet been learned, such as the law of supply and demand in economics and Ohm's law in electricity. It gradually progresses to narrower, more detailed, precise, complex principles, such as those that relate to maximizing profits on the supply side (e.g., marginal revenues equaling marginal costs) and those that relate to consumer preferences on the demand side of the law of supply and demand. This is done until the desired level of complexity has been reached. Again, this pattern of sequencing can be done in either a topical or spiral fashion. You identify all of these principles and their inclusivity/complexity relationships by conducting a theoretical analysis (Reigeluth, 1987), which yields a theoretical structure (see Figure 2.8). It is worth noting that the more detailed principles are more complex and more difficult to learn.

Other Sequences

The three types of elaboration sequences just described are each based on a single type of relationship within the content. There are likely additional elaboration sequences that fit the basic principles of epitomizing and elaborating described earlier, as well as many sequences that do not (such as the historical sequence, which is based on the chronological relationship among events). But even more important is the utility of thinking about sequencing strategies for different types of courses, in addition to ones for different types of relationships. Often such strategies will be combinations of ones based on relationships, but not always.

The following are some of the types of common courses we have identified that seem likely to benefit from different types of course sequences, but there are surely many more that need to be identified:

- history courses, such as European history or courses on the history of a particular field or discipline, such as physical therapy or economics
- courses on the theory and practice of a particular field, such as physical therapy or electronics
- appreciation courses, such as music appreciation or art appreciation
- philosophy courses, such as the philosophy of education
- science courses, such as biology and physics
- skill courses, such as algebra, English composition, or electronic troubleshooting

It is beyond the scope of this chapter to explore differences in sequencing strategies for these common types of courses, partly because we have been unable to find much work on them.

When and Why to Use Elaboration Sequences

In both training and education contexts much instruction focuses on complex cognitive tasks. The strengths of the SCM sequence for such tasks are as follows:

- SCM enables learners to understand complex tasks holistically by acquiring the skills of an expert for a real-world version of the task from the very first module of the course.
- This understanding in turn enhances the motivation of learners and, therefore, the quality (effectiveness and efficiency) of the instruction.
- The holistic understanding of the task also results in the formation of a stable cognitive schema to which more complex capabilities and understandings can be assimilated. This is especially valuable for learning a complex cognitive task.
- Because the learners start with a real version of the task from the beginning, the SCM is ideally suited to situated learning, problem-based learning, computer-based simulations, and on-the-job training.
- The SCM can be used with highly directive instruction, highly constructivist instruction, or anything in between.

The strengths of the conceptual and theoretical elaboration sequences are these:

- They help to build the cognitive scaffolding (schemata) that makes subsequent, more complex understandings much easier to attain and retain.
- The enhancement of understanding aids motivation.
- These sequences can be used in either directive or constructivist approaches to instruction.

The limitations of the elaboration sequences are the following:

- The content (task or domain expertise) must be fairly complex and large to make the approach worthwhile. With smaller amounts of content, these approaches will not make much difference in the quality of the instruction.
- The elaboration sequences must be used with other sequencing strategies that provide guidance for within-module sequencing. For example, procedural tasks require a combination of procedural and hierarchical approaches for within-module sequencing. As an instructional theory that synthesizes existing knowledge about sequencing, the elaboration theory includes guidelines for using those other approaches with the elaboration approaches.

The net effect is that the elaboration sequences are powerful methods for complex tasks and domains, but they are a bit more complex and hence more difficult to learn, though not much more difficult to use once they are learned. Furthermore, the SCM task analysis procedures and the elaboration sequence content analysis procedures are both very efficient (see Reigeluth, 2006). Because these procedures allow task/content analysis and sequence design to be done simultaneously, it is possible to do *rapid prototyping* so that the first module can be designed and developed before any task or content analysis is done for the remaining modules of the course or curriculum. A rapid prototype can provide a good sample for inspection and approval by clients, higher management, and other stakeholders, as well as for formative evaluation and revision of the prototype, that can strongly improve the design of the remaining modules.

CONCLUSIONS

This review shows several of the major instructional design techniques for ordering instructional content, based on the nature of the content and its interrelationships. It also shows that much remains to be understood about how to sequence instruction for different domains.

The later chapters describe increasingly useful models, but they are ones that need to be developed further to support the needs of instructional design in the field. They are complex enough to support the development of new instructional methods beyond the ones presented here and help validate, illustrate, and teach these design principles.

The following are some general guidelines and principles for sequencing, organized by the order in which decisions need to be made.

Is Sequencing Important?

Decide whether sequencing is likely to make a difference (item 3.2 in Table 2.1). To make this decision, you need to analyze the amount of content and the degree of relationship among the elements of the content (item 3.1 in Table 2.1). If you are teaching a small amount of content (less than about 1 hour of instruction) or you are teaching unrelated topics, then sequencing is not likely to make a difference in school settings, and you can skip the rest of these guidelines and just use your common sense. Be sure to include in

the decision-making process the major people who will be implementing the instruction (item 3.4 in Table 2.1). Once you have made the decision, evaluate it by consulting more than one person who is experienced in teaching this content or task (item 3.3 in Table 2.1). They may be the same people you included in the activity for item 3.4 in Table 2.1.

What Kind of Sequence?

If sequencing is likely to make a difference, then you need to decide what kind of sequence to use (e.g., procedural, hierarchical, or elaboration). To do so, you need to analyze the nature of the content (item 3.1). Again, you should include experienced instructors and other end users in the decision-making process (items 3.4 and 3.3, respectively). Considerations for making this decision were described earlier in this chapter.

Design the Scope and Sequence

Once you have decided on the kind of sequence to use, then you need to apply the corresponding scope and sequence methodology to the content (item 3.2). To do this, you need to perform the appropriate type of content or task analysis (e.g., the procedural sequence requires procedural analysis, the hierarchical sequence requires learning prerequisite analysis, and so forth; item 3.1, Table 2.1). The process of conducting the content analysis simultaneously yields decisions about what content to teach (scope), how to cluster it into learning episodes (grouping), and what order to teach those learning episodes (sequence). The following are some general principles that can facilitate making these decisions.

The first factor to consider for sequencing is the size of each learning episode (set of related knowledge and skills). If the learning episode is too big, the learners may forget the early instruction before they have had a chance to review and synthesize what they have just learned. On the other hand, if the learning episode is too small, it will fragment the instruction. The size of each learning episode should also be influenced by the time constraints (if any) of the instructional situation (item 3.1). For example, if you are constrained to 2-hour blocks of time for teaching, then each learning episode should contain 2 hours worth of instructional content (or multiples of 2). Again, you should include end users and other stakeholders in the decision-making process (item 3.4) and have experienced instructors evaluate the resulting sequence (item 3.3).

Second, in addition to considering the size of each learning episode, the components of each learning episode should be considered. The components should be selected based on the relationships among learning episodes that you wish to utilize for your sequence. If you use a procedural sequence, you should include all those steps (and only those steps) that are performed in the same period of time. If you use a hierarchical sequence, you should include only those skills that are prerequisites for the same skill (or set of skills).

Third, the order of the learning episodes should be considered. Presenting too much complexity too soon or presenting the learning episodes in an illogical order will discourage the learner, slow down the learning process, and reduce the chances of mastering the topic or task. The order of these episodes will also depend on the relationship chosen. If you choose a procedural sequence, each set of steps (which constitutes a learning episode) should be taught in the order in which an expert performs it.

Design the Within-Episode Sequences

Once you have finalized the content for your learning episodes and sequenced them, you need to order the content within each learning episode (item 3.2). The sequencing of elements such as prerequisites and relevant information, understandings, and attitudes can influence the quality of the instruction. For example, if you teach nothing but the prerequisite skills (which are less interesting) in the first half of the learning session, learners may become bored and give up before they taste the real flavor of the topic or task, and they may forget the earlier ones before they have an opportunity to use them.

Various principles of sequencing are likely to be relevant here, such as "Teach prerequisites immediately before they are needed" (the just-in-time principle) and "Teach understanding before efficient procedures." Each of these principles requires a different type of analysis of the content (item 3.1). And, of course, you should include end users and other stakeholders in the decision-making process (item 3.4) and have experienced instructors evaluate the resulting within-learning-episode sequences (item 3.3). Reigeluth (2006) addresses further considerations for making these decisions.

The components and the order of each learning episode are strongly interrelated. The order will be influenced by the components. Therefore, the order should be selected by first determining which relationships should be emphasized and thus the components each learning episode should have. Some guidance for making this decision was presented earlier in this chapter.

What's Next?

Further research on sequencing instruction will need to advance our knowledge of sequencing strategies for different types of courses, such as those mentioned earlier (history, theory and practice, appreciation, philosophy, etc.). Additional research is also needed on how best to identify heuristic knowledge, which is often tacit knowledge unbeknownst to the expert (see, e.g., Dehoney, 1995; Lee & Reigeluth, 2003; Schraagen, Chipman, & Shalin, 2000). This requires advances in the heuristic task analysis process. Finally, research is needed on applying the principles of the Elaboration Theory to the affective domain.

PROJECTS AND OPEN PROBLEMS

1. Would any of the elaboration sequences (conceptual, theoretical, or simplifying conditions) be appropriate for a course that you teach (or have taught or might teach)? If so, which one? Prepare an outline of the learning episodes and their sequence.

2. What additional course-sequencing strategies can you think of, besides those listed earlier (historical, theory and practice, appreciation, philosophy, etc.), that are not offered by the hierarchical, procedural, and elaboration sequences? What major guidelines would you offer for such a course? Feel free to email your ideas to me at reigelut@indiana.edu.

3. How would you apply Elaboration Theory principles to teaching attitudes and values, such as the values of hard work, service to others, and integrity?

4. How can the theory and tools from later chapters help teachers in schools to improve their instruction? Interview a teacher to learn what that

person needs from a theory to teach more effectively.

5. Consider how to teach teachers about sequencing strategies. What would be a good order? Create a figure like Figure 2.3 or 2.5 for teaching sequencing strategies.

References

Anderson, J. R. (1983). *The architecture of cognition.* Cambridge, MA: Harvard University Press.

Anderson, R. C. (1984). Some reflections on the acquisition of knowledge. *Educational Researcher, 13*(9), 5–10.

Ausubel, D. P. (1968). *Educational psychology: A cognitive view.* New York: Holt, Rinehart, and Winston.

Banathy, B. H. (1996). *Designing social systems in a changing world.* New York: Plenum.

Beissner, K. L., & Reigeluth, C. M. (1994). A case study on course sequencing with multiple strands using the elaboration theory. *Performance Improvement Quarterly, 7*(2), 38–61.

Bruner, J. S. (1960). *The process of education.* New York: Random House.

Carr-Chellman, A. A., & Savoy, M. R. (2003). Using the user-design research for building school communities. *School Community Journal, 13*(2), 99–118.

Carr-Chellman, A. A. (in press). *User-design in instructional design.* Mahwah, NJ: Erlbaum.

Dehoney, J. (1995, February 8–12). *Cognitive task analysis: Implications for the theory and practice of instructional design.* Paper presented at the Association for Educational Communications and Technology, Anaheim, CA.

Gagné, R. M. (1965). *The conditions of learning* (2d ed.). New York: Holt, Rinehart, and Winston.

Gagné, R. M. (1968). Learning hierarchies. *Educational Psychology, 6,* 1–9.

Gagné, R. M., Briggs, L. J., & Wager, W. W. (1992). *Principles of instructional design* (4th ed.). New York: Harcourt Brace Jovanovich College Publishers.

Goleman, D. (1995). *Emotional intelligence: Why it can matter more than IQ.* New York: Bantam.

Greenberg, M. T., Kusche, C. A., Cook, E. T., & Quamma, J. P. (1995). Promoting emotional competence in school-aged children: The effects of the PATHS curriculum, *Developmental Psychopathology, 7,* 117–136.

Indiana Curriculum Advisory Council. (1991). *Indiana schooling for the twenty-first century.* Indianapolis: Indiana State Department of Education.

Kaufman, R. A., & English, F. W. (1979). *Needs assessment: Concept and application.* Englewood Cliffs, NJ: Educational Technology Publications.

Kaufman, R. A., Rojas, A. M., & Mayer, H. (1993). *Needs assessment: A user's guide.* Englewood Cliffs, NJ: Educational Technology Publications.

Lee, J. Y., & Reigeluth, C. M. (2003). Formative research on the heuristic task analysis process. *Educational Technology Research & Development, 51*(4), 5–24.

Leshin, C. B., Pollock, J., and Reigeluth, C. M. (1992). *Instructional design strategies and tactics.* Englewood Cliffs, NJ: Educational Technology Publications.

Mechner, F. (1967). Behavioral analysis and instructional sequencing. In P. Lange (Ed.), *Programmed instruction: 66th yearbook of the National Society for the Study of Education, Part II* (pp. 81–103). Chicago: University of Chicago Press.

Merrill, P. F. (1976). Task analysis: An information processing approach. *NSPI Journal, 15*(2), 7–11.

Merrill, P. F. (1980). Analysis of a procedural task. *NSPI Journal, 19*(2), 11–15.

Osin, L., & Lesgold, A. (1996). A proposal for the reengineering of the educational system. *Review of Educational Research, 66*(4), 621–656.

Polanyi, M. (1983). *The tacit dimension.* Garden City, NY: Doubleday.

Posner, G. J., & Strike, K. A. (1976). A categorization scheme for principles of sequencing content. *Review of Educational Research, 46,* 665–690.

Reigeluth, C. M. (1987). Lesson blueprints based on the elaboration theory of instruction. In C. M. Reigeluth (Ed.), *Instructional theories in action: Lessons illustrating selected theories and models* (pp. 245–288). Hillsdale, NJ: Erlbaum.

Reigeluth, C. M. (1992). Elaborating the elaboration theory. *Educational Technology Research & Development, 40*(3), 80–86.

Reigeluth, C. M. (2006). *Scope and sequence decisions for quality instruction.* Unpublished manuscript.

Reigeluth, C. M., & Darwazeh, A. N. (1982). The elaboration theory's procedure for designing instruction: A conceptual approach. *Journal of Instructional Development, 5*(3), 22–32.

Reigeluth, C. M., & Kim, Y. (1993, April). Recent advances in task analysis and sequencing. Paper presented at the NSPI national conference, Chicago.

Reigeluth, C. M., & Kim, Y. (1995, February 8–12). Rapid prototyping for task analysis and sequencing with the simplifying conditions method. Paper presented at the annual meeting of the Association for Educational Communications and Technology (session #520).

Reigeluth, C. M., & Rodgers, C. A. (1980). The Elaboration Theory of Instruction: Prescriptions for task analysis and design. *NSPI Journal, 19*(1), 16–26.

Resnick, L. B., & Ford, W. W. (1978). The analysis of tasks for instruction: An information-processing approach. In T. A. Brigham and A. C. Catania (Eds.), *Handbook of applied behavior analysis: Social and instructional processes* (pp. 378–409). New York: Irvington.

Rossett, A. (1987). *Training needs assessment.* Englewood Cliffs, NJ: Educational Technology Publications.

Rummelhart, D. E., & Ortony, A. (1977). The representation of knowledge in memory. In R. C. Anderson, R. J. Spiro, & W. W. Montague (Eds.), *Schooling and the acquisition of knowledge* (pp. 99–135). Hillsdale, NJ: Erlbaum.

Scandura, J. M. (1973). Structural learning and the design of educational materials. *Educational Technology, 8*(8), 7–13.

Schraagen, J. M., Chipman, S. F., & Shalin, V. L. (Eds.) (2000). *Cognitive task analysis.* Mahwah, NJ: Erlbaum.

Senge, P. M. (1990). *The fifth discipline: The art and practice of the learning organization.* New York: Currency Doubleday.

Vygotskii, L. S. (1986). *Thought and language* (A. Kozulin, Trans. and Ed.). Cambridge, MA: MIT Press.

Chapter 3

The Necessity of Order in Machine Learning: Is Order in Order?

A. Cornuéjols

In myriad human-tailored activities, whether in a classroom or listening to a story, human learners receive selected pieces of information presented in a chosen order and pace. This is what it takes to facilitate learning. Yet, when machine learners exhibited sequencing effects, showing that some data sampling, ordering, and tempo are better than others, seemingly simple questions had suddenly to be thought anew: What are good training data? How to select them? How to present them? Why is it that there are sequencing effects? How to measure them? Should we try to avoid them or take advantage of them? This chapter presents ideas and research directions that are currently studied in the machine learning field to answer these questions and others. As any other science, machine learning strives to develop models that stress fundamental aspects of the phenomenon under study. The basic concepts and models developed in machine learning are presented here, as well as some of the findings that may have significance and counterparts in related disciplines interested in learning and education.

Imagine this new Kibur's nightmare. The game that says, "Order an experience and experience order." How deceptively simple it looks. You just have a box with a transparent top, a landscape-like rubber surface inside, a ball rolling on this surface, and a few knobs on the side. You are told that after you have turned all the knobs on the side, in whatever order suits you, the ball has to be located just under a mark on the top of the box. Each knob, when turned, has an effect on the rubber surface and modifies its shape, rotating it along some axis or accentuating wells and mountains, and the rolling ball, in consequence, changes its position. Once every knob has been turned, it is known that the lowest point on the rubber surface is located below the mark on the top side of the box. The trick is that the ball, which descends only in the local well, will not necessarily be found in the lowest spot of the surface. Only by carefully selecting the order of the knobs' turning will the ball be guided to its desired place. How should you then go about selecting one of the very many ($n!$ if there are n knobs) possible orderings?

You play a little bit, get older if not order, and start to notice patterns. There is, for instance, one knob that can be turned at any time without affecting the final position of the ball; another knob must be turned third if success is to be obtained. By carefully selecting experiments, you learn the laws of your Kibur's box. Or so you believe.

Now comes the time when you are ready for variants. In one of these, you must manage to place your ball under other selected spots on the transparent top. This time you may choose whatever knobs you wish without having to turn all of them. Does that sound easier? Go ahead and try it. Then, there is this ultimate experience. You change the ball and place a new one inside the box, with a kind a Velcro-like covering that makes it slow in its changes of location on the slopes of the surface. Now you are ready to experiment with out-of-equilibrium control. To guide your ball, you can play with the speed of the surface transformations. A world full of new possibilities and challenges has opened up. You now have to control the choice of the knobs to turn, the order in which you turn them, and even the intervals between each turn. Experience order — or experience an ordeal? You begin to wonder.

In many learning situations, the sequence of training experiences is a key parameter. In education, for instance, teachers pay a great deal of attention to the teaching schedule. In particular, they carefully select the order of the exercises. So will the students themselves when preparing for an exam. Clearly, some choices and orders of exercises are better than others, while the delay (hours, days, or weeks) between problem-solving sessions is also of importance. This is true not only of human learning and concept acquisition. It has also been found that rats, taught to press a lever to obtain food, learn more quickly when rewarded first for partial performance of the desired response (for instance, simply for facing the end of the cage in which the lever sits) and then for increasingly more precise behavior.

In fact, some artificial learning systems that are coming of age now are equally sensitive to the sequencing of data presentation. The same questions abound for machine learners as for the natural organisms. What kind of sequencing effects show up in learning? Why are some learners (artificial or natural) affected while others are not? Are there general rules for choosing the most appropriate teaching sequence given a particular learner and a specific goal? These questions are difficult ones. The hope for the scientists involved in this research is that the more easily controllable machine-learning setting will provide results that will hold for large classes of learning systems, including natural ones, providing levers for further investigations in the natural learning area.

This chapter is intended to give a flavor of the research directions and the state of the art in machine learning regarding these questions. However, because the approach followed in machine learning is specific and original, it is interesting to first sketch a general perspective, one that may seem somewhat abstract and distant from natural and artificial learning systems but that nevertheless highlights crucial questions and essential parameters that play a role in sequential learning. This sketch puts in perspective the approaches and findings in machine learning and its links with the corresponding issues in psychology and the educational sciences. I thus ask the reader to spend some time examining these issues in a general and abstract setting and in a sense to go back to our Kibur's game.

WHAT DOES MACHINE LEARNING TELL US ABOUT LEARNING?

Machine learning is a very young discipline compared to other scientific fields, say physics or chemistry (see, for instance, Mitchell, 1997; Russell & Norvig, 2003; or Cornuéjols & Miclet, 2002, for the Francophones). The first computer models to incorporate learning or adaptive capacities first appeared in the 1950s. They explored cybernetic turtles and automatic checker players. It was not until the 1980s that a significant number of researchers dedicated themselves to this discipline. Yet, if one looks on the Internet to examine the content of the courses offered all around the world on machine learning, one will find that there is a large core of shared material and, more importantly, that there seems to be a consensus on what learning is and what constitutes the main lessons to be remembered about machine learning. This is extraordinary given the sheer complexity of the subject: learning. Has machine learning found what has eluded philosophy, psychology, and neurobiology for centuries? In this perspective, let us examine the course taken by machine learning over the last half century.

The first attempts at programming learning systems were oriented toward adaptive behaviors, either in cybernetic turtles that learned to exit a labyrinth or in the adaptation to opponents in checkers. The "learner" was at times subjected to reinforcement signals, positive or negative, and the learner's task was to maximize a kind of cumulated gain over time. These earlier systems were aimed at demonstrating the possibility of machine adaptation. They implemented clever heuristics at a time when almost no theory about adaptive systems even existed. In addition, they were following cybernetics with little or no concern for knowledge and reasoning. The 1960s witnessed the development of the then new field of "pattern recognition," where the problem was (and is) to find ways of recognizing instances of types of objects by observing simple characteristics or features of these instances. A theoretical account emerged, mostly of a statistical nature, and new algorithms were developed, among them the illustrious perceptron (see Rosenblatt, 1962; Minsky & Papert, 1988), ancestor of the now so commonly used formal neural networks. I will return to this approach to learning because, in more than one way, the current point of view is only a continuation of it.

Toward the end of the 1960s, the pattern recognition approach to learning was overshadowed by a new interest in cognitive aspects. This transition was inspired by the dominant artificial intelligence tradition, which put an emphasis on knowledge representation, rule-based inferencing, and more generally symbolic manipulations as the basis of intellectual activity. The work on machine learning changed in nature during the period that extends to the early 1980s. Doctoral dissertations, which represent the common quantum of activity in science, tended to aim at producing computer models of cognitive activities measured in human subjects, such as analogy making, learning the basis of geometry, or making conjectures in algebra. The hypotheses tested in these works were related to the division between working memory and semantic memory, the role of procedural versus declarative knowledge, the structuring of knowledge in memory, and so on. Consistent with cognitive science but in contrast with the current dominant view in machine learning, learning was considered as an ongoing activity. In addition, because the learner was supposed to learn something from a teacher that was cognitively equivalent, learning was considered successful to the extent that the learner correctly identified the concepts that the teacher had in mind.

This period was in many ways the golden age of the collaboration between cognitive science and machine learning. It did not last, however, for at least two reasons. First, the cognitive architectures developed in these computer programs, impressive as they were, depended too much on ad hoc tunings of the many parameters hidden in the system. It was difficult to extract general guiding principles from these experiments, let alone a general theory of learning. There were, therefore, doubts about the very nature of the scientific investigation associated with machine learning. Second, just at this time, the parallel distributed processing revolution (also called the neoconnectionist period) appeared. With it, everything changed. It brought the pattern recognition paradigm back in machine learning, with the idea that learning is essentially the search for a good approximation of some hidden concept known from a training sample. Also, because neural networks are adaptive systems based on differential equations and optimization techniques, this neoconnectionist revolution attracted theoretically oriented computer scientists to the field and as a consequence put more and more emphasis on convergence problems and complexity issues. More than

twenty years later, we are still mostly in the wake of this turning point.

According to this simplified perspective, learning chiefly comes in three guises: supervised learning, nonsupervised learning, and reinforcement learning. Because supervised learning has received most of the attention and has shaped the whole approach to learning, I start by describing the main ideas behind it.

The task in *supervised learning* can be defined in simple terms: A learning agent receives training data in the form of pairs (x_i, y_i), where x_i is an example described by a set (a vector; thus it is in bold) of simple characteristics, often called features, and y_i is its associated output value, which can be of various forms depending on the learning task. For instance, examples could be descriptions of objects or situations that are to be assigned to one of a predefined set of classes, as in an optical character recognizer that must output the name of the character ("A" through "Z") corresponding to the input digitalized image. This is accordingly called a *classification task*. In the case of a Boolean output, one speaks of a *concept learning* task since the system is supposed to recognize instances of a concept rather than anything else. If the output is taken from a continuous range of values, as is the case in the prediction of a trade market index, for instance, then one speaks of a *regression task*. In all cases, the output value is supposed to be computed from the corresponding input according to a hidden function (possibly corrupted by noise) or a hidden dependency, as is the case for a probabilistic dependency. The task of the learner is, from a limited collection of training data, to discover this dependency or at least to find a good approximation of it.

To be well posed, this problem needs additional constraints. First, the hidden or target dependency must be fixed a priori or at least changing sufficiently slowly that regularities can be reliably identified in the data. Second, except for very specific protocols where the data are supposed to be complete in some sense, it is unrealistic to demand perfect identification of the target dependency from the learner. A good approximation is enough. But what does that mean? In supervised learning, it is assumed that the ultimate goal is that the system makes predictions as accurately as possible for future events that can happen in the same universe as the one in which the learner was trained. This requirement has two parts. The first one measures the goodness of fit of the agent's prediction compared to the actual output for a given event. This

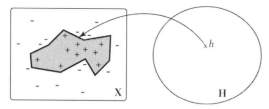

FIGURE 3.1. Inductive concept learning involves exploring a hypothesis space H to find a hypothesis h that describes a region of the example space X coherent with the known training instances.

"loss function" can, for instance, be a 0–1 function where a correct prediction counts 0, and 1 otherwise. One can then get the number of mistakes on a given set of test data. The loss function can also be the squared difference of the prediction and the correct output, or it can take the form of a loss matrix that counts errors of different types differently. For instance, as in medicine, a false negative could be more costly than a false positive. The second part allows one to compute the expected cost of using the agent's knowledge in the universe that includes unseen events. It takes the form of a probability density function over the events in the universe.

Thus, supervised learning can be seen as the search for a hypothesis as close as possible to the target dependency (see Figure 3.1), which means that its expected cost for as yet unseen events will be minimal. The theoretical analysis of supervised learning therefore involves three essential questions:

- First, given that one cannot directly compute the expected cost associated with a candidate hypothesis that one seeks to minimize, what should be the optimizing criterion defined on the basis of the available information?
- Second, in which space should one look for candidate hypotheses? Are there conditions on this hypothesis space, or is any space appropriate?
- Third, how should the exploration of the hypothesis space be organized to find a hypothesis optimizing the criteria of interest?

I address these three questions in turn.

Several methods of evaluating hypotheses have been proposed for inductive purposes; they all revolve around three main "inductive criteria" that correspond to seemingly intuitive and reasonable inductive principles:

- The first evaluation method says that *the best hypothesis is the one that most closely fits the data*. The underlying reason is that a hypothesis that fits the known data well should also fit the unknowns. This principle is called the *empirical risk minimization principle*, where the empirical risk measures the misfit, also called the loss, on the known data.
- The second one favors *the hypotheses that are the most likely given the data*. This requires estimating both a prior probability with regard to the hypotheses and conditional probabilities. The maximum likelihood principle is one well-known variant. It states that if all the hypotheses are equally likely before the observation of the training data, then one should choose the most likely one once the training data have been accounted for. In other words, one should choose the hypothesis that can most easily explain the data.
- The third one is inspired by information and communication theories and states that the best hypothesis is the one that allows one to transmit with as few bits as possible the information contained in the training data. In essence, it is closely related to the intuitive notion that *the best explanation of a set of phenomena is the simplest one*.

Depending on one's background, inclination, and requirements of the problem in question, a researcher will adopt one or the other of these inductive principles. Fortunately, there are strong links between them, and the choice of one particular principle does not usually have a large impact on the result.

Now that potential evaluation criteria have been defined for the candidate hypotheses, how should we choose the hypothesis space over which the evaluation will take place to select the best or at least a promising hypothesis? Apart from feasibility concerns, why should we not choose the largest or richest possible hypothesis space, in the hope that in this way we are assured that such a hypothesis space contains at least one hypothesis very close, if not identical, to the target dependency?

The study of inductive learning in fact shows that there is a fundamental trade-off between the richness of the hypothesis space, in some sense that can be technically defined, and the required number of training data needed to compute a good hypothesis. In essence, the richer the hypothesis space, the weaker the link between the estimated value of one hypothesis on the basis of the training data and its real value. Only more training data or insightful information from experts can tighten this link. This is why so much of the discussion and arguments in machine learning revolves around the choice of the hypothesis space and of the related knowledge representation language. The problem, of course, is that a too constrained hypothesis space can prevent finding a good hypothesis therein. Part of the game in inductive learning is, therefore, to adaptively select the best hypothesis space.

Finally, there is the issue of the actual exploration of the hypothesis space, once chosen, to find a good—or even the best—hypothesis according to the selected inductive criterion. The search procedure critically depends upon the structure or absence thereof that the hypothesis space can be endowed with. There are three main possibilities for the search.

The first one occurs when a relation of relative generality can be defined over the space of hypotheses. In this way, it is possible, by directly considering their expressions, to determine whether one hypothesis is more general or more specific than another one—or is simply not comparable. More importantly, it is usually possible to define generalization and specialization operators that allow one to obtain hypotheses more general or more specific than a given one. If available, this generality relation is very helpful in that it allows one to explore the hypothesis space in an informed way by following meaningful directions. For instance, if a given candidate hypothesis does not cover or explain some known positive instance of the target concept, then only a more general hypothesis is acceptable. The exploration of the hypothesis space can then be carried out by applying generalization operators to the incorrect hypothesis. In contrast, specialization operators should be used if the candidate hypothesis wrongly covers negative instances of the target concept. This is the basis of what is often called "symbolic machine learning." The difficulty of defining a relation of generality over the hypothesis space is more than counterbalanced by the resulting much greater efficiency of the search procedure and the accompanying comprehensibility of the learning process.

The second possibility corresponds to the case in which no generality relationship can be found over the hypothesis space. For instance, the use of neural networks does not allow for such a generality relationship to be defined. In that case, one has to rely on less powerful search procedures. In effect, this means procedures that are based on gradient descent techniques. Using the chosen inductive criterion, one estimates the merit of the current candidate hypothesis and its immediate neighbors and follows the direction that leads to the seemingly greater improvement. The notorious back-propagation algorithms for neural networks or the genetic algorithm mechanisms are nothing other than variants of gradient-based search procedures. For their greater range of applicability, one pays for their relative inefficiency and opaque character.

Finally, it may not even be possible to define a hypothesis space, per se, distinct from the example space. Learning then does not output any more hypotheses about the world but only decisions based on comparisons between a current input and known instances. The famous nearest neighbor technique, which decides that an input is of the same class as the class of the nearest known example, is an instance of this family of algorithms. This corresponds to the weakest possible type of learning. To give good results, it requires the knowledge of numerous examples.

The framework for inductive learning that I have sketched here has similar counterparts in unsupervised learning and somewhat in reinforcement learning as well. It has provided a sound theoretical basis for induction. This, in turn, can be used to explain the properties of well-known learning algorithms that were first obtained heuristically, but it has also led to new powerful inductive algorithms that were motivated from theoretical interrogations, such as the so-called support vector machines (see Vapnik, 1995; Schölkopf, Burges, & Smola, 1999), or the boosting metalearning technique (see Freund & Schapire, 1999). There are now myriads of applications for learning techniques that go under the generic name of data mining. Machine learning is thus a well-established field with a seemingly strong theoretical basis.

Hence, has machine learning uncovered truths that escaped the notice of philosophy, psychology, and biology? On one hand, it can be argued that machine learning has at least provided grounds for some of the claims of philosophy regarding the nature of knowledge and its acquisition. Against pure empiricism, induction requires prior knowledge, if only in the form of a constrained hypothesis space. In addition, there is a kind of conservation law at play in induction. The more a priori knowledge there is, the easier learning is and the fewer data are needed, and vice versa. The statistical study of machine learning allows quantifying this trade-off. One corollary is that, if a cognitive agent is ready to accept any theory of the world, then it becomes unable to learn by induction from data alone. This is deeply connected to Opper's claim that science is characterized by the possibility of refuting theories. If everything is conceivable, then for any set of data there exists a model for it, and one can no longer avail oneself of the good fit between the model and the learning data to guarantee its relevance for future unknown events.

On the other hand, the algorithms produced in machine learning during the last few decades seem quite remote from what can be expected to account for natural cognition. For one thing, there is virtually no notion of knowledge organization in these methods. Learning is supposed to arise on a blank slate, albeit a constrained one, and its output is not supposed to be used for subsequent learning episodes. Neither is there any hierarchy in the "knowledge" produced. Learning is not conceived as an ongoing activity but rather as a one-shot process more akin to data analysis than to a gradual discovery development or even to an adaptive process. Indeed, this timeless point of view of learning resides also at the core of the current theories of induction. Thus, the theory that establishes a link between the empirical fit of the candidate hypothesis with respect to the data and its expected value on unseen events becomes essentially inoperative if the data are not supposed to be independent of each other. This requirement is obviously at odds with most natural learning settings, where either the learner is actively searching for data or where learning occurs under the guidance of a teacher who is carefully choosing the data and their order of presentation. If only for this reason, it would be interesting to remove the blinders of the current dominant theory in machine learning and study learning as a more historical and interactive process.

To sum up, even if the successes of machine learning so far can justifiably be considered impressive, they are nonetheless too often limited to a narrow range of situations. Thus, learning is seen as a passive process with data arriving independently of each other from a stationary environment. Learning is a one-shot activity with training occurring once before testing. Finally, the current theories about learning are mostly

done as worst-case analyses; they suppose that the environment behaves as an adversary trying to conceal its regularities from the learner. In addition, they are unable to account for incremental learning.

From this severe assessment, it seems that machine learning is not yet in a position to offer vistas on incremental learning and ordering effects. In the following section I extract relevant seeds from recent inquiries in machine learning.

EMPIRICAL FINDINGS: DATA + SEQUENCES = VARIATIONS

Even though machine learning has not overly concerned itself with the ongoing character of learning, practical considerations sometimes impose resorting to incremental learning. For instance, there are situations in which the data are not entirely available before decisions must be made, causing learning to be distributed over time. But even in cases where the whole data set is on hand, it can happen that, due to its size, the learning algorithm cannot practically handle it all and must split the data into smaller samples, starting by finding regularities in the first sample and then using others sequentially to check and modify if needed any regularity that is found. There is, therefore, a collection of empirical findings about what is called *on-line learning*.

One of the most documented and studied spectacular effects is observed with artificial neural networks. These systems are made of numerous elementary computing elements called "neurons" that are often organized in successive layers through which information flows from input units to output units via connections (see Figure 3.2). In supervised learning, input and output units are repeatedly clipped with the values associated with the training examples, and the strength of the connections in the network are progressively modified using a gradient descent technique to reproduce the correct output for each example's input. If the neural network has been well tailored and if the data are representative of the phenomenon, then generalization can occur from the particular training set to unseen inputs.

In neural networks, there are two types of learning algorithms: those that take the whole training set into consideration to compute a total signal error that is used for the gradient descent method, and those that compute local error signals, one for each example in

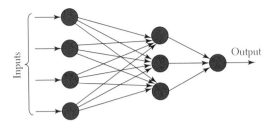

FIGURE 3.2. Example of a feed-forward neural network. The input signal is transmitted from one layer of neurons to the next one via weighted connections.

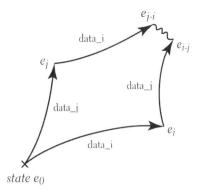

FIGURE 3.3. From an initial state e_0, two orderings of data$_i$ and data$_j$ can lead in general to two different learner states. Which information should then be transmitted from one state to the next one so that $e_{i-j} = e_{j-i}$?

turn. In both cases, the training set must be presented to the system many times before convergence of the connection strengths occurs. However, what happens then if new instances become available? Can we continue learning by concentrating on these new instances without repeating the former ones as, it seems, is routinely done in natural brains? The answer, obtained through numerous experiments, is a resounding no. When an artificial neural network is exposed to new examples, it tends to completely forget what has been learned before, a phenomenon aptly named "catastrophic forgetting" (see French, 1997). Something in these artificial neural networks wreaks havoc. Researchers have attempted to remedy this by acting in two directions: either by manipulating the data and repeating at least part of the former data in the new data set presentations, or by modifying the learning algorithm itself. It has been postulated that one reason for this undesirable behavior is indeed the distributed character of the memory in neural network. By somewhat limiting this distributed processing, a more graceful behavior is obtained in incremental learning. For more information, see Lane's chapter (this volume).

These efforts, however, are partial and only scratch the surface of important questions. For instance, which information, in on-line learning, is transmitted from one state of the learner to the next one? More intriguingly, what happens if two pieces of data are presented in two different orders? Is the result of learning the same (see Figure 3.3)?

One can imagine that if the learner perfectly accumulates its past experience, then no forgetting occurs. The learner passes all of this information from one state to the next, adding in the process more and more information as training data are made available. Then, of course, the system is insensitive to the order of presentation of the data. However, surely, learning can

involve much more sophisticated mechanisms than pure memorization of data. Is it still possible to identify the "current of information" flowing from one state to the next? Can we determine the conditions that are necessary or sufficient or both, regarding the data and/or the learner, for order independence in learning?

Incremental learning systems other than neural networks have been devised out of curiosity or for reasons of applicability to real-world problems. For instance, incremental versions of decision trees for inductive algorithms (see Utgoff, 1989, 1994) have been published and tested. In unsupervised learning, many algorithms behave incrementally by selecting "seeds" among the training data from where groups or hierarchical categories are built. Always the yardstick against which these systems have been compared is the nonincremental version. Variations in the learning output resulting from the order of the training data presentation, also called ordering effects, accompanying these incremental learners have been considered as deviations from the true best obtainable learning results. Thus, research efforts have turned toward the reduction of these effects. It did not occur that the sequence of the data can encode useful information that only learners prone to ordering effects could detect or that nonincremental learning is necessarily an ideal. The same outlook also dominates theoretical studies on on-line learning, the question being there to measure the "regret," or the difference in performance, between an on-line learner and the corresponding off-line one when given identical training data.

In this frame of thought, various heuristics have therefore been proposed to reduce ordering effects. Foremost among them is the proposal that training examples be presented in as uncorrelated an order as possible. For instance, in unsupervised learning, one should try to present examples of each category in turn so that a category does not establish itself too strongly before instances of other categories are observed. But a more radical solution is, rather than to play on the training data order, to modify the incremental learning algorithm. One solution is indeed to keep in memory all of the past data and recompute at any time the current optimum, given all the data observed so far. For instance, the decision tree inducer ID5 (see Utgoff, 1994) is an on-line version of the standard induction algorithm ID3 (see Quinlan, 1986), where enough information about past data is kept in memory to ensure that the same tree that would be induced by ID3 is produced by ID5. On the other hand, the system ID4, which does not memorize as much information as ID5, is prone to ordering effects (see Utgoff, 1989).

One can see, therefore, that there is an interplay between the training data and the learning algorithm that affects the importance of ordering effects.

SEQUENCING EFFECTS AND LEARNING

Given a learning task defined by a space of potential examples together with their attached output values (in the case of supervised learning) and a cost function over the prediction made by the learner, *sequencing effects* arise when the result of learning is affected by at least one of the following parameters: (1) *sampling*, that is the choice of the training data, (2) the *order* of presentation of these data, and (3) the *speed* of presentation.

Sequencing effects abound in natural learning situations. It is obvious to any teacher that the learning material, the order in which it is presented, and the speed of presentation of this material are all of paramount importance in the making of a good lesson. Not all students are equally affected by the possible variations of these parameters, but all are, at least to some degree. This seems equally true in animal learning. In fact, it is difficult to envision any learning process that would not be sensitive to sequencing effects.

It is clear why learning must, in general, be sensitive to sampling, that is, to the choice of the learn-ing inputs. Indeed, following what was mentioned earlier on inductive supervised learning, each candidate hypothesis is evaluated with respect to the available training data via the inductive criteria. Usually, when one changes the particular training set, one also de facto changes the respective values of the hypotheses, possibly leading to a different choice of the optimal hypothesis. In technical terms, this is called the variance. It is usually the case that the variance is directly linked to the richness of the hypothesis space, increasing when the richness increases.

The dependency of learning on the order and the speed of presentation of the data calls for other considerations that can be related to the search procedure used for finding hypotheses that are good under the inductive criteria. Two main parameters can be identified in this respect. The first one is associated with the *memorization of the information contained in the data observed so far*. If no information is discarded, then, in principle, it is possible to restore the entire collection of the past data and, therefore, to cancel the effects due to their order of presentation. On the other hand, forgetting aspects of the past data can prevent one from finding the same optimum of the inductive criteria since it is now computed from different data. Because forgetting is usually a function of the order of the data presentation and possibly of its duration (see Pavlik's chapter, this volume), the result of learning can be affected as well by the same factors.

The second parameter is linked to the *properties of the search procedure* used for the exploration of the hypothesis space. Even if no information on the training data is lost, if the search procedure is not guaranteed to return the optimal hypothesis but, for instance, only a local one, then the order in which the data are processed can lead to different results. This is illustrated in Figure 3.4 for a gradient method. If, in addition, the search procedure exhibits inertia due to limits on computational resources, then the order and speed issues acquire even greater importance.

Sampling, order, and speed of presentation thus define a three-dimensional control parameter space (see Figure 3.5). A number of research forays in machine learning explore this space, even if, admittedly, in a still very limited way. This is the topic of the next section. Along the way, it will be interesting to consider a set of questions and examine what light, if any, machine learning research sheds on them.

These questions include obvious ones about the controllability of learning:

Landscape after data + data$_i$

Landscape after data + data$_i$ + data$_j$

Landscape after data + data$_j$

Landscape after data + data$_j$ + data$_i$

FIGURE 3.4. The optimization landscape changes with each new piece of data and may differ depending on the order of presentation of the data.

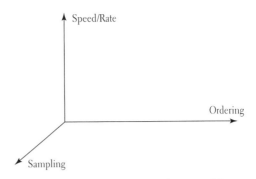

FIGURE 3.5. The three-dimensional space of the control parameters for ordering effects in incremental learning.

- Are there general strategies for determining—either a priori or on-line—the most appropriate data sample, order, and speed of the presentation of examples?
- Are there advantages to ordering effects? If so, how can we profit from them?
- More specifically, does the choice of data sample, order, and speed of presentation facilitate learning more—or simply learning more easily?
- Under what conditions, with regard to either the data or the learner, can incremental learning be rendered order independent?

There are also questions related to the learning process as an ongoing activity:

- Are there harmful pieces of data? What characterizes them? How do they affect learning? How do learners recover from them?
- What are the conditions for positive or negative transfer from one learning step or task to the next one?
- Is it sometimes necessary or useful to retrace steps in learning, for instance, reconsidering past hypotheses or past data sets?
- Would it be possible to infer an unknown concept in such a way that only better and better hypotheses are inferred? And, more generally, can monotonic learning always be successful?
- How does prior knowledge affect sequencing effects?
- What kind of relationships, if any, exist between the information content of the data, the training

sequence, the properties of the learner, and ordering effects?

CONTROLLING SEQUENCING EFFECTS: A MACHINE LEARNING PERSPECTIVE

Before considering ways of controlling incremental learning, a preliminary question needs to be addressed: How do we measure or evaluate different learning trajectories?

Under the classical model in machine learning, only the result of learning matters; the vagaries during the learning process are deemed of no consequence. However, this point of view seems too limited in the study of incremental learning because one aspect of interest is the ease of learning, not merely the end product or even the rate of convergence to the final hypothesis or the final level of performance. Several other performance criteria have thus been defined to assess the merits of various learning strategies.

Some merely quantify the degradation of performance compared to one-shot, nonincremental learning, which results from the lack of information during learning. This is the "regret" notion. It is usually cast into a game theoretical framework in which one compares the gain of a set of various "players," that is, learners, over a given sequence of training data.

Other criteria quantify the whole learning trajectory underlining specific aspects. For instance:

- the number of needed training instances
- the number of mistakes the learner made during training (This mostly applies in concept learning

tasks, where the learner tries to identify a target concept. For each new input, the learner is first asked to give its class according to its current knowledge, before being given the correct answer. Each mistake is counted.)
- the number of mind changes of the learner during training (In the machine learning perspective, a *mind change* occurs whenever the learner changes its mind about the best hypothesis or model of the data observed so far.)
- the memory size required during learning

It is then possible to analyze learning settings where either the data sample, the order or speed of presentation, or the set of parameters controlling the learners is varied.

Active Learning

In active learning, the learner is not passively waiting for the data to come but has, to varying degrees, some autonomy in the search for information. In the weaker setting, the learner can choose examples only among a predefined training data set. For instance, this could apply to the case in which data are abundant, but the cost of labeling each example is high so that only the data selected by the learner will be submitted to the expert. Two approaches are possible based on whether the learner must make its choices prior to learning or whether it can make its decisions piecewise while learning.

In the first case, this amounts to changing the input distribution. Because the selection of the more useful data must be done before learning, the choice is usually made on the basis of a crude preliminary data analysis phase. For instance, one may try to eliminate redundant examples or discard seemingly irrelevant attributes describing the examples. Or one may want to detect and retain prototypes, for instance, centers of groups of data points, in the hope that these encode most of the information without be overly affected by noise or spurious effects in the original data sets. The question is whether such a "filter" method, roughly independent of the learning algorithm, can be devised in a general way. It is in fact not the case, and no filter is universally useful. It all depends on the kind of regularities that are searched for in the data.

In the second case, the selection of the next data point to query is made on the basis of the current candidate hypothesis. In concept learning, there are two main approaches. One is to modify the distribution of the input data from one run to the next, as in the boosting method (Freund & Schapire, 1999). In a sense, this is not really incremental learning but rather an iterative process where more and more weight is given to examples that were not correctly classified in the previous run. The final decision function results from a weighted sum of the hypotheses learned at every step.

The second approach properly belongs to the incremental scheme with new examples processed on-line. Again, one can distinguish two principal mechanisms. The first one is to try to gain as much information as possible with each new data point. This can be done simply by selecting data points in regions where one does not yet have data, or where the performance so far is bad, or where previously found data resulted in learning. One can also try to measure the uncertainty affecting the current candidate hypotheses and select data that reduce uncertainty as much as possible. Technically, this can be done in several ways. For instance:

- One can try to reduce the number of remaining candidate hypotheses, which is called the version space in concept learning. The difficulty here is first to evaluate the "volume" of the space and second to identify one optimal example, that is, one that allows the elimination of approximately one half of the version space.
- Another solution consists in measuring the disagreement among hypotheses sampled from the current version space on potential training examples and retaining one example for which this disagreement is maximal.
- A third method, not limited to concept learning (i.e., only two classes), is to compute the entropy of each potential class for each remaining instance and each possible labeling of them. One then selects the instance that maximally reduces the entropy. This can be computationally expensive.

There are other proposed techniques, but all of them revolve around the idea of trying, one way or another, to reduce as much as possible the uncertainty about the remaining candidate hypotheses.

Another approach does not take into account the whole version space but focuses instead on the current candidate hypothesis. In this framework, one tries to get more details about the hypothesis where differences in prediction are more critical. For instance, when the hypothesis can be seen as a decision function separating the space of examples in two regions, there can be regions where positive and negative instances are close to each other and where, therefore, it is crucial that the decision boundary be well informed. Active learning consists then in selecting data points close to that estimated boundary to accurately define it.

One borderline case is that of reinforcement learning. There, an agent perceiving part of its environment and choosing actions that modify its state in the environment tries to identify courses of actions, called policies, that maximize a cumulative gain over time. Initially the agent knows very little about the environment, and it must learn its characteristics while acting. To discover an optimal or near-optimal policy, the agent usually must control a trade-off between exploring the world (so that it does not miss valuable opportunities) and exploits its current knowledge about the world. Here, the data points correspond to states of the agent in the world, and they must be tested to discover what opportunities they offer in terms of gain. It was found that, under some stationary conditions with regard to the environment, the optimal sampling strategy is to greedily select the seemingly most promising states, except for a small, diminishing proportion of time. Strictly speaking, this guarantees correct learning only in the limit of infinitely many visits of each state.

More interesting are the studies of learning games using reinforcement learning. There the question arises as to what is the best progression of "teachers." Should one start by confronting novice players before playing against experts? Or should there be a period of self-play: the machine against the machine? No definite answer has been found, even if it has been generally observed that facing players of increasing competence is better than the other way around. This question more properly belongs to the general issue of teachability discussed later.

Finally, other active learning paradigms have been investigated, particularly in theoretical terms. In one, called the "membership query" model, the learner queries any data point and is told whether the queried example belongs to the concept (see Angluin, 1988). In the "equivalence query" model, the learner can ask whether one hypothesis is the correct one, and the "oracle" either answers "yes" or provides a counter-example (see Angluin, 1988). One interesting result is that, if the learner can test hypotheses that are outside the set of target concepts, then learning can possibly require fewer training data than if it is required to stay within this set.

Overall, when active learning consists in selecting examples to label from a given set of unlabeled data, theoretical results show that the number of training data can be reduced substantially if they are selected carefully. In some cases, this can make the difference between tractable and intractable learning. However, these studies look at only the acceleration of learning, not at differences in what can be learned with different orders of presentation of the training data. Several chapters here examine learners doing something like this.

From a conceptual point of view, the study of active learning is very important because it forces researchers to turn away from the assumption that data are identically and independently distributed, which is at the basis of most of the theoretical constructions so far. One can expect radically novel ideas when this assumption is fully removed.

The Control Parameters of the Learner

When an external agent, rather than the learner, controls a part of the learning process, there exist two broad classes of possible interferences with the learning process. Either one tries to change the learner's characteristics or one tries to control the sequence of inputs. The latter case, called teachability, is dealt with latter.

There are many control parameters to a learning system. The question is to identify, at a sufficiently high level, the ones that can play a key role in sequencing effects. Because learning can be seen as the search for an optimal hypothesis in a given space under an inductive criteria defined over the training set, three means to control learning readily appear. The first one corresponds to a change of the hypothesis space. The second consists in modifying the optimization landscape. This can be done by changing either the training set (for instance, by a forgetting mechanism) or the inductive criteria. Finally, one can also fiddle with the exploration process. For instance, in the case of a gradient search, slowing down the search process can prevent the system from having time to find the local optimum, which, in turn, can introduce sequencing effects.

Not all of these possibilities have been investigated in machine learning. Mostly there have been some theoretical studies dealing with the impact on learning of quantities such as:

- the memory capacity (particularly the trade-off between short-term and long-term memory)
- the number of mind changes allowed to the learner before it has to settle for a definitive hypothesis
- the number of errors allowed during learning
- the computational resources

Some studies have also dealt with the effect of imposing some monotonic constraint on learning, such as not allowing new candidate hypotheses to be considered that are in error on some past data points.

Overall, the findings are generally valid only in very restricted conditions, and it is difficult to interpret or generalize them. One can cite, for instance, the result that, in inductive concept learning, order independence is possible only if no forgetting of the training data occurs. This underlines the fact that order independence is a rather stringent and unreasonable restriction on learning.

How can learning be optimized through better ordering, given that the learner and the target concept are known in advance? Or, what is the optimal ordering for a given learner? Those are questions that do not yet have answers.

Teachability

In teachability studies, the problem is how to select the best training data and/or the order of presentation such that learning of a given target concept (or target class of concepts) is facilitated. One question in particular is to quantify the minimal sequence of training data needed to teach a target concept to a learner (see Goldman & Mathias, 1996). This can be in terms of the sample size required or the minimal number of mistakes the learner is to make before reaching the correct hypothesis. Obviously the notion of a learner has to be more precisely defined. It can be some given learner, the characteristics of which are known to the teacher, or it can be any learner or the worst possible learner. In these cases, the learner should still obey some constraints. In machine learning, one often requires that the learner consider only hypotheses that

are coherent with the data, for example, that they cover all positive instances and no negative ones.

The size of the minimal training set needed to teach a coherent learner is called the "teaching dimension." It obviously depends on the types of laws that Nature and the learner may consider. For instance, if the possible hypotheses take the form of convex rectangles in two dimensions and if the learner always outputs the most general hypothesis consistent with all past training inputs, then it suffices to provide the learner with the two inputs associated with two opposites vertices of the target rectangle. Therefore, it is apparent that the problem is to determine the right encoding of the target law within the instance language and given some knowledge about the learner's functioning.

While relatively little empirical work has been reported on this question, theoreticians have pondered with anguish the line separating teaching from cheating. One can indeed see teaching as a kind of encoding operation by which a teacher tries to transmit some information to the learner using a coded message: the training data. If, however, nothing prevents the teacher and the learner from having agreed beforehand on some private code, then it is easy for the teacher to transmit the identity of the hypothesis in this secret code, thus completely bypassing a true learning mechanism. Much consideration has been given to cleverly defining the rules of the teaching game so as to prevent any possibility of collusion. One must acknowledge that, overall, this has been detrimental to the search for reasonable scenarios and to obtaining interesting results. In fear of forbidden collusion between learner and teacher, the theoretical settings devised by researchers have actually prohibited any possibility of a constructive cooperation and address only scenarios in which the learner becomes obstinate and adversarial, trying as hard as possible not to learn! In the present state of affairs, waiting for renewed theoretical approaches, the more interesting ideas come from the study of heuristics designed for empirical experiments.

One early proposal is to select for teaching what are called "near-miss" examples (see Winston, 1970). These examples (positive or negative) differ from the current best candidate hypothesis by as few relevant aspects as possible because the idea is to help the learner to focus on relevant differences between the current hypothesis and the target concept. The difficulty here—to transfer that principle to natural learning–is that a perfect knowledge of the learner and of its current set of candidate hypotheses is required. Other proposals are described in more general terms. For instance, one idea is to provide the data in increasing order of complexity. One could translate this into "teach simple things first." (See Gobet and Lane in this volume for an example application of this.)

However, the task remains to define a reliable complexity criterion. Some concepts can be easy for one learner, while being unfathomable to another or to the same learner at another time. Most current research defines complexity in terms of superficial syntactical complexity. This certainly is unsatisfactory, and there remains a long way to go between such crude criteria and the more sophisticated principles used, for example, in educational science, where concerns for things such as the historical genesis of the subject matter or its epistemology are everyday life.

There is nonetheless one promising research direction called hierarchical learning (see Barto & Mahadevan, 2003; Murphy & Lassaline, 1997; and Rivest & Sloan, 1994). The idea is to teach subconcepts before higher knowledge structures. This has been tested for the learning of concepts expressed in first-order logic, where one can identify logical subexpressions. Once again, the teacher must know the definition of the target concept and at the same time identify subconcepts and relevant corresponding training data.

As one can see, teaching requires knowledge of the domain, the learning target, and some characteristics of the learner. This suggests a trade-off between the complexity of teaching and the complexity of learning. This is one open question among many for which the study of machine learning has yet to provide answers. We are far from being able to compute the best way to teach Newtonian mechanics or French grammar to human students or artificial learners.

CONCLUSIONS

Artificial intelligence needs to study sequencing effects for many reasons. First, natural learning systems (be they human or not) learn over time, and all seem prone to sequencing effects, in particular related to the order and speed of the learning inputs and tasks. If artificial intelligence is to be part of the overall scientific effort toward understanding cognition and especially natural cognition, it cannot ignore these aspects of learning.

Second, if only on practical and engineering grounds, artificial intelligence must increasingly deal with incremental learning. The huge databases now readily available can no longer be handled in one shot. They have to be analyzed in a piecemeal fashion and, thus, at least partially sequentially. This implies that choices will have to be made regarding the selection of training data subsets and their order of presentation. Likewise, many learning systems are now embedded in long-life computer systems and must confront sequences of inputs, drifting environmental conditions, and evaluative tasks. Per force therefore, artificial intelligence engineers will become increasingly aware of sequencing effects and will have to find intelligent ways to cope with them.

Finally, there are reasons to believe that deep issues in cognition and information theory are connected with the study of incremental learning and sequencing effects. For instance, there has been much debate about the redundancy in a set of information. But this question becomes even more interesting when it is discussed in the context of a sequence of information because then the place in the sequence has to be taken into account and, even more, the possibility for misleading pieces of information must be examined.

While it has been always considered that a piece of information could at worst be useless, it should now be acknowledged that it can have a *negative* impact. There is simply no theory of information at the moment offering a framework ready to account for this in general. Related to this issue is the problem of transfer, positive or negative, between learning tasks. This is still infrequently studied in artificial intelligence and only in the context of independent computer simulations for very limited sets of learning tasks involving relatively poor prior knowledge. For a view of this from cognitive science, see Singley and Anderson (1989) and Ritter and Bibby (2001). It is obvious that if one is seriously interested in understanding and controlling transfer in learning (for instance, in the hope of enhancing the efficiency of the educational system), much more research must be done in this area.

More generally, the study of incremental learning and sequencing effects should shed new light on fundamental questions such as these: What is the impact of forgetting? Can it be helpful in some cases? What kind of data should preferably be dispensed with in case of memory size constraints? What is the best teaching strategy? What is the trade-off between the complexity of learning and the complexity of teaching?

With regard to these questions, there are two ways to assess the current status of machine learning research. The first one pessimistically considers the blindness of the current dominant paradigm in machine learning concerning incremental learning and sequencing effects, as well as the lack of interest so far from the practitioners. In addition, machine learning so far is mostly limited to the learning of one concept, using a single learning mechanism with little prior knowledge. This is indeed a poor framework for the study of something as complex as learning can be in natural systems. The second way optimistically regards this state of affairs as an opportunity to open up new and interesting directions for research, which could have a major impact on the development of cognitive science as a whole. If it is true that machine learning research currently has little to offer regarding on-line and long-life learning, it nevertheless provides tremendous opportunities for research in this area, if only because artificial learners and artificial contexts are more easily controllable than natural ones. (See Ohlsson, this volume, for an example application.)

In effect, machine learning research has already brought us several interesting concepts. Most prominently, it has stressed the benefit of distinguishing between the properties of the hypothesis space—its richness and the valuation scheme associated with it—and the characteristics of the actual search procedure in this space, guided by the training data. This in turn suggests two important factors related to sequencing effects, namely forgetting and the non-optimality of the search procedure. Both are key parameters than need to be thoroughly understood if one is to master sequencing effects. Indeed, in retrospect, it is hard to believe that learning and memorization can be studied without regard to forgetting. There is thus no doubt that sequencing effects are deeply associated with the fundamental properties of learning. They therefore deserve to be actively examined.

It is foreseeable that machine learning research will increasingly turn toward the study of incremental learning (see Figure 3.6). Among the reasons for this new focus are the current interest in text mining—and what are texts if not complex *sequences* of data?—the growing concern for computer-aided education, and the design of more complex learning systems embedded in long-life artificial systems.

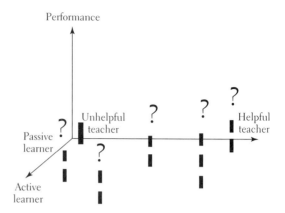

FIGURE 3.6. So far, in machine learning we have performance measures only for passive learners and unhelpful teachers. Future work should provide us with more insights into other mixtures of learning parameters.

There is hope, therefore, that someday in the not-too-distant future, we will be more knowledgeable about sequencing effects, learning trajectories, and the design of teaching sequences. We should be careful, however, not to be overly optimistic. It will never be easy to craft optimal or even good teaching sequences. After all, it is quite difficult to find a sequence of appropriate operations for transforming a Rubik's cube back to its original configuration. Finding a sequence of inputs that carefully guides a complex learner toward some goal state will be at least as difficult. In some sense, education and the Kibur's megagame are not that different from the Rubik's cube game. We have thus a lot of fun and frustration waiting for us.

PROJECTS AND OPEN PROBLEMS

1. Explain why the candidate elimination algorithm of Mitchell (1997) is not subject to the order of presentation of the data.

    Propose changes to the algorithm that would make it order sensitive.

2. Use the SNNS software freely available on the Internet (www-ra.informatik.uni-tuebingen.de/SNNS/) to learn the letters in the data set provided in the letters.pat file available with the software. First, learn the whole set of 26 letters. This should typically require a few hundred epochs to get an accuracy better than 99%.

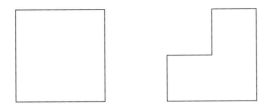

FIGURE 3.7. A square that must be split into 5 equal parts (left). The amputated square (one fourth has been removed) that has to be split into 2, 3, and then 4 equal parts (right).

Next, learn first one half of the 26 letters, and—only when these are learned with high accuracy—learn the second half. What do you observe happens to the recognition of the letters learned in the first stage?

Test other incremental learning protocols (e.g., learn the first half, then the second, then the first half again; or learn the letters in sequence, presenting each one of them at least 100 times before processing the next one). What do you observe? What could explain these behaviors? What would be a good strategy for learning the whole set when the first half has to be learned first?

3. Human learners are also subject to ordering effects. For instance, if asked to split a square into five equal parts, human subjects answer quickly and without hesitation (see the left side of Figure 3.7).

On the other hand, humans have considerable trouble if they have been asked beforehand to solve the following sequence of problems: Split the amputated square (see the right side of Figure 3.7) first into two equal parts, then into three equal parts and then into four equal parts.

Replicate this experiment with your friends. Try to figure out what might explain this behavior. Try then to invent other sequences of tasks that can produce significant order effects.

References

Angluin, D. (1988). Queries and concept learning. *Machine Learning, 2*, 319–342.

Barto, A., & Mahadevan, S. (2003). Recent advances in hierarchical reinforcement learning. *Discrete Event Dynamic Systems, 13*(4), 341–379.

Cornuéjols, A., & Miclet, L. (2002). *L'apprentissage artificiel: Méthodes et concepts.* Paris: Eyrolles.

French, R. (1997). Catastrophic forgetting in connectionist networks. *Trends in Cognitive Science, 3,* 128–135.

Freund, Y., & Schapire, R. (1999). A short introduction to boosting. *Journal of Japanese Society for Artificial Intelligence, 14,* 771–780.

Goldman, S., & Mathias, D. (1996). Teaching a smarter learner. *Journal of Computer and System Sciences, 52,* 255–267.

Minsky, M., & Papert, S. (1988). *Perceptrons: An introduction to computational geometry* (2d ed.). Cambridge, MA: MIT Press.

Mitchell, T. (1997). *Machine learning.* New York: McGraw-Hill.

Murphy, G., & Lassaline, M. (1997). Hierarchical structure in concepts and the basic level of categorization. In K. Lambert and D. Schanks (Eds.), *Knowledge, concepts, and categories* (pp. 93–131). Hove, UK: Psychology Press.

Opper, M. (1999). A Bayesian approach to online learning. In D. Saad (Ed.), *On-line learning in neural networks* (pp. 363–378). New York: Cambridge University Press.

Quinlan, J. (1986). Induction of decision trees. *Mach Learn, 1,* 81–106.

Ritter, F. E., & Bibby, P. (2001). Modeling how and when learning happens in a simple fault-finding task. In *Proceedings of ICCM 2001, Fourth International Conference on Cognitive Modeling* (pp. 187–192). Mahwah, NJ: Erlbaum.

Rivest, R., & Sloan, R. (1994). A formal model of hierarchical concept learning. *Information and Computation, 114*(1), 88–114.

Rosenblatt, F. (1962). *Principles of neurodynamics: Perceptrons and the theory of brain mechanisms.* Washington, DC: Spartan.

Russell, S., & Norvig, P. (2003): *Artificial intelligence. A modern approach* (2d ed.). Englewood Cliffs, NJ: Prentice Hall.

Schölkopf, B., Burges, C., & Smola, A. (1999) *Advances in kernel methods: Support vector learning.* Cambridge, MA: MIT Press.

Singley, M. K., & Anderson, J. R. (1989). *The transfer of cognitive skill.* Cambridge, MA: Harvard University Press.

Utgoff, P. (1989). Incremental induction of decision trees. *Machine Learning, 4,* 161–186.

Utgoff, P. (1994). An improved algorithm for incremental induction of decision trees. In *Machine learning: Proceedings of the Eleventh International Conference* (pp. 318–325). New Brunswick, NJ: Morgan-Kaufmann.

Vapnik, V. (1995). *The nature of statistical learning theory.* Berlin: Springer.

Winston, P. H. (1970). Learning structural descriptions from examples. (MIT Technical Report AI-TR-231). Cambridge, MA: MIT.

Chapter 4

Rules of Order: Process Models of Human Learning

Josef Nerb
Frank E. Ritter
Pat Langley

To fully understand sequential effects on learning in humans, we need a comprehensive theory of cognition. Such a theory should be complete enough to perform the task of interest and to learn like humans while doing so. These theories, called process models or cognitive models, can be broken down into aspects that do not change between tasks—the architecture—and aspects that do change—the knowledge. Where such models have been used to understand sequence effects on learning, they have proven to be very powerful. As an example, we present a model of behavior on a simple task that shows how an appropriate order can lead to significantly (16%) faster learning. However, despite their power, process models remain difficult to apply routinely. In response, we also discuss an alternative approach—abstract models—that may be more appropriate in some contexts.

Science is concerned not only with data, as was discussed in the previous chapter, but also with models or theories that explain those data. Because human cognition is dynamic and involves change over time, accounts of cognition often take the form of process models, which are sometimes called cognitive models. In this chapter we review the form such models have taken and their relation to order effects in learning.

We begin by discussing the connection between artificial intelligence (AI) systems (e.g., as reviewed by Cornuéjols, Chapter 3), including those from machine learning and computational models of human behavior, including some illustrations of the latter. After this, we present a computational model of order effects on a cognitive task, cast within a particular but simplified theoretical framework. Next we explore more broadly the possible sources of order effects within such models and then briefly consider an alternative approach that models human behavior at a more abstract level. We close with some open problems in the area of modeling order effects and a charge to new modelers.

PROCESS MODELS IN COGNITIVE SCIENCE

Many sciences use process models to explain the behavior of complex, dynamic systems. For example, physics often uses the formalism of differential equations to describe the relationships among quantitative variables (say, heat and temperature in a furnace) over time. Process models of human behavior have somewhat different requirements, as what changes over time are not primarily continuous variables but rather qualitative structures in short- and long-term memory, as well as in motivational state.

Fortunately, computer languages provide formalisms that can be used to model the symbolic aspects of human cognition in the same way that differential equations are used in physics. Moreover, the field of AI has developed a variety of representations, performance mechanisms, and learning methods that can operate on many of the tasks that confront humans. Some AI work has little relevance to cognitive science because it makes no effort to constrain its methods to match psychological phenomena, but other AI systems have been developed with this goal explicitly in mind, and one can use them as computational models of human behavior. Indeed, some of the earliest AI systems, including EPAM (Feigenbaum & Simon, 1984) and GPS (Newell, Shaw, & Simon, 1962) fall into this category.

The Advantages of Formal Models

The advantage of formal models over informal ones is the same in cognitive science as in any other field. Rather than being sufficiently vague to handle almost any empirical result, detailed models of the processes that generate behavior lead to specific predictions that can be shown to be incorrect.[1] Such results can thus lead to improved models that account for problematic findings and make new predictions, leading to iterative progress toward more complete theories. Formal models also let us examine the internal states and mechanisms in the model that gave rise to the observed behavior, such as order effects. This lets us predict the effects of different conditions, such as alternative orders, without running subjects.

Another advantage of having a model's detailed behavior at hand is that it assists in analyzing a subject's behavior. In particular, it lets us partition behavior into portions that the model can explain and those that it cannot, thus identifying anomalous observations. This in turn helps indicate where the model is incorrect and suggests where to improve it. Finally, a well-developed, parameterized model can be used to classify subjects by their characteristics (e.g., Daily, Lovett, & Reder, 2001), providing an account of individual differences.

Types of Process Models

Before examining how computational models can explain order effects observed in human learning, we must briefly review the major types. Early process models were compared to psychological data, but they incorporated rather idiosyncratic mechanisms and structures that were rarely shared within the research community. Over the past decade, researchers have imposed an increasing number of theoretical constraints across sets of models. These often take the form of cognitive architectures (Newell, 1990), which posit the structures and mechanisms of the cognitive system that are common across tasks. A cognitive architecture provides a framework for describing the sources of thought and behavior, including order effects.

Although there exist numerous computational models for aspects of cognition such as categorization and long-term memory retrieval, we focus here on frameworks for modeling more complex sequential tasks like problem solving and natural language. One widespread class of architectures used for such tasks is known as production systems (G. Jones, Ritter, & Wood, 2000; Neches, Langley, & Klahr, 1987; Young, 1979). This framework includes a long-term memory that contains productions or condition-action rules, which changes only slowly with learning, as well as a short-term or working memory, which is far more dynamic. What varies across models in this framework is the contents of long-term memory.

A production system operates in cycles, matching its rules in each step against the contents of short-term memory (which may include representations of the environment), selecting one or more rules to apply, using their actions to alter short-term memory or the environment, and then iterating. Various learning methods exist for combining, generalizing, specializing, or otherwise modifying the rules in long-term memory. For example, a common approach involves making a larger rule out of several smaller ones that applied in sequence. This new rule can reduce the load on working memory and increase the speed of processing. If the choice of which smaller rules to apply was learned from extensive problem solving, the new rule can also constitute new knowledge about how to constrain future behavior. Examples of production systems that learn include Pavlik's ACT-R model (Chapter 10) and Ohlsson's HS system (Chapter 11).

A second well-studied framework for modeling sequential behavior is recurrent neural networks (for an introduction see Bechtel & Abrahamsen, 2002). Such models include a long-term memory composed of

---

1. Moreover, AI models actually carry out the tasks they address, thus opening up many possibilities for applications (e.g., Anderson & Gluck, 2001; Ritter et al., 2003).

nodes, directed links connecting nodes, and weights on the links, with short-term memory consisting of temporary activations on the nodes. What varies across tasks are the number and connectivity of the nodes and the weights on links. Lane (Chapter 5) reviews this approach in more detail. A recurrent network also operates in cycles. On each cycle it uses the activations of input nodes (at the lowest level) and the weight of links to compute the activations of higher-level nodes, ultimately calculating activation levels for output nodes that determine actions. The activations for some higher-level nodes then replace those for the input nodes, and the next cycle begins. Learning typically occurs by propagating errors (differences between the desired and output values) downward through the network and modifying the weights to reduce these errors in the future.

Although production systems and recurrent neural networks are not the only classes of models used to model sequential human behavior, they are certainly the most widely used. Other architectural frameworks, including case-based and probabilistic ones, differ in their assumptions about representation, knowledge retrieval, and learning but can be described using the terms of cognitive architecture and knowledge. Indeed, the most remarkable aspect of these architectures is not their differences but their similarities. All of them operate in cycles, in some sense matching procedural knowledge against the contents of declarative memory, taking actions to alter it, and then repeating the process. Their learning methods, despite their differences in operation, also tend to give similar effects, such as mastering simpler structures before more complex ones. (We return to this observation later in the chapter.)

A SIMPLE MODEL OF ORDER EFFECTS

An example model that produces an order effect in learning will illustrate how one can use a cognitive architecture to understand human behavior and ground the rest of the discussion in more concrete terms. We first present the model's structure and mechanisms, after which we explain its behavior on a simple task that shows how order effects can arise.

We will assume that the example model is based upon a simple architecture that incorporates ideas from two existing frameworks, notably Soar (Newell, 1990) and ACT-R (Anderson et al., 2004). Figure 4.1 shows the components of this generic architecture, which includes a long-term memory encoded as production rules, which matches against the current goal stack and the contents of short-term memory. The rules are strengthened when they match or resolve problems within the goal stack, such as achieving or filling in some goal. A

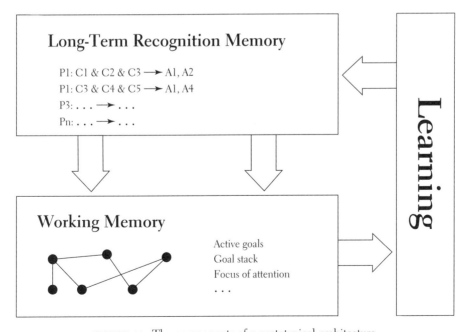

FIGURE 4.1. The components of a prototypical architecture.

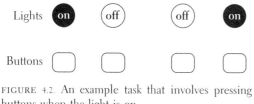

Lights on off off on

Buttons

FIGURE 4.2. An example task that involves pressing buttons when the light is on.

structural learning mechanism adds new rules to long-term memory, which alters future performance.

The Simple Lights and Buttons Task

To illustrate some of these concepts, consider a task that involves pushing buttons underneath lights that are on. A simple version uses four lights and four buttons, two per hand. If a light is on, the subject presses the corresponding button, as shown in Figure 4.2. In total, there are 16 different patterns of lights that require 16 different responses, assuming that not pushing all four buttons is a possible response. Seibel (1963), who studied a more complex version of this task, found that subjects become faster at this task the longer they practiced it.

The Model

Our model in the prototypical architecture assumes a hierarchical decomposition of the task and of the knowledge needed to perform it. To master the task with both hands, which entails subtasks for each hand,

mastery for each button must be achieved; to master a button, the subject must observe the light and make the appropriate action with regard to the button (press it if the light is on but do not press it if the light is off). Figure 4.3 depicts this organization by grouping the lights in pairs. We have based this simple model on a previous one (Newell & Rosenbloom, 1981; Rosenbloom & Newell, 1987).

The model predicts that the time taken to press the appropriate lights depends on the production rules available in long-term memory and also that learning occurs in a cumulative manner, in that combined responses across fingers can be acquired only when the subresponses are known. The lowest-level response, for an individual light, is atomic and thus always known. Learning combined responses requires acquiring new rules denoted by nodes e, f, and g in Figure 4.3. At the outset, the first set of lights thus takes a total of seven steps. The model takes one step to do each of the four lights, one step to compose each of the two pairs, and one step to compose the four-light set. Recognizing each pair saves two steps, and recognizing the whole four-light set saves six steps.

Defining the task knowledge and how it is used lets us describe a way to create a good learning sequence. An efficient training order for this model draws as much as possible on what is known and provides opportunities for acquiring the maximum number of rules each time. In contrast, a poor learning sequence provides fewer opportunities for learning. For instance,

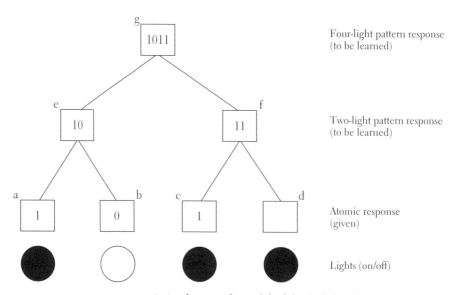

FIGURE 4.3. A simple example model of the Seibel task.

TABLE 4.1. How Two Different Sequences With the Same Items but in a Different Order Can Lead to Different Learning

An Efficient Sequence for Learning			Less Efficient Sequence for Learning		
Stim. #	Stimuli	Patterns Learned	Stim. #	Stimuli	Patterns Learned
0	oo oo	ooL ooR	1	oo ox	ooL oxR
5	ox ox	oxL oxR	2	oo xo	xoR
10	xo xo	xoL xoR	3	oo xx	xxR
15	xx xx	xxL xxR	0	oo oo	ooR
1	oo ox	ooox	4	ox oo	oxL
2	oo xo	ooxo	5	ox ox	oxox
3	oo xx	ooxx	10	xo xo	xoL
4	ox oo	oxoo	15	xx xx	xxL

Learned:	8 two-light patterns	Learned:	8 two-light patterns
	4 four-light patterns		1 four-pattern
% learned	50%	% learned	37.5%

There are 24 things to learn in this simple world (8 two-light patterns and 16 four-light patterns). The symbol "x" indicates lights that are on, whereas "o" indicates lights that are off. Stimuli numbers are based on the set of 16 different four-light patterns.

repeatedly practicing the same two-light pattern on one of the hands while the other hand learns a new two-light pattern does not lead to the acquisition of higher-level knowledge (a four-light pattern) as quickly as with the more efficient order in which new patterns are learned by both hands during each trial.

Table 4.1 gives an example of both an efficient and a less efficient learning sequence for the task. In general, the most efficient approach for this architecture on this task, at least with this knowledge and representation, is to keep the learning mechanism busy. Less efficient sequences let the subtasks be repeated without learning, particularly precluding higher-level learning from occurring. For example, when the remaining eight unseen items are presented, the learner with the bad sequence must be shown three additional trials to catch up with the efficient sequence, giving a total of 19 instead of 16 trials, which amounts to a 16% slower learning rate.

Despite the simplicity of both task and model, they are complex enough to exhibit order effects. Moreover, the task is similar to many others that occur in the real world, in which component knowledge must be mastered before more advanced knowledge can be acquired. This effect can be found in existing Soar models of job shop scheduling (Nerb, Ritter, & Krems, 1999), blood typing (Johnson, Krems, & Amra, 1994), circuit troubleshooting (Ritter & Bibby, 2001), and language acquisition (Lewis, 1998).

This simple example shows that several things—the structure of the task, the internal representation, the performance process, the order of stimuli, and the learning mechanism—interact to create order effects. A complete account of such effects must specify each of these components.

ASPECTS OF PROCESS MODELS THAT CAN EXPLAIN ORDER EFFECTS

Ideally, process models do not just explain but also predict data, including the effects of training order. A well-crafted computational account of human behavior can suggest novel conditions under which phenomena of interest occur. One advantage of casting models within a constrained theory of the cognitive architecture is that they are more likely to produce such predictions.

Order effects can also arise from processing that leaves changes in the process model's state or mechanisms that interact with later processing (like soap left on poorly rinsed pots that influence later cooking). In this section we consider five possible factors within cognitive architectures that can explain and predict such effects: (a) forgetting, (b) not forgetting, (c) memory overload, (d) changes to the internal processes, and (e) time constraints that arise in rapidly changing environments. Undoubtedly, other sources of explanation are possible, but these seem likely to account for many of the cases in which training order influences learning.

Forgetting

Order effects can occur whenever structures cannot be retrieved later, say, due to decay over time or interference from other structures. A model may also assume that activations decay over time or that retrieval can fail due to shifts of attention. Order effects appear when an interaction between a pair of cognitive elements facilitates or hinders the learning of these elements, when those elements are forgotten over time, or when the time interval between processing the elements is not fixed. For example, suppose one is learning about a country A and its capital B. Knowing A facilitates learning B and vice versa, but facilitation occurs only if A is still active in memory when B is learned. Because forgetting is a function of time, sequences in which A and B appear close to each other should produce faster learning than ones in which A and B are distant. Pavlik's chapter (Chapter 10) explores this idea in some detail.

Many learning models rely on the co-occurrence of elements in dynamic memories. For example, the composition mechanism in ACT-R (Anderson, 1993; G. Jones, Ritter, & Wood, 2000) uses information about the elements matched by successively applied rules to create a new rule. Similarly, the chunking mechanism in Soar (Newell, 1990) uses dependencies among elements in working memory before and after it solves a problem to determine the content of new production rules. Finally, recurrent neural networks (Elman, 1989) change weights on links only to the extent that the nodes from which they emanate were active. Factors that influence the retrieval of either of such pairs will also influence learning.

Einstellung (Not Forgetting)

Another source of order effects is reliance on strategies that have proved successful in the past. Once a person has found some way to solve a problem, that person often continues to utilize the same solution even when other responses may work better in new situations. Such Einstellung behavior occurs more often when the person encounters problems in certain orders.

The classical example for such effects are sequences of arithmetical water jug puzzles. Luchins (1942) showed that, depending on the order in which subjects solved such problems, subjects used more or less efficient strategies to solve later problems (for a more recent demonstration of the effect, see Luchins & Luchins, 1991). If an individual is given a series of problems (Set A) and devises a strategy that works, that person tends to use the same strategy on other problems (Set B) even when a simpler solution is possible. However, if presented with problems from Set B first, the individual nearly always finds the more elegant solution.

Cognitive scientists have developed a number of process models for Einstellung that incorporate various learning mechanisms. These include composing sets of production rules into larger ones (Neves & Anderson, 1981) and analogical reasoning based on earlier solutions (Gick & Holyoak, 1980; R. M. Jones & Langley, 2005). Scheiter and Gerjets (Chapter 14) examine a related concept. What these models have in common are methods that create new long-term structures from individual experiences, which they then prefer to utilize in new situations rather than searching for more efficient solutions.

Cognitive Overload

A third factor that can underlie effects of training order is cognitive load. Sweller (1988, 1994, Chapter 15) has developed the most extensive theory of how demands on working memory affect problem solving and learning. His account provides a framework for investigations into instructional design by considering both the structure of information and the cognitive processes that let learners interpret that information. The theory assumes that working memory demands stem from three additive sources: the material being learned (intrinsic cognitive load); the manner in which information is presented (extraneous or ineffective load); and resources devoted to learning and automation (germane or effective cognitive load).

In this framework, a well-designed learning sequence maximizes resources that can be devoted to germane cognitive load. Intrinsic cognitive load depends on the complexity of the material being learned: It is high if relevant elements interact with each other and low if they can be learned independently. Effective instructional design therefore minimizes extraneous cognitive load during learning, as well as the load from the interfaces themselves. In a series of studies, Sweller and his colleagues have shown how different cognitive loads imposed by external structuring (including ordering) of tasks can facilitate or hinder learning. Of crucial interest here are the kinds and timing of instructions and learning aids that will encourage effective learning (Bass, Baxter, & Ritter, 1995).

A further source for order effects within this framework has to do with intrinsic cognitive load, which was initially considered as given and static, as well as irreducible. A more recent view, however, assumes that intrinsic cognitive load may itself be a function of the task-subject interaction. In particular, the learner's level of expertise may correspond to alterations in intrinsic cognitive load. An interesting outcome of research in this area is the so-called expertise reversal effect, indicating that instructional techniques that are effective with novices can become ineffective when used with more experienced learners (Kalyuga, Ayres, Chandler, & Sweller, 2003; Renkl & Atkinson, Chapter 7). An overview of both the theoretical and empirical status of the theory is given by Paas, Renkl, and Sweller (2003, 2004).

Changes to Internal Processes

At the moment, most architectures provide the same mechanisms and information-processing capabilities across situations and time. This assumption is at odds with common sense and, more importantly, with findings from psychological research. Fatigue is a simple and intuitive example of how the way we process information changes: We process information differently when alert than we do when we are tired. Likewise, motivational and emotional states can change perception and information processing. Order effects can arise because different sequences of training material can lead to different emotional or motivational states. For instance, a sequence might be more or less boring for learners, thereby influencing their motivation for further learning and problem solving.

The work of Isen (2000) provides psychological evidence for effects of mood on information processing. She showed that different moods lead to different levels of success in problem solving and learning. Positive mood leads to more creativity (or at least more variance in behavior), and negative mood leads to more accurate behavior. A good mood lets the problem solver work more flexibly, whereas a bad mood makes the problem solver eager to get positive reinforcement as soon as possible. The order of problems can lead to these modes. For example, difficult tasks given early in a sequence can lead to frustration and other negative emotional states (see Bower, 1981;

Nerb & Spada, 2001; Thagard & Nerb, 2002, for further psychological evidence that cognitions influence and are influenced by emotions).

Recently, however, there has been growing interest in the study of emotions within cognitive science and especially within artificial intelligence (e.g., Cañamero & Hudlicka, 2004; Minsky, 2006; Norman, Ortony, & Russell, 2003; Picard, 1997; Silverman, 2004). As a result of these efforts, some computational models of the role of emotions during reasoning and problem solving have emerged; example models are Cathexis (Velásquez, 1998), EMA (Gratch & Marsella, 2004), HOTCO (Thagard, 2003), and DEBECO (Nerb, 2004, in press). None of these models are concerned explicitly with order effects. However, order effects in learning will result if within these models emotions have lingering effects on cognitive mechanisms. Altogether, this is a fascinating new development and a growing field of research that has huge potential for changing the study of learning and problem solving (Kort, Reilly, & Picard, 2001).

Time Constraints in Rapidly Changing Environments

The order in which a learner attempts tasks is often important in highly interactive, externally paced environments that require timely responses. If the situation is novel enough or if the response is complicated enough, the learner will not be able to respond before the situation changes and the learner loses a chance to learn from that context. For example, in video games, the player must hit a target before it disappears. If this is not accomplished in time, then the player may not be able to acquire even a partial response, and the task can remain impossible.

One way to avoid this problem is to change the order of tasks. If learners encounter easier situations before harder ones, then they will be able to respond more often and thus able to learn from the outcomes. Moreover, learning on easy tasks can reduce the time needed to respond in more complicated situations, thus allowing responses and learning in them as well. For this reason, such part-task training, which presents component tasks before the complete task, is a common approach to training in real-time environments (Donchin, 1989).

This account predicts that part-task training would be beneficial in the lights and buttons domain if the button pushes had a deadline. When a task required pushing many buttons, a novice would not initially be able to respond in time. However, presenting tasks that involve a single light, followed by those with pairs of lights, and so forth up to the full set would allow learning on early trials. This approach would support learning on the later trials because the partial responses would be available for combination into more complex ones.

FROM CONCRETE MODELS
TO ABSTRACT MODELS

As we have seen, process models in cognitive science typically take the form of a running AI system that performs some task and that is also constrained to carry out the task in much the same way as humans. However, two problems can arise with this approach that can be solved by using a somewhat different form of process model.

The first problem is the difficulty in creating a complete AI model, which is not always straightforward. Developing a system that performs the task requires that one specify a complete algorithm and a way for the model to interact with the task. The modeler must have substantial programming skills. The model must also be run, which is usually straightforward but can be time consuming if one applies it to a wide range of tasks or desires expected or average behavior. One may also have to interpret or code the results of the model's behavior.

The second problem is that, in order to develop a complete, running model, one must often make arbitrary assumptions about structures or processes that have no theoretical content. Even when the model fits the data well, its success may not be due to its core theoretical assumptions but rather to its arbitrary components. An example of this occurred with context effects in letter perception, where the encoding of the stimuli by the modelers appears to have been more important than the processes used in the model itself (McClelland & Rumelhart, 1981; Richman & Simon, 1989).

A response to these difficulties is to develop an abstract process model of the phenomena. Unlike the "concrete" information-processing models we have been discussing, an abstract model makes fewer commitments about structures and processes, which means that it cannot actually perform the task but rather represents behavior at a more basic level. Whereas concrete models characterize what humans will do and the details of their reasoning processes, abstract models are often used to predict quantitative measures such as the time to make choices and how much is learned.

Cognitive scientists have developed abstract models of learning and problem solving (Atwood & Polson, 1976; Ohlsson, 1995; Schooler & Hertwig, 2005), sensory-motor behavior (Langley, 1996), categorization (Langley, 1999), and decision making (Young, 1998), but one of the earliest is due to Rosenbloom and Newell (1987) for the lights and buttons (Seibel, 1963) task described earlier. They initially presented a concrete production system model to explain the power law of practice (how reaction times decrease with practice but at a decreasing rate). For reasons of computational efficiency, they used an abstract model based on the production system model to compute the reaction times for a series of trials for comparison with the human data.

Abstract models can be much easier to use. Later work by Ritter (1988) utilized another abstract model to compute the expected value for each trial on this task. In each case, the predictions of the abstract model were easier to manipulate and could be derived around 100,000 times faster (5 seconds vs. 100 runs $\times$ 5 hours per run $\times$ 3,600 seconds/hour) than the concrete rule-based model that actually performed the task.

One drawback of abstract models as typically used is that they average over different training sequences and thus cannot account for order effects. However, there is nothing inherent in the abstract approach that forces such averaging over all tasks. If one's goal is average learning curves, they may be the only practical way to achieve this end. For example, Nerb, Ritter, and Krems (1999) report a concrete model of behavior on a more complex problem-solving task that provides reasonable timing predictions for sequences of problems for individual subjects. Each trial takes more than a minute to run, with learning taking place over a sequence of 25 trials, and 100 runs would be required to achieve a reliable average. An abstract modeling approach could achieve this result far more efficiently.

To illustrate this point, let us consider an abstract model that captures the essential features of the concrete lights and buttons model. Rather than running the concrete model repeatedly to compute the expected average time across trials for the first two test trials, Trials 9 and 10, we can compute the expected time, assuming a uniform distribution of all the possible stimuli.

As shown at the top of Table 4.2, the efficient sequence starts with a better knowledge base. It can

TABLE 4.2. Expected Time for Stimuli 9 and 10 if They Are Presented Randomly, Along With the Stored Knowledge After the Training Sequences in Table 4.1

After the efficient sequence there are in the model:	After the less efficient sequence there are in the model:
8 two-light patterns	8 two-light patterns
4 four-light patterns	1 four-light pattern

On Trial 9

(no learning situation)	(no learning situation)
4/16 four-light patterns known	1/16 four-light patterns known
× 1 model cycle if matched	× 1 model cycle if matched
(learning situation)	(learning situation)
75% chance of learning a new four-light pattern	93% chance of learning a new four-light pattern
12/16 unknown four-light patterns	15/16 unknown four-light patterns
× 3 model cycles (two-light patterns)	× 3 model cycles (two-light patterns)
2.5 model cycles expected response time (.25 × 1 cycle) + (.75 × 3 cycles)	2.97 model cycles expected response time (.065 × 1 cycle) + (.925 × 3 cycles)

After Trial 9

8 two-light patterns	8 two-light patterns
4.75 four-light patterns	1.93 four-light patterns

On Trial 10

(no learning situation)	(no learning situation)
4.75/16 patterns known	1.93/16 pattern known
× 1 model cycle if all matched	× 1 model cycle if all matched
(learning situation)	(learning situation)
70% chance of learning a new four-light pattern	88% chance of learning a new four-light pattern
11.25/16 unknown patterns	15/16 unknown patterns
× 3 model cycles (two-light patterns)	× 3 model cycles (two-light patterns)
2.4 model cycles expected response time (.30 × 1) + (.70 × 3)	2.76 model cycles expected response time (.12 × 1) + (.80 × 3)

recognize each of two-light patterns and a quarter of the four-light patterns. The inefficient sequence can recognize all the subpatterns but not as many larger patterns. In Trial 9, the efficient sequence has a greater chance of applying a four-light pattern than the inefficient sequence. The inefficient sequence, on the other hand, has a greater chance to learn a new pattern. This effect carries into Trial 10. With repeated trials, the two will converge, with the more efficient sequence always being faster but by an ever decreasing amount.

This abstract model provides several lessons. First, it illustrates how seemingly similar but theoretically different sequences can lead to different learning. Second, it illustrates how abstract models can be used and how easily they can represent a process model and its predictions.

CONCLUSIONS

Although process models of human behavior, including learning, have existed for almost five decades, considerable work still remains to be done. In closing, we briefly consider some open questions with respect to computational models of order effects that readers may wish to explore on their own.

Experimental Tests of Predictions

One advantage of process models is that they let one make predictions about behavior in new situations, which can then suggest additional experiments that can either support or disconfirm the model. Some useful activities of this sort would include the following.

1. Identify situations in which the model's predictions about the effects of training order disagree with common sense and design an experiment to determine which is correct. Results that agree with the model provide more compelling evidence than ones for studies that simply agree with intuitions. For example, in the lights and buttons task, consider what would happen if half of the stimuli were not presented until after extensive practice (Simon, personal communication, 1988). Most models would consider them as fairly new stimuli, but would human subjects treat them in this way?

2. Identify situations in which competing models make different predictions about order effects and design an experiment to discriminate between them. Such studies tell more about the nature of human learning than ones in which the models agree. For example, in the lights and buttons task, one could create two different problem representations. If the two representations predicted different behavior, an experiment might help resolve the apparent contradiction.

3. Identify aspects of a process model that explain order effects (as discussed earlier) and design experiments that vary task characteristics to determine which aspects are responsible. Such studies can lead to the gradual refinement of process models that can make increasingly specific predictions.

4. Identify situations in which a process model indicates that the learner's background knowledge will mitigate or eliminate order effects and design experiments to test this prediction. Such studies can reveal more information about the role of expertise in learning than experiments focusing on simple novice-to-expert transitions. In the lights and buttons task, one might expect pianists to exhibit weaker order effects because they have extensive knowledge about keys.

Of course, these types of experiments are not specific to the study of order effects; they can be equally useful in understanding other aspects of human behavior. However, the empirical study of sequencing has been so rare, especially in the context of evaluating process models, that they seem especially worthwhile.

Developing Models and Architectures

Because there are relatively few process models of order effects, another important activity is the creation and refinement of such models. Some likely work of this sort would include the following.

1. Identify a simple order effect and develop a model that explains it. For example, create a model that explains the benefits of part-task training (Mane & Donchin, 1989), which emphasizes the teaching of the component skills of a task before teaching how to integrate them. After creating the model, consider what suggestions it makes for instruction in the area. The model need not be concrete, but it should be clear enough to predict implications such as relative learning rates.

2. Identify an order effect that has not yet been explained and develop a concrete process model that explains it within an existing architectural framework. An even better approach would involve modeling the effect within different architectures and, if they share underlying features, designing an abstract model that subsumes them.

3. Identify places in an existing architecture where the introduction of resource or timing limitations would suggest new order effects, then develop concrete models that instantiate this prediction for a specific task or set of tasks.

Again, these types of activities apply to any class of psychological phenomena, but order effects have received so little attention that they seem an especially fertile area to use in constructing and constraining our theories of the human cognitive architecture.

General Advice

In addition to these suggestions of open problems in the study of order effects, we offer some general advice to erstwhile cognitive modelers. First, we encourage researchers to select a theoretical framework, ideally one that takes a clear position on the nature of the human cognitive architecture, and to develop models within that framework. If researchers are new to the area, then they should not work in isolation but rather collaborate with a scientist or group experienced with using that framework. At the same time, they should not focus their attention on this framework to the exclusion of all others; understanding alternative theories and their relation to one's own is also part of the scientific process. For further advice, see Ritter (2004).

Second, computational modelers should also remember that it is essential to relate their systems to phenomena. A model should always make a connection with observations of some sort. Moreover, like other disciplines, cognitive science operates not by attempting to confirm its theories but rather by gaining insights into ways to improve them (Grant, 1962). The construction, evaluation, and analysis of process models is an important means to this end.

ACKNOWLEDGMENTS

Support for this work has also been provided to the second author by the DERA, contract number 2024/004, by the Economic and Social Research Council (ESRC) Centre for Research in Development, Instruction, and Training, and ONR contracts N00014-03-1-0248 and N00014-02-1-0021. The views expressed here are those of the authors, and an acknowledgement here does not indicate an endorsement of this report from the sponsors listed.

References

Anderson, J. R. (1993). *Rules of the mind.* Hillsdale, NJ: Erlbaum.

Anderson, J. R., Bothell, D., Byrne, M. D., Douglass, S., Lebière, C., & Qin, Y. (2004). An integrated theory of the mind. *Psychological Review, 111,* 1036–1060.

Anderson, J. R., & Gluck, K. (2001). What role do cognitive architectures play in intelligent tutoring systems? In D. Klahr & S. M. Carver (Eds.), *Cognition and instruction: Twenty-five years of progress* (pp. 227–262). Mahwah, NJ: Erlbaum.

Atwood, M. E., & Polson, P. G. (1976). A process model for water jug problems. *Cognitive Psychology, 8,* 191–216.

Bass, E. J., Baxter, G. D., & Ritter, F. E. (1995). Using cognitive models to control simulations of complex systems. *AISB Quarterly, 93,* 18–25.

Bechtel, W., & Abrahamsen, A. (2002). *Connectionism and the mind: Parallel processing, dynamics, and evolution in networks* (2d ed.). Malden, MA: Blackwell.

Bower, G. H. (1981). Mood and memory. *American Psychologist, 36,* 129–148.

Cañamero, L., & Hudlicka, E. (2004). *Architectures for modeling emotion: Cross-disciplinary foundations.*

AAAI Spring Symposium Series. Menlo Park, CA: AAAI.

Daily, L. Z., Lovett, M. C., & Reder, L. M. (2001). Modeling individual differences in working memory performance: A source activation account in ACT-R. *Cognitive Science, 25,* 315–353.

Donchin, E. (1989). The learning strategies project: Introductory remarks. Special issue: The learning strategies program: An examination of the strategies in skill acquisition. *Acta Psychologica, 71*(1–3), 1–15.

Elman, J. L. (1989). Distributed representations, simple recurrent networks, and grammatical structure. *Machine Learning, 7,* 195–225.

Feigenbaum, J. R., & Simon, H. A. (1984). EPAM-like models of recognition and learning. *Cognitive Science, 8,* 305–336.

Gick, M. L., & Holyoak, K. J. (1980). Analogical problem solving. *Cognitive Psychology, 12,* 306–355.

Grant, D. A. (1962). Testing the null hypothesis and the strategy and tactics of investigating theoretical models. *Psychological Review, 69,* 54–61.

Gratch, J., & Marsella, S. (2004). A domain-independent framework for modeling emotion. *Journal of Cognitive Systems Research, 5,* 269–306.

Isen, A. (2000). Positive affect and decision making. In M. Lewis & J. M. Haviland (Eds.), *Handbook of emotions* (2d ed.) (pp. 417–435). New York: Guilford.

Johnson, T. R., Krems, J., & Amra, N. K. (1994). A computational model of human abductive skill and its acquisition. In *Proceedings of the annual conference of the Cognitive Science Society* (pp. 463–468). Mahwah, NJ: Erlbaum.

Jones, G., Ritter, F. E., & Wood, D. J. (2000). Using a cognitive architecture to examine what develops. *Psychological Science, 11,* 93–100.

Jones, R. M., & Langley, P. (2005). A constrained architecture for learning and problem solving. *Computational Intelligence, 21*(4), 480–502.

Kalyuga, S., Ayres, P., Chandler, P., & Sweller, J. (2003). The expertise reversal effect. *Educational Psychologist, 38,* 23–32.

Kort, B., Reilly, R., & Picard, R. W. (2001). An affective model of interplay between emotions and learning: Reengineering educational pedagogy—building a learning companion. In T. Okamoto, R. Hartley, & J. P. K. Kinshuk (Eds.), *International conference on advanced learning technology: Issues, achievements, and challenges* (pp. 43–48). IEEE Computer Society.

Langley, P. (1996). An abstract computational model of learning selective sensing skills. In *Proceedings of the eighteenth annual conference of the Cognitive Science Society* (pp. 385–390). Hillsdale, NJ: Erlbaum.

Langley, P. (1999). Concrete and abstract models of category learning. In *Proceedings of the twenty-first annual conference of the Cognitive Science Society* (pp. 288–293). Mahwah, NJ: Erlbaum.

Lewis, R. L. (1998). Leaping off the garden path: Reanalysis and limited repair parsing. In J. D. Fodor & F. Ferreira (Eds.), *Reanalysis in sentence processing* (pp. 247–284). Boston: Kluwer.

Luchins, A. S. (1942). Mechanization in problem solving. *Psychological Monographs, 54.*

Luchins, A. S., & Luchins, E. H. (1991). Task complexity and order effects in computer presentation of water-jar problems. *Journal of General Psychology, 118,* 45–72.

Mane, A. M., & Donchin, E. (1989). The space fortress game. Special issue: The learning strategies program: An examination of the strategies in skill acquisition. *Acta Psychologica, 71*(1–3), 17–22.

McClelland, J. L., & Rumelhart, D. E. (1981). An interactive activation model of context effects in letter perception: Part I: An account of basic findings. *Psychological Review, 88,* 375–407.

Minsky, M. L. (2006). *The emotion machine: Commonsense thinking, artificial intelligence, and the future of the human mind.* New York: Simon & Schuster.

Neches, R., Langley, P., & Klahr, D. (1987). Learning, development, and production systems. In D. Klahr, P. Langley, & R. Neches (Eds.), *Production system models of learning and development* (pp. 1–53). Cambridge, MA: MIT Press.

Nerb, J. (2004). How desire coherence and belief coherence lead to emotions: A constraint satisfaction model of the appraisal process. In L. Cañamero & E. Hudlicka (Eds.), *Architectures for modeling emotion: Cross-disciplinary foundations.* AAAI Spring Symposium Series (pp. 96–103). Menlo Park, CA: AAAI.

Nerb, J. (in press). Exploring the dynamics of the appraisal-emotion relationship: A constraint satisfaction model of the appraisal process. *Cognition and Emotion.*

Nerb, J., Ritter, F. E., & Krems, J. F. (1999). Knowledge level learning and the power law: A Soar model of skill acquisition. *Kognitionswissenschaft* [Journal of the German Cognitive Science Society], 8, 20–29.

Nerb, J., & Spada, H. (2001). Evaluation of environmental problems: A coherence model of cognition and emotion. *Cognition and Emotion, 15,* 521–551.

Neves, D. M., & Anderson, J. R. (1981). Knowledge compilation: Mechanisms for the automatization of cognitive skills. In J. R. Anderson (Ed.), *Cognitive skills and their acquisition* (pp. 57–84). Hillsdale, NJ: Erlbaum.

Newell, A. (1990). *Unified theories of cognition.* Cambridge, MA: Harvard University Press.

Newell, A., & Rosenbloom, P. S. (1981). Mechanism of skill acquisition and the law of practice. In J. R. Anderson (Ed.), *Cognitive skills and their acquisition* (1–56). Hillsdale, NJ: Erlbaum.

Newell, A., Shaw, J. C., & Simon, H. A. (1962). The process of creative thinking. In H. E. Gruber, G. Terrell, & M. Wertheimer (Eds.), *Contemporary approaches to creative thinking* (pp. 63–119). New York: Lieber-Atherton. (Reprinted in H. A. Simon, [1979], *Models of Thought* [pp. 144–174]. New Haven, CT: Yale University Press.)

Norman, D. A., Ortony, A., & Russell, D. M. (2003). Affect and machine design: Lessons for the development of autonomous machines. *IBM Systems Journal, 42,* 38–44.

Ohlsson, S. (1995). Abstract computer models: Toward a new method for theorizing about adaptive agents. In N. Lavrac & S. Wrobel (Eds.), *Machine learning: ECML-95* (pp. 33–52). Berlin: Springer.

Paas, F., Renkl, A., & Sweller, J. (2003). Cognitive load theory and instructional design: Recent developments. *Educational Psychologist, 38,* 1–4.

Paas, F., Renkl, A., & Sweller, J. (2004). Cognitive load theory: Instructional implications of the interaction between information structures and cognitive architecture. *Instructional Science, 32,* 1–8.

Picard, R. W. (1997). *Affective computing.* Cambridge, MA: MIT Press.

Richman, H. B., & Simon, H. A. (1989). Context effects in letter perception: Comparison of two models. *Psychological Review, 96,* 417–432.

Ritter, F. E. (1988). Extending the Seibel-Soar model. In *Proceedings of the Soar V Workshop,* Carnegie Mellon University, June 1986.

Ritter, F. E. (2004). Choosing and getting started with a cognitive architecture to test and use human-machine interfaces. *MMI-Interaktiv-Journal, 7,* 17–37. Retrieved November 21, 2006, from http://useworld.net/mmiij/musimms

Ritter, F. E., & Bibby, P. (2001). Modeling how and when learning happens in a simple fault-finding task. In *Fourth international conference on cognitive modeling* (pp. 187–192). Mahwah, NJ: Erlbaum.

Ritter, F. E., Shadbolt, N. R., Elliman, D., Young, R. M., Gobet, F., & Baxter, G. D. (2003). Techniques for modeling human performance in synthetic environments: A supplementary review. Wright-Patterson Air Force Base, OH: Human Systems Information Analysis Center (HSIAC).

Rosenbloom, P. S., & Newell, A. (1987). Learning by chunking: A production system model of practice. In D. Klahr, P. Langley, & R. Neches (Eds.), *Production system models of learning and development* (pp. 221–288). Cambridge, MA: MIT Press.

Schooler, L. J., & Hertwig, R. (2005). How forgetting aids heuristic inference. *Psychological Review, 112,* 610–628.

Seibel, R. (1963). Discrimination reaction time for a 1,023-alternative task. *Journal of Experimental Psychology, 66,* 215–226.

Silverman, B. G. (2004). Human performance simulation. In J. W. Ness, D. R. Ritzer, & V. Tepe (Eds.), *The science and simulation of human performance* (pp. 469–498). Amsterdam: Elsevier.

Sweller, J. (1988). Cognitive load during problem solving: Effects on learning. *Cognitive Science, 12,* 257–285.

Sweller, J. (1994). Cognitive load theory, learning diffi-culty, and instructional design. *Learning and Instruction, 4*, 295–312.

Thagard, P. (2003). Why wasn't O. J. convicted? Emotional coherence in legal inference. *Cognition and Emotion, 17*, 361–383.

Thagard, P., & Nerb, J. (2002). Emotional gestalts: Appraisal, change, and emotional coherence. *Personality and Social Psychology Review, 6*, 274–282.

Velásquez, J. D. (1998). Modeling emotion-based decision-making. In *Proceedings of the 1998 AAAI Fall Symposium: Emotional and Intelligent: The Tangled Knot of Cognition*. Orlando: AAAI Press.

Young, R. M. (1979). Production systems for modeling human cognition. In D. Michie (Ed.), *Expert systems in the micro-electronic age* (pp. 35–45). Edinburgh: Edinburgh University Press. (Reprinted in *Educational computing*, pp. 209–220, by E. Scanlon & T. O'Shea, Eds., 1987, New York: Wiley)

Young, R. M. (1998). Rational analysis of exploratory choice. In M. Oaksford & N. Chater (Eds.), *Rational models of cognition* (pp. 469–500). New York: Oxford University Press.

Chapter 5

Order Out of Chaos: Order in Neural Networks

Peter C. R. Lane

Neural networks are a popular model for learning, in part because of their basic similarity to neural assemblies in the human brain. They capture many useful effects, such as learning from complex data, robustness to noise or damage, and variations in the data set. Within this chapter, we consider how neural networks can be used to capture order effects. Along the way, we will meet two radically different types of neural network, and find that demonstrating the presence of order effects in all situations is not always simple!

Neural networks are a popular model for learning, in part because of their basic similarity to neural assemblies in the human brain. They capture many useful effects, such as learning from complex data, robustness to noise or damage, and variations in the dataset. In this chapter we consider how neural networks can be used to capture order effects. We will also discuss two radically different types of neural networks and discover that demonstrating the presence of order effects in all situations is not always simple.

Neural networks are a form of learning algorithm with a basic representation loosely modeled on the neuronal structure in the human brain. Neurons in the human brain are interconnected by axons and synapses, which become vast webs of immense computational power. The human body contains approximately ten thousand million neurons, each of which may have up to ten thousand connections to other neurons.

The artificial neural network is a much simpler affair, with individual neurons having a number of both input and output links. A neuron has an activation that is carried to other neurons by its output links. A link between two neurons is weighted, so only a proportion of the output from the source neuron reaches the destination neuron. A neuron takes the weighted inputs from the incoming links and performs a calculation on them to determine its output. The basic structure of a neuron is shown in Figure 5.1, which depicts a neuron with a number of input links and a single output link. Notice the bias input, which is an input connected to a predetermined input value.

Neural networks are a popular model for human cognition, and researchers have applied the model to many areas, including language learning, implicit learning, categorization, and semantic comprehension. The classic books that helped generate much of the popularity are those by Rumelhart and McClelland (1986). Other texts referred to in this chapter include those by Elman et al. (1996) and Levine (2000). A good introductory text, including simulation software, is that of McLeod, Plunkett, and Rolls (1998). Further discussion of neural networks may be found in the chapters

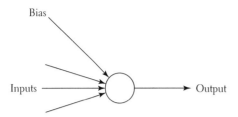

FIGURE 5.1. Figure of a simple neuron.

by Cornéujols and by Nerb, Ritter, and Langley in this book, and O'Reilly and Munkata (2000).

All learning algorithms, including neural networks, are affected by order effects in one way or another. My aim in this chapter is to consider how order effects are used or manipulated within neural networks. As described by Langley (1995), order effects may be present in three distinct areas of a learning algorithm: its features, instances, or concepts. Features are the components that make up the description of an individual instance or item. Usually with neural networks, we assume that an individual instance is presented all at once, in parallel, and so feature order is rarely important.

More interesting for neural networks are the effects of changing the order of presentation of individual instances. The question here is whether a new instance affects what has already been learned; this is known as the plasticity-stability dimension of learning. This question can be developed further by considering the concepts underlying whole groups of instances and whether reordering the presentation of concepts has any effect on what the network learns.

Although order effects are important for almost any model of learning, they take on greater importance in certain applications. Here I take two important general aspects of learning and discuss how order effects arise and affect the behavior of the network. I first consider the plasticity-stability dimension and the effects of instance order, with a look at the adaptive resonance theory (ART) of Grossberg and Carpenter (Figure 5.2). Next I consider the effects of order on concept learning and include a look at Elman's experiments in language learning.

ADAPTIVE RESONANCE THEORY

Adaptive resonance theory, which is based on the work of Grossberg, addresses the way in which adaptive resonant feedback can work between two layers of neu-

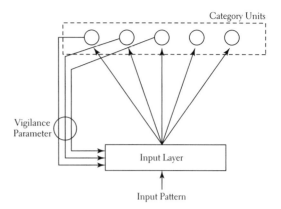

FIGURE 5.2. Example ART network.

rons. A good introduction to ART can be found in Levine (2000), and more technical material is presented in Carpenter, Grossberg, and Reynolds (1991), Carpenter, Grossberg, and Rosen (1991), and Wasserman (1989). Our starting point, as well as our interest in ART, is its solution to the basic dilemma of real-world learning. An agent in the world must be able to absorb new information when it is encountered but must also be able to retain existing memories. The problem is to strike a balance between being flexible enough to change and yet stable enough to remain the same.

For example, we all learned multiplication tables at school. This information is important to us, and we would like it to remain stable. But what happens when we meet someone who is adamant that 8 times 8 is actually 71? In this case, we should probably err on the side of stability. However, if told that we should now be learning our multiplication tables in the base of 9 instead of 10, we may need to be more flexible in our answers.

When we work with neural networks, the real-world dilemma is often not much of an issue. This is because datasets are initially fixed, and a network is trained separately from its use in performing a task. However, any form of real-world application, where learning may be incremental, brings the plasticity-stability problem to the fore. It is worth emphasizing that this problem is not one solely for neural networks; it is a general problem that all learners, including humans, must address.

An ART network is designed to maintain adaptivity in the light of new experience, while retaining knowledge already acquired. This is achieved by seeing how similar the current input is to the network's previous knowledge: Information that is not similar to previous knowledge is learned by creating new parts of the network, allowing the network to learn new information quickly in a plastic manner. Information similar to what has been learned before is instead acquired by gently modifying existing parts of the network, allowing the network to retain its earlier knowledge in a stable manner.

I now consider a version of ART that learns to group similar objects together, forming categories.

Structure of an ART Network

The ART network is composed of two distinct layers of units, with sets of links progressing in each direction; Figure 5.2 illustrates the network. The initial layer, which is the input layer, accepts the values for the binary features to learn. The top layer is the set of category units. Bottom-up links from the input to the category units hold weightings, determining the degree of fit of the input to each category. Top-down links from the category to the input units hold the definition of the category in terms of its accepted range of input values. Control is modulated by a vigilance parameter, which defines the degree to which an input must match the definition of a category for it to be admitted as belonging to that category.

Categorizing an Example

Initially, the category units are said to be uncommitted, and all of their definitions, the top-down links, hold the most general description, being all set to 1. When an input vector is presented, the activation of each category unit is computed as the dot product of the bottom-up weighted links with the input. The category unit with the maximum activation dominates and passes its definition (via the top-down links) for consideration against the input. A measure of similarity is computed, measuring the degree to which the input matches the category. If this is above the level set by the vigilance parameter, the category unit is said to "resonate." If it is not valid, the category unit shuts off for this input presentation, and the unit with the next highest level of activation now dominates and is checked as before.

Learning

A valid unit will now begin to learn by modifying the bottom-up and top-down links in light of the current input. The definition of the category will be contracted by changing to the logical *And* of the input and previous definition. Thus, only bits set in both will be retained. This principle means the definition will retain only data that are true for all of the examples. The bottom-up weights are modified in a fashion based upon this. Once a category unit has done some learning, it is said to be committed, and it is the committed units that hold the knowledge of the network.

The structure of the learning cycle is such that many similar patterns will become grouped together, and the resultant category definition should be able to generalize with future examples. This will work, along with providing a unique definition for any unexpected patterns, which demand their own category definition. Whether this was the first or last pattern, future learning will not corrupt its definition.

Illustration

To illustrate the operation of an ART network, let us look at the process of learning to recognize letters. For our training data, we will use five examples of letters, depicted on an 8×8 grid of 64 binary-valued bits. Figure 5.3 illustrates these five letters; note the two distorted examples of the letter E, which are used for testing the generality of the concepts.

First, let us consider how the network adapts when presented with each of the five patterns in turn, assuming a value of 0.9 for the vigilance parameter; remember that the vigilance parameter determines how alike a concept and input instance must be for the two to resonate.

What we are interested in is the set of committed concepts acquired by the ART network. These committed concepts and their order of acquisition are depicted in Figure 5.4.

In step 1, the first example, the letter C is presented to the network. Because all of the concepts are uncommitted, the network selects one at random and commits it fully to the new observed letter, the C. Figure 5.4 shows the committed concept in the first row.

In step 2, the second example, the letter B is presented to the network. The match between the input example and the committed concept is below the level set by the vigilance parameter, and so a new

FIGURE 5.3. Five example letters (C, B, E, E, E).

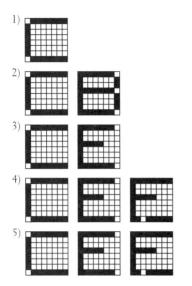

FIGURE 5.4. Learning some sample patterns with the vigilance parameter set to 0.9.

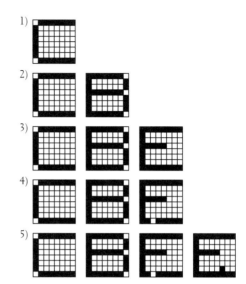

FIGURE 5.5. Learning some sample patterns with the vigilance parameter set to 0.95.

uncommitted concept is selected. The uncommitted concept is committed to the new observed letter.

In step 3, the third example, the letter E is presented. The match between the input example and the previously committed concept for B exceeds the level set by the vigilance parameter. The concept is thus modified, with each bit remaining set only if is also set in the current input example. This has the effect of reducing the B toward the E, but notice that the top and bottom lines of the E are shorter than the training example. Generalization of the stored concept has occurred.

In step 4, the fourth example, the first distorted E is presented. The match between it and the committed concepts is smaller than the level set by the vigilance parameter, and so a new uncommitted concept is selected and uncommitted.

In step 5, the final example, the second distorted E is presented. It matches and thus resonates with the last committed concept, but no new learning is required, and so the stored concepts remain the same.

As a second example of learning, let us consider how the network adapts when presented with the same five patterns in the same order but assuming a value of 0.95 for the vigilance parameter. The committed concepts are depicted for each step in Figure 5.5.

The main difference from the former example occurs in step 3. The higher level of the vigilance parameter means that the stored pattern for B and the

input pattern for E are not sufficiently similar for the two to resonate. Thus, a new uncommitted concept is used to store the input pattern, and the higher level of vigilance has decreased the degree to which the concepts are grouped together. By the end of the training sequence, the network has developed four concepts: one for each of the three letters, plus one for the distorted E patterns.

Order Effects

It is now instructive to see how order effects appear when training an ART network with the same instances but arranged in a different order. The simplest possible example to illustrate this uses training examples with simple on-off features. The two examples (1 1 0 0 0) and (1 1 1 0 0) refer to two training examples with five features and the suggested pattern of on and off for those features. Figure 5.6 shows the two categories created when training with these two examples; note that, depending on the order of the instances, the network either creates one category or two. What is happening here?

The explanation lies in the internal workings of the ART system during the computation of a resonant category. The similarity measure used by the standard ART network computes the agreement between the overlap of the input instance, the most active category definition, and the input instance. Mathematically, if

Net 1 - trained with (1 1 0 0 0) and then (1 1 1 0 0)
Committed categories
Category 1, definition #(1 1 0 0 0)
End of categories

Net 2 - trained with (1 1 1 0 0) and then (1 1 0 0 0)
Committed categories
Category 1, definition #(1 1 1 0 0)
Category 2, definition #(1 1 0 0 0)
End of categories

FIGURE 5.6. Demonstrating order effects in ART.

we write I as the input instance and C as the retrieved category definition, the similarity measure is computed as follows:

$$\frac{|I \cap C|}{|I|}$$

This measure is asymmetrical, meaning that putting the example (1 1 0 0 0) as I and (1 1 1 0 0) as C produces a similarity measure of 1, whereas the other way around would produce a measure of 2/3. If readers follow the algorithm, they will observe how ART generates different numbers of categories, as Figure 5.6 illustrates.

DISCUSSION OF ADAPTIVE RESONANCE THEORY

The full theory of ART, based upon a consideration of the physics of neural activation, provides for rates of learning and committal in the network. A neuron may modify its weights either slowly or quickly. Typically, it is believed that short stimulations of a neuron will not provide it with enough time to learn new behavior. Committal is said to be slow and is relied upon to allow for deactivating categories and seeking new ones without affecting those considered.

Thinking again about the two sequences of learning shown in Figures 5.4 and 5.5, we can see the dilemma for a learner between plasticity and stability. The plasticity of the network learning enables it to store different concepts and group together variations of a distorted E pattern into a single concept. However, as the example in Figure 5.4 shows, a high level of plasticity has meant that the B concept could not be distinguished from the E concept at this level. The difference between these two sequences is entirely due to the difference in the setting of the vigilance

parameter: A high level of vigilance prefers separate concepts, whereas a low level prefers grouped concepts. How should we set the vigilance parameter?

In general, this is a hard problem to solve, and it is usually determined by experimentation with your chosen data set. However, if you instead try "supervised" learning, where there are predetermined categories into which you want the network to separate the input patterns, the problem becomes easier. In supervised learning, you use the predetermined categories to judge the appropriateness of combining two patterns into one concept. For example, the B and E patterns in the earlier illustration were combined, although we would prefer them to be separate. By combining two ART networks into an architecture known as ARTMAP, we enable the network to determine its own setting for the vigilance parameter in response to the given categories. This extension is not described here but can be found in Carpenter, Grossberg, and Reynolds (1991).

The ART algorithm naturally produces order effects, as we have observed. An important aspect is the asymmetry in the similarity measure. This asymmetry arises because ART is motivated as a model of real neuronal activation. There are techniques to remove the order effects by using a symmetric similarity measure, and readers may explore these extensions.

RECURRENT NEURAL NETWORKS

We now consider an important model of concept learning known as the simple recurrent network (SRN), and specifically the model developed by Elman (1991, 1993). Figure 5.7 illustrates the basic architecture of an SRN.

Structure and Operation of a Simple Recurrent Network

The SRN is composed of three layers of neurons and a "context" layer, which is used for the recurrence. The basic functioning of the network is as follows. First, the input activation is placed onto the input neurons. This input activation is passed through the weighted links to the hidden units. The hidden units also receive weighted input from the context units, whose output I discuss in a moment. The hidden units apply their activation function to the weighted input, and their output is passed to the output units. The output

Output

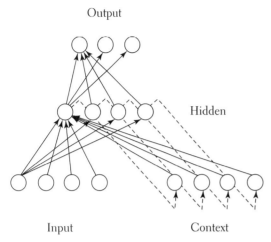

Hidden

Input   Context

FIGURE 5.7. A simple recurrent network (after Elman, 1991). Not all of the links between the layers are shown.

units sum the weighted activation received from the hidden units and generate their output activation. Finally, the activation in each of the hidden units is copied (note the dotted lines) to the corresponding unit in the context layer. This copied activation forms the output of the context unit for the next cycle.

The context units are the key to the SRN's behavior because they enable the network to acquire information about sequences of input patterns. During the first time step, information about the first input pattern is copied to the context units. This copied information is then combined with the second input pattern, so that the output is computed in response to the first and second input patterns. The combined information from the first and second input patterns is then copied to the context units, where it is combined with the third input pattern, and so on.

Learning

An SRN learns by being trained in a "supervised manner." Supervision means that the network is trained by a teacher, who determines what the correct output is to the training data. One of the more important applications for the SRN was language acquisition. Here, the task for the network is to learn to predict the next word appearing in a sentence. For example, given the sentence "The boy chases the . . . ," the network would have to fill in the dots with a suitable word. The teacher then supplies the expected word,

say "dog," and the network must learn that this sentence is typically concluded with the word "dog."

Later on I describe how the network handles the many possible conclusions to such sentences, but first let us consider the process by which the network modifies its internal connections in response to the given example. The basic process is known as *back propagation of error* and is explained in detail in many textbooks: Good examples are Mitchell (1997) and McLeod et al. (1998).

Training proceeds after the propagation of input forward, as described in the previous section. The network then compares its computed output with the teacher-supplied target output: The difference between the two is known as the error. The next step is to compute the error terms for the hidden units. This is accomplished by calculating the proportion of error for each hidden unit in the output error. The computation uses the activation function of the hidden units, as well as the weights of the hidden-to-output unit links.

A neural network learns by encoding information into the weights on its links. After computing the error terms for the output and hidden units, the weights can be updated, with the change in the current weight being the product of the input activation to each link and the error on the destination unit of the link. A learning rate term controls the amount of learning that occurs at any step.

Learning proceeds with many small adjustments to the weights in response to specific training sequences. Over time, the weights gradually converge to values that encode the information in the training sequences. Now, let us see how and what an SRN can learn, before I discuss the implications of this form of learning.

Illustration

Elman explores the ability of the SRN to learn various properties of natural language. One goal of his experiments is to discover the strengths and weaknesses of the SRN in this area and to draw conclusions about language learning more generally. To this end, one of his experiments explored the ability of an SRN to learn grammatical agreement between words. The agreement is trained and tested by considering a pool of sentences, such as the following:

"dog sees cat," "boy sees dog who sees cat," "boys see dogs who see girls who hear," "boy who girls see hears"

These examples are not quite "real" sentences in the sense that they are examples of things that people might actually say. However, they do present sequences of nouns and verbs in interesting, language-like ways. One of the key properties is that verbs must agree with their nouns. The agreement is particularly important in sentences such as the last one, where the final verb "hears" must agree in number with its subject, the noun "boy."

Using a sentence-generator program, it is relatively easy to generate large numbers of sentences of the form described above. Elman uses a continuous sequence of 10,000 such sentences, training an SRN to predict every word in the sequence. What was interesting here, especially in the context of this chapter, was that the network was unable to learn the full task from the complete set of sentences. Hence, a new training regimen was devised, in which the "easier" sentences, without any "who" clauses, were presented to the network first and were then followed by sentences with progressively more layers of "who" clauses. This new regimen is known as "starting small" and reflects an ordering in the conceptual information.

Let us consider this in more detail. What Elman is claiming is that, before learning a sentence such as "boy who sees girl chases dog," the learner must already know sentences such as "boy chases dog." If we look in more detail at what has to be learned, we can understand the problem more closely. First, we must put ourselves in the mind of the computer learner, which, quite literally, knows nothing at all about language. This is not easy to do because our human minds are very complex, and we readily assume things for which there is as yet very little evidence. Second, we must consider what it means to learn about this subset of language. If we knew this language, we would know that certain words, such as "boy," "girl," or "dog" are nouns and fulfill a certain role in a sentence. Words such as "who" are sometimes relative pronouns, while "chases," "sees," and so on are verbs: Relative pronouns and verbs fulfill a role in sentences that differs from the role nouns play. (We can ignore the problem of agreement between nouns and verbs for the moment.)

The words emphasized earlier, such as nouns and verbs, are descriptions of categories of words. The learner must somehow group words into these categories, even if the learner does not know the names for them. So, the learner's task is twofold: Find the categories for the words, and then work out the acceptable orders for these categories, which make up sentences. The twofold nature of the task perhaps makes clear the nature of the problem that order effects generate. Because the learner must assign words to categories and then work out the acceptable orders for the categories, it is better to have words from a simpler set of acceptable orders; in other words, starting from a simpler sentence structure will support the learner in assigning words to the correct categories. This is why first seeing lots of sentences such as "boy chases dog" enables the learner to figure out the nouns and verbs of the language before attempting to recognize these categories in more complex sentences.

DISCUSSION OF SIMPLE RECURRENT NETWORKS

The arguments for starting small made by Elman (1991, 1993) and Elman et al. (1996) have an intuitive appeal. The SRN is trained on the simplest sentences, which enables it to resolve the basic interactions between words (such as noun-verb agreement and simple sentence structure) before extending these to apply across the "who" clauses. Indeed, such arguments are readily adaptable to educational settings, where students are taught in a hierarchical fashion, with the basic building blocks presented before the more complex ideas are introduced.

However, one problem from a linguistic point of view is to understand how such a training regimen may be provided. Consider a child learning language, who will be exposed to the full complexity of adult language without the benefit of having simple sentences being presented first. How can the learning model be extended to such settings?

Elman provides an answer, using the SRN as an example. The complexity of the sentences is due to the length of the dependencies that are present. The "starting small" regimen structures the learning so that only short dependencies can be learned first and the longer ones are learned later. Instead of structuring the training regimen, can the learning algorithm be modified to produce a similar effect? The answer is yes. The SRN learns dependencies based on the contents of its context units. If these context units are "emptied" by setting their activations to zero, then they effectively forget all that has gone before. Elman's proposal is that, initially in learning, the context units get emptied after almost every word. As learning progresses, the context units are emptied less regularly. After some time, the context units are not emptied at all, enabling the SRN to learn about long dependencies. By modifying the learning algorithm, Elman manages to reproduce the effect of modifying the order of concepts.

The complexity of these learning issues is illustrated in the discussions by authors such as Rohde and Plaut (1997, 1999), who found it difficult to replicate the order effects demonstrated by Elman. Indeed, they managed to train SRNs to handle more complex grammatical structures without the benefit of starting small.

Whatever the final verdict on SRNs and the need to structure the training regimen or modify the learning algorithm may be, the experiments by Elman have highlighted the need to consider order effects in training networks to handle complex tasks.

GENERAL DISCUSSION

Any learning algorithm develops an internal representation of some domain of knowledge, given training instances from that domain. As the algorithm is given in each training instance, it must consider how much to modify its previously developed knowledge. The response of a learning algorithm to the plasticity-stability problem will depend most directly on how it represents knowledge and more subtly on how its target domain is structured. I now consider more generally the way in which these aspects manifest themselves in the two network types described earlier.

The first and clearest manifestation of order effects occurs in those learning algorithms that "commit" themselves to a specific internal representation given in the initial training instances. The ART network is a clear example of this. As soon as it is presented with a training instance, the ART network commits one of its category units to represent the instance. Fine-tuning will later modify the instance to cover a broader set of examples, but essentially the concept is committed from an early point, and there is no way for the ART network to undo its decision. Because of this, and also because of asymmetries in its comparison function, the ART network will learn different sets of concepts for different orders of the same instances.

Another good example of a learning algorithm that commits quickly is the EPAM architecture, discussed by Gobet and Lane in this book. There, the internal representation used by the learning algorithm is a decision tree. No decision, once learned, can be retracted. This means that EPAM is particularly sensitive to the order of presentation of the training examples. That chapter also considers the educational implications of this effect.

Thus our first reason for the presence of order effects involves the architectural properties of the learning algorithm, particularly the rapid commitment of the learning algorithm to specific information. However, removing this property (by allowing the learning algorithm to gradually modify any and all of the elements of its internal representation) does not guarantee an absence of order effects.

The second manifestation of order effects concerns those learning algorithms that tackle complex domains, where dependencies are present in the information to be learned. The SRN learning sentences from a simple language provides an example of this. Although the SRN may modify every weight in its network with each training instance, it still exhibits order effects. These are observed in the ease with which it learns complex concepts, given a different ordering of the training instances. In this case, learning clearly begins with word classes, then progresses to simple dependencies, and finally tackles dependencies over longer sequences.

Domain complexities are likely to lead to order effects in learning regardless of which learning algorithm is used. Other chapters in this book cover this question in more detail.

CONCLUSION

I have discussed the role of order effects in neural networks and explored in some detail two specific examples: adaptive-resonance theory networks and simple recurrent networks. As we have seen, order effects can arise in neural network modeling and can be exploited. However, some of the order effects are harder to capture due to the manner in which information is learned and stored in neural networks. In particular, the slow learning rates and parallel operation of the standard neural-network models make it impossible to cleanly separate learning into fixed stages. We might suggest that one of the challenges for neural-network research still remains to resolve the acquisition and evolution of identifiable concepts in a manner suggestive of human behavior in response to order.

PROJECTS AND OPEN PROBLEMS

Here are some exercises and open questions to help you develop your thinking in this area.

1. Create your own implementation of an ART network to model performance on a task such as categorizing further examples of the letters used in this chapter.

2. Recreate the training sequences illustrated here in categorizing simple letters, and see what happens with 3–10 different settings for the vigilance parameter. Discuss the settings, and try to explain what has happened.

3. Using the mathematical notation used earlier, we can define a symmetric similarity measure for ART networks as:

$$\frac{|I \cap C|}{|I \,||\, C|}$$

Explore the effect of this measure on the training sequences used in this chapter. You should be able to work through the examples from Figure 5.7 by hand. (The new measure is technically called a cross-correlation.)

4. Modify the network so that it can learn sequential information, perhaps by adding a concept layer in a manner like the SRN.

5. Explore the development of concepts in an SRN by modifying its training sequence. Several of the chapters in this book can help you wit possible data sets, approaches, and training sequences.

References

Carpenter, G. A., Grossberg, S., & Reynolds, J. H. (1991). ARTMAP: Supervised real-time learning and classification of nonstationary data by a self-organizing neural network. *Neural Networks, 4,* 565–588.

Carpenter, G. A., Grossberg, S., & Rosen, D. B. (1991). ART-2A: An adaptive resonance algorithm for rapid category learning and recognition. *Neural Networks, 4,* 493–504.

Elman, J. L. (1991). Distributed representations, simple recurrent networks, and grammatical structure. *Machine Learning, 7,* 195–225.

Elman, J. L. (1993). Learning and development in neural networks: The importance of starting small. *Cognition, 48,* 71–99.

Elman, J. L., Bates, E. A., Johnson, M. H., Karmilo-Smith, A., Parisi, D., & Plunkett, K. (1996). Rethinking innateness: A connectionist perspective on development. Cambridge, MA: MIT Press.

Langley, P. (1995). Order effects in incremental learning. In P. Reimann & H. Spada (Eds.), *Learning in humans and machines: Towards an interdisciplinary learning science* (pp. 154–165). Oxford, UK: Elsevier.

Levine, D. S. (2000). *Introduction to neural and cognitive modeling* (2d ed.). Mahwah, NJ: Erlbaum.

McLeod, P., Plunkett, K., & Rolls, E. T. (1998). *Introduction to connectionist modeling of cognitive processes.* New York: Oxford University Press.

Mitchell, T. (1997). *Machine learning.* New York: McGraw-Hill.

O'Reilly, R. C., & Munkata, Y. (2000). *Computational explorations in cognitive neuroscience: Understanding the mind by simulating the brain.* Cambridge, MA: MIT Press.

Rohde, D. L. T., & Plaut, D. C. (1997). Simple recurrent networks and natural language: How important is starting small? In *Proceedings of the Nineteenth Annual Conference of the Cognitive Science Society* (pp. 656–661). Hillsdale, NJ: Erlbaum.

Rohde, D. L. T., & Plaut, D. C. (1999). Language acquisition in the absence of explicit negative evidence: How important is starting small? *Cognition, 72,* 67–109.

Rumelhart, D. E., & McClelland, J. L. (Eds.). (1986). *Parallel distributed processing: Vol. 1 and 2.* Cambridge, MA: MIT Press.

Wasserman, P. D. (1989). *Neural computing: Theory and practice.* New York: Van Nostrand Reinhold.

Chapter 6

Getting Things in Order: Collecting and Analyzing Data on Learning

Frank E. Ritter
Josef Nerb
Erno Lehtinen

Where shall we start to study order effects in learning? A natural place is to observe learners. We present here a review of the types of data collection and analysis methodologies that have been used to study order effects in learning. The most detailed measurements were developed and are typically used in experimental psychology. They can also form the basis for higher level measurements, such as scores in games. Sequential data, while less often used, are important because they retain the sequential nature of observations; and order effects are based on sequences. In areas where experimental data cannot always be obtained, other observational techniques are employed. Once gathered, these data can be compared with theories, which can be grouped into two types: (a) static descriptions that describe the data without being able to reproduce the behavior, and (b) process models that perform the task that subjects do and thus make predictions of their actions. These process models typically are implemented as a computational system. They provide a more powerful, dynamic description, but one that is inherently more difficult to use.

Where shall we start to study order effects in learning? A natural place is with data. In this chapter we review several of the types of data for studying order effects in learning, as well as a selection of existing, well-established methodologies for collecting and studying such data. Some of these methodologies are often underused, however, so this chapter may encourage the use of these deserving (but often expensive in time or equipment) data collection and analysis methodologies. We present approaches from psychology, education, and machine learning, which, we believe, can fruitfully be applied in other disciplines.

We are interested in data that can show that order effects occur and give us insight into how they occur. In addition, of course, we would like the data to be robust; that is, they should be reproducible and reliable. This will sometimes imply special techniques for data gathering.

We will discuss several themes and issues in exploring the types of data that can be used. First, when studying sequential phenomena, it is important to keep the sequential nature of the data intact. Second, there is a trade-off between the detail and the amount of data that can be gathered and analyzed with a given number of resources. For example, you can see that chapters here that gather a lot of data per subject and do very detailed analyses use fewer subjects than studies that gather less information per subject or perform more automatic analyses. Third, we present several data types and a discussion of corresponding, appropriate analysis techniques. Fourth, we turn to the issue of different experimental designs for studying order effects. The end of the chapter discusses how your data can be embedded within broader theories of human learning and problem solving.

Retaining the Sequential Nature of the Data

It is not strictly necessary to maintain the sequential order of the data to study order effects themselves. Order effects can often be found simply by looking at how subjects perform after receiving stimuli in two different orders. It is necessary to keep the sequential aspects of the data in mind to be able to observe where and when these order effects appear (they might be very important as well). In addition, and theoretically more important, our understanding how the order effects occur is greatly assisted by having intermediate measures of performance that retain the sequential nature of behavior.

Figure 6.1 illustrates an order effect. It shows how performance (typically an inverse of response time) might vary with two different learning orders. If you measure after two units, there is not an order effect because the stimuli are not equivalent. If you measure after three or four units of time, there is an order effect. At five units of time, there is not an order effect for E, but there remain the difference performance effects on the intermediate stimuli (D is most prominent), and there are likely to be residual effects in many learning systems.

Retaining the sequential nature of data is not dependent upon the kind of data that are gathered, although most types have traditionally either discarded the sequential information (e.g., reaction times) or retained their sequential order (e.g., verbal protocols). In the case presented in Figure 6.1, the data must be retained for the units, as well as for their order. To be sure, you always can collect sequences of elementary data, such as sequences of reaction times, test scores, and verbal utterances, and keep them as sequences. (We present examples of those data sequences later on.)

Efforts have been made to extend the use of sequential data. Exploratory sequential data analysis (ESDA) in human-computer interaction studies (Sanderson & Fisher, 1994) and in the social sciences in general (Clarke & Crossland, 1985) allows you to see intermediate order effects.

Data Granularity

Of course, choosing the appropriate level of data to examine is crucial. If you use detailed enough data, you can often see a large number of intermediate order effects, as you see learners on different paths arriving at the same level of performance (see again Figure 6.1). VanLehn's results (this book) suggest this is possible. More finely grained data will also provide greater insight into the learning mechanisms.

There are trade-offs, however. Having more data often means that data collection will become more cumbersome and the analysis more complicated. In addition, as we know from the statistical theory of mental test scores (Lord & Novick, 1968), single observations are less reliable than an aggregation over a set of similar observations. Thus, using aggregated data by collapsing blocks of multiple observations over time increases the statistical power of your research at the cost of ignoring potential interesting interactions within the collapsed blocks (e.g., order effects). Newell and Simon (personal communication) often said that the most interesting trials were the practice trials before starting the experiment proper because these were where subjects learned.[1]

TYPES OF DATA: THEIR GATHERING AND ANALYSIS

We next examine several types of data in detail. This is not to say that there are not other types, just that these are either the most natural or are particularly good examples. This includes simple quantitative measurements, qualitative measures, measures from students, and data from models and automatic learners.

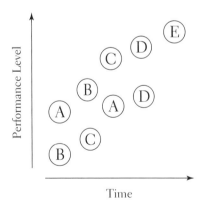

FIGURE 6.1. Order effects are visible after measuring after ABC vs. BCA and after ABCD vs. BCAD, but there is no effect after ABCDE vs. BCADE.

---

1. We have followed Roediger's (2004) use of "subjects" to refer to subjects because experimenters are also participants.

Simple Quantitative Measures

Measures such as time to complete a task (response times) and quality of performance (percent correct) are not the most exciting way to study order effects, but they are a good place to start because they are simple and clear. When they are taken at the end of two stimuli orders, they can provide the first indication that order effects are occurring in learning. Learning curves, such as those shown in Figure 6.1, are often generated from repeated assessing of those simple performance measures. Reaction times are also among the most traditional ways of studying behavior. Especially in applied research, time to perform a task can be crucial because it represents money or consumes other resources. Time can be measured with a stopwatch, with keystroke loggers (e.g., RUI [Recording User Input]; Kukreja, Stevenson, & Ritter, 2006), or from video recordings (e.g., MacSHAPA; Sanderson, McNeese, & Zaff, 1994).

In part-task training, complex tasks are broken down into smaller units that can be efficiently trained in isolation. The effects of part-task training are typically examined through time to learn and task performance. The goal, then, is to find a decomposition and an optimal training sequence for those smaller units that minimize the cost of learning the total task (see, e.g., Donchin, 1989, for a relatively complex task; and Pavlik, this volume, for a relatively simple task example that examines only training order, not decomposition).

Other often-used simple measures include the number of correct and incorrect responses. Many of the chapters here start with these measures. In general, these simple quantitative measures can be a useful indicator and summary of order effects that you will often wish to see, but they will not tell you much about how and why the effects occurred.

Derived Measures

Simple measures can be combined to create more complex ones. A good example of a derived measure is velocity (as it is derived from distance and time). Examples in behavior would include sums, differences, and ratios of reaction times or similar manipulations of other kinds of indirect measures. There are several interesting kinds of derived measures to keep in mind, which we explain next.

Hybrid Measures

To create scores provided to people who are learning a procedural task, we can often combine several measures (e.g., scoring 5 points for each second to complete a task and 10 points per widget). The highly motivating learning experiences called video games, for example, often use these. A problem with these measures is that they are ad hoc, and thus they often fail to meet the assumptions necessary for inferential statistical tests (for an account of when and how several measures can be combined meaningfully see Krantz, Luce, Suppes, & Tversky, 1971, or other good statistics books). These scores are nevertheless common practice in the classroom; for example, many tests give points for knowing different types of knowledge. From an applied point of view, they may be initially useful as a summary of performance. For further theoretical analysis, however, you will need to keep the components separate and check for possible interaction before you build combined scores.

Change as a Measurement

In order to change the impact of learning on performance, it is sometimes useful to compute differences in performance. These may include differences in time to successfully complete a task (has learning changed the speed of performance?), differences in error rates, or differences in other quantitative measures you are using. Turn taking is another derived measure, for a turn is defined in relation to another action. But always be aware of problems in inferential statistics using differences as a dependent variable!

Other interesting change measures include interaction patterns, which can be represented with a variety of grammars (e.g., Olson, Herbsleb, & Rueter, 1994) and can be analyzed to find precursors for behaviors using lag sequential analyses (e.g., Gottman & Roy, 1990)

Applying Codes to Measures: Qualitative Measures

When studying the impact of learning, sometimes it is useful to study how performance changes qualitatively, such as in strategy shifts. This can be done by building meaningful categories and coding the subject's behavior. These codes (categories) can then be analyzed as other data.

An example of this type of study is research examining the level of aspiration in a series of tasks of varying difficulty. In a study by Salonen and Louhenkilpi (1989), students solved anagram tasks in an experimental situation in which they were required to select a series of tasks from five levels of difficulty. Students had to select and solve several tasks and had restricted time for each one. In the middle of the series they were given superficially similar but impossible tasks. The effect of induced failures was different for students with different motivational tendencies. Some slightly lowered their aspiration level after the failures but raised it again after the later success. Others responded to failures by decreasing their aspiration level and kept selecting the easiest tasks independently of occasional success during later trials. Their selections were videotaped, and the students were interviewed after each selection. These qualitative data were combined with the quantitative data of selecting sequences and successes. (This data-and-analysis approach is similar to work reported in VanLehn's chapter.)

In another study (Lehtinen, Olkinuora, & Salonen 1986), students solved problems involving the addition and subtraction of fractions. In this study impossible tasks were also presented in the middle of the series. Qualitative differences in the problem-solving processes before and after induced failures were observed. Some of the students solved the problems without showing any effect of the induced failures, whereas the problem-solving processes of other students grew worse after the induced failures. This might suggest possible mechanisms for order effects in learning (in this case, emotional responses; also see Belavkin & Ritter, 2004) and highlights the effect of order on motivation and the role of motivation in learning.

Protocols and Theoretical Frameworks

All measurements are taken within a theoretical framework, even if one might not be aware of it. Some measurements, however, are taken within a larger and more explicit framework than others. Protocol data (sequences of behavior) typically provide a rich account of all kinds of behavioral observations. As an important area of measurement that can be used to study learning, protocols often need to have their measurement theory made more explicit.

Protocols allow us to look at the time course of learning and are usually able to provide additional information on processing and learning, which many types of data do not address. Many types of protocols are related to an explicit theoretical framework and form an important method for studying learning processes. Examples of protocol data include the sequential recording of verbal utterances during problem solving (e.g., VanLehn, this volume), mouse and keyboard events while working with a computer (e.g., Pavlik, this volume; Swaak & De Jong this volume; Scheiter & Gerjets, this volume), or eye movements during reading. To find regularities within such vast records one needs a theoretical framework to provide guidance.

Each type of protocol data comes with a theoretical framework of how and why it can be used. Verbal protocols—often called talk-aloud protocols—are perhaps the best known. Verbal protocols are utilized within a strong framework (Ericsson & Simon, 1993) and make several explicit assumptions about how subjects can access working memory and how they can report by "talking aloud." Verbal protocols can provide cues about what information subjects are using and point to strategies the subjects employed. Eye movements have been studied as well (from early work summarized by Monty & Senders, 1976, and Rayner, 1989, to more recent work such as Byrne, 2001; Anderson, Bothell, & Douglass, 2004; and Hornof & Halverson, 2003) and help us understand how order effects occur by suggesting what information subjects have paid attention to and in what order. These protocols can include mouse movements (where they are different from task actions), but these, too, require a theory to support a less direct measurement theory (Baccino & Kennedy, 1995; Ritter & Larkin, 1994).

In educational psychology, the units of analyses have typically been larger than in experimental cognitive psychology, and thus the data acquisition methods are somewhat different. They can include stimulated recall interviews, where students, for example, watch a videotape of the sequence of their own activities and try to explain the meaning and intention of different acts (Järvelä, 1996). (This is a type of retrospective verbal protocol; see Ericsson & Simon, 1993).

So far, gathering and analyzing all of the various types of protocols have been difficult enough that they have not been used as often as one might like. However, the theories supporting the use of protocols are robust, and protocols can detail the microstructure of how order effects can occur and often provide insight into the mechanisms that give rise to order effects.

Machine Learning Data

The behavior of machine learning algorithms, for example, as noted by Cornuéjols (this volume), can be examined in pretty much the same way as human subjects (Cohen, 1995; Kibler & Langley, 1988). Very often the same measures can be taken. Machine learning algorithms, however, are nearly always easier to study than human subjects because the algorithms are typically faster to run than subjects, and they do not have to be recruited to do the task. You can easily control for confounding variables, and you do not have to be concerned with factors related to the social psychology of the experiment (such as demand characteristics or experimenter expectancy effects). In addition, it is easy to reset the learning algorithm and run it over a new input stimuli set or with changes in the model's parameters (representing different subjects or subject populations). The analyst can also take additional direct measurements of the learner's internal state and directly observe the mechanisms that generated it. When doing this, it is important to save the machine learning data and to note the conditions under which they were gathered. We include some guidelines as an appendix to this chapter.

There appear to be two outstanding limitations, however, to studying machine learning algorithms. The first is that they cannot provide abstractions or reflections about their behavior in a general way. While introspection is not a reliable data-gathering technique, subjects' insights can nevertheless be helpful. It would be useful to have descriptions and summaries of the model's mental state, particularly when this is complex or time based and changing. The second problem is that machine learning tends to be simple, done with a single type of data, a single knowledge base, a single learning algorithm, and a single and permanent learning goal (i.e., the machine is always and directly motivated). Although there are exceptions to each of these, in general these shortcomings often limit the application to human learning and represent areas for further work for machine learning.

TYPES OF EXPERIMENTAL DESIGNS

We can outline several experimental designs for studying order effects. Note, however, that experimental designs are usually concerned with eliminating order effects by averaging over different sequences. More information on experimental design can be found in standard textbooks (e.g., Calfee, 1985; Campbell & Stanley, 1963).

The Same Tasks Presented in Different Orders

The simplest design for studying order effects is just to present the same task in different orders to different groups (between-groups design). Where this is possible, the use of simple direct measures of performance can detect whether different orders have an effect. With richer performance measures, such as verbal protocols, one might start to address how these different orders give rise to different behavior. Presenting the different orders to the same group (within-group design) is generally not applicable in learning studies, simply because subjects have learned after the first order.

It is also worth noting a direct and powerful trade-off: The more data you collect for a single subject, either by the number or type of trials or the density of the data, the fewer subjects that can be run for a given project size. With increased density or complexity of data, more interesting questions can be answered. However, the work then relies more on previous work (theories) to define how the initial results are to be interpreted, such as protocol theory, and the data gathering has more constraints on it. Furthermore, the analyses become more complex and difficult to perform.

An example from survey research helps illustrate the simplest form of a between-subject design for studying order effects. Imagine a questionnaire with two items for assessing life happiness. Respondents have to indicate their happiness with life in general either before or after they have reported how happy they are with a specific domain of their life, namely dating. The dependent variable of interest is how dating affects general life happiness, which is indicated by the correlation between dating happiness and general happiness. The correlations will differ in the two conditions (the correlation is higher when dating happiness is assessed after general happiness). The usual explanation for this order effect is that subjects interpret general life happiness as "life happiness beside dating happiness" when they first have been asked for dating happiness. For a richer discussion of those issues see Strack (1992).

Another example of order that is more closely related to learning is Asch's (1946) classical finding about impression formation in personal perception. Asch showed that a person will be viewed as more likeable when described as "intelligent-industrious-impulsive-critical-stubborn-envious" than when described by the same list of traits presented in the opposite order. In Asch's view, this primacy effect occurs because some of the traits gain a positive meaning when preceded by a positive trait (such as intelligent) but gain a negative meaning when preceded by a negative trait (such as envious). The trait adjectives thus seem to be differently colored in meaning depending on their context. This kind of experiment again uses a simple between-subjects design.

As another example of learning effects, consider industrial training programs that differ only in the order of presenting the material; in these programs, subjects in different groups end up with different performance levels. Langley (1995) notes that the effects of two orders sometimes converge with time (see the "canceling out effect" in Figure 6.1, where further learning eventually cancels out the order effect seen in the first four stimuli). But keep in mind that the worst-trained group will meanwhile be unnecessarily less productive until it catches up. This often matters!

Teaching Sequences in
Educational Psychology

In education psychology it is seldom possible (or meaningful) to carry out experiments where exactly the same information can be presented in different orders. Often in these experiments the order and content cannot be completely independent variables, but order already results in some changes in the content. An example of this kind of design is provided by studies of the effects of so-called advanced organizers in learning texts (Griffin & Tulbert, 1995). Advanced organizers at the beginning of the text do not bring any additional information to the text but activate some prior knowledge and learning aims before reading. Exactly the same text or picture could be presented, for example, at the end of the text, but this is not often the case in studies of the effects of advanced organizers.

On a more general level, sequence effects have been studied in comparisons of different instructional approaches such as discipline-based vs. problem-based methods in medical education (e.g., Schmidt, Machiels-Bongaerts, Cate, Venekamp, & Boshuizen, 1996). In principle, the same content can be taught but in very different orders. Discipline-based models start with the teaching of the theoretical basis of different medical disciplines. This knowledge is later used in solving case problems, whereas the problem-based models start with authentic problems, and the students have to study basic science subjects when solving these problems. From a methodological point of view, however, these two approaches can almost never be examined as a pure sequence effect because of the real-world limitations of presenting exactly the same material.

Observational Methods for Interacting
With Computers

In educational psychology many order-sensitive experimental designs have been used where the learning sequence is not an independent but a dependent variable. Hypertext and instrumented readers (now called browsers) make it possible to follow students' personal reading sequences and problem-solving strategies and then to compare these techniques with the learning results. Britt, Rouet, and Perfetti (1996) used hypertext documents and instrumented browsers to present educational material. The format and the browser made it possible to record the students' reading sequences, which could then be analyzed with respect to learning and performance (see Scheiter & Gerjets, as well as Swaak & de Jong, this volume, for examples of this approach).

Another approach to work in this area—when you have access to the user's computer—is to use a keystroke logger such as RUI (Kukreja, Stevenson, & Ritter, in press). Keystroke loggers record the user's keystrokes for later analysis and some, such as RUI, allow playback. This permits any piece of software to be studied. There are also commercial versions available that work with video data as well. Research in usability studies has provided further tools and methodological notes in this area.

Repeated Surveys

In certain areas, true experiments are not possible because the situation cannot be independently manipulated. Repeated measurements by means of surveys and finding carefully matched cases can be used to analyze longer-term and more intricate order effects in complex social behavior and education. For example, developmental psychologists have to note the order of the development of skills; they can only survey the skill progression, not manipulate it. If they want to study the effects of the order of skill acquisition, they must observe many different, naturally occurring orders. The same elements will not always appear in each learning sequence (do all children hear the same words from their parents?), but we suspect that for many purposes they can be treated as equivalent on a more abstract level. Typically, the measurements brought to theoretical analysis are not the items themselves (such as performance on individual math problems) but higher-level derived measures (such as a score on a standardized exam).

Surveys can also be carried out in the midst of another design. Subjects can be queried while performing a task with questions or requests or self-reports designed to measure their internal state in some way (for example, their motivational state; Feurzeig & Ritter, 1988). Scheiter and Gerjets (this volume) do this to study how students reorder problems on exams.

TYPES OF ANALYSES: STEPS TOWARD THEORIES

How can the data on order effects be summarized? There are numerous examples of summary analyses in the other chapters in this volume, such as process models in psychology and machine learning algorithms in computer science. Here we address some of the preliminary analyses that need to be performed so that we understand the data before creating such models. These analyses can be used to summarize knowledge of and to predict order effects.

Simple Data Descriptions

The first step in nearly any set of analyses is to create a set of simple descriptive statistics of the data, such as the response time for each task in each order and the number of errors per condition. It is often very useful to visualize the data in the form of a graph or a plot. This is part of a fairly large and well-defined area of exploratory data analysis (for example, Tukey, 1977, and Tufte, 1990), which applies to sequential data as well. Sanderson and Fisher (1994) provide an overview of exploratory sequential data analysis (ESDA). Papers in their special issue on ESDA provide several examples (Frohlich, Drew, & Monk, 1994; Olson, Herbsleb, & Rueter, 1994; Ritter & Larkin, 1994; Vortac, Edwards, & Manning, 1994).

Simple descriptive statistical analyses are not always applicable when sequential data have been gathered. Keeping the sequential nature of the data precludes many averaging analyses, so creating graphic displays becomes more important. The user can try to create transition networks as behavioral summaries, such as Markov models, which show the frequency and types of transitions (Rauterberg, 1993; also see Sun & Giles, 1998, for more sequence learning models). More complex transition diagrams may include other features of the data such as the frequency of each category (Olson, Herbsleb, & Rueter, 1994).

Applying inferential statistics in this area can be a bit tricky. Often the assumptions of such analyses are violated by sequential data, such as independence. The best way to proceed is often to come up with a theory and then simply work to improve it, not prove it (Grant, 1962).

Microgenetic Analyses of Verbal and Other Protocols

An extreme version of data analysis is to keep the sequential nature of the data completely intact, not using averages but analyzing the data as a sequence of individual points. If simple reaction times are used as the data points, learning curves are generated because learning nearly always occurs (Ritter & Schooler, 2001).

Richer, nonnumeric data are often kept as sequential data. Here, a sequential analysis of the data can extract more information and provide more direct information on how behavior is generated than reaction time means. This type of analysis includes protocol analysis (Ericsson & Simon, 1993; Newell & Simon, 1972) and microgenetic analysis (Agre & Shrager, 1990; Siegler, 1987; VanLehn, this volume). These analyses typically print or plot the data in series. The analyst then examines the data by hand-looking for higher-order patterns, such as strategies and strategy changes. This is a tedious form of analysis, but it often provides the most insight into behavior and its causes. The initial analyses are tied to data rather closely here, with the final analysis often designed to help create or test formal information-processing models.

Information-Processing Process Models

The analysis of order effects should lead to information-processing theories that can make predictions about where, when, and how order effects will occur. These theories typically perform the task of interest, providing a description of the knowledge and mechanisms sufficient to perform it. They typically describe intermediate internal states, the time course of processing, and near alternative actions. They do this in a very inspectable and objective way, thereby yielding a much richer theory to test than a verbal theory.

These information-processing models have been created in at least two traditions: machine learning, which emphasizes doing the task well, and cognitive modeling, which emphasizes doing the task the way humans do. Summaries of theories are described in the other chapters on machine learning (Cornuéjols) and process models (Nerb et al.; Lane) and are used in many of the chapters (e.g., Gobet & Lane; Pavlik; Ohlsson). We briefly preview them here and describe how they can influence data collection.

Process models make many predictions and many types of predictions, and nearly any type of data gathered can be compared with their performance. It is thus very easy to see where these types of theories are not matched by the data; consequently, many people believe that this makes them bad theories. We believe that this viewpoint could not be more incorrect. If you are trying to create a theory that will predict behavior, you need to create one that makes strong predictions about behavior, which these theories do. Being able to see where the theory does not correspond to the data allows you to improve or reject the theory. Theories that cannot be seen to be wrong cannot be improved and, even worse, cannot be falsified. And, let us be fair, theories that do not make predictions are even more wrong for not making them. A more complete description of this theory development view is available from Grant (1962). Creating the model thus first points out what kinds of data to gather to validate and improve the model (Kieras, Wood, & Meyer, 1997).

CONCLUSIONS

Because we cannot prove a theory, what is the role of data, and what means do we have for organizing our understanding of order effects as theories? We believe that there are two complementary ways. The first is simply to test your theories to show that they are worth taking seriously and to find out where they are incomplete and could be improved (Grant, 1962). This approach does not end (how could it?) but is repeated until the theory is sufficient. The theory will remain incomplete and wrong in some way (for example, it will always be able to take account of further phenomena).

PROJECTS AND OPEN PROBLEMS

1. Take your favorite task and design an experiment to study order effects. Can you augment the design of an existing experiment to look at order effects? Which experimental design would you use? What measurements would you take? What would taking different types of data mean? How would you analyze them? Would what you learn be worth the effort? If you are taking sequential measurements, how will you deal with the complexity? (See websites for software and software reviews in this area of sequential data analyses.)

A second method is to create broader theories. Here, the breadth of the theory counts, as well as its depth. This approach, first argued for by Newell (1990), is for unified theories of cognition (UTCs). These theories are intended to include emotions, perception, and social interaction, so they might be better labeled unified theories of behavior. Practically, UTCs are currently studies on how to integrate theories and use a cognitive architecture. This approach is taken up in more detail in the introductory chapters that discuss models and the chapters on models in the second section of this book.

2. How can we choose appropriate data to test our theories? Find a task in psychology, machine learning, education, or your own field. What are the typical measurements? What would be an unconventional measurement to take in your field that is routinely used in one of the other fields?

   If there are theories or software to do so easily, run a pilot study creating and using this new technique for your area. An example of this would be to modify a machine learning algorithm or cognitive model (instead of a subject, typically) to "talk aloud" while it solves a task (this has been done only twice to our knowledge; Johnson, 1994, and Ohlsson, 1980).

3. Can unified theories be correct? Does psychology need a uniform theory, or are first-year

undergraduates correct in saying that human behavior is too complex to understand, let alone
predict? What are some of the arguments for and
against UTCs, based on the data that are available? Prepare a 10-minute presentation.

APPENDIX: GUIDELINES FOR
RUNNING MODELS AS SUBJECTS

Running models as subjects deserves some attention
because it seems that everyone knows how to do it, but
when it comes time to reexamine the model runs or
reanalyze the results, problems appear. Here we provide some guidance on how to run a model like a
subject. The details will, of course, vary depending on
the size of the model and the number of runs. For
example, if the model simulates 90 hours of data, you
might keep less than the full record of its behavior. If
you are running the model 10,000 times, you might
also not keep a full record of every run. Otherwise, it
appears to us that model traces need to be considered
to be as good as or better than empirical data.

There can be many objectives when running a
model. One important reason is to understand it, and
another might be to illustrate how the model works so
that you can explain how the mechanisms give rise
to behavior (VanLehn, Brown, & Greeno, 1984). Another major purpose for running a model is to generate predictions of behavior for comparison with data
for validation and model development. And finally,
an important reason is predicting human behavior. In
this case you probably have run the model for comparison with human data to validate the model. At this
point you may or may not want or need to compare it
with human data.

In all of these cases, the predictions of the model
should be clear. If your model is deterministic, then
you have to run your model only once. Some Soar
models work this way. If your model has stochastic
(random) elements, you either need to compute what
its expected value is using iterative equations (which
we have succeeded in doing only once; Ritter, 1988)
or to sample the model's behavior enough times that
its predictions are clear.

Ideally, you would like a point prediction and a
prediction of variance for each measure. Too often
predictions are sampled predictions (that is, the model's prediction is only an estimate of its final prediction because the model has not been run enough

times). Computing these predictions means running
the model and saving its results. We have provided
some suggestions for how to do this.

Suggestions

1. Save a copy of the model. "Freeze" it, so that at a
later time the model, its cognitive architecture (if applicable), and any task apparatus that it uses can be run
or at least examined. This is similar to taking down
study details like the experimental methods section of
a paper for the model. Put this frozen copy in a separate directory from the model you are developing.

2. The model code should be documented to be
at least as clear as good programs are. Dismal (www
.gnu.org/software/dismal) provides an example that
we can point to. Thus, model code should have an
author, date, preamble, required libraries and base
systems, table of contents of the model, and variables,
and these should be presented as major sections. A
README file should tell someone from another location how to load and run the model. This approach
is based on a theory of how to write more readable
code (Oman & Cook, 1990).

3. Record a trace of the model in enough detail to
enable later analyses. This entails recording individual differences and assigning a subject ID. It will thus
be possible to run the model later, perhaps, if you need
additional data. However, if you are using a batch of
runs or if the model takes a while to run, it will be very
useful to have the longer trace available. If even larger
traces are available, it is good insurance to record a few
of these. These traces will also be helpful if at a later
time you find something interesting in the model's
behavior or if you want to report another aspect of
the model's behavior. If you are running the model to
represent different subject conditions, these traces
should be separately recorded, labeled, and stored.

4. Each run of the model, the trace, and any summary measures should be stored in the same manner
as subject data. That is, store only one run per file if
possible, and do not modify it later.

5. The number of times to run a model poses an
interesting question. In nearly all cases, models are
theories, and as such their predictions should be and
can be made very clear. Nearly all science theory we
know of does not talk about sampling the theory,
which is assumed to be fixed, but sampling data from
the world. Thus, the model should ideally be run
until its predictions are clear.

If your model is deterministic, running it once is enough. If it has random components and is not deterministic, however, once is not enough. Increasing the number of model runs is nearly always much less expensive than increasing the number of subjects. It is clear to us (Ritter, Quigley & Klein, 2005) that several of the heuristics currently being used to determine the number of runs (e.g., "10" and "the number of subjects") are not appropriate. Examining a limited number of subjects arises because of resource limitations; also, they are data and need to be treated differently. Model runs typically are not as limited.

A way to decide how many runs to perform is both necessary and possible. After looking at power and sample sizes, we believe that 100 runs will often prove sufficient for examining predictions for Cohen's medium (0.2) effect sizes. Power calculations will enable you to compute how many runs you need to make to obtain a given effect size and a given confidence level of finding a difference. Currently, 100 runs is more than most models are run. Power calculations suggest that 10,000 runs should nearly always be more than sufficient, but this can be problematic when the model takes a relatively long time to run.

ACKNOWLEDGMENTS

Georg Jahn, Mike Schoelles, and William Stevenson provided useful comments on this chapter, and Mike was particularly helpful with the Appendix. Support for this work has also been provided to the first author by DERA, contract number 2024/004; by the ESRC Centre for Research in Development, Instruction, and Training; and ONR contracts N00014-03-1-0248 and N00014-02-1-0021.

References

Agre, P. E., & Shrager, J. (1990). Routine evolution as the microgenetic basis of skill acquisition. In *Proceedings of the 12th Annual Conference of the Cognitive Science Society* (pp. 694–701). Hillsdale, NJ: Erlbaum.

Anderson, J. R., Bothell, D., & Douglass, S. (2004). Eye movements do not reflect retrieval. *Psychological Science, 15*, 225–231.

Asch, S. E. (1946). Forming impressions of personality, *Journal of Abnormal and Social Psychology, 41*, 303–314.

Baccino, T., & Kennedy, A. (1995). MICELAB: Spatial processing of mouse movement in Turbo-Pascal. *Behavior Research Methods, Instruments, and Computers, 27*(1), 76–78.

Belavkin, R. V., & Ritter, F. E. (2004). OPTIMIST: A new conflict-resolution algorithm for ACT-R. In *Proceedings of the Sixth International Conference on Cognitive Modeling* (pp. 40–45). Mahwah, NJ: Erlbaum.

Britt, M. A., Rouet, J. F., & Perfetti, C. A. (1996). Using hypertext to study and reason about historical evidence. In J. F. Rouet, J. J. Levonen, A. Dillon, & J. R. Spiro (Eds.), *Hypertext and cognition* (pp. 43–72). Mahway, NJ: Erlbaum.

Byrne, M. D. (2001). ACT-R/PM and menu selection: Applying a cognitive architecture to HCI. *International Journal of Human-Computer Studies, 55*, 41–84.

Calfee, R. C. (1985). *Experimental methods in psychology.* New York: Holt, Rinehart, and Winston.

Campbell, D. T., & Stanley, J. C. (1963). *Experimental and quasi-experimental designs for research.* Boston: Houghton Mifflin.

Clarke, D. D., & Crossland, J. (1985). *Action systems: An introduction to the analysis of complex behaviour.* London: Methuen.

Cohen, P. R. (1995). *Empirical methods for artificial intelligence.* Cambridge, MA: MIT Press.

Donchin, E., 1989. The Learning Strategies Project: Introductory remarks. Special issue: The Learning Strategies Program: An examination of the strategies in skill acquisition. *Acta Psychologica, 71*(1–3), 1–15.

Ericsson, K. A., & Simon, H. A. (1993). *Verbal protocol analysis: Verbal reports as data.* Cambridge, MA: MIT Press.

Feurzeig, W., & Ritter, F. (1988). Understanding reflective problem solving. In J. Psotka, L. D. Massey, & S. A. Mutter (Eds.), *Intelligent tutoring systems:Lessons learned* (pp. 285–301). Hillsdale, NJ: Erlbaum.

Frohlich, D., Drew, P., & Monk, A. (1994). Management of repair in human-computer interaction. *Human-Computer Interaction, 9*(3–4), 385–425.

Gottman, J. M., & Roy, A. K. (1990). *Sequential analysis: A guide for behavioral researchers.* New York: Cambridge University Press.

Grant, D. A. (1962). Testing the null hypothesis and the strategy and tactics of investigating theoretical models. *Psychological Review, 69*, 54–61.

Griffin, C. C. & Tulbert, B. L. (1995). The effect of graphic organizers on students' comprehension and recall of expository text: A review of the research and implications for practice. *Reading and Writing Quarterly, 11*, 73–89.

Hornof, A. J., & Halverson, T. (2003). Cognitive strategies and eye movements for searching hierarchical computer displays. In *ACM CHI 2003: Conference on Human Factors in Computing Systems* (pp. 249–256). New York: ACM.

Järvelä, S. (1996). *Cognitive apprenticeship model in a complex technology-based learning environment:*

Socioemotional processes in learning interaction. Joensuu, Finland: Joensuu University Press.

Johnson, W. L. (1994). Agents that learn to explain themselves. In *The 12th National Conference on Artificial Intelligence (AAAI)* (pp. 1257–1263). Menlo Park, CA: American Association for Artificial Intelligence.

Kibler, D., & Langley, P. (1988). Machine learning as an experimental science. In *Proceedings of the Third European Working Session on Learning* (pp. 81–92). Glasgow: Pittman. (Reprinted in *Readings in machine learning* (pp. 38–44), by J. W. Shavlik & T. G. Dietterich, Eds., 1990, San Francisco: Morgan-Kaufmann.)

Kieras, D. E., Wood, S. D., & Meyer, D. E. (1997). Predictive engineering models based on the EPIC architecture for a multimodal high-performance human-computer interaction task. *Transactions on Computer-Human Interaction, 4*(3), 230–275.

Krantz, D. H., Luce, R. D., Suppes, P., & Tversky, A. (1971). *Foundations of measurement: Vol. 1.* New York: Academic Press.

Kukreja, U., Stevenson, W. E., & Ritter, F. E. (2006). RUI—Recording user input from interfaces under Windows. *Behavior Research Methods, 38,* 656–659.

Langley, P. (1995). Order effects in incremental learning. In P. Reimann & H. Spada (Eds.), *Learning in humans and machines* (pp. 154–167). Kidlington, UK: Pergamon.

Lehtinen, E., Olkinuora, E., & Salonen, P. (Eds.). (1986). The research project on interactive formation of learning difficulties: Report III: A preliminary review of empirical results, Tom. B, No. 171. Turku, Finland: University of Turku.

Lord, F. M., & Novick, M. R. (1968). *Statistical theories of mental test scores.* Reading, MA: Addison-Wesley.

Monty, R. A., & Senders, J. W. (Eds.). (1976). *Eye movements and psychological processes.* Hillsdale, NJ: Erlbaum.

Newell, A. (1990). *Unified theories of cognition.* Cambridge, MA: Harvard University Press.

Newell, A., & Simon, H. A. (1972). *Human problem solving.* Englewood Cliffs, NJ: Prentice-Hall.

Ohlsson, S. (1980). *Competence and strategy in reasoning with common spatial concepts: A study of problem solving in a semantically rich domain.* Unpublished doctoral dissertation. Also published as #6 in the working papers of the Cognitive Seminar, Department of Psychology, University of Stockholm, Stockholm.

Olson, G. M., Herbsleb, J. D., & Rueter, H. H. (1994). Characterizing the sequential structure of interactive behaviors through statistical and grammatical techniques. *Human-Computer Interaction, 9*(3–4), 427–472.

Oman, P. W., & Cook, C. R. (1990). Typographic style is more than cosmetic. *Communications of the ACM, 33*(5), 506–520.

Rauterberg, M. (1993). AMME: An automatic mental model evaluation to analyze user behavior traced in a finite, discrete state space. *Ergonomics, 36*(11), 1369–1380.

Rayner, K. (1989). *The psychology of reading.* Englewood Cliffs, NJ: Prentice Hall.

Ritter, F. E. (1988, September). Extending the Seibel-Soar model. Presented at the Soar V Workshop held at Carnegie-Mellon University, Pittsburgh, PA.

Ritter, F. E., & Larkin, J. H. (1994). Using process models to summarize sequences of human actions. *Human-Computer Interaction, 9*(3–4), 345–383.

Ritter, F. E., Klein, L. C., & Quigley, K. S. (2005). *Determining the number of model runs: Treating cognitive models as theories by not sampling their behavior.* Unpublished manuscript.

Ritter, F. E., & Schooler, L. J. (2001). The learning curve. In *International encyclopedia of the social and behavioral sciences* (pp. 8602–8605). Amsterdam: Pergamon.

Roediger, R. (2004). What should they be called? *APS Observer, 17*(4), 5, 46–48. Retrieved September 29, 2006, from http://www.psychologicalscience.org/observer/getArticle.cfm?id=1549

Salonen, P., Lehtinen, E., & Olkinuora, E. (1998). Expectations and beyond: The development of motivation and learning in a classroom context. In J. Brophy (Ed.), *Advances in research on teaching: Vol. 7. Expectations in the classroom* (pp. 111–150). Greenwich, CT: JAI.

Salonen, P., & Louhenkilpi, T. (1989, September 4–7). Dynamic assessment of coping with failure, regulation of aspiration level, and comprehension skills. Study I: The effects of failure on the regulation of aspiration level. In M. Carretero, A. López - Manjon, I. Pozo, J. Alonso-Tapia, & A. Rosa (Eds.), *Third European Conference for Research on Learning and Instruction* (p. 95). Facultad Psicologia, Universidad Autonoma de Madrid.

Sanderson, P. M., & Fisher, C. A. (1994). Exploratory sequential data analysis: Foundations. *Human-Computer Interaction, 9*(3–4), 251–317.

Sanderson, P. M., McNeese, M. O., & Zaff, B. S. (1994). Handling complex real-world data with two cognitive engineering tools: COGENT and MacSHAPA. *Behavior Research Methods, Instruments, and Computers, 26*(2), 117–124.

Schmidt, H. G., Machiels-Bongaerts, M., Cate, T. J., Venekamp, R., & Boshuizen, H. P. (1996). The development of diagnostic competence: Comparison of a problem-based, an integrated, and a conventional medical curriculum. *Academic Medicine, 71*(6), 658–664.

Siegler, R. S. (1987). The perils of averaging data over strategies: An example from children's addition. *Journal of Experimental Psychology, 115,* 250–264.

Strack, F. (1992). Order effects in survey research: Activative and informative functions of preceding questions. In N. Schwarz & S. Sudman (Eds.), *Context effects in social and psychological research* (pp. 23–34). New York: Springer.

Sun, R., & Giles, C. L. (1998). *Sequence learning.* Berlin: Springer.

Tufte, E. R. (1990). *Envisioning information.* Cheshire, CT: Graphics Press.

Tukey, J. W. (1977). *Exploratory data analysis.* Reading, MA: Addison-Wesley.

VanLehn, K., Brown, J. S., & Greeno, J. (1984). Competitive argumentation in computational theories of cognition. In W. Kintsch, J. R. Miller, & P. G. Polson (Eds.), *Methods and tactics in cognitive science* (pp. 235–262). Hillsdale, NJ: Erlbaum.

Vortac, O. U., Edwards, M. B., & Manning, C. A. (1994). Sequences of actions for individual and teams of air-traffic controllers. *Human-Computer Interaction, 9*(3–4), 319–343.

Part II

Fundamental Explanations of Order: Example Models

Chapter 7

An Example Order for Cognitive Skill Acquisition

Alexander Renkl
Robert K. Atkinson

This chapter addresses the question of how to structure and order instructional events to foster cognitive skill acquisition. We introduce a corresponding instructional model that is based on a larger experimental research program examining example-based skill acquisition. We then propose a specific order of learning activities that closely relates to different stages of cognitive skill acquisition. In the early stages of skill acquisition, when the major goal is to gain an understanding of the domain, the learner is presented with worked-out examples. In time, the worked-out steps are gradually faded and problem-solving demands are introduced. Finally, learners solve problems on their own, which is an appropriate learning activity in later stages of cognitive skill acquisition. In combination with this fading procedure, we show that there is also a particular order for introducing various types of self-explanation prompts and instructional explanations over the course of this transition. This chapter presents both the theoretical rationale and the empirical basis for this instructional model. Finally, it outlines directions for further research, for example, adapting the order of instructional events to individual learners.

Numerous experimental studies have documented that providing worked-out examples is an effective instructional means for fostering the initial acquisition of cognitive skills in well-structured domains such as mathematics, physics, or programming (e.g., Lisp). However, this finding immediately raises some questions with respect to the ordering of instructional events. Obviously, at some point in skill acquisition, learners need to actually solve problems in order to optimize their proficiency. The present chapter addresses the question of how to order instructional events—from studying examples to later problem solving—to foster the acquisition of cognitive skills in well-structured domains.

In this chapter we first provide an overview of the various stages of cognitive skill acquisition in order to situate learning from worked-out examples in the course of learning a new skill. Second, we define more precisely what we mean by learning from worked-out examples, provide reasons for its effectiveness, and discuss the relevance of self-explanations and instructional explanations as factors moderating the effectiveness of studying examples. Third, we discuss the problem of structuring the transition from studying examples to problem solving. Fourth, we describe a preliminary instructional model of example-based skill acquisition that currently guides our research. Finally, we outline a set of research questions intended to guide future research, such as adapting the proposed fading procedure to individual learners.

COGNITIVE SKILL ACQUISITION

In this chapter we concentrate on skill acquisition in well-structured domains such as mathematics, physics, and computer programming. According to a variety of researchers, the process by which cognitive skills are acquired is usually divided into several similar phases, albeit the specifics vary across theories (e.g., Anderson, 1983; Sweller, van Merrienboer, & Paas, 1998; Van-Lehn, 1996). From an instructional point of view, Van-Lehn's (1996) definition of these phases is especially attractive because it dovetails nicely with an example-based process of skill acquisition.

VanLehn (1996) distinguishes among early, inter-mediate, and late phases of skill acquisition. During the *early phase*, learners attempt to gain a basic under-standing of the domain without necessarily striving to apply the acquired knowledge. This phase corresponds to the study of instructional materials (typically texts) that provide knowledge about principles in an example-based skill acquisition process. During the *intermediate phase*, learners turn their attention to learning how to solve problems. Specifically, learning is focused on how abstract principles are used to solve concrete problems. One potential outcome of this phase is that flaws in the learners' knowledge base—such as a lack of cer-tain elements and relations, as well as the presence of misunderstandings—are corrected. In the context of example-based instruction, learners first study a set of examples before turning to problem solving. It is im-portant to note, however, that the construction of a sound knowledge base is not a quasi-automatic by-product of studying examples or solving problems. In fact, learners have to actively self-explain the solutions; that is, they have to reason about the rationales of the solutions (Chi, Bassok, Lewis, Reimann, & Glaser, 1989; Neuman & Schwarz, 1998; Renkl, 1997; VanLehn, 1996). Finally, the learners enter the *late stage*, in which speed and accuracy are heightened by practice. During this phase, engaging in actual problem solving—as opposed to reflective cognitive activities, such as gen-erating self-explanations—is crucial (Pirolli & Recker, 1994).

Of course, these three stages have no precise boundaries, especially in the case of learners who are attempting to acquire a complex cognitive skill that en-compasses multiple subcomponents. Under these cir-cumstances, learners may be entering the late stage in the acquisition of one of the skill's subcomponents while simultaneously operating in the early or inter-mediate phase of acquiring the skill's other subcom-ponents. Thus, learners may be in different stages at the same time with respect to different subcomponents.

LEARNING FROM WORKED-OUT EXAMPLES

Worked-out examples typically consist of three ele-ments: a problem formulation, solution steps, and the final solution. They are typically employed in math-ematics or physics textbooks in the following fashion: (a) a principle (or a rule or theorem) is introduced; (b) a worked-out example is provided; and (c) one or more to-be-solved problems are supplied. Thus, worked-out examples are designed to support initial skill ac-quisition. Many studies have shown, however, that the potential of learning from such examples is not real-ized using a traditional instructional approach in-volving the presentation of a single example. Instead, it is more effective to use a series of examples or to pair them with practice problems as in the classical studies of Sweller and colleagues (e.g., Sweller & Cooper [1985]) before presenting a set of instructional items consisting only of problems to be solved (for an over-view see Atkinson, Derry, Renkl, & Wortham, 2000).

The major difference between an example-based approach (several examples before problem solving) and the traditional approach (just one example) in-volves the intermediate stage of skill acquisition. In both approaches, the basic domain principles are typ-ically introduced by a text, and in the later stage, when greater speed and accuracy are the focus, learners are required to solve problems; becoming a proficient programmer by simply studying worked-out exam-ples without actually writing and testing some code is impossible. However, the two approaches make use of different means to accomplish the main goal of the intermediate stage, where the focus is on under-standing how to apply domain principles in solving problems. In the traditional method, the learners are expected to gain understanding through solving prob-lems, whereas in the example-based approach the ob-jective is to ensure substantial understanding prior to the introduction of problem-solving demands.

Why Is Example-Based Learning Effective?

In the beginning stages of a learning process, the learner's low level of prior domain knowledge has two consequences: (a) The learner is unable to apply do-main- or task-specific solution procedures; thus, general problem-solving strategies must be employed instead;

and (b) representing the problem in working memory requires substantial resources because the lack of knowledge prevents effective chunking of information (cf. Sweller et al., 1998). In this situation, when learners are confronted with problems to solve, they usually adopt a means-ends-analysis strategy. This tactic demands a considerable working memory capacity because the learner has to keep in mind the following aspects of the problem: current problem state, goal state, differences between these states, operators that reduce the differences between the goal state and the present state, and subgoals. Although the means-ends analysis can be an effective problem-solving strategy, it unfortunately does not directly foster understanding. Thus, this approach imposes an unproductive cognitive load, and, as a consequence, there is little or no remaining room for processes that contribute to understanding, such as generating self-explanations. In contrast, when studying worked-out examples, the learner is freed from performance demands and can concentrate on gaining understanding. This cognitive-load explanation accounting for the advantage of example-based learning was directly tested in a recent experiment employing a dual-task paradigm (Renkl, Gruber, Weber, Lerche, & Schweizer, 2003). The results of this experiment fully supported the cognitive-load hypothesis.

When Does Example-Based Learning Become Ineffective?

Although studying examples plays an important role in initial skill acquisition, empirical evidence indicates that problem solving is superior to studying examples in later phases. For instance, Kalyuga, Chandler, Tuovinen, and Sweller (2001) analyzed mechanical trade apprentices' learning about relay circuits and their programming in different stages of cognitive skill acquisition. Although in the initial phase, learning from worked-out examples was superior to problem solving, this advantage faded over time. In fact, the authors found that when learners had ample experience in this domain, learning by solving problems was superior to studying examples. Thus, there was a reversal of the worked-example effect across the phases of skill acquisition (see also Kalyuga, Ayres, Chandler, & Sweller, 2003). This reversal effect clearly implies the existence of an instructional order effect (Langley, 1995), as specific learning opportunities and materials

have to be sequenced in an order that fits the growing level of the learners' expertise.

Clearly, this raises the following question: What is a sensible ordering of learning opportunities? In the intermediate phase of skill acquisition, relieving learners of performance demands and instead providing them an opportunity to reflect on solution procedures by providing worked-out examples is effective because the main learning goal is to gain an understanding of how to apply domain principles and relate them to solution procedures. In the late stage of skill acquisition, the major goal is to increase speed and accuracy. At a minimum, some subcomponents of the skill should be automated during this phase, and, as was previously suggested, when automaticity is the goal, reflecting on worked-out solutions is not very helpful. Instead, solving problems or their subgoals is the major path by which speed and accuracy can be enhanced. In a nutshell, learning opportunities should be ordered in a way that first fosters reflections for understanding, followed by practice opportunities intended to promote automaticity.

Self-Explanations

Of course, the use of worked-out examples does not guarantee effective learning. It is crucial that learners actively explain the example solutions to themselves. Active reflection in this manner is especially important for learners as they transition from the early phase into the intermediate phase. As evidence, studies by Chi et al. (1989) and by Renkl (1997) related learning outcomes to the learners' self-explanation activities. They documented that successful learners were likely to engage in the following activities: (a) generation of *principle-based explanations*, whereby learners assign meaning to operators by identifying the underlying domain principle, a process that in turn fosters a principle-based understanding of an example's solution; and (b) *explication of goal-operator combinations*, whereby learners assign meaning to operators by identifying the subgoals achieved by these operators, a practice that helps in identifying the goal structure of certain problem types and knowledge of relevant operators.

Renkl (1997) found that these two types of self-explanations are especially effective when the learners' prior knowledge is low. In addition, he documented that an effective way to learn is to *anticipate* or predict the solution steps of a worked-out example (before actually examining the respective worked-out steps) and then to compare the prediction with the solution step provided in the example. This act of anticipating requires learners to solve parts of the problem. However, such anticipation appeared to be effective only when the learners had a relatively high level of prior knowledge, that is, when they were reasonably well advanced in the course of skill acquisition.

Although the aforementioned research is correlational in nature, there is also experimental evidence that corroborates the critical role of self-explanations in example-based learning. Bielaczyc, Pirolli, and Brown (1995) employed learning materials consisting of text and worked-out examples on Lisp programming. In an experimental group, participants were explicitly trained to generate self-explanations while studying examples. The training consisted of the following components: (a) introducing and encouraging self-explanations, (b) learning from watching a student modeling self-explaining on videotape, and (c) verifying the participants' ability to provide elaborated self-explanations (Bielaczyc et al., 1995). The control-group learners also received some training (e.g., viewing a student modeling self-explaining), but this intervention was more implicit (e.g., no explicit training in the application of self-explanation strategies). The authors found that the explicit training was substantially more effective than the implicit training in fostering self-explanations in students' studying examples and text. Consequently, the learning outcomes (programming performance) were superior in the explicit-training group.

In another study, Renkl, Stark, Gruber, and Mandl (1998) explicitly focused on *principle-based self-explanations* and *explication of goal-operator combinations*. Half of the learners received a short self-explanation training (10–15 min.) that included the following components: (a) information on the importance of self-explanations, (b) modeling how to generate self-explanations (one worked-out example), and (c) coached practice with self-explanations (another worked-out example). Participants in the control condition received thinking-aloud training. After these interventions, all of the participants independently learned from a set of worked-out examples. For learning materials, Renkl et al. used examples drawn from the domain of compound interest and real interest calculation. The explicit-training intervention had a strong effect on self-explanation activities and learning outcomes (assessed by performance on

transfer problems). In the case of near transfer (transfer to isomorphic problems), the authors found an aptitude-treatment interaction, where learners with low prior topic knowledge tended to profit the most from the training. This finding provides additional support for the assumption that principle-based self-explanations and explication of goal-operator combinations are particularly helpful in the very beginning of skill acquisition when prior knowledge is low.

Stark (1999) took up the finding of Renkl (1997) that learners with high prior knowledge profited from anticipating. In his study, Stark first presented his learners with a set of completely worked-out examples in a computer-based learning environment. After acquiring some knowledge by studying these examples, half of the learners went on to study completely worked-out examples, whereas the others were given examples that included blanks to be filled in. In some sense, these blanks forced the learners to *anticipate* the next solution step on their own. By providing the correct step after the anticipation, the learners received feedback from the learning environment. Stark found that this type of required anticipation coupled with feedback fostered learning. This finding confirmed the previously stated assumption that after acquiring some knowledge, anticipating is an effective learning activity.

Cooper, Tindall-Ford, Chandler, and Sweller (2001) provide further evidence supporting the assumption that anticipating is a particularly beneficial activity for learners with some prior knowledge. These authors employed an instructional method involving example-based learning that induced an activity similar to anticipating. Instead of anticipating a step, they instructed their learners to imagine a previously learned solution path. Again, it was found that this mental problem solving fostered learning only when the learner had a high level of prior knowledge.

In summary, empirical evidence suggests that self-explanations are of major importance for effective learning from worked-out examples. In addition, different types of self-explanations should be employed in a specific order: It is sensible to first elicit principle-based and goal-operator self-explanations and later, when some knowledge has been acquired, to elicit the anticipation of solution steps.

Instructional Explanations

Whereas self-explanations are of major importance in example-based learning, research has shown that the effects of instructional explanations are often disappointing (e.g., Brown & Kane, 1988; Chi, 1996; Schworm & Renkl, 2002; Stark, Gruber, Mandl, & Hinkofer, 2001). On the one hand, it seems to be more effective to prompt self-explanations than to offer instructional ones. On the other hand, it is important to consider that relying solely on self-explanations entails several disadvantages. For instance, it is very likely that learners will at times be unable to explain a specific solution step or their given self-explanations will be incorrect.

Renkl (2002) has developed a set of instructional principles designed to support the spontaneous self-explanation activity by providing instructional explanations. The central principles related to the design of effective instructional explanations were these: (a) Provision on learner demand: Instructional explanations should be presented on learner demand. This should ensure that the instructional explanations are appropriately timed and are actually used in the learners' ongoing knowledge-construction activities. (b) Minimalism: In order to facilitate their processing, instructional explanations should be concise. Explanations that are integrated in help systems of computer-based learning programs are often not used because they are too long, too redundant, and too labor-intensive to process. (c) Focus on principles: With respect to the content of instructional explanations, their focus should be on the underlying principles of the respective content subdomain. This claim is supported by the significance of principle-based explanations when studying worked-out examples. Based on a study with college students who were studying probability, Renkl demonstrated that instructional explanations designed according to these principles fostered the average learning outcomes.

Atkinson and Renkl (2001) experimentally investigated instructional explanations similar to those of Renkl (2002) (in both studies: college students; domain: probability). The results supplemented Renkl's findings in the following ways: (a) It is equally effective to provide instructional explanations on learner demand or in reaction to a learner's error when filling in a blank in a worked-out example; and (b) It is especially important to help the learners to relate the explanation to the example at hand by integrating the explanations into the example and making the connection between the example and the explanation obvious. Figure 7.1 shows the type of instructional explanation that proved to be helpful. This explanation is minimalist, integrated,

focused on principles, and related to the example. Moreover, it is provided on learner demand or in reaction to a learner's error.

In summary, instructional explanations are typically of very restricted use in example-based learning. In order to be effective, it is critical that instructional explanations not be provided at arbitrary points in the learning processes but carefully introduced into the ordering of instructional events. Specifically, they should follow errors committed by the learners or should appear when learners request help. In addition, they should be focused on principles, minimalist, integrated, and related to the example under study.

FROM STUDYING EXAMPLES TO PROBLEM SOLVING: IMPLEMENTING THE RIGHT ORDER FOR LEARNING

Although Stark (1999) demonstrated how to integrate problem-solving elements into the study of examples, he did not provide a satisfying answer to the question of how to structure the transition between studying examples in the early stages of skill acquisition to problem solving in the later stages. In response, Renkl, Atkinson, Maier, and Staley (2002) and Renkl and Atkinson (2003) proposed the following transition procedure: First, a complete example is presented. Second, an isomorphic incomplete example is presented in which one single solution step is omitted (see Figure 7.2 for a worked-out example whose last step was omitted); after trying to solve the problem, the learner receives feedback about the correct solution. Then, in the following isomorphic examples, the number of blanks is increased step by step until only the problem formulation is left, that is, a problem to be solved. For instance, for an example/problem type with *three* solution steps, the following instructional procedure is proposed:

(1) problem formulation
     (pf) worked step   worked step   worked step

(2) pf   worked step   worked step   faded step

(3) pf   worked step   faded step   faded step

(4) pf   faded step   faded step   faded step

This way implements a smooth transition from studying examples to working on incomplete examples

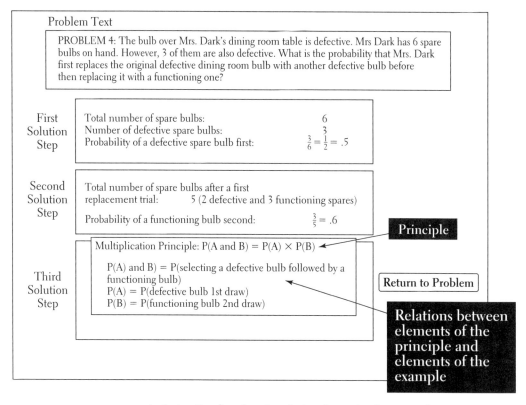

Problem Text

PROBLEM 4: The bulb over Mrs. Dark's dining room table is defective. Mrs Dark has 6 spare bulbs on hand. However, 3 of them are also defective. What is the probability that Mrs. Dark first replaces the original defective dining room bulb with another defective bulb before then replacing it with a functioning one?

First Solution Step

Total number of spare bulbs: 6
Number of defective spare bulbs: 3
Probability of a defective spare bulb first: $\frac{3}{6} = \frac{1}{2} = .5$

Second Solution Step

Total number of spare bulbs after a first replacement trial: 5 (2 defective and 3 functioning spares)

Probability of a functioning bulb second: $\frac{3}{5} = .6$

Principle

Third Solution Step

Multiplication Principle: P(A and B) = P(A) × P(B)

P(A) and B) = P(selecting a defective bulb followed by a functioning bulb)
P(A) = P(defective bulb 1st draw)
P(B) = P(functioning bulb 2nd draw)

Return to Problem

Relations between elements of the principle and elements of the example

FIGURE 7.1. An instructional explanation during the study of an example.

to problem solving is implemented. When problem-solving demands are gradually increased, the learners should retain sufficient cognitive capacity to successfully cope with these demands and thereby be able to focus on gaining understanding.

Renkl et al. (2002) documented the effectiveness of such a *fading procedure* — in comparison to the tried-and-tested method of using example-problem pairs — in a field study (ninth graders; domain: physics) and two laboratory experiments (college students; domain: probability). In a subsequent study, Renkl, Atkinson, and Große (2004) replicated this finding (college students; domain: probability).

Jones and Fleischman (2001; Fleischman & Jones, 2002) took up our finding that fading fosters learning and modeled this effect within the Cascade framework (VanLehn, Jones, & Chi, 1992; VanLehn & Jones, 1993). Their results also confirmed the effectiveness of the proposed fading procedure.

In addition to further replicating the fading effect, Atkinson, Renkl, and Merrill (2003) showed that combining fading with prompting for principle-based self-explanations leads to very favorable learning outcomes (college students; domain: probability). In their study, learners were required to select the principle underlying a step from a list at each step that was completely worked out (at the faded step the learners were just to fill in the step); after selecting the principle, the correct one was displayed so that the learners received feedback (see Figure 7.3). For the three-step problems that Atkinson et al. used, the following instructional procedure was employed in the condition with fading and prompting:

(1)	problem formulation (pf)	worked + prompting	worked + prompting	worked + prompting
(2)	pf	worked + prompting	worked + prompting	faded
(3)	pf	worked + prompting	faded	faded
(4)	pf	faded	faded	faded

The experimental results from a laboratory study showed that both instructional procedures employed by Atkinson et al. (i.e., fading and prompting) contributed additively to the learning outcomes. Thus,

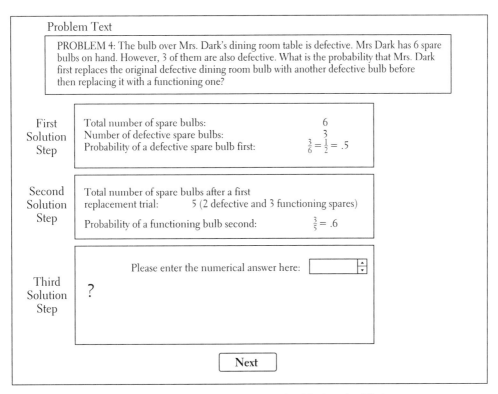

FIGURE 7.2. A worked-out example with a blank to be filled in.

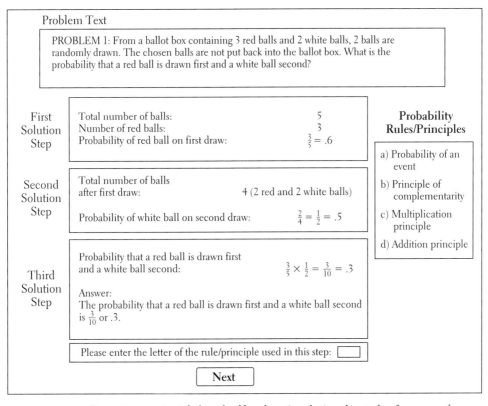

FIGURE 7.3. Prompting a principle-based self-explanation during the study of an example.

the two can be fruitfully combined. Additionally, the authors documented the robustness of this prompting effect by replicating it across two settings: in the laboratory with college students and in the field with high school students learning probability.

TOWARD A MODEL ON ORDERING INSTRUCTIONAL EVENTS IN EXAMPLE-BASED LEARNING

In this section, we integrate the previously discussed findings on example-based learning into an instructional model (see Figure 7.4). The model contains several main elements derived from experimental findings that we, in most cases, replicated in our studies on example-based learning.

1. *Sequence of isomorphic examples/problems.* After the introduction of one or more domain principles, worked-out examples are provided (see Figure 7.4). The use of more than one example before problem solving is the heart of an example-based approach (cf. Atkinson et al., 2000).

2. *Priority of self-explanation activities.* While learners are studying the examples, no instructional explanations are provided initially. Instead, the learners are required to explain the examples to themselves. At all worked-out steps, a prompt for principle-based explanations is provided. The learners receive feedback about the correctness of their self-explanations (e.g., Atkinson et al., 2003).

3. *Fading worked-out steps.* After the initial completely worked-out example, an example with one missing solution step is provided, which requires the learners to engage in anticipation. The learners receive feedback about their anticipation by providing the correct solution step. In the following examples, the number of blanks is successively increased until a problem is left that the learner has to solve completely without assistance. In this fashion, a smooth transition from studying examples to problem solving is implemented (e.g., Renkl et al., 2002).

4. *Instructional explanations as backup.* In the case of an incorrect anticipation, the learner may have insufficient understanding with respect to the corresponding solution step to solve the problem step correctly. Therefore, a principle-based instructional explanation is provided in order to repair that knowledge gap. These explanations are carefully designed (e.g., in a minimalist way, integrated into the example) in order to prevent the problems that are typically associated with instructional explanations (e.g., Atkinson & Renkl, 2001).

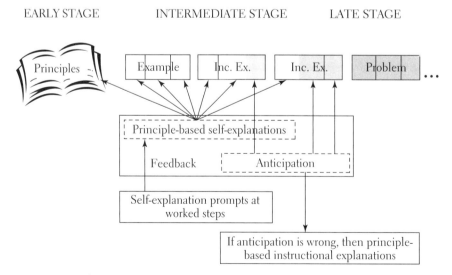

FIGURE 7.4. Ordering in example-based cognitive skill acquisition: toward an instructional model (Inc. Ex.: incomplete example).

This model can be classified as an instructional order model due to three important characteristics: (a) It prescribes a specific order of worked-out examples, incomplete examples, and problems to be solved over the course of skill acquisition; (b) It suggests that different types of self-explanations should be elicited in a specific order (i.e., first principle-based explanations, then anticipations); and (c) It proposes a way of prioritizing self-explanations and instructional explanations such that fostering the former should be the highest priority and only in specific instances, such as errors or help requests from the learners, should instructional explanations be provided.

PROJECTS AND OPEN PROBLEMS

Project: Design your own learning environment and implement the model guidelines. Our instructional model is implemented in the domain of probability. However, it can also be employed in a variety of domains that consist of problems with algorithmic solutions. Conduct some pilot tests with your new learning environment and have the participants think aloud while interacting with it. This will provide you with a better understanding of the actual learning processes involved with an example-based learning environment.

Outlook

In recent years, a significant empirically based knowledge base has accumulated. It has implications for the enhancement of cognitive skill acquisition by (a) ordering certain instructional events in order to foster example processing and (b) structuring a smooth transition from studying examples in initial learning to problem solving in later stages. We integrated these research findings into an instructional model, albeit a preliminary one. To ensure a comprehensive instructional model of example-based cognitive skill acquisition, several aspects of the model should be supplemented in the future.

1. To date, the order of learning opportunities prescribed by our fading rationale has not been sensitive to individual differences in knowledge state. Some learners may have acquired enough knowledge after the initial complete example that it makes sense to fade more than one step in the second example. On the other hand, others may need an additional complete example before they can productively try to anticipate solution steps. For such different learners, we argue that diverse orders of learning opportunities should be employed. To be able to accomplish such order adaptations, an "intelligent module" that estimates a learner's knowledge with respect to certain steps would be necessary (cf. Pavlik, this book). We are presently developing such a module in which the estimate is derived from the results of a prior knowledge test and the correctness of self-explanations. When, after a certain step that is correctly self-explained, the probability is high that the learner has acquired the relevant knowledge, the corresponding step in the next isomorphic example is faded. Empirical studies will demonstrate to what extent such individual adaptation of ordering worked, and faded steps will then lead to better learning outcomes.

Project: Develop and empirically test an adaptive fading procedure. For instance, an adaptive fading procedure could follow a rationale similar to the one outlined in this section. It might also be feasible to give students an opportunity to choose which steps they would like to solve on their own in the next example. Which theories could provide a rationale for such an adaptive fading procedure?

2. The worked-out examples that we have used so far in our studies were designed according to research findings on effective example design (cf. Atkinson et al., 2000). For example, the single subgoals in the solution procedures were made salient in our instructional materials because salient subgoals support self-explanation activities, such as explication of goal-operator combinations (Catrambone, 1996, 1998). In addition, with our fading procedure we interspersed studying worked-out solution steps with problem-solving elements, which also proved to be effective (e.g., Stark, Gruber, Renkl, & Mandl, 2000; Trafton & Reiser, 1993). However, we did not systematically include guidelines for designing examples into our model. This is especially important because productive self-explanations can be fostered or hampered, depending on example design (Renkl, 2005; Renkl & Atkinson, 2002).

3. Our present fading procedure is effective when the goal is to teach a method for solving a certain problem type. Often, however, it is important to explicitly teach

the differentiation between related problem types that
learners often confuse. Quilici and Mayer (1996) have
developed a rationale for combining and ordering
worked-out examples in order to foster the differentiation between such problem types. Specifically, they
advocate independently varying surface features (e.g.,
cover stories, objects, numbers) and structural features
(which are relevant for selecting a certain solution
method) in a sequence of examples. How to integrate
such a procedure into our instructional model to help
learners differentiate problem types is also a task to be
addressed in the future.

> **Project:** Develop and pilot test an idea about how
> to combine a fading procedure with an instructional
> procedure that fosters the differentiation of related
> problem types. One possible approach would be to
> juxtapose two faded example sequences. Another
> possibility is to design a faded example sequence that
> uses different problem types. Be sure to develop a
> theoretical rationale for your solution.

Although there are some significant open questions, our instructional model can serve as a guideline
to order different types of learning events in example-
based learning environments. By addressing the previously mentioned issues in the near future, we intend
to develop a comprehensive, empirically based instructional model of example-based skill acquisition.

References

Anderson, J. R. (1983). *The architecture of cognition.*
Cambridge, MA: Harvard University Press.
Atkinson, R. K., Derry, S. J., Renkl, A., & Wortham, D. W.
(2000). Learning from examples: Instructional prin-
ciples from the worked examples research. *Review of
Educational Research, 70,* 181–214.
Atkinson, R. K., & Renkl, A. (2001). The provision of
instructional explanations in example-based learning:
An analysis from a cognitive load perspective. In
A. Renkl, J. Sweller, & F. Paas (cochairs), *Cognitive
load and instructional design.* Symposium conducted
at the Ninth European Conference for Research on
Learning and Instruction, Fribourg, Switzerland.
Atkinson, R. K., Renkl, A., & Merrill, M. M. (2003). Tran-
sitioning from studying examples to solving problems:
Combining fading with prompting fosters learning.
Journal of Educational Psychology, 95, 774–783.
Bielaczyc, K., Pirolli, P., & Brown, A. L. (1995). Train-
ing in self-explanation and self-regulation strategies:
Investigating the effects of knowledge acquisition ac-

tivities on problem solving. *Cognition and Instruction, 13,* 221–252.
Brown, A. L., & Kane, M. J. (1988). Preschool children
can learn to transfer: Learning to learn and learning
from examples. *Cognitive Psychol, 20,* 493–523.
Catrambone, R. (1996). Generalizing solution procedures learned from examples. *Journal of Experimental Psychology: Learning, Memory, and Cognition,
22,* 1020–1031.
Catrambone, R. (1998). The subgoal learning model:
Creating better examples so that students can solve
novel problems. *Journal of Experimental Psychology: General, 127,* 355–376.
Chi, M. T. H. (1996). Constructing self-explanations
and scaffolded explanations in tutoring. *Applied
Cognitive Psychology, 10,* S33–S49.
Chi, M. T. H., Bassok, M., Lewis, M. W., Reimann, P., &
Glaser, R. (1989). Self-explanations: How students
study and use examples in learning to solve prob-
lems. *Cognitive Science, 13,* 145–182.
Cooper, G., Tindall-Ford, S., Chandler, P., & Sweller, J.
(2001). Learning by imagining. *Journal of Experimental Psychology: Applied, 7,* 68–82.
Fleischman, E. S., & Jones, R. M. (2002). Why example
fading works: A qualitative analysis using Cascade. In
W. D. Gray & C. D. Schunn (Eds.), *Proceedings of the
Twenty-fourth Annual Conference of the Cognitive Science Society* (pp. 298–303). Mahwah, NJ: Erlbaum.
Jones, R. M., & Fleischman, E. S. (2001). Cascade
explains and informs the utility of fading exam-
ples to problems. In J. D. Moore & K. Stenning
(Eds.), *Proceedings of the Twenty-third Annual
Conference of the Cognitive Science Society* (pp.
459–464). Mahwah, NJ: Erlbaum.
Kalyuga, S., Ayres, P., Chandler, P., & Sweller, J.
(2003). The expertise reversal effect. *Educational
Psychologist, 38,* 23–32.
Kalyuga, S., Chandler, P., Tuovinen, J., & Sweller, J.
(2001). When problem solving is superior to
studying worked examples. *Journal of Educational
Psychology, 93,* 579–588.
Langley, P. (1995). Order effects in incremental learning. In P. Reimann & H. Spada (Eds.), *Learning in
humans and machines: Towards an interdisciplinary
learning science* (pp. 154–165). Oxford: Elsevier.
Neuman, Y., & Schwarz, B. (1998). Is self-explanation
while solving problems helpful? The case of analogical problem solving. *British Journal of Educational Psychology, 68,* 15–24.
Pirolli, P., & Recker, M. (1994). Learning strategies and
transfer in the domain of programming. *Cognition
and Instruction, 12,* 235–275.
Quilici, J. L., & Mayer, R. E. (1996). Role of examples
in how students learn to categorize statistics word
problems. *Journal of Educational Psychology, 88,*
144–161.
Renkl, A. (1997). Learning from worked-out examples: A
study on individual differences. *Cognitive Science,
21,* 1–29.

Renkl, A. (2002). Learning from worked-out examples: Instructional explanations supplement self-explanations. *Learning and Instruction, 12,* 529–556.

Renkl, A. (2005). The worked-out-example principle in multimedia learning. In R. Mayer (Ed.), *Cambridge handbook of multimedia learning* (pp. 229–246). New York: Cambridge University Press.

Renkl, A., & Atkinson, R. K. (2002). Learning from examples: Fostering self-explanations in computer-based learning environments. *Interactive Learning Environments, 10,* 105–119.

Renkl, A., & Atkinson, R. K. (2003). Structuring the transition from example study to problem solving in cognitive skills acquisition: A cognitive load perspective. *Educational Psychologist, 38,* 15–22.

Renkl, A., Atkinson, R. K., & Große, C. S. (2004). How fading worked solution steps works: A cognitive load perspective. *Instructional Science, 32,* 59–82.

Renkl, A., Atkinson, R. K., Maier, U. H., & Staley, R. (2002). From example study to problem solving: Smooth transitions help learning. *Journal of Experimental Education, 70,* 293–315.

Renkl, A., Gruber, H., Weber, S., Lerche, T., & Schweizer, K. (2003). Cognitive Load beim Lernen aus Lösungsbeispielen [Cognitive load during learning from worked-out examples]. *Zeitschrift für Pädagogische Psychologie, 17,* 93–101.

Renkl, A., Stark, R., Gruber, H., & Mandl, H. (1998). Learning from worked-out examples: The effects of example variability and elicited self-explanations. *Contemporary Educational Psychology, 23,* 90–108.

Schworm, S., & Renkl, A. (2002). Learning by solved example problems: Instructional explanations reduce self-explanation activity. In W. D. Gray & C. D. Schunn (Eds.), *Proceedings of the Twenty-fourth Annual Conference of the Cognitive Science Society* (pp. 816–821). Mahwah, NJ: Erlbaum.

Stark, R. (1999). *Lernen mit Lösungsbeispielen: Der Einfluß unvollständiger Lösungsschritte auf Beispielelaboration, Motivation, und Lernerfolg* [Learning by worked-out examples: The impact of incomplete solution steps on example elaboration, motivation, and learning outcomes]. Bern, Switzerland: Huber.

Stark, R., Gruber, H., Mandl, H., & Hinkofer, L. (2001). Wege zur Optimierung eines beispielbasierten Instruktionsansatzes: Der Einfluss multipler Perspektiven und instruktionaler Erklärungen auf den Erwerb von Handlungskompetenz [Ways to optimize an example-based instructional approach: The effects of multiple perspectives and instructional explanations on cognitive skill acquisition]. *Unterrichtswissenschaft, 29,* 26–40.

Stark, R., Gruber, H., Renkl, A., & Mandl, H. (2000). Instruktionale Effekte einer kombinierten Lernmethode: Zahlt sich die Kombination von Lösungsbeispielen und Problemlöseaufgaben aus? [Instructional effects of a combined learning method: Does the combination of worked-out examples and problems to be solved pay off?] *Zeitschrift für Pädagogische Psychologie, 14,* 206–218.

Sweller, J., & Cooper, G. A. (1985). The use of worked examples as a substitute for problem solving in learning algebra. *Cognition and Instruction, 2,* 59–89.

Sweller, J., Merriënboer, J. J. G. van, & Paas, F. G. (1998). Cognitive architecture and instructional design. *Educational Psychology Review, 10,* 251–296.

Trafton, J. G., & Reiser, B. J. (1993). The contributions of studying examples and solving problems to skill acquisition. In M. Polson (Ed.), *Proceedings of the Fifteenth Annual Conference of the Cognitive Science Society* (pp. 1017–1022). Hillsdale, NJ: Erlbaum.

VanLehn, K. (1996). Cognitive skill acquisition. *Annual Review of Psychology, 47,* 513–539.

VanLehn, K., & Jones, R. M. (1993). Learning by explaining examples to oneself: A computational model. In S. Chipman & A. L. Meyrowitz (Eds.), *Foundations of knowledge acquisition: Cognitive models of complex learning* (pp. 25–82). Boston: Kluwer.

VanLehn, K., Jones, R. M., & Chi, M. T. H. (1992). A model of the self-explanation effect. *Journal of the Learning Sciences, 2,* 1–59.

Chapter 8

An Ordered Chaos: How Do Order Effects Arise in a Cognitive Model?

Fernand Gobet
Peter C. R. Lane

This chapter discusses how order effects arise within EPAM, an influential computational theory of cognition developed by Feigenbaum and Simon. EPAM acquires knowledge by constructing a discrimination network indexing chunks, closely integrating perception and memory. After a brief description of the theory, including its learning mechanisms, we focus on three ways order effects occur in EPAM: (a) as a function of attention; (b) as a function of the learning mechanisms; and (c) as a function of the ordering of stimuli in the environment. We illustrate these three cases with the paired-associate task in verbal learning and with an experiment using artificial material. In the discussion, we address some of the implications of this work for education, including how to order hierarchically arrangeable material, and the need to focus learners on important and relevant features.

Chapter 2 by Cornuéjols presents some current research in machine learning, and Chapter 5 by Nerb et al. discusses several process models that have been used to simulate human behavior. In this chapter we consider the origins of order effects in a detailed theory of human cognition. This theory arose early in the development of the field now known as artificial intelligence (AI), and it is worth considering in brief the context from which it emerged. At the time (the 1950s and 1960s), AI was generally seen as an attempt to model the way in which the human mind represents and uses knowledge. Therefore, the early AI systems were, in many respects, cognitive models. Two broad ideas were explored in those models that learned: one set of models required explicit, supervised instructions; the other, operating more "unconsciously," extracted patterns in an unsupervised manner.

The models based on supervised learning relied to a large extent on simplified forms of human tutoring. A good example of such a model is Winston's W system (Winston, 1975, 1992), which learned con-

ceptual maps for identifying complex and varied visual forms of abstract entities such as an arch. In this model, the quality of the conceptual map built by the system depended on that of the presented examples. Winston developed the idea of a "near miss" to define the optimal presentation sequence; the near miss would make some feature salient, which the learner would then use to induce some property of the concept being learned. For example, given an initial example of an arch, the second example might be a "nonarch," without a gap between the supporting pillars. This example fails to be an arch in only one property—the lack of a gap between the pillars—and so this is extracted by the learner and emphasized as an important property of an arch.

Unfortunately, such a level of supervision depends on the teacher possessing full knowledge of the domain and the learner having an optimal internal representation of the domain. But even more so, it relies on the internal matching process of the learner extracting precisely those features that the teacher intended to be the most salient conceptual differences between the two examples. The requirement of absolute knowledge by the teacher of both the domain and the learner has meant that such fine-grained supervised instruction did not scale up well to more complex systems or environments. Other cognitive models from this period rely on a less-supervised instruction routine and allow the individual learner greater scope in building up an internal representation of the presented examples. The teacher supervises the learner's overall performance rather than the details of the knowledge gained. This approach to computer instruction is followed in the field now known as machine learning.

In this chapter we discuss one of these less-supervised theories of human cognition, one based directly on perception. The theory, known as EPAM (Elementary Perceiver and Memorizer), relies on an attentional mechanism and short-term memory to extract perceptual chunks from the observed data and then stores these chunks in a discrimination network for distinguishing between training examples.[1] EPAM has been used to account for certain data on the effect of order in learning. This chapter presents a simplified version of EPAM's learning mechanisms and some experiments that examined the way in which the order of training examples affects the content and performance of the discrimination network learned. Thus, this chapter covers a single topic in relatively great detail, showing how order effects arise in an established cognitive model.

A COGNITIVE MODEL OF PERCEPTION AND MEMORY

The cognitive model we discuss in this chapter was initially proposed in Edward Feigenbaum's 1959 PhD dissertation. Feigenbaum introduced a theory of high-level perception and memory, which he called EPAM. The basic elements of EPAM include low-level perception, a short-term memory, attentional mechanisms, and a discrimination network for indexing items in long-term memory. Although EPAM includes all of these elements in a complete theory of cognition, most of the interest in the theory has focused on the discrimination network. Many of the amendments to EPAM address variations on the learning mechanisms possible in acquiring this network; the various improvements and

amendments may be followed in Feigenbaum (1963), Feigenbaum and Simon (1962, 1984), Richman and Simon (1989), and Richman, Staszewski, and Simon (1995). A more recent outgrowth of this line of research is CHREST (Chunk Hierarchy and REtrieval STructures), for which the reader can consult Gobet (1993, 1996), Gobet and Lane (2004, 2005), Gobet and Simon (2000), and Gobet et al. (2001).

This section begins with an overview of EPAM and its basic assumptions, considering any implications for the way stimuli order might affect learning and processing. Then we describe in more detail how the discrimination network is used to represent and learn about information acquired by perception.

Overview

Figure 8.1 contains a schematic overview of the five basic areas of the EPAM architecture: processes for acquiring low-level perceptual information, short-term memory (STM) and attentional mechanisms, processes for extracting high-level features from the low-level information, its indexing in a discrimination network, and the link from this network into other items of long-term memory, such as productions or schemas. The STM mediates the amount of processing that can occur in any of these areas and guides the attentional mechanisms, which, in this case, are eye fixation points. As an implemented theory, EPAM has little to say about feature extraction: Implementations assume merely that it occurs and supplies suitable features for discrimination. Also, as a theory of perception, EPAM has had little to say about the contents of long-term memory, although Richman et al. (1995), Gobet (1996), and Gobet and Simon (2000) discuss ways in which traditional models of semantic memory can be implemented within the theory.

The central processing of the EPAM architecture therefore revolves around the acquisition of a discrimination network while the attentional mechanisms retrieve high-level perceptual features from the outside world. For the purposes of this chapter, we assume that the sole role of the discrimination network is to distinguish perceptually distinct phenomena from one another.

Feigenbaum was supervised by Herbert Simon, and thus EPAM has some features that arise from Si-

---

1. Although our emphasis is about its use as a theory of human cognition, EPAM can also be considered a set of algorithms for machine learning. The system is available at http://homepages.feis.herts.ac.uk/~comqpcl/chrest-shell.html

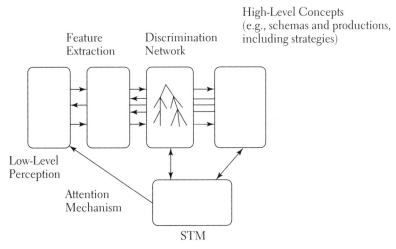

FIGURE 8.1. Overview of the EPAM architecture.

mon's view of human cognition as expressed in, for example, Simon (1981). One of these is that seriality plays an important role. The central processing is all assumed to operate in a serial fashion; that is, the eye fixates on an object, features are extracted and processed in the discrimination network, and then a further eye fixation is made, and so on. In addition, the STM operates as a queue, in which the first elements to enter are also the first to leave; the STM, as suggested by Miller (1956), has a limited capacity, which experiments with EPAM have shown to consist of between three and seven chunks. Further influences from Simon include the fact that learning is sufficient to generate satisfactory but not necessarily optimal performance, and processing is constrained by capacity and time limits. The limitations include various time parameters, which permit direct empirical tests. Examples include the length of time required for eye fixations and the processing of information in the discrimination network.

Hierarchical Representation of Objects

In EPAM, all information is stored as an ordered list of features. For example, the word "cat" may be stored as the ordered list of letters c, a, and t. These features are initially extracted from the image by using the attentional mechanisms and feature extraction module. However, these features may also be adjusted to suit what has been learned previously. For example,

once the system has learned words such as "cat," the sentence "the cat sat on the mat" would be represented as an ordered list of words and not individual letters. We can see this more clearly after considering both the discrimination network built up by the learning mechanisms within the cognitive model and its role in guiding perception.

Searching and Creating the Discrimination Network

The information experienced by the cognitive model is stored within the discrimination network. This network consists of *nodes*, which contain the internal representations (known as *images*) of the experienced data. The nodes are interconnected by *links*, which contain *tests* by which a given item is sorted through the network. In this chapter we assume that tests are simply chunks from the discrimination network, that is, individual letters or words. Each test applies simply to the next letter (or set of letters) in the stimulus. In the broader theory of EPAM, more complex tests are possible in which, for example, color is tested.

Figure 8.2 contains an example network in which the black circles depict separate nodes, and the node images are contained in ellipses next to them. Note that an image need not contain the same information as the set of tests that reaches that node. For example, the node reached after the test "t" from the root node has "time" as its image, and not just "t." The reason

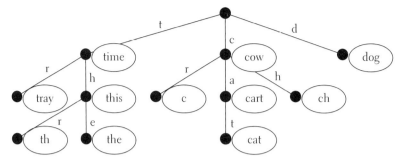

FIGURE 8.2. Example of a discrimination network.

for this will become clear when we describe the process of familiarization.

An item is sorted through a network as follows: Starting from the root node of the network, the links from that node are examined to see whether any of the tests apply to the next letter (or letters) of the current item. If so, then that link is followed, and the node reached becomes the new current node; this procedure is repeated from this current node until no further links can be followed.

The learning procedure is illustrated in Figure 8.3 and proceeds as follows: Once an item has been sorted through the network, it is compared to the image in the node reached. If the item and image agree but there is more information in the item than in the image, then *familiarization* occurs, in which further information

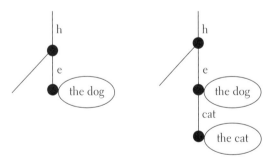

FIGURE 8.3. Examples of learning. Only a fragment of the entire network is shown. *Left*: Presenting "the dog" leads to familiarization, by which information is added to the current node; note that the entire word "dog" can be added to the image as it appears elsewhere in the network. *Right*: Subsequently presenting "the cat" leads to discrimination, by which an extra link and node are added to the network; note that the link can use the whole word "cat" as a test as it appears elsewhere in the network.

from the item is added to the image. If the item and image disagree in some feature, then *discrimination* occurs, in which a new node and a new link are added to the network. Estimates have been made from human data of the time each of these operations requires: for discrimination, about 8 seconds, and for familiarization, around 2 seconds (Feigenbaum & Simon, 1984).

One further important aspect is the way the model determines the test to be added to the new link during discrimination. At the point of discrimination, the model will have sorted the new item to a node, and it will mismatch some feature in the image there. In order to progress, the model must create a test from the information in the new item. It does this by sorting the mismatching features of the new item through the discrimination network. The node reached from these mismatching features is used as the test on the link. For example, "cat" was used as the test in Figure 8.3. Thus, tests may be formed from lists of features and not just single features; for example, in the textual domain, tests may be words and not discrete letters. We provide some pseudocode in the Appendix to this chapter for readers who wish to construct their own implementation of this discrimination network algorithm.

EPAM as a Psychological Theory

As a psychological theory, EPAM has several strengths. It is a simple and parsimonious theory, which has few degrees of freedom (mainly subjects' strategies). It makes quantitative predictions and is able to simulate in detail a wealth of empirical phenomena in various domains, such as verbal learning (Feigenbaum & Simon, 1984), context effect in letter perception (Richman & Simon, 1989), concept formation (Gobet, Richman, Staszewski, & Simon, 1997), and expert behavior (Gobet & Simon, 2000; Richman, Gobet,

Staszewski, & Simon, 1996; Richman, Staszewski, & Simon, 1995; Simon & Gilmartin, 1973). The most recent addition to the EPAM family, CHREST, has enabled detailed simulations in domains such as expert behavior (de Groot and Gobet, 1996; Gobet, 1993; Gobet, de Voogt, & Retschitzki, 2004; Gobet & Waters, 2003), the acquisition of syntactic structures (Freudenthal, Pine, & Gobet, 2006), and vocabulary (Jones, Gobet, & Pine, 2005), the learning and use of multiple diagrammatic representations (Lane, Cheng, & Gobet, 2000), concept formation (Lane & Gobet, 2005), and the integration of low-level perception with expectations (Lane, Sykes, & Gobet, 2003). The recursive structure of EPAM's network captures a key feature of human cognition, and its redundancy (small variations of the same information can be stored in various nodes) ensures that EPAM is not brittle or oversensitive to details. Finally, its learning mechanisms and the emphasis on serial processes make it an ideal candidate for studying effects of order in learning.

ORDER EFFECTS

There are three main sources of order effects in EPAM: (a) ordering of the attentional strategies used; (b) effects arising from routines that train the discrimination network; and (c) ordering of the stimuli in the environment (e.g., the curriculum). All three are similar in the sense that they change the form of the discrimination network by altering the order of appearance of examples and their features. Each of these three effects may be explored by using computer simulations and, to a certain extent, experiments with human subjects. We illustrate the first two effects with the paired-associate task in verbal learning, which was used in the initial EPAM publications to demonstrate its ability to emulate human performance. Two order effects were observed in these experiments: the serial position effect, in which a subject initially learns items in salient positions (the effect of an attentional strategy), and forgetting, in which a subject's previously correct knowledge is somehow lost (the effect of the learning routines). The third order effect is investigated in a simple set of experiments that explore the effects of stimuli order.

Paired-Associate Task in Verbal Learning

The role of order effects was indirectly explored in the first publications on EPAM (Feigenbaum & Simon,

1962). Feigenbaum and Simon were interested in simulating aspects of the paired-associate task in verbal learning. In this task, items are presented in pairs (stimulus-response), and subjects try to learn the appropriate response given a particular stimulus. For example, during the first presentation of the list, the experimenter may present pairs such as

[DAG—BIF]

[TOF—QET]

[DAT—TEK]

During a later presentation of the list, only the stimuli are presented, and the subjects have to propose a response. The correct pair is then displayed as feedback. For example:

[DAG—?]

[DAG—BIF]

[TOF—?]

[TOF—QET]

The list is presented as many times as required until some level of success is attained; for instance, the subjects may be required to make two consecutive correct passes. Two of the numerous *anticipation learning* phenomena observed in the human data and simulated by Feigenbaum and Simon are of interest here. We next discuss the serial position effect, which is a result of attentional strategies, and the phenomenon of forgetting and then remembering again, which is a result of EPAM's learning mechanisms. When modeling such experiments in EPAM, we assume that the discrimination network is learning to distinguish between the stimuli. The nodes are then linked to their appropriate responses, which are stored elsewhere in long-term memory.

Serial Position Effect

When subjects are presented with a list of items, such as the stimulus-response pairs above, they will pay attention to some items before others. Of interest here is that the initial item that subjects focus on is not selected arbitrarily. In the simplest case, they will notice any item that stands out, such as a brightly colored word, and remember it before noticing the other items. This effect, known as the Von Restorff effect (Hunt,

1995), is found with the other senses, too: Subjects pay attention to loud sounds first. In the absence of any particularly prominent feature, subjects will begin from "anchor points," in this case, the beginning and end of the list. This leads to the serial position effect, where the items close to the beginning and end of the list are learned better than the items in the middle.

Feigenbaum and Simon (1984) showed that two postulates of EPAM account for the serial position effect. First, it takes a constant amount of time to create a new node in memory (experiments have shown this requires roughly 8 seconds). This limitation means that subjects simply do not have enough time to memorize entire lists of novel items; thus they tend to learn more about what they notice most. The second reason to account for the serial position effect is the attentional strategy the subject uses to select which item to pay attention to first. The default strategy that subjects most often use is to begin from the anchor points, though this may be overridden by particularly salient items. In addition, subjects may consciously decide to look at the items in the middle of the list first, for example. Evidence for the role of attentional strategies on the ordering of learning has been discussed in Feigenbaum and Simon (1984) and Gregg and Simon (1967).

Forgetting and Remembering Again

Another, almost curious, phenomenon that has been observed in subjects is that learned information may sometimes be forgotten and then remembered later on. For instance, Feigenbaum and Simon (1984) discussed how subjects may correctly recall the response to a given stimulus on one trial, t, then incorrectly recall the response to the same stimulus on trial $t+1$, but then get the correct response on trial $t+2$. Because the discrimination network, which stores all of the information learned by the cognitive model, cannot delete or erase information, one might wonder whether the model can explain such phenomena.

However, Feigenbaum and Simon provide an explanation based on the learning mechanisms that create the discrimination network. The basic idea is that, as the discrimination network is modified, additional test links may be added to any node. For instance, consider Figure 8.4. At the beginning, the stimulus DAG is sorted to a node using a single test on its first letter (d); that node indexes the correct response, BIF (indicated by the dashed line). As further learning occurs within the network, additional links are added to this node. As the second panel of Figure 8.4 shows, this may result in DAG now being sorted to a deeper level than before, using tests on its two first letters (first d and then a). Thus, the model will be considered to have "forgotten" the correct response, BIF, whereas what has really happened is that the response has been bypassed. With additional learning, a new node may be created, using tests on all three letters of the stimulus (first d, then a, and finally g), and the correct response may be associated with this new node. We leave as an exercise to the reader to show how this mechanism can be used to explain oscillation, where the cycle of knowing-forgetting-knowing occurs several times.

Experimental Exploration of Order Effects

In this section we show how one may explore order effects arising from the environment by using a rela-

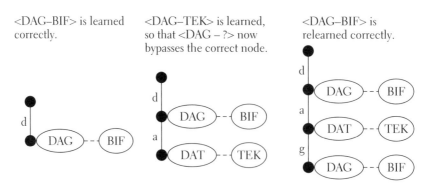

FIGURE 8.4. Learning, forgetting (by-passing), and learning again.

tively simple experimental setup. We are interested in how changes in the order in which the discrimination network receives data to process affects the network. To investigate this, we choose a simple target domain, train the model with different orders of items from that domain, and then investigate the changes in observed performance of the resulting networks.

The Data to Learn

The experiment here tests EPAM's ability to distinguish patterns consisting of ordered sequences of random digits. For simplicity, we assume that only the digits 0 to 4 may appear in each sequence; example patterns would then be (0), (3), (2 1), (4 1 2), and so forth. The discrimination network will identify each pattern using individual digits or series of digits (chunks) as tests, with patterns forming the images at the nodes in the network.

We present the discrimination network with a dataset consisting of a number of patterns. We investigate three kinds of order on the dataset: small first, large first, and random. "Small" and "large" refer to the length of the pattern. Therefore, "small first" means that the learner sees the patterns in the dataset in order of increasing size; "large first," in order of decreasing size; and "random," in arbitrary order. For example, the random sequence of patterns ((0) (4 1 2) (2 1) (0 4 2 1 1)) would be ordered small first as ((0) (2 1) (4 1 2) (0 4 2 1 1)) and large first as ((0 4 2 1 1) (4 1 2) (2 1) (0)).

Testing for Order Effects

To test for order effects, we present EPAM with a dataset of patterns in the three different orders. We then compare the learned networks first by their performance and second by contrasting their form and content. We illustrate this procedure by comparing the networks learned for datasets consisting of up to 10,000 patterns, each pattern of at most 10 digits, and each digit one of 0, 1, 2, 3, or 4. We first generate a database of 10,000 random patterns and then select subsequences of this database for training the network. We thus produce separately trained networks for sequences of 1,000 patterns, 2,000 patterns, and so on up to the full 10,000 patterns. For each length of sequence we produce three networks, one for each ordering of the patterns. After training, each network's performance is measured by testing it on the entire database, with learning turned off.

For each pattern, the discrimination network must first sort the pattern through its tests and assign it to an appropriate node. At that node only two things can occur: Either the pattern matches the image at the node, or it mismatches. If the pattern matches the image, then we say that the pattern was correctly sorted, though we distinguish those cases where the image is an exact match from those where it is only a subset. If the pattern mismatches the image, then the pattern was incorrectly sorted. Figure 8.5 shows graphs of the performance for the three orderings based on increasing numbers of patterns from the dataset; the top graph reports the proportion of nodes reached at which the item and the image in the node matched exactly, and the lower graph the proportion in which the item was a subset of the image in the node. It can be seen that the small-first ordering performs substantially worse than the other orders in terms of exact matching but is clearly superior in terms of subset matching; note that the range of the vertical axis differs.

The next point of interest is how well the learned networks from each order compare with one another. We use two measures. The first simply adds up the number of nodes in the network, and the second counts the average number of tests used to index each example in the test set. Because each test will require a certain amount of time to be applied, the latter test helps measure the resources required by the network when in use. Figure 8.6 contains graphs showing how these two quantities vary across the networks. The number of nodes in each network does not change much for the separate orders, but the small-first order requires a noticeably greater number of tests for sorting of test items.

Discussion

The results in the graphs indicate that the different orders do indeed produce different discrimination networks and consequently varying levels of performance. We have seen that the small-first order produces a deeper network, that is, one requiring more tests. This occurs because, on average, each pattern is longer than the preceding ones during training. Therefore the network will discriminate among the longer patterns at a greater depth. This also explains the performance differences. The small-first order works

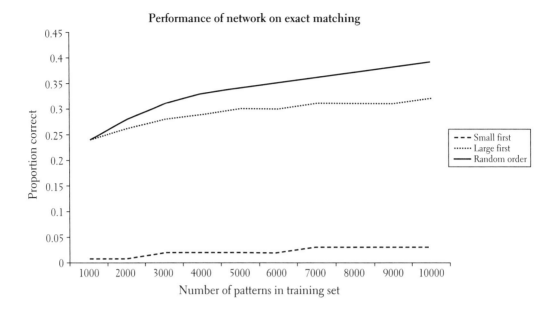

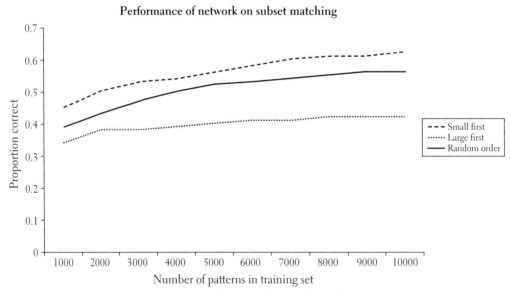

FIGURE 8.5. Performance of the network given three different orderings.

poorly for exact matching because there are more of the larger patterns, and, because these appear only at the end of the training set, there is not enough time for familiarization to learn them completely. In addition, the small patterns, because they do not appear later in the training, will not be properly familiarized.

EPAM AND INSTRUCTION: THE BROADER VIEW

We have seen that order effects arise due to different orderings of stimuli. There are a number of consequences of this. On the positive side, it should be possible to order stimuli such that many primitives

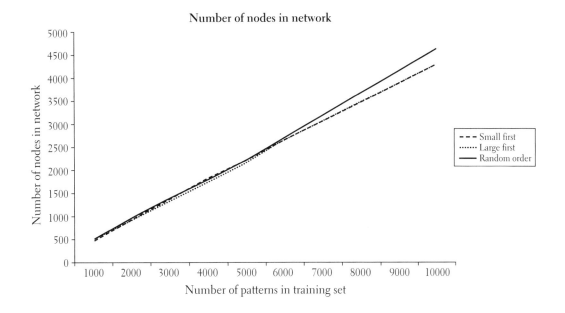

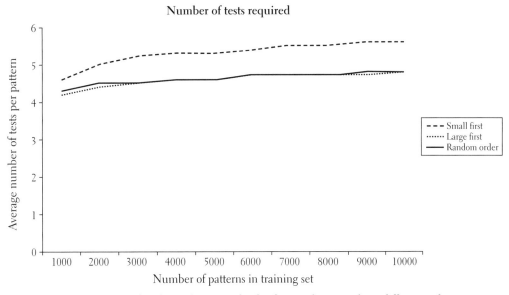

FIGURE 8.6. Number of nodes and average depth of networks given three different orderings.

and useful chunks will be learned first and thus support the acquisition of more complex information. On the negative side, if stimuli are inappropriately ordered, then learning may become progressively harder and result in suboptimal performance. One of the clearest predictions that EPAM makes is that relearning a domain with a new organization is very difficult because the structure of the discrimination network must be completely altered. We briefly consider how such findings relate to education.

A common claim in education (e.g., Anderson, 1990; Gagné, 1973) is that knowledge is organized hierarchically and that teaching should move from simple chunks of knowledge to more advanced knowledge (see also Chapter 7 of this book, by Renkl and Atkinson and Chapter 2 by Reigeluth). EPAM agrees with the hierarchical organization of knowledge, but when extrapolating (perhaps boldly) from our simulations in a simple domain to real-life settings, one would conclude that the need for hierarchical teaching is at least open to discussion and almost surely will vary from one domain of instruction to another and as a function of the goals of instruction.

Attentional strategies and the ordering of instances in the environment are crucial for EPAM because, as a self-organizing system, EPAM develops both as a function of its current state and of the input of the environment. Therefore, any deficiencies in learning, such as attending to irrelevant features of the environment, will lead to a poor network and thus poor performance. Further, attempting to correct previous learning will require massive and costly restructuring of knowledge (Gobet & Wood, 1999; Gobet, 2005).

Note that EPAM's view of sequential effects on learning is not shared by all theories of learning. For example, Anderson (1987, p. 457) states that, for the ACT tutors, "nothing about problem sequence is special, except that it is important to minimize the number of new productions to be learned simultaneously." This difference seems to come from the way information is stored in both systems: as a hierarchical structure in EPAM and as a flat, modular organization of productions with ACT. As a consequence, the two theories have different implications for the design of effective instructional systems (Gobet & Wood, 1999).

CONCLUSIONS

We are now in a position to answer the questions raised in the title: How do order effects arise in cognition, and can cognition do anything about them? Order effects arise in our example cognitive model, EPAM, because its learning mechanisms are incremental. That is, on seeing an item of data, the learning mechanism will add to whatever is already present in long-term memory. How and what is added from a given item of data will depend upon what is already present in the discrimination network. Thus, order effects arise as a natural consequence of the incremental mechanisms within the cognitive model.

Of interest is whether these order effects may be eliminated by continued experience. In a number of simple situations we have seen that order effects manifest themselves quite strongly in the performance of

the system and subjects. These effects have some interesting consequences for instruction, as was discussed in the previous section. However, the impact and correction of order effects in more complex domains are still open research topics.

PROJECTS AND OPEN PROBLEMS

To explore the topics this chapter raises, we have included two sets of possible problems and exercises.

Easy

1. Implement the discrimination network learning procedure described in this chapter.

2. Replicate the experiments described here (broadly defined), and verify that you obtain similar results.

3. Extend the experiments by varying the parameters. For example, increase the set of numbers that may appear in the patterns and the number of elements in each pattern. Do the learned networks contain more nodes or fewer? Is performance as good as before, or does it take longer to improve?

Hard

1. Write a parallel implementation of EPAM, and find out whether order effects are still present.

2. Gobet (1996) and Gobet and Simon (2000) suggest that chunks that recur often evolve into more complex data structures similar to schemata, which they called templates. Read their papers and discuss how the presence of such structures influences ordering effects.

3. Investigate other measures of the quality of the discrimination network. For example, information theory allows us to predict the optimum size of the network and sets of features for indexing any specified dataset. Are the networks learned by EPAM nearly optimum? If not, could better networks be learned with a better ordering of the training data?

APPENDIX: PSEUDOCODE FOR
DISCRIMINATION NETWORK

We provide a simplified version of the training routines for EPAM's discrimination network. Information is held in two separate data structures:

Node: *Node-image* stores a chunk for this node.
Node-links stores the set of links from this node.
Link: *Link-test* holds a test.
Link-node holds the node reached from this link.

Root-node holds the initial node for the discrimination network.
High-level functions, for calling EPAM:

```
Procedure   Recognize-pattern (target)
            Find-node (target, root-
                node)
Procedure   Learn (target)
  Let found-node be find-node (target,
    root-node)
  If node-image (found-node) ⊆ target
    Then familiarize (found-node,
      target)
    Else discriminate (found-node,
      target)
```

Searching:

```
Procedure   Find-node (target, current_
                node)
  While (unconsidered links in
    current_node)
    If target satisfies link-test
      Then find-node (target, link-
        node)
    If no links left and no link satisfied,
    Return current_node
```

Learning:

```
Procedure   Familiarize (found-node,
                target)
  Add to node-image (found-node) a
    feature from target
```

```
Procedure   Discriminate (found-node,
                target)
  Let new-feature be select-mismatch-
    feature (target, node-image
    (found-node))
  Create a new-node with an empty
    image.
  Create a new-link with a link-test =
    new-feature and link-node =
    new-node.
  Add new-link to node-links (found-
    node)
Procedure   Select-mismatch-feature
                (target, found-image)
  Let mismatch be difference of target
    and found-image
  Let new-node be Find-node (mismatch)
  If a new-node is found with nonempty
    node-image
    Then return node-image (new-node)
    Else learn (mismatch)
```

References

Anderson, J. R. (1987). Production systems, learning, and tutoring. In D. Klahr, P. Langley, & R. Neches (Eds.), *Production systems models of learning and development* (pp. 437–458). Cambridge, MA: MIT Press.

Anderson, J. R. (1990). *Cognitive psychology and its implications* (3d ed.). New York: Freeman.

de Groot, A. D., & Gobet, F. (1996). *Perception and memory in chess: Heuristics of the professional eye.* Assen, the Netherlands: Van Gorcum.

Feigenbaum, E. A. (1963). The simulation of verbal learning behavior. In E. A. Feigenbaum & J. Feldman (Eds.), *Computers and thought* (pp. 297–309). New York: McGraw-Hill.

Feigenbaum, E. A., & Simon, H. A. (1962). A theory of the serial position effect. *British Journal of Psychology, 53,* 307–320.

Feigenbaum, E. A., & Simon, H. A. (1984). EPAM-like models of recognition and learning. *Cognitive Science, 8,* 305–336.

Freudenthal, D., Pine, J. M., & Gobet, F. (2006). Modelling the development of children's use of optional infinitives in English and Dutch using MOSAIC. *Cognitive Science, 30,* 277–310.

Gagné, R. M. (1973). Learning and instructional sequence. *Review of Research in Education, 1,* 3–33.

Gobet, F. (1993). A computer model of chess memory. *Proceedings of Fifteenth Annual Meeting of the Cognitive Science Society* (pp. 463–468). Hillsdale, NJ: Erlbaum.

Gobet, F. (1996). Discrimination nets, production systems and semantic networks: Elements of a unified framework. *Proceedings of the Second International Conference on the Learning Sciences* (pp. 398–403). Evanston: Northwestern University.

Gobet, F. (2005). Chunking models of expertise: Implications for education. *Applied Cognitive Psychology, 19,* 183–204.

Gobet, F., de Voogt, A. J., & Retschitzki, J. (2004). *Moves in mind: The psychology of board games.* Hove, UK: Psychology Press.

Gobet, F., & Lane, P. C. R. (2004). CHREST tutorial: Simulations of human learning. In *Proceedings of the Twenty-sixth Annual Meeting of the Cognitive Science Society* (p. 3). Mahwah, NJ: Erlbaum.

Gobet, F., & Lane, P. C. R. (2005). The CHREST architecture of cognition: Listening to empirical data. In D. Davis (Ed.), *Visions of mind: Architectures for cognition and affect* (pp. 204–224). Hershey, PA: Information Science Publishing.

Gobet, F., Lane, P. C. R., Croker, S., Cheng, P. C. H., Jones, G., Oliver, I., & Pine, J. M. (2001). Chunking mechanisms in human learning. *Trends in Cognitive Science, 5,* 236–243.

Gobet, F., Richman, H., Staszewski, J. J., & Simon, H. A. (1997). Goals, representations, and strategies in a concept attainment task: The EPAM model. *Psychology of Learning and Motivation, 37,* 265–290.

Gobet, F., & Simon, H. A. (2000). Five seconds or sixty? Role of presentation time in expert memory. *Cognitive Science, 24,* 651–682.

Gobet, F., & Waters, A. J. (2003). The role of constraints in expert memory. *Journal of Experimental: Learning, Memory, and Cognition, 29,* 1082–1094.

Gobet, F., & Wood, D. J. (1999). Expertise, models of learning, and computer-based tutoring. *Computers and Education, 33,* 189–207.

Gregg, L. W., & Simon, H. A. (1967). An information-processing explanation of one-trial and incremental learning. *Journal of Verbal Learning and Verbal Behavior, 6,* 780–787.

Hunt, R. R. (1995). The subtlety of distinctiveness: What von Restorff really did. *Psychonomic Bulletin & Review, 2,* 105–112.

Jones, G., Gobet, F., & Pine, J. (2005). Modelling vocabulary acquisition: An explanation of the link between the phonological loop and long-term memory. *Journal of Artificial Intelligence and Simulation of Behavior, 1,* 509–522.

Lane, P. C. R., Cheng, P. C. H., & Gobet, F. (2000). CHREST+: Investigating how humans learn to solve problems using diagrams. *AISB Quarterly, 103,* 24–30.

Lane, P. C. R., & Gobet, F. (2005). Discovering predictive variables when evolving cognitive models. In S. Singh, M. Singh, C. Apte, & P. Perner (Eds.), *Proceedings of the Third International Conference on Advances in Pattern Recognition: Part I* (pp. 108–117). Berlin: Springer.

Lane, P. C. R., Sykes, A. K., & Gobet, F. (2003). Combining low-level perception with expectations in CHREST. In F. Schmalhofer, R. M. Young, & G. Katz (Eds.), *Proceedings of EuroCogSci 03: The European Cognitive Science Conference 2003* (pp. 205–210). Mahwah, NJ: Erlbaum.

Miller, G. A. (1956). The magical number seven, plus or minus two: Some limits on our capacity for processing information. *Psychological Review, 63,* 81–97.

Richman, H. B., Gobet, F., Staszewski, J. J., & Simon, H. A. (1996). Perceptual and memory processes in the acquisition of expert performance: The EPAM model. In K. A. Ericsson (Ed.), *The road to excellence: The acquisition of expert performance in the arts and sciences, sports, and games* (pp. 167–187). Mahwah, NJ.: Erlbaum.

Richman, H. B., & Simon, H. A. (1989). Context effects in letter perception: Comparison of two theories. *Psychological Review, 96,* 417–432.

Richman, H. B., Staszewski, J., & Simon, H. A. (1995). Simulation of expert memory with EPAM IV. *Psychological Review, 102,* 305–330.

Simon, H. A. (1981). *The sciences of the artificial.* Cambridge, MA: MIT Press.

Simon, H. A. (1989). *Models of thought: Vol. 2.* New Haven, CT: Yale University Press.

Simon, H. A., & Gilmartin, K. J. (1973). A simulation of memory for chess positions. *Cognitive Psychology, 5,* 29–46.

Winston, P. H. (1975). Learning structural descriptions from examples. In P. H. Winston (Ed.), *The psychology of computer vision* (pp. 157–209). New York: McGraw-Hill.

Winston, P. H. (1992). *Artificial intelligence* (3d ed.). Reading, MA: Addison-Wesley.

Chapter 9

Learning in Order: Steps of Acquiring the Concept of the Day/Night Cycle

Katharina Morik
Martin Mühlenbrock

Scientific discovery is a research endeavor to enhance our understanding of scientific activity through experiments with computational models. Early approaches developed algorithms of learning from observations. These carefully investigated a single, clearly separable phenomenon. More recently, scientific discovery broadened its scope to include complex theories. However, the discovery process remained restricted to a single learning step. We believe that scientific discovery encompasses sequences of learning steps, a perspective that is also true in life-long learning. Shifting from historical scientific breakthroughs to human scientific activity allows us to exploit psychological results for our study of long-term learning processes. This chapter investigates scientific activity as multistep theory evolution. A computational model of children's explanations of the day/night cycle is used for experiments that indicate possible (and impossible) sequences of learning steps as well as their complexity of transitions.

Scientific discovery has fascinated machine learning researchers from the very beginning. They hoped to explain how research produces substantially new insights and to automate discoveries or at least computationally support them. The process of discovery was considered an extremely difficult form of *learning from observations* (Carbonell, Michalski, & Mitchell, 1983). In this view, discovery aims to summarize data by quantitative or qualitative laws. The BACON system is a typical example of this approach (Langley, 1981). It covers a method for introducing hidden variables that shorten the comprehensive characterization of the observations. The COPER system can even determine the relevance of a variable when its value is not changing (Kokar, 1986). Most often, computational studies of empirical discovery rediscovered physical or chemical laws. BACON and ABACUS (Falkenhainer & Michalski, 1986), for instance, rediscovered among others the gas law and that of falling bodies. The STAHL system (Zytkow & Simon, 1986) found componential models for chemical re-

actions. The methods of automated empirical discovery and their applications worked on a single phenomenon as expressed by measurements. Relationships with other phenomena and the need to combine diverse findings to formulate a theory were not considered in these approaches, although the researchers mention that theory constrains the exploratory analysis of the data. The reason for the admitted neglect of theory may well be the complexity of representing several related concepts. Whereas one concept—or a hierarchy of concepts with subsumption as the only relation between the concepts—can easily be represented in propositional logic, a theory consists of relationships between those hierarchical concepts and requires some restricted first-order representation formalism. Now that efficient learning algorithms for restricted first-order logic have been developed, we can broaden our view of the discovery process and look at the evolution of scientific theories.

One early work describes scientific discovery as a process of *theory evolution* and illustrates its method of learning and theory revision with the discovery of the equator (Emde, Habel, & Rollinger, 1983). Data from the northern hemisphere of the earth led to the realization that temperatures in more northerly regions are lower than those of more southerly regions. Data from the southern hemisphere are summarized by the opposite rule. The contradiction can be explained when introducing a concept that we call the equator and enriching the rules by an additional premise, north or south of the equator. Belief revision methods for the discovery of chemical laws were also implemented in the STAHLp system (Rose & Langley, 1986). The idea of theory revision as a driving force of learning was further developed and psychologically motivated in Wrobel (1994a, 1994b). Well based on computational theory, Wrobel's tool, KRT, detects contradictions in a knowledge base, determines the rules that produced them, and finds a syntactically minimal revision of the rule base that repairs the knowledge base. Esposito, Malerba, Semeraro, Vosniadou, and Ioannides (1999) exploit Wrobel's ideas for a computational simulation of children learning the concept of force. The transition from a naive theory to a scientific one can be computationally modeled by revisions. Filippo Neri has presented a representation of a pupil's explanatory model of physical phenomena and a mechanism that detects differences between models (2000). To our knowledge, in all computational simulations of theory evolution, only one step is modeled. This one step leads from a naive theory to the target one. It may be implemented either by an incremental procedure that handles one input (observation) at a time or in batch mode, where all input data are used without intermediate results. In both cases, however, the discovery process is limited to the transition from one theory to another. Sequences of theories in the evolution of the current scientific one are not investigated. Thus, ordering effects are not analyzed in the context of theory development.

The one-step approach to theory evolution is in conflict with the history of science, as well as our own experience of the scientific process. We consider scientific discovery an outcome of life-long *scientific activity*. The subject of computational modeling is no longer restricted to a first and a final theory. Intermediate theories are no longer merely technical artifacts but also require interpretation. Only those intermediate theories are to be constructed computationally that can be observed in human scientific activity. How can we constrain the theory evolution such that only

sensible intermediate theories are constructed? How are these characterized; that is, what distinguishes a sensible intermediate theory from a senseless one? To answer these questions we must generalize the issue of theory evolution from a one-step to a multistep approach. We need to find principles that organize sequences of transitions in the most efficient way.

Orderings of intermediate theories shed light on the orderings of training input. If contradictions are a driving force of theory evolution, instructions should point out contradictions between the current theory and the observations. By solving the contradiction, the learner develops a new theory. However, revision is a complex process and may be too complex to handle. Therefore, instructions that demand a too complex revision do not have any effect on the learner's model. Thus, instructions should be ordered such that the revision does not exceed the learner's capacity but leads to an intermediate model, which can then be changed by the next instruction. From this point of view, possible orderings of intermediate theories determine adequate orderings of instructional inputs. The investigation of observed transitions of theories with respect to their cognitive complexity thus contributes to the explanation of the ordering effects of instructions.

In this chapter, we describe a case study of scientific activity as multistep theory evolution. The discovery process is modeled as long-term learning with revision as a driving force. The history of astronomy illustrates a theory evolution with intermediate knowledge states. The geocentric model with the earth as a stationary center and the planets and the sun moving around it was held from Plato's time until Copernicus refuted it. The contradicting observations of the retrograde motion of the stars and parallactic shifts of varying degree were explained in different ways. Copernicus and then Galileo moved to the heliocentric model, which posited the sun as the stationary center, with the earth moving around it. This conceptual change was possible because of the development of better telescopes, as well as changes in religious belief. A computational model of the history of astronomy is difficult because revisions of Christian beliefs are involved. For a case study that allows us to investigate scientific activity as a multistep theory evolution, we look for well-documented material that focuses on astronomical explanations. If we take seriously the common saying of "the child as a scientist," we indeed find such material. Thus, we have computationally modeled empirical data about various explanations of the day/night cycle given by children of different ages (Morik, 1996). The psychological material describes a learning period of 5 years. It is taken from Vosniadou and Brewer (1992, 1994) and does not investigate individual development but rather developmental states and their sequence. Sixty children (20 from the first, third, and fifth grades, with mean ages of 6.9, 9.9, and 11.0 years) attending an elementary school in Urbana, Illinois, were investigated. The materials consisted of a 48-item questionnaire. The children explained their understanding of the day/night cycle. The interviews are snapshots of an ongoing learning process. For the scientific investigation of life-long learning, the snapshots form landmarks.

To explore the paths between the landmarks, we have performed a careful computer simulation and built computational models of the observed knowledge states. This includes the formal modeling of spatio-temporal concepts and implementation of the concepts of problem solving (i.e., forming on demand an explanation of the observations). The formal model makes explicit an understanding of the empirical data (the children's explanations). It raises questions and points to missing data or knowledge about what the children actually had in mind. The computational model must reproduce the observations of the empirical study; that is, it has to meet the landmarks. Then, learning operators in the sense of Siegler (1991) were formalized. Because we used the MOBAL system for our simulation (Morik, Wrobel, Kietz, & Emde, 1993), we could readily apply a set of learning and knowledge revision tools. Thus, systematic experiments could be undertaken that are impossible to carry out with human subjects. Different inputs into the simulated theory were applied in different instructional orders. Because the topic of our investigation is a multistep theory evolution, all of the transitions between the formally modeled knowledge states have been simulated. It is interesting to characterize those transitions that correspond to psychologically assumed actual transitions. The questions guiding our experiments are:

• What is the nature of intermediate explanations? Are they motivated by the structure of the domain, by the complexity of the transition from the naive explanation to the scientific one, or by the cognitive capabilities that must be acquired before the scientific explanation can be learned?
• Can we give a formal account of the difficulties of different explanations of the day/night cycle?

Is there a formal way to characterize the reasons the naive explanations are simpler than the scientific ones?
• What distinguishes transition sequences that were observed empirically from other transitions that seem not to happen in children's thinking? Are there formal distinctions that clearly separate simulated transitions that correspond to children's development from those that do not correspond to children's development?

In this chapter, we first report on the multistep evolution of a theory that explains the day/night cycle. Psychological studies on children's development of explanations for this phenomenon are related to the history of science. Second, we present our computational models for different explanations of the day/night cycle and their validation. Third, we describe our experiments. We conclude by showing how our experiments help to answer the preceding questions, which, in turn, explain why some instruction orderings successfully lead to the target theory, whereas others fail.

EXPLAINING ASTRONOMICAL PHENOMENA: THE DAY/NIGHT CYCLE

The earth is a huge sphere in space. Is it really? How do you know? Well, the concept of the earth as a huge sphere in space is usually acquired sometime during childhood. But it is not the very first conception of the earth that is acquired at a young age. Before children learn the scientifically accepted concepts of the earth, the sun, and the moon, they hold alternative concepts of the celestial bodies, for example, that the earth is flat and that it is supported by an infinite ground (Nussbaum, 1979; Mali & Howe, 1979; Sneider & Pulos, 1983; Vosniadou & Brewer, 1992). And it seems plausible to assume that these alternative notions heavily influence further learning in astronomy (Vosniadou, 1991; Nussbaum, 1985). Empirical research on children's understanding of astronomical phenomena has shown a considerable resemblance between the development of their alternative conceptions and the development of astronomical theories in the history of science.

In the second century of the Christian calendar, the Egyptian mathematician Ptolemy developed a theory that governed thinking in astronomy for more than a millennium. Ptolemy's theory corresponds to

Plato's astronomical theory and Aristotle's physical principles by posting the earth as the center of the universe, with the moon, the sun, and the other planets revolving around it. By postulating such orbits, Ptolemy was able to explain a large number of observations in connection with the celestial bodies. Except for minor revisions, Ptolemy's view remained unchallenged until the year 1543, when Copernicus's *De Revolutionibus Orbium Coelestium* was published. According to Copernicus, the sun constitutes the center of the universe, and the earth and the other planets revolve around it, whereas the moon revolves around the earth. However, it was more than a hundred years before Copernicus's view, extended by Galileo, was generally accepted.

The shift from the geocentric view of Ptolomy to the heliocentric view of Copernicus has also been found in children's individual explanations of the day/night cycle. According to Nussbaum (1985), the shift from a geocentric to a heliocentric view in children is related to a shift of perspective from an *absolute* organization of space toward a *relative* organization of space. This means that the scientific explanation for the alternation of day and night can be acquired only if one interprets the spatial concept *down* as related to the center of the earth and not in relation to some flat, infinite ground. It has been shown that children's initial conceptions of the earth and other celestial bodies remain rather stable toward new and contradictory information. In a study subsequent to a course in earth science and astronomy (Sadler, 1987), the rate of misconceptions was as high as in the control group without further teaching (though the rate of *scientific* expressions such as *orbit* or *tilt* was considerably higher). In contrast to the theory-building in the history of astronomy, many more illustrative observations are available to children, and there further exists a generally accepted theory of the celestial bodies that is to be assimilated with the individually differing views.

In recent years, children's explanations of the day/night cycle have been investigated in a number of empirical studies (Klein, 1982; Viglietta, 1986; Sadler, 1987; Baxter, 1989). Children's explanations ranged, for instance, from "The sun goes to another country or another planet," "The sun goes into the ground," "The sun goes to the other side of the earth," "The sun goes out" (becomes extinct), and "The moon covers the sun" to the correct explanation, "The earth rotates around its axis." In a comprehensive psychological study (Vosniadou & Brewer, 1994), 16 different explanations for the alternation of day and night have been found (see Table 9.1).

For instance, one of the explanations for the alteration between day and night is that the sun is occluded by clouds, which is the first explanation in Table 9.1. A child that used this explanantion in the psychological study was Tamara, a fifth-grade student (Vosniadou & Brewer, 1994, p. 150):

INVESTIGATOR: Now can you make it so it is day for that person?

CHILD: He's outside the earth.

I: Where should he be?

C: In here. (see Figure 9.1)

I: Ok now, make it daytime for him.

C: The sun is out here, but it looks like it's in the earth, when it shines . . .

I: Ok. What happens at night?

C: The clouds cover it up.

I: Tell me once more how it happens.

C: 'Cause at 12 o'clock it's dark.

Another explanation is that the sun and the moon move down to the other side of the earth (explanation C in Table 9.1). These are the answers given by Timothy, a first-grader, to the question "Now make it so that it is day for that person. Good! Now make it so that it is night for that person" (Vosniadou & Brewer, 1994, p. 150):

I: Tell me once more how it happens.

C: When the moon comes up and the sun goes down. (see Figure 9.2)

I: Where was the moon before?

C: Under the earth.

I: What time was it when it goes under the earth?

C: Day.

Vosniadou and Brewer (1994) grouped the models into three categories (see also Table 9.1):

- Initial models are consistent with observations and cultural information that derive from everyday experience.
- Synthetic models represent attempts to reconcile the scientific explanation of the day/night cycle with aspects of the initial model.

TABLE 9.1. Children's explanations for the day/night cycle according to Vosniadou & Brewer (1994)

	Explanations	Status	Grade 1	Grade 3	Grade 5	Total	
A.	The sun is occluded by clouds or darkness.	initial	2	1	1	4	7%
B.	The sun and the moon move up/down on the ground.	initial	7	0	0	7	12%
C.	The sun and the moon move to the other side of the earth.	initial	2	0	0	2	3%
D.	Sun and moon move up/down unspecified as to earth side.	initial	3	0	0	3	5%
E.	The sun moves out in space.	initial	1	1	0	2	3%
F.	The sun and the moon revolve around the earth every day.	synthetic	0	1	0	1	2%
G.	The earth and the moon revolve around the sun every day.	synthetic	0	1	0	1	2%
H.	The earth rotates up/down; the sun and moon are fixed at opposite sides.	synthetic	1	3	7	11	18%
I.	The earth rotates up/down; the sun is fixed but the moon moves.	synthetic	0	1	3	4	7%
J.	The earth rotates around its axis; the sun and the moon are fixed at opposite sides.	synthetic	0	1	1	2	3%
K.	The earth turns around its axis; the sun is fixed but the moon moves.	scientific	0	1	0	1	2%
L.	The earth turns in an unspecified direction; the sun is fixed but the moon may or may not move.		1	1	1	3	5%
M.	Mixed: The earth rotates and the sun moves up/down.		1	0	4	5	8%
N.	Mixed: The earth rotates and revolves.		1	2	2	5	8%
O.	Mixed general.		0	5	1	6	10%
P.	Undetermined.		1	2	0	3	5%
Total			20	20	20	60	100%

FIGURE 9.1. Drawing of a child (Tamara) for explanation A (The sun is occluded by clouds or darkness.) Reprinted with permission of the Cognitive Science Society.

• The scientific model is consistent with the currently accepted scientific view.

It appears that most of the younger children form initial mental models of the day/night cycle that are based on their everyday experience. The presence of synthetic models shows that the process of acquiring the scientific explanation is a slow and gradual one.

THE COMPUTATIONAL MODEL OF EXPLANATIONS FOR THE DAY/NIGHT CYCLE

The 16 explanations for the day/night cycle presented in Vosniadou and Brewer (1994) differ in terms of comprehensiveness. For instance, the explanation

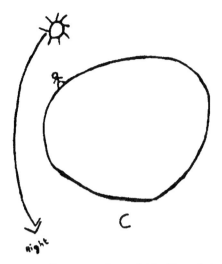

FIGURE 9.2. Drawing of a child (Timothy) for explanation C (The sun and the moon move to the other side of the earth.) Reprinted with permission of Cognitive Science Society.

"The sun goes to the other side of the earth" is more detailed with respect to the objects and spatial relations than the explanation "The sun moves somehow" or "I don't know." Thus, not all of the 16 explanations are suited for a deep modeling of the underlying concepts. In fact, 9 of them are sufficiently detailed and have been represented as computational models (cf. Mühlenbrock, 1994a, 1994b). These computational models are listed in Table 9.2.

Of the 16 explanations, 5 (explanations L to P) were considered mixed or undetermined. These explanations cannot be modeled because they provide insufficient information. Interestingly, in the experiments with the computational models that are described later, mixed explanations have also been generated. Explanation D is another that is partially determined, because the children did not specify whether the sun goes down to the ground or to the other side of the earth. Because both of these explanations are already covered by explanations B and C, explanation D has not been modeled.

Among the remaining 10 explanations there are pairs of categories that differ only concerning the movement of the moon. These are, for instance, explanations J and K. Because the stars do not play a role in the children's explanantions, the moon plays a role in only some of their explanantions, and the way the moon appears and disappears is not different from the way the sun appears and disappears, only the sun is used for discrimination in the models. This means that explanantions H and I, as well as J and K, are covered by models 8 and 9, respectively.

Finally, explanation B is differentiated into two models (i.e., models 2 and 3) because they are based on two different principles. The first one is that an object disappears when it is submerged into something else such as a stone dug into sand, whereas in the second explanation the disappearance is based on the fact that one object is hidden behind another one, such as a ball that rolls behind a wall. This leaves a total of nine different models (Table 9.2). Models 1 to 4 have been classified initial, models 5 to 8 synthetic, and model 9 represents the scientific explanation for the day/night cycle.

For the modeling, the obvious objects in this domain are the sun, the earth (ground), and clouds. Less obvious but nonetheless included in the explanations is a designated person (me), who observes the events

TABLE 9.2. Computational models of the children's explanations as given in Table 9.1

Models	Status	Explanations
1. Clouds cover the sun	initial	A
2. The sun goes down into the ground	initial	B1
3. The sun moves behind hills	initial	B2
4. The sun goes far away	initial	E
5. The sun moves to the other side of the earth	synthetic	C
6. The sun revolves around the earth	synthetic	F
7. The earth revolves around the sun	synthetic	G
8. The earth turns up and down	synthetic	H, I
9. The earth rotates	scientifc	J, K

taking place. It is an important part of the model that the observer be located within it. The point of view always refers to the observer's location. For instance, "the sun is far away" actually means "the sun is far away from me." The objects have been represented as constants as described above, namely the sun, the earth, clouds, and the observer. Predicates are used to represent the relevant objects' features, such as observing, shining, opaque, and solid, or relations between objects, such as bigger. In addition, the explanations implicitly contain separate points (intervals) in time where things sometimes change and are sometimes constant.

In the day/night cycle, the relevant temporal distinctions are between two states (state0 and state1) and two events (event0 and event1), which are characterized as day and night or sunset and sunrise, respectively, in a valid derivation (explanation) of the day/night cycle. A temporal structure is imposed on these temporal objects by means of predicates such as next_state, state_seq, and cycle (cf. Figure 9.3). The spatial structure is expressed in terms such as *behind*, *other side*, and *around*. Its representation is based on the general predicates in and complementary, which describe relationships between objects and the areas (directions) relevant to them. A sample spatial relation is shown in Figure 9.4, which can be represented as in (object1,area1,object2,state) and particularly in(sun,up,earth,state0) in the day/night cycle domain.

These predicates, together with the constants, form the basic layer of the conceptual structure. More complex relations are formed by means of rules and integrity constraints. Rules express propositions that are true for all objects of a certain type. Hence, variables

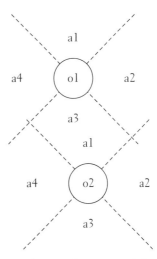

FIGURE 9.4. The spatial structure of the domain.

(written in capital letters) occur in rules. When a rule is applied, the variables are unified with particular objects (constants). For instance, the following rule

```
in(O1,A1,O2,S1) & in(O1,A2,O2,S2) &
state_seq(S1,E,S2) & ne(A1,A2) & not
(stationary(O1,E)) → moves(O1,O2,E)
```

states that, if an object (O1) is in another area (A2) as before (A1) after an event (E) and this object is not stationary, then this object moves in the mentioned event. Depending on what is considered stationary, the variable O1 can be unified with a constant—the sun, clouds, or earth, for instance.

Integrity constraints are used to prevent cycles and check the consistency of the rule base. The integrity constraint

```
not(in(O1,A,O2,S1)) & in(O1,A,O2,S2) &
state_seq(S1,E,S2) & stationary(O1,E)
& stationary(O2,E) ↝
```

says that, if an object (O1) is in a certain area (A) of another object (O2) at state S1 and it has not been there before an event (E) and both objects are stationary, then the consistency of the explanation is violated. A complete list of all of the rules and constraints can be found in Morik and Mühlenbrock (1999).

In the next layer are concepts for certain kinds of movements (moves, revolves, rotates) and of (dis)appearance (covers, uncovers, hides,

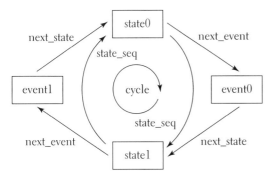

FIGURE 9.3. The temporal structure of the domain.

unhides). Finally, these relate to day and night and the `day_night_cycle`. Using these concepts, the nine different models for the day/night cycle have been represented by formulating appropriate facts for each of them so that the system derives an explanation according to the specific models (see Appendix A of this chapter for the specific facts of the nine models).

We validated the computational model by asking the same questions as were asked of the children and checked the system's answers. The central question ("Where is the sun at night?") is queried by

```
in(sun,X,Y,Z) & night(me,Z)
```

and results in different answers according to the explanation of the day/night cycle (cf. Table 9.3): Model 1 (Clouds cover the sun) answers that the sun is above the clouds, the earth, and "me" (the observer). Here, X is unified with X, Z is unified with `state1`, and three facts are stated, unifying Y with `cloud`, `earth`, and me, respectively. In model 3 (The sun goes behind hills) the sun is also above the earth, but it is in the same direction (`right`) with regard to the hills as the hills are to me; thus the hills are between me and the sun. Model 4 (The sun goes far away) says that the sun is above the earth and me and beyond the visual range. In all the other models, including the scientific explanation, the sun is below the earth and below the observer (i.e., on the other side of the earth).

In the formal models, an explanation for the day/night cycle is represented as a derivation tree for the predicate `day_night_cycle`. A sample derivation is shown in Figure 9.5, which represents the scientific explanation for the day/night cycle (model 9 in Table 9.2) It shows how many facts and rules make up model 9. Thus, it is plausible that this is hard to learn. The fact

```
day_night_cycle(me,state0,event0,
state1,event1)
```

is inferred from the rotational movement of the earth

```
rotates_acw(earth,sun,event0)
```

and of the observer

```
rotates_acw(me,sun,event0)
```

and from the coverage of the sun by the earth

```
covers(earth,sun,me,event0),
```

which leads to the disappearance of the sun

```
disappears(sun,me,event0).
```

It is worth noting that, although the observer ("me") occurs in most of these facts, the explanation of the day/night cycle is not bound to just this constant. In fact, another observer (e.g., `someone_else`, who stays on the other side of the earth) may be added to the model by additional facts stating the relevant temporal and local relations. Then model 9 will

TABLE 9.3. Querying the models "Where is the sun at night?", i.e., ?- in(sun, X, Y, Z) & night(me, Z)

Models	Answers	English Translation
1	in(sun,up,cloud,state1) in(sun,up,earth,state1) in(sun,up,me,state1)	"The sun is up but behind clouds."
3	in(sun,right,hill,state1) in(sun,right,me,state1) in(sun,up,earth,state1)	"The sun is up but behind hills."
4	in(sun,up,earth,state1) in(sun,up,me,state1) in(sun,up,visual_range,state1)	"The sun is up but too far away."
2, 5, 6, 7, 8, 9	in(sun,down,earth,state1) in(sun,down,me,state1)	"The sun is below the earth and below me."

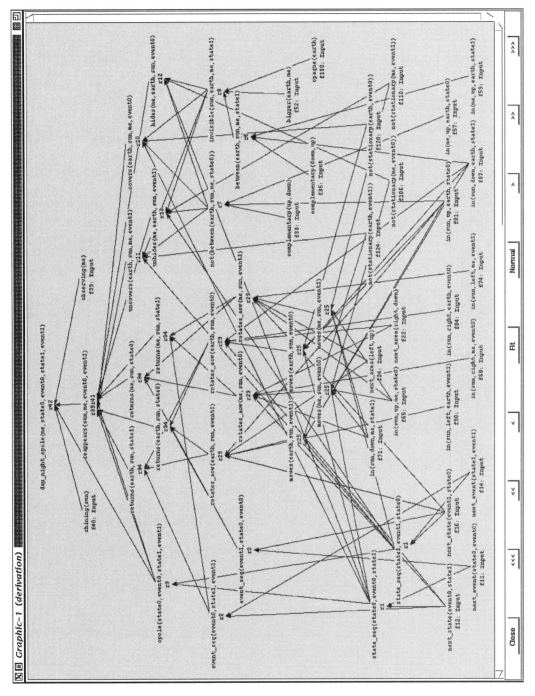

FIGURE 9.5. Derivation of the day/night cycle in the scientific model.

derive that it is day for the second observer when it is night for the first one and vice versa:

```
night(me,state1), day(me,state0)
day(someone_else,state1), night(someone_
else,state0)
```

This holds only for the synthetic models and the scientific model because in the initial models it will lead to contradictions with the prevailing definition of the earth.

As can be easily seen in Figure 9.5, an explanation is quite a complex structure. It relates general knowledge about a temporal scheme (the derivation of `cycle` in the leftmost part of the graphic), the meaning of spatial relations (the derivation of `covers`, `uncovers` in the rightmost part of the diagram), and movements (in the middle of the diagram). The specific knowledge about the sun, the earth, and the observer makes rule application possible. For instance, the movement `moves(earth, sun, event1)` is possible only because the earth is assumed not to be stationary. The more specific characterization of the movement ascribes areas to the involved objects (particularly a `down` area with regard to the earth). It takes a lot of knowledge and inferencing to conclude `between(earth, sun, me, state1)`! Further inference is necessary to link this with the reappearance of the sun in the morning. The short answers of the system are thus based on a complex explanation.

EXPERIMENTS IN MULTISTEP LEARNING

We performed experiments with sequences of transitions from one explanation to another. Using the knowledge revision component, we found, in all of the nonscientific explanations, contradictions of the scientific explanation. Those statements of the scientific explanation that are in conflict with the respective other explanation are candidate instructions. Hence, the ordering effects of the instruction sequences refer to this set. We experimented with all subsets of the candidate instructions, that is, the corrections of a teacher. Inputting instructions to an explanation leads to a new state of knowledge because of the revisions. Now, two cases can be distinguished. First, the revised knowledge is no longer capable of predicting that there will be a sunrise (bringing daylight) followed by a sunset and moonlight. In this case, the child will stick

to the unrevised knowledge and simply ignore the teacher's input. Second, the revised knowledge is a new explanation for the day/night cycle. We tested every explanation together with its corresponding instructions. Those that led from one model to another are the following:

```
solid(earth)
not(opaque(cloud))
in(sun,down, earth, state1)
in(sun, left, earth, event0)
in(sun, right, earth, event1)
in(earth, down, sun, state1)
not(stationary(earth, event0))
not(stationary(earth, event1))
stationary(sun,event0)
```

We call these statements *true instructions*. We found that only some of the possible transitions are possible by presenting true instructions. For instance, to move from one naive explanation to another naive explanation, a wrong statement must be input. Thus, in Figure 9.6, there are no transitions between the naive explanations.

The addition of scientific information about the day/night cycle to the initial and synthetic models leads to contradictions. The system places contradictions in an agenda for revision purposes. Figure 9.7 lists contradictions between the scientific model and model 1 (`Clouds cover the sun`). There are also violations of integrity constraints. Some scientific facts are critical for the destruction of a wrong explanation. These are exactly the ones to be given, if the instruc-

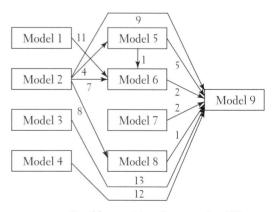

FIGURE 9.6. Possible transitions between the different models and their costs.

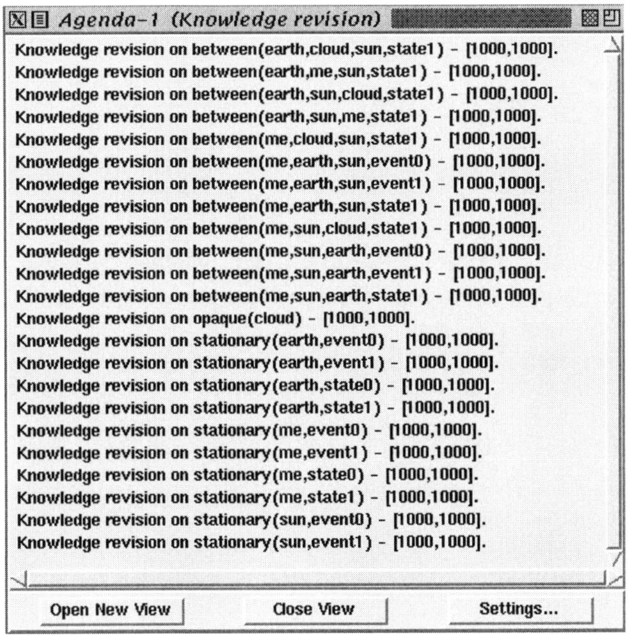

```
┌──────────────────────────────────────────────────────────────┐
│ ⊠ ▤  Agenda-1  (Knowledge revision) ▨▨▨▨▨▨▨▨▨▨  ▨ 已       │
├──────────────────────────────────────────────────────────────┤
│ Knowledge revision on between(earth,cloud,sun,state1) – [1000,1000].  │
│ Knowledge revision on between(earth,me,sun,state1) – [1000,1000].     │
│ Knowledge revision on between(earth,sun,cloud,state1) – [1000,1000].  │
│ Knowledge revision on between(earth,sun,me,state1) – [1000,1000].     │
│ Knowledge revision on between(me,cloud,sun,state1) – [1000,1000].     │
│ Knowledge revision on between(me,earth,sun,event0) – [1000,1000].     │
│ Knowledge revision on between(me,earth,sun,event1) – [1000,1000].     │
│ Knowledge revision on between(me,earth,sun,state1) – [1000,1000].     │
│ Knowledge revision on between(me,sun,cloud,state1) – [1000,1000].     │
│ Knowledge revision on between(me,sun,earth,event0) – [1000,1000].     │
│ Knowledge revision on between(me,sun,earth,event1) – [1000,1000].     │
│ Knowledge revision on between(me,sun,earth,state1) – [1000,1000].     │
│ Knowledge revision on opaque(cloud) – [1000,1000].                   │
│ Knowledge revision on stationary(earth,event0) – [1000,1000].        │
│ Knowledge revision on stationary(earth,event1) – [1000,1000].        │
│ Knowledge revision on stationary(earth,state0) – [1000,1000].        │
│ Knowledge revision on stationary(earth,state1) – [1000,1000].        │
│ Knowledge revision on stationary(me,event0) – [1000,1000].           │
│ Knowledge revision on stationary(me,event1) – [1000,1000].           │
│ Knowledge revision on stationary(me,state0) – [1000,1000].           │
│ Knowledge revision on stationary(me,state1) – [1000,1000].           │
│ Knowledge revision on stationary(sun,event0) – [1000,1000].          │
│ Knowledge revision on stationary(sun,event1) – [1000,1000].          │
├──────────────────────────────────────────────────────────────┤
│   Open New View    │    Close View    │    Settings...    │
└──────────────────────────────────────────────────────────────┘
```

FIGURE 9.7. Contradictions between Model 1 and Model 9.

tion aims at an efficient sequence of model transitions. In model 1, for instance, the addition of not(opaque(cloud)) brings about the complete retraction of the derivation of day_night_cycle. Thus, depending on the current model, the next best instruction can be determined.

When adding further scientific facts, the system asks for revisions and deletions of facts. This process eventually leads to the creation of the scientific explanation for the day/night cycle. Intermediately, the system may derive an explanation according to model 6, depending on the sequence of input facts (cf. Table 9.4). So far, we know which subsets of the true instructions are responsible for model transitions. We see an ordering of subsets of instructions, in which the first subset leads from a naive model (model 1) to an intermediate model (model 6), and the second subset leads from the intermediate model to the scientific

TABLE 9.4. Possible transitions between models 1, 6 and 9 and impossible transition between models 1 and 5

Transitions[a]	Instructions	Operations[b]
$1 \rightarrow 6$	not(opaque(cloud))	–
	in(sun,down,earth,state1)	4 ∅ 1⟳
	in(sun,left,earth,event0)	2 ∅ 1⟳
	in(sun,right,earth,event1)	2 ∅ 1⟳
$6 \rightarrow 9$	stationary(sun,event0)	–
	not(stationary(earth,event0))	1∅
	not(stationary(earth,event1))	1∅
$1 \not\rightarrow 5$	in(sun,left,earth,event0)	!!
	in(sun,left,earth,event1)	!!

[a] transitions: possible ($\rightarrow$) and impossible ($\not\rightarrow$)

[b] operations: deletion (∅) and revision (⟳): unscientific facts (!!) and destructive facts (–)

one (model 9). Similarly, the instruction subsets for all other instructions are determined. This clearly determines sets of instructions that effectively change the current explanation and lead to a new model.

Having determined effective subsets of instructions for each model, we ask about efficient instruction sets. The formal representation allows us to measure the complexity of the transitions. For each of the possible transitions we count the total number of revisions necessary and calculate the number per input. We found that the number of revisions per input is more or less the same. A more interesting point is to compare the complexity of the direct transition from a naive explanation to the scientific one with the complexity of the transition from a naive explanation to an intermediate one or from an intermediate one to the scientific one (see Table 9.5 for the complexity of the direct and indirect transition from explanation 1 to the scientific explanation). Is there a threshold n such that transitions from initial models to intermediate ones require up to n revisions, but direct transition from intermediate models to the scientific one require more than n revisions? The overall number of revisions that must be performed to reach an intermediate explanation ranged between 4 and 11. The number of revisions for moving from an intermediate to the scientific explanation ranged between 1 and 5. The number of revisions when moving from an initial to the

scientific explanation ranged between 9 and 13. If we assume $n = 8$, it is true (for all but one transition) that no transition via intermediate models demands more than n revisions, but direct transitions from any initial model to the scientific one demands more than n transitions. The exception to the rule is the transition from model 1 to intermediate model 6, which demands 11 revisions. However, there is no set of true instructions that would lead from model 1 to model 9.

The question is now whether there is any individual child that moved from explanation 1 (Clouds hide the sun at night) to explanation 6 (The sun revolves around the earth). Here, empirical studies of individual developments are needed. We hypothesize that transitions of more than n revisions will not be observed. Multistep learning can be viewed as easing the task of discovering a complex model by dividing it into a sequence of less complex tasks. Our computational model cannot prove that the discovery of a complex explanation cannot be learned in one step by children or scientists. What our computational model states is that

- not all transitions between explanations are possible
- transitions between explanatory models have different degrees of difficulty

CONCLUSIONS

We have developed a computational model of children's explanations of the day/night cycle. The model describes each of the explanation types such that the system gives the same answers as did the children (assuming a clear relationship between the natural language answers and those in formal language). This means that the computational model in fact expresses the empirical data (i.e., the snapshots of the children's ongoing learning process, which have been found in the interviews, are met by the computational model). The computational model, in fact, reproduces the observations of the empirical study. However, this does not mean that the children make the same logical inferences as the computational system. Moreover, the computer—or more specifically, the inference system—is employed as a representational formalism for explicitly describing the different explanations. In contrast to the natural-language representation of the explanations given by the psychological study, the

TABLE 9.5. Costs of transitions between models

Transitions	$1 \to 6$	$6 \to 9$	$1 \to 9$
starting facts	295	244	295
input facts	4	3	7
treatments[a]	11	2	13
final facts	244	250	250
equal facts	215	233	210
deleted facts[b]	80	11	85
new facts[c]	29	17	40
effect[d]	2.75	0.67	1.86
deletion[e]	20	3.67	12.14
renewal[f]	7.25	5.67	5.71

[a] deletions ($\emptyset$) and revisions ($\circlearrowleft$)

[b] difference starting facts − equal facts

[c] difference final facts − equal facts

[d] difference treatments / input facts

[e] quotient deleted facts / input facts

[f] quotient new facts / input facts

computer-based representation is much more practical as it makes explicit the consequences of the explanations, as well as the contradictions between the explanations that are otherwise hidden.

Transitions from one explanation to another have been modeled. The process of transition from one theory to another could be modeled using the knowledge revision operator. Interestingly, revision did not delete all of the facts from a previous explanation. Thus, some of the facts from former explanations remained in the current one. Practically, this made necessary a program that determines the type of the current explanation. The results of our experiments suggest that statements from former explanations often remain in the learner's current knowledge state. The computational model precisely distinguishes between facts that are to be deleted in the course of knowledge revision and those that remain untouched.

Precisely defined, sensible (intermediate) theories are knowledge states that are capable of deriving a sensible explanation of a phenomenon. For the day/night cycle, this means that the fact

```
day_night_cycle(me,state0,event0,
state1,event1)
```

must be derivable. There were some contradiction resolutions that did not lead to a set of beliefs that were allowed to derive this fact. Those sets of beliefs are not considered models of the day/night cycle. For instance, giving the instructions

```
not(stationary(earth, event0))
not stationary(earth, event1))
stationary(sun, event0)
```

would leave someone who believed model 1 in the desperate state of no longer being able to explain the day/night cycle and would not lead to changing to another model.

In contrast to most other computational investigations of conceptual change, we have investigated *sequences of transitions* in order to determine adequate orderings of instructions. Viewing the explanation types of children as landmarks, the experiments explore paths between landmarks. The transitions were triggered by true input facts that contradict the current explanation of the day/night cycle. True input facts are facts from the scientifically correct model (model 9). However, we found that not all true input facts from the correct model lead to revisions of the initial and synthetic models; rather, some leave the learner in a desperate state. Identifying the set of true input facts that have an effect on the initial and synthetic models has been one of the major tasks of this approach. Using true input facts, not all transitions are possible. In other words, some transitions are possible only by using false facts. In particular, the transition from one naive explanation to another requires false assumptions. It is also interesting that, when using true facts, no transition from any of the naive explanations leads to the explanation that the earth revolves around the sun (model 7). We suspect the child who gave this explanation was parrotting a true statement without having understood it (i.e., without embedding it into its conceptual structure).

Characterizing the possible paths to the landmark of current scientific knowledge, we used complexity measures of the revision process. We found that the one-step transition from a naive to the scientific explanation is more complex than the step from a naive to an intermediate explanation and the step from an intermediate explanation to the scientific one. We measured the difficulty of the transition from one explanation to another in terms of the number of necessary revisions. Does this correspond to a threshold of complexity that can be observed in human thinking? This question has to be answered by further empirical investigations. What computer science offers is a precise notion of complexity, which we tailored to multistep learning here.

Our case study suggests answers to the questions that we asked at the beginning:

- An intermediate explanation explains the phenomenon. However, it leads to a contradiction when confronted with some true facts.
- Intermediate explanations divide the long path from a naive theory to a correct theory into tractable pieces. The complexity of the transition from a naive to an intermediate explanation is less than that of the transition from a naive explanation to an advanced theory.
- The difficulty of theory evolution can be measured by the number of facts and rules that are handled by knowledge revision.
- Transition sequences are constrained by two aspects: the complexity of each step (efficiency) and the derivability of an explanation by the resulting knowledge state (effectiveness).

Our case study shows how computer science can help to analyze multistep learning. Further empirical research is needed to generalize and verify the tentative answers.

We may now turn our findings into explanations of the ordering effects of instruction sequences. Instructions that do not contradict the current explanation have no effect at all. Instructions that contradict the current model such that their resolution does not lead to a new model almost stop the learning process because the learner then has no explanation at all and does not know what to revise (the desperate case). Instructions that contradict the current model such that their resolution leads to a new model effectively enhance learning. If we look again at Figure 9.6, we see that, depending on the ordering of instructions, model 2 can become model 5 or model 6. The easiest learning path with respect to the costs of transitions is from model 2 to model 5, then to model 6, and finally to model 9 (seven revisions), where the other possible transitions from model 2 to the scientific one require nine revisions. In this way, our computational simulation with all subsets of the true instructions not only states ordering effects formally but also explains them.

For education, our experiments determine the optimal path from initial models 1 and 2 to the scientific model, together with their instructions with regard to order. Because such a clear rule of how to order instructions requires a formal modeling of the overall domain with all the explanatory models, it is not a practical approach for planning instruction orders. However, teachers could well take our findings into account when designing a sequence of propositions by which to guide pupils to current knowledge. By understanding the effectiveness and efficiency issues underlying ordering effect, teachers could visualize a structure analogous to that of Figure 9.6 and estimate the costs.

PROJECTS AND OPEN PROBLEMS

1. Examine Table 9.2 and Figure 9.6, and comment on how to teach a mixed classroom of students given that students may hold different models.

2. Describe another domain where model progression like the day/night cycle may occur and may influence learning.

3. Examine a group of children (or adults!) and summarize what models they hold about the day/night cycle.

4. Create a model of how people understand thermostats after surveying people about how they work, and after making sure you know how they work.

APPENDIX: MODELS AND SPECIFIC FACTS

```
infinite (earth, down)
infinite (earth, left)
infinite (earth, right)

covers (cloud, sun, me, event0)
hides (sun, cloud, me, event0)
moves (cloud, sun, event0)
uncovers (cloud, sun, me, event1)
unhides (sun, cloud, me, event1)
moves (cloud, sun, event1)
```

FIGURE 9.8. Model 1. Clouds cover the sun (initial).

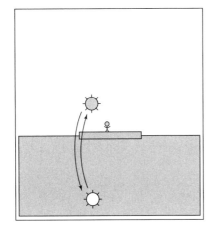

```
infinite (earth, down)
infinite (earth, left)
infinite (earth, right)

hides (sun, earth, me, event0)
revolves_acw (sun, earth, event0)
unhides (sun, earth, me, event1)
revolves_cw (sun, earth, event1)
```

FIGURE 9.9. Model 2. The sun goes down into the ground (initial).

```
infinite (earth, down)
infinite (earth, left)
infinite (earth, right)

hides (sun, hill, me, event0)
revolves_cw (sun, hill, event0)
unhides (sun, hill, me, event1)
revolves_acw (sun, hill, event1)
```

FIGURE 9.10. Model 3. The sun moves behind the hills (initial).

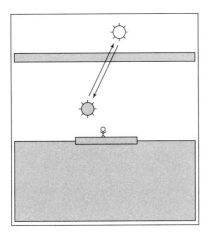

```
infinite (earth, down)
infinite (earth, left)
infinite (earth, right)

hides (sun, visual_range, me, event0)
moves (sun, visual_range, event0)
unhides (sun, visual_range, me, event1)
moves (sun, visual_range, event1)
```

FIGURE 9.11. Model 4. The sun goes far away (initial).

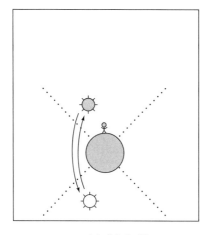

```
hides (sun, earth, me, event0)
revolves_acw (sun, earth, event0)
unhides (sun, earth, me, event1)
revolves_cw (sun, earth, event1)
```

FIGURE 9.12. Model 5. The sun moves to the other side of the earth (synthetic).

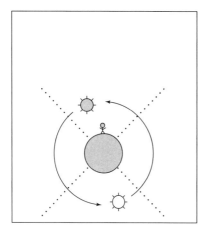

```
hides (sun, earth, me, event0)
revolves_acw (sun, earth, event0)
unhides (sun, earth, me, event1)
revolves_acw (sun, earth, event1)
```

FIGURE 9.13. Model 6. The sun revolves around the earth (synthetic).

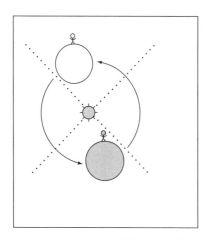

```
covers (earth, sun, me, event0)
hides (me, earth, sun, event0)
revolves_acw (earth, sun, event0)
rotates_cw (earth, sun, event0)
revolves_cw (me, sun, event, event0)
rotates _acw (me, sun, event0)
uncovers (earth, sun, me, event1)
unhides (me, earth, sun, event1)
revolves_acw (earth, sun, event1)
rotates_cw (earth, sun, event1)
revolves_acw (me, sun, event1)
rotates_cw (me, sun, event1)
```

FIGURE 9.14. Model 7. The earth revolves around the sun (synthetic).

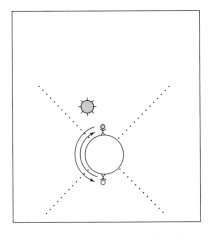

```
covers (earth, sun, me, event0)
hides (me, earth, sun, event0)
rotates_acw (earth, sun, event0)
rotates_acw (me, sun, event0)
uncovers (earth, sun, event1)
unhides (me, earth, sun, event1)
rotates_cw (earth, sun, event1)
rotates_cw (me, sun, event1)
```

FIGURE 9.15. Model 8. The earth turns up and down (synthetic).

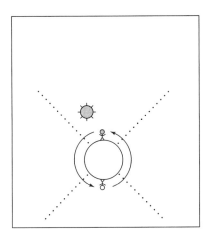

```
covers (earth, sun, me, event0)
hides (me, earth, sun, event0)
rotates_acw (earth, sun, event0)
rotates_acw (me, sun, event0)
uncovers (earth, sun, me, event1)
unhides (me, earth, sun, event1)
rotates_acw (earth, sun, event1)
rotates_acw (me, sun, event1)
```

FIGURE 9.16. Model 9. The earth rotates (scientific).

References

Baxter, J. (1989). Children's understanding of familiar astronomical events. *International Journal of Science Education, 11,* 502–513.

Carbonell, J., Michalski, R. S., & Mitchell, T. (1983). An overview of machine learning. In R. S. Michalski, J. G. Carbonell, and T. M. Mitchell (Eds.), *Machine learning: An artificial intelligence approach: Vol. 1,* ch. 1 (pp. 3–25). Palo Alto, CA: Morgan-Kaufmann.

Emde, W., Habel, C. U., & Rollinger, C.-R. (1983). The discovery of the equator or concept-driven learning. In *Proceedings of the Eighth International Joint Conference on Artificial Intelligence* (pp. 455–458). Los Altos, CA: Morgan-Kaufman.

Esposito, F., Malerba, D., Semeraro, G., Vosniadou, S., & Ioannides, C. (1999). Conceptual change as a logical revision process: A machine learning perspective. In S. Vosniadou & D. Kayser (Eds.), *Modelling changes in understanding: Case studies in physical reasoning* (pp. 106–137). New York: Pergamon.

Falkenhainer, B. C., & Michalski, R. S. (1986). Integrating quantitative and qualitative discovery: The ABACUS system. *Machine Learning, 1:* 367–401.

Klein, C. A. (1982). Children's concepts of the earth and the sun: A cross-cultural study. *Science Education, 65*(1): 95–107.

Kokar, M. (1986). Determining arguments of invariant functional descriptions. *Machine Learning, 1*(4): 403–422.

Langley, P. (1981). Data-driven discovery of physical laws. *Cognitive Science, 5:* 31–54.

Mali, G. B., & Howe, A. (1979). Development of earth and gravity concepts among Nepali children. *Science Education, 63*(5): 685–691.

Morik, K. (1996). A developmental case study on sequential learning: The day-night cycle. In P. Reimann & H. Spada (Eds.), *Learning in humans and machines:*

Towards an interdisciplinary learning science, ch. 12 (pp. 212–227). New York: Pergamon.

Morik, K. & Mühlenbrock, M. (1999). Conceptual change in the explanations of phenomena in astronomy. In S. Vosniadou & D. Kayser (Eds.), *Modelling changes in understanding: Case studies in physical reasoning.* (pp.). New York: Pergamon.

Morik, K., Wrobel, S., Kietz, J.-U., & Emde, W. (1993). *Knowledge acquisition and machine learning: Theory, methods, and applications.* London: Academic Press.

Mühlenbrock, M. (1994a). Computational models of learning in astronomy. In R. Cooper & S. Grant (Eds.), *AISB 1994 workshop series: Computational models of cognition and cognitive function* (pp. 19–29). Society for the Study of Artificial Intelligence and Simulation of Behaviour (SSAISB).

Mühlenbrock, M. (1994b). Menschliches und maschinelles Lernen: Bildung und Revision von Begriffsstrukturen zum Tag/Nachtzyklus [Learning in humans and machines: Forming and revising concept structures for the day/night cycle]. Unpublished Master's thesis, Universität Dortmund, Fachbereich Informatik, Lehrstuhl VIII.

Neri, F. (2000). Multilevel knowledge in modeling qualitative physics learning. *Machine Learning*, 38(1–2): 181–211.

Nussbaum, J. (1979). Children's conceptions of the earth as a cosmic body: A cross-age study. *Science Education*, 63(1): 83–93.

Nussbaum, J. (1985). The earth as a cosmic body. In R. Driver, E. Guesne, & A. Tiberghien (Eds.), *Children's ideas in science*, ch. 9 (pp. 170–192). Philadelphia: Open University Press.

Rose, D., & Langley, P. (August 1986). STAHLp: Belief revision in scientific discovery. In *Proceedings of the*

Fifth National Conference of the AAAI (pp. 528–532). Philadelphia: Morgan-Kaufman.

Sadler, P. M. (1987). Misconceptions in astronomy. In J. D. Novak (Ed.), *Second International Seminar on Misconceptions and Educational Strategies in Science and Mathematics*, Vol. 3 (pp. 422–424). Ithaca, NY: Cornell University.

Siegler, R. S. (1991). *Childrens's thinking* (2d ed.). Englewood Cliffs, NJ: Prentice-Hall.

Sneider, C. & Pulos, S. (1983). Children's cosmographies: Understanding the earth's shape and gravity. *Science Education*, 67(2): 205–221.

Viglietta, M. L. (1986). Earth, sky, and motion: Some questions to identify pupils' ideas. In J. J. Hunt (Ed.), *GIREP-86: Cosmos: An educational challenge* (pp. 369–370). Nordwijk, the Netherlands: European Space Agency.

Vosniadou, S. (1991). Designing curricula for conceptual restructuring: Lessons from the study of knowledge acquisition in astronomy. *Journal of Curriculum Studies*, 2(3): 219–237.

Vosniadou, S., & Brewer, W. (1992). Mental models of the earth: A study of conceptual change in childhood. *Cognitive Psychology*, 24: 535–585.

Vosniadou, S., & Brewer, W. F. (1994). Mental models of the day/night cycle. *Cognitive Science*, 18: 123–183.

Wrobel, S. (1994a). *Concept formation and knowledge revision.* Boston: Kluwer Academic Publishers.

Wrobel, S. (1994b). Concept formation during interactive theory revision. *Machine Learning*, 14(2): 169–192.

Zytkow, J., & Simon, H. (1986). A theory of historical discovery: The construction of componential models. *Machine Learning*, 1(1): 107–137.

Chapter 10

Timing Is in Order: Modeling Order Effects in the Learning of Information

Philip I. Pavlik Jr.

Simple memorization of information, because it does not have the complexity of more conceptual learning, provides a paradigm for investigating how primitive memory processes may underlie order effects in higher-level tasks. For instance, the superiority of distributed vs. massed practice implies an order effect because it suggests that any learning that has a repetitive memory component must be spaced widely to maximize retention. This chapter examines this effect and discusses recent research in which a mathematical model of both learning and forgetting was applied to optimizing the learning of facts. The model explains why it is always important to consider forgetting functions as well as learning curves for any learning procedure. One important implication of this model is that while learning per trial is generally greater with wider spacing, the increased time necessary to complete widely spaced practices means that it is difficult to fully apply in practice. These results suggest that investigations of order effects in the learning of more complex domains must consider the spacing of practice to the extent that there is a repetitive memory component to the task.

Repetition is an important component of many types of learning. Even though learning occasionally takes only one trial in humans, given a long enough retention interval, it is uncontroversial to suggest that most cognitive skills (particularly those with a memory component) need repetition to become durable. However, it is not easy to determine how much repetition is needed to achieve durability for any given skill because of the interaction between forgetting and the spacing of practice. This fact is made clear by the vast literature on how the spacing of practice (be it more massed or more distributed) affects the amount of practice needed to attain desired levels of skill ability and durability. One key finding of this work is that, while learning occurs more slowly with spaced practice compared to massed practice, it also is more durable (Pavlik & Anderson, 2005).

This chapter considers the spacing effect and its implications for those interested in finding the optimal order of practice. In contrast with most results in the spacing literature (which suggest that, given a need for maximal durability, spacing should be as wide as possible), an implication of the research discussed here is that, to achieve optimal learning efficiency, it will often be the case that spacing should be more massed, particularly when practicing newly learned skills.

To explore the effects of spaced practice in isolation, researchers have found it necessary to use tasks unlike the more conceptual and inductive tasks traditionally considered when discussing order effects in incremental learning. One that isolates spacing effects well is paired-associate learning. In this task, research subjects memorize the response to a cue over the course of repeated trials (e.g., gato = cat). Studies of this kind have varied the amount of spacing between repetitions of an item and then examined the effects at various retention intervals (e.g., Young, 1971; Glenberg, 1976; Pavlik & Anderson, 2005). Many studies of this type have initially introduced fact items with a presentation of both members of the pair and then presented repetitions by giving tests with feedback. This sort of experiment produces learning curves and forgetting functions that allow a detailed analysis of the effects of spacing and repetition.

While one might suspect that any task that has a repetitive memory component would benefit from an understanding of the principles governing this simpler paradigm, Langley (1995) has said that studies of paired-associate learning do not attend to many of the factors examined in more complex incremental learning. Despite this, however, his definitions of incremental learning and order effects do not seem to exclude this simpler task from consideration. Specifically, the paired-associate memory task appears to be incremental at the level of the individual item and to have order effects at the level of the set of items. According to Langley, learning a paired-associate must be an incremental learning task because the "learner inputs one training experience at a time, does not reprocess any previous experience and retains only one knowledge structure in memory." Following this definition of incremental learning, Langley proposed that there is an order effect in learning if different orders of learning produce different knowledge structures. Indeed, a good deal of research on paired-associate learning has demonstrated that the order of practice for a set of items being learned (whether items are spaced or massed) results in knowledge structures of different strength and durability (Peterson, Wampler, Kirkpatrick, & Saltzman, 1963; Young, 1971; Glenberg, 1976; Bahrick, 1979; Pavlik & Anderson, 2005). This shows that the overall task of learning a set of paired-associates produces an order effect.

Langley (1995) went on to describe three levels at which these order effects can occur. First is the attribute level, which describes how the order of processing the attributes of each instance may affect learning. In paired-associate fact learning, one might expect the attribute level of analysis to be applicable to different subject strategies of cue-response processing. As Langley suggests, attentional resources in a task are limited, and therefore, when learning a paired-associate, the processing order of cue and response may have important effects on the efficiency of processing.

Second is the instance level, which describes the effect of the order in which each instance of a concept is learned. In paired-associate learning this is the level at which we see order effects most clearly in the learning of an overall set of items. For instance, if the task were to learn 20 paired-associates, spacing effect research suggests that the optimal strategy is to cycle through the entire set so that the spacing of repetition for each item is maximal. In contrast, a strategy of massing practice for each item (given the same number of total repetitions) would be expected to result in much less durable knowledge structures.

Third is the concept level, which describes how the order of learning individual concepts affects overall performance. In paired-associate learning this corresponds to the way in which the learning of each item might affect the learning of other items. Insights into order effects can be found at this level as well because paired-associates are sometimes difficult to discriminate and orderings of practice that space confusable items more closely may promote this discrimination and thus improve performance (Nesbitt & Yamamoto, 1991).

However, while interactions at the concept level may be significant, most paired-associate literature treats the pairs as independent items and abstracts away from this level. Thus, the *overall* task of learning a set of items is not usually considered to have order effects at the concept level according to Langley's definition because the knowledge structures (the paired-associates) are better characterized as separate. Despite this, the overall task clearly has instance-level order effects as discussed earlier. Further, these instance-level order effects are interesting because many complex tasks have some independence of component concepts.

OPTIMAL ORDER OF PRACTICE

One of the best examples of these instance-level order effects is Atkinson (1972). In this experiment, a Markov model of paired-associate learning was used to optimize the learner's performance over a fixed number of trials. The effect of applying this model during a learning session was assessed one week later during a testing session. In this Markov model, paired-associates were thought to be in one of three states: permanently learned, temporarily learned, or unlearned. Depending on practice or forgetting, items could move from state to state with varying transition probabilities. Optimization in this model involved training the item (for each trial) that had the greatest probability of moving from a lower state to the permanently learned state.

Breaking down the Atkinson (1972) model reveals that it worked by identifying the most unlearned item before every trial. In both of his optimization conditions, the essential strategy was to train this weakest item because it had the greatest probability of moving to the permanently learned state.[1] This is clearly shown by the data Atkinson presented, in which the most effective conditions on the testing session produce correspondingly poor performance during the learning session.

In fact, the spacing effect can be interpreted as resulting in a memory benefit for the same reason that Atkinson's model succeeded by training the weakest items. Because maximal spacing results in maximal forgetting between repetitions, it also, on average, results in training the weakest item with each practice. The only important difference between cycling the items to achieve the widest possible spacing and the Atkinson routine was that the Atkinson routine incorporated sensitivity to item differences and subject performance in order to more accurately determine which item was weakest at any time.

Pavlik and Anderson (2005) provided a theory and model to explain why a practice (defined as any successful recall or study opportunity of the paired-associate) of the weakest item would result in maximal learning at all retention intervals and used this same mechanism to explain spacing effects. In this model the long-term benefit for a practice trial is determined by the current strength of the memory for the item that is being practiced. Pavlik and Anderson's model corresponds with a body of work (e.g., Whitten & Bjork, 1977) that suggests that the more difficult a practice event is, the more durable the learning that results. (Poorly learned items are difficult, and thus practicing them results in more durable retention than practicing well-learned items.) In the model, this effect manifests itself through the forgetting rate, which is higher for the contribution of a practice for a well-learned item and lower for the contribution of a practice for a poorly learned item. This mechanism produces the spacing effect because maximal spacing results in each item being weaker (due to forgetting) on repetition, and it also explains why a procedure of training the weakest item for each

trial is optimal. According to this theory, Atkinson (1972) succeeds by paying attention to the mechanism behind the spacing effect at a finer level than is achieved by just providing maximal spacing.

Atkinson (1972) is not the full story on optimization, however, because his work involves an optimization over a fixed number of trials. At least since Smallwood (1962), it has been clear that optimizing the learning per trial is only optimal given a fixed cost per trial. However, this assumption of a fixed cost for each trial is unreasonable because, in a drill procedure (where practice consists of a test of an item followed by a study opportunity if incorrect), the time cost per trial is much shorter for well-learned items and inflated for poorly learned items. Part of this is due to the need for a study opportunity following incorrect responses, and part is due to the longer latencies typically found with recall that is more difficult.

Because trials take a variable amount of time, an optimization like Atkinson's (1972) may not have been optimal because it considered all trials as having equal cost (in the experiment the approximate fixed cost per trial was 20 s). However, it may be that subjects in Atkinson's experiment spent a larger fraction of this 20-s period on task in the optimization conditions compared with conditions where learning was easier. Perhaps, if time on task were controlled, training the weakest item would not be optimal. If one wants to properly control time on task, the trial duration must be under the subject's control, and optimality needs to be defined over a fixed interval rather than a fixed number of trials.

Optimizing over a fixed interval, however, requires a model that estimates the true learning rate (a function of learning per unit of time) and thus allows the selection of the most efficient item to practice. Computing this true learning rate for items in the learning set requires some model of retrieval latency, something Atkinson's (1972) model lacked. Because the Adaptive Character of Thought–Rational cognitive architecture's (ACT-R, Anderson & Lebière, 1998) declarative memory equations include such a model, however, they lend themselves to computing a true learning rate. Thus, ACT-R provides us the tools we need to design and test a procedure for the optimization of paired-associate learning.

---

1. This is an overall characterization and varied somewhat based on individual item parameters in one of Atkinson's optimization conditions.

EXTENDED ACT-R MODEL

The model used, an extension of the ACT-R theory, captures three main effects in memory. The original ACT-R model captures the recency and frequency effects; in other words, performance is better the more recently or frequently a memory item is practiced. A recent extension of ACT-R (Pavlik & Anderson, 2005) captures the spacing effect. Importantly, this extension also captures both the spacing by practice interaction (that more practice leads to a greater spacing effect) and the spacing by retention interval interaction (that longer retention intervals result in larger spacing effects), effects shown by Underwood (1970) and Bahrick (1979).

In addition, the model has been extended to capture the fact that memory items are not equally difficult for each subject to learn (Pavlik & Anderson, 2004). This extension allows the model to capture three kinds of item and individual differences. Item differences reflect that some items are more or less difficult than others. Subject differences reflect that some subjects have greater overall facility in the task. Finally, subject/item differences reflect that there is consistent variation in how difficult a particular item is for a particular subject.

These practice effects, item differences, and individual differences are captured by an activation equation that represents the strength of an item in memory as the sum of these differences and the benefit from a number of individual memory strengthenings each of which corresponds to a past practice event (either a memory retrieval or study event). Equation 1 proposes that each time an item is practiced, the activation of the item, m_n, receives an increment in strength that decays as a power function of time.

$$m_n(t_{1...n}) = \beta_s + \beta_i + \beta_{si} + \ln\left(\sum_{i=1}^{n} t_i^{-d_i}\right) \quad (1)$$

To deal with the spacing effect, we developed an equation in which decay for the ith trial, d_i, is a function of the activation at the time it occurs. The implication of this is that higher activation at the time of a practice will result in the benefit of *that* practice decaying more quickly. On the other hand, if activation is low, decay will proceed more slowly. It is important to note that *every practice has its own d_i that controls the forgetting of that practice.* Specifically, we propose Equation 2 to specify how the decay rate d_i is calculated for the ith presentation of an item as a function of the activation m_{i-1} at the time the presentation occurred. Equation 1 shows how the activation m_n after n presentations depends on these decay rates, d_is, for the past trials.

$$d_i(m_{i-1}) = ce^{m_{i-1}} + a \quad (2)$$

The β parameters are the new addition for this chapter to capture item and individual differences. They capture any deviation of the overall model from the data for any particular sequence of tests with an item for a subject. They represent differences at the level of the subject (β_s), item (β_i), and subject/item (β_{si}). Unlike the a, c, and other parameters in the model, one does not make a single estimate of these values but rather finds their distributions across subjects, items, or items within a subject. This information is used to make decisions about how to allocate practice. For instance, by finding the distribution of β_{si} one is able to estimate the β_{si} value for any particular item over the course of learning and use this information to more effectively allocate practice.

In Equation 2, c is the decay scale parameter, and a is the intercept of the decay function. For the first practice of any sequence, $d_1 = a$ because m_0 is equal to negative infinity before any practice occurs. These equations are recursive because to calculate any particular m_n one must have previously calculated all prior m_ns to calculate the d_is needed. These equations result in a steady decrease in the long-run retention benefit for more presentations in a sequence of closely spaced presentations. As spacing gets wider in such a sequence, activation has time to decrease between presentations, decay is then lower for new presentations, and long-run effects do not decrease as much. (An example of how these equations are used, including the h parameter discussed below, is included in the Appendix.)

In ACT-R, an item in declarative memory will be retrieved if its activation is above a threshold. However, because activation is noisy, recall is uncertain. An item with activation m (as given by Equation 1) has a probability of recall described by Equation 3. Equation 3 is the standard ACT-R function, which assumes a logistic distribution of activation noise for activation values.

$$p(m) = \frac{1}{1 + e^{\frac{\tau - m}{s}}} \quad (3)$$

In this equation, τ is the threshold parameter, and s describes the noise in activation estimates from

Equation 1. Effectively, the s parameter describes the sensitivity of recall to changes in activation.

The time to retrieve in ACT-R is:

$$l(m) = Fe^{-m} + fixed\ time\ cost \qquad (4)$$

In this equation F is the latency scalar. Fixed time cost usually refers to the fixed time cost of perceptual motor encoding and response.

Because the β parameters in Equation 1 will vary across subjects and items, they play a role similar to that of the s parameter in Equation 3. Most ACT-R models have dealt with item and individual differences (noise at the level of the item, subject, or subject/item) through the s parameter. For instance, a larger s parameter can represent that some items are learned early in a particular set and some are learned later. Indeed, in an aggregate dataset, s will capture at least four kinds of variability: random trial-to-trial noise, subject variability, item variability, and item/subject variability. The β parameters let us remove from s all variability except the trial-to-trial noise.

So, when finding the individual β parameters for all of the sequences of practice that compose an aggregate dataset, one finds that the best-fitting model also needs a much lower s parameter. When s is low, the transition from low correctness to high correctness will be sharp. This will make the model's description of the learning and forgetting of individual items appear more all or none; however, real valued changes in activation levels still underlie these transitions. This is similar to the idea that learning curves in aggregate data are the result of all-or-none learning at the level of the individual item. However, in the model, the aggregate learning curves come both from the averaging of sequences with different β parameters and from the fact that while s is low, the model still represents activation as a continuous value.

Finally, Anderson, Fincham, and Douglass (1999) found that while Equation 1 could account for practice and forgetting during an experiment, it could not fit retention data over long intervals (up to one year). Because of this, they supposed that intervening events between sessions erode memories more slowly than during an experimental session. This slower forgetting was modeled by scaling time as if it were slower outside the experiment. Forgetting is then dependent on the "psychological time" between presentations rather than the real time. This is implemented by multiplying the portion of time that occurs between sessions by

the h parameter when calculating recall. Essentially, this means that time in the model is best considered a measure of destructive interfering events. The decay rate can then be considered a measure of the fragility of memories to the corrosive effect of these other events. An example of how this h parameter is integrated into Equation 1 will be useful and is provided in the Appendix.

A COMPARISON WITH ALL
OR NONE MODELS

It is interesting to compare this incremental ACT-R model with more traditional all-or-none models of learning. As reviewed by Crowder (1976), Rock (1957) initiated the all-or-none versus incremental learning debate by noticing that, given a set of items to be learned, what appears to be incremental learning of the set might actually be caused by the averaging of results for individual items, each of which is learned in an all-or-none fashion with some probability for each practice. The idea is that if you have three items, and one is learned on the first practice, one on the second practice, and the last on the third practice; then when one averages this situation it looks as if there is an incremental increase of 33.3% per practice in recall ability, despite the fact that the learning was all or none for the individual items. Rock and later Estes, Hopkins, and Crothers (1960) tried to prove that this is what was going on in the experimental literature.

Rock (1957) used a word-learning procedure in which, in the experimental condition, new words were inserted after each pass through the list for words that were not recalled correctly. In contrast, in the control condition the same set of words was used for each pass. The idea was that the control condition would have an advantage if the incremental theory were correct because individuals will get incremental practice on failed words, rather than having to start fresh with new words for each pass. Unfortunately, this design has a selection issue because it forces the control condition subjects to learn the most difficult items, while conceivably experimental subjects would keep getting new words inserted for any hard words they do not recall in a pass. Williams (1961) showed that this selection effect was likely to be the cause of Rock's result.

Estes et al. (1960) tried to show all-or-none effects using an RTT protocol, where each item was presented once for study and then tested twice. According to

Estes's interpretation of the all-or-none theory, items recalled on the first trial should also be recalled on the second trial, whereas items not recalled should be likewise not recalled on the second trial. According to his understanding of incremental theory, items should have nearly the same probability for each trial of the two tests. Of course, the experiment followed Estes's predictions, but again the issue of the differential difficulty of items was glossed over in the analysis of incremental theory. It seems likely that Estes's results were caused by the fact that easy items were often gotten correct twice, the second time being made easier by the practice from the first recall, while difficult items were gotten incorrect twice, the second time having no advantage from practice after the first failure and suffering a yet longer retention interval.

In both cases, what is being challenged is a straw man conceptualization of incremental theory. When noise in item difficulty is introduced in an incremental model (in the model here this is done with the β parameters), it becomes easy to capture the results of Rock (1957) and Estes et al. (1960) since this differential difficulty results in behavior that certainly appears all or none when combined with the recall equation and a low s.

Perhaps the strongest reason to doubt an all-or-none model, however, has to do with what it implies for retrieval, learning, and forgetting. For retrieval, it is very hard to reconcile the findings of recognition memory and priming with the notion that a memory is all or none. It is well known, for instance, that memories can be accurately recognized when recall is impossible. Nevertheless, the all-or-none model seems to require the strange assumption that no learning has occurred unless a recall is successful. This becomes particularly confusing because such an assessment of recall might occur at any duration, and it certainly matters what the duration is. If only 1 second passes after learning, recall will be very high, indicating the learning had an effect; however, if 10 minutes pass, learning appears to have had no effect. Similarly perplexing is the issue of overlearning. While overlearning has been shown to have an effect (e.g., Rohrer, Taylor, Pashler, Wixted, &

Cepeda, 2005), the all-or-none model has no easy explanation for this phenomenon. It is axiomatic that if recall strength is "all," then adding to it will provide no benefit. Relearning is no less difficult to conceptualize because the implication is that if an item is learned and then forgotten, relearning should be no easier the second time around.[2]

APPLYING THE MODEL

To understand how the ACT-R model is applied, it is useful to consider two intuitions from the model. The first one is about the benefit of spaced practice. One can see from Equations 1 and 2 that it should be straightforward to calculate the gain in activation at any particular retention interval for a practice at the current time. Because of this, the model provides a clear measure of the memory gain for practice. One can also see that, according to the model, this gain depends on the activation strength of the memory at the time of practice. Because decay is lower when memory strength is lower, this gain increases monotonically (given an appropriately long retention interval) as spacing increases because spacing allows more forgetting.

The second intuition from the model has to do with the cost of spaced practice. As captured in Equation 4, retrieval latency increases monotonically with the decrease in memory strength. While one might consider other measures of cost, the time on task is perhaps the most straightforward measure of the cost of each practice. As Equation 4 makes clear, this cost increases as memory strength decreases. Further, wider spacing also leads to more errors, which require costly study practice that would be unnecessary if correctness was higher due to narrower spacing.

These intuitions can be integrated mathematically to determine the true learning rate. As Smallwood (1962) has explained, any true optimization must maximize the learning rate, which is the gain/cost. Simplifying the fraction obtained from doing this calculation on the measures from the model gives us the activation gain at test per second of practice. Because

2. The overall suggestion of Rohrer et al. (2005), that overlearning is not a good idea, can be seriously questioned according to the logic of the ACT-R model. First, in their Experiment 1, the conclusion that overlearning trials are not effective does not account for the fact that overlearning trials are much faster given free responding. Given this fact, the small advantage of overlearning that Rohrer et al. found becomes more significant. Second, in their Experiment 2, the narrower spacing of the overlearning condition may have caused the faster forgetting for overlearning that was found, similar to Pavlik and Anderson (2005).

the model captures the strength of individual items for any subject through the β parameters, this learning rate (measuring learning at test for each second of current practice for the item) can be calculated for all items at any time for a subject in an experiment.

Indeed, if one ignores the logarithm in Equation 1, a simplified version (which closely approximates the full version) of the activation gain at test per second of practice is shown in Equation 5.

$$gain_n(r, m_n) = \frac{r^{-(cm_n + a)}}{p(m_n)(Fe^{-m_n} + fixed\,success\,cost)} \quad (5) \\ + (1 - p(m_n))\,(fixed\,failure\,cost)$$

Interestingly, the activation value (m_n) that maximizes this quantity is constant. This is because Equation 5, given a fixed value for retention interval (r), depends only on activation. This means that, when a practice for an item is scheduled so it occurs at this activation, the efficiency of the practice will be maximal for the specified retention interval. For the parameter values used in the following experiment, this optimal practice threshold activation ($m_n = -0.38$) corresponded to a 0.95 probability of correctness. Thus, according to this analysis, it is maximally efficient to test the items in the experiment when there is an expectation of getting them correct 95% of the time. This point is optimal because, if items were trained below this value, the time cost would be too large relative to the gain, while if they were trained above this value, the gain would be too small relative to the time cost.

This 95%-correct value for an item assumes that β has been determined based on prior practice with the item. Given no specific information about an item, the initially optimal level is 78%, assuming $s = 0.253$ in Equation 3 (this estimate of s comes from an early version of the model in Pavlik and Anderson, 2005). Because of this, practice will be expected to begin at a level of about 78% in the optimization condition in the following experiment and rise across a sequence of practices to a final maintenance level of 95%.

Having this equality makes implementing this efficiency optimization rather straightforward. For each trial, the experimental software computes the activation of all of the items in the learning set for the subject. Unpracticed items are assumed to have a 0% chance of recall, and therefore their activation is negative infinity. At the beginning of a session, no items have been practiced, so a random unpracticed item is chosen.

Because the probability of recall for the unpracticed item is 0%, it is introduced with a study trial. Once items have been introduced, they are susceptible to forgetting, so their activations are constantly dropping, depending on the decay rates. The algorithm selects for practice any item that falls below this optimal practice threshold activation. Given two or more items dropping below this threshold, the one with the lowest activation is chosen. The goal of this selection policy is to practice items as near as possible to the practice threshold activation, while preventing items from slipping far below the target as would a policy of picking the nearest possible item to the practice threshold.

Often during these selections, all of the items in the set will be above the practice threshold activation. In this case, practice for these items is not optimal. However, this creates a logical and ideal opportunity to introduce new items as a side effect of the selection strategy. Thus, the optimization algorithm provides an elegant solution to the perplexing question of how many items should be in the learning set. This number is controlled by how well each item has been learned. When the set is well learned, items will be above practice threshold activation, and new items will be introduced. To the extent that the set is less well learned, previously practiced items will be falling below practice threshold activation more often, and new items will be introduced less often.

This characteristic of the model seems to correspond with the discussion in Chapter 12, in which VanLehn describes the importance of maintaining a single disjunct per lesson; and it can also be seen as operationalizing Sweller's (Chapter 15) Cognitive Load theory. Here we can define the lesson as the single drill trial of the paired-associate item. Given this definition, the algorithm can be understood as trying to train items such that all prior items are well learned (and thus no longer disjuncts) before presenting a new item (disjunct). If an item is not well learned because of forgetting, it qualifies as a disjunct again and is practiced as soon as possible.

One side effect of this procedure is that, given an average item, the algorithm predicts that an expanding schedule of practice will be optimal. This is because items with fewer accumulated practices will be forgotten relatively quickly. Because of this, they will drop below the practice threshold activation and receive more practice. As practices accumulate, the activation strength will become more stable and will decrease below the practice threshold more slowly.

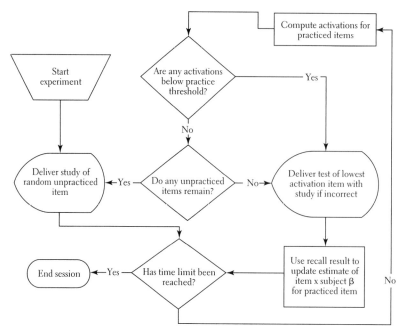

FIGURE 10.1. Flowchart of optimization algorithm.

Because of this, each additional practice will occur at a wider spacing than the previous practice.

The optimization in the following experiment works through these principles using Equation 5 according to the flowchart shown in Figure 10.1.

EXPERIMENT

The experiment to test this routine took place in two sessions separated by one day. During Session 1, subjects went through 1 hour of practice divided into between-subjects conditions. For Session 2, all of the subjects were recalled to assess the effects of these conditions.

The experiment had two main goals. The first was to determine how the optimization algorithm compared with a policy of using the widest spacing possible. In this comparison policy one simply cycles through the set of items. The widest spacing seemed to be the most straightforward control to compare with the optimization described because the expected gain per trial increases monotonically with increasing spacing (given a long retention interval), as shown by Pavlik and Anderson (2005).

The second goal was to examine the effect of mnemonic strategy training on performance. Pavlik and

Anderson (2005) found that postexperimental interviews suggested that more than 80% of subjects used a mnemonic strategy. However, according to self-report, these strategies were often somewhat haphazard. To alleviate this issue, this experiment also looked at the effect of brief training in the keyword mnemonic method (Atkinson, 1975) before the experiment (5- to 10-minute description of the keyword method with three examples). This mnemonic training might provide three benefits. First, it might improve performance. Second, it could reduce the between-subject variability in performance. Finally, it might result in subjects behaving in a more homogeneous manner and thus reduce the methodological issue of averaging over methods between subjects.

The design of this study was therefore a 2×2 between-subjects comparison of the scheduling condition (optimized or widest spacing) and the strategy condition (mnemonic training or free-strategy instructions).

The first session practice differed according to the scheduling condition. Of the 100 word pairs used in each condition, the subjects learned all 100 in the widest spacing condition. These pairs were introduced with study trials for all of the items, and then the items were cycled with drill trials (test trials that included study if incorrect). To prevent sequence learning, items were perturbed in groups of 20 for each cycle through the list, so the actual spacing in this condition was between 80 and 118. In the optimization condition, new words were introduced randomly using study trials according to the rules of the algorithm. Following this introduction, the rules of the optimization determined the spacing of drill trial repetitions.

The optimization used overall a, c, τ, h, and s parameters determined from the dataset in Pavlik and Anderson (2005). Fixed latency costs and the F parameter were estimated from data described in Pavlik and Anderson (2004). Item β parameters and subject/item β distribution were estimated using data from both of these experiments. Item β parameters were used to bias activation (Equation 1) when making scheduling decisions. The subject/item β distribution was used to adjust the subject/item β for each item for each subject as the program monitored performance. Initially, subject/item β values were set at 0, but given the prior information about the distribution (which was assumed to be normal), a Bayesian procedure was used to update the estimates based on the history of performance. Finally, the subject β values were estimated by averaging current subject/item β estimates after every 150 trials. This average was then used as the prior mean for subject/item βs for previously untested items. The goal of using β in all of these cases was simply to get better estimates of activation so as to better choose the most efficient item to study according to Equation 5.

During the second session, all of the items were tested three times to determine the effects of conditions. The second-session tests were randomized on the first pass through the list, and this order was further randomized in sequential groups of 20 to determine the sequence for the second and third passes through the list.

Each test trial (for both Session 1 and 2) consisted of presenting the cue foreign word with a space in which to type the English translation (the response). After the subject entered a translation or no answer, the next trial began unless the response was incorrect, in which case another study trial for the item was presented before the next item test. Study trials in the experiment (both after incorrect responses and for the introduction) lasted between 3 and 10 seconds. The subject determined when the study was complete by pressing the "enter" key after at least 3 seconds had elapsed. Test trials timed out at 10 seconds, though most of the responses were made in less than 5 seconds. Between these events, there were half-second intertrial prompt screens.

Sixty-four subjects (16 in each between-subjects cell) were paid to complete the experiment and received a small bonus depending on their performance. All of the subjects promised not to study the items during the 1-day retention interval. Four subjects (the worst performers in each of the between-subject cells) were viewed as outliers, and their data were discarded.

SIMULATION

Before actually running the experiment, I used the model to simulate it in order to produce predictions for the scheduling conditions. The simulation assumed 500 subjects in each condition running through the experiment I have described. Because I had no clear notion of the effects of the mnemonics, mnemonic conditions were not simulated. Each simulated subject had a randomly generated subject β to model individual ability, a randomly selected set of item βs (drawn from the actual distribution), and a randomly generated set of subject/item βs. Parameter values were as described in Pavlik and Anderson (2004, 2005). The simulated subjects (behaving according to the ACT-R equations) were optimized by the algorithm, but the simulation replicated learning only on the first session and the first recall trial of the second session. This simulation used Equation 4 to simulate latencies and Equation 5 to make decisions according to the expected latencies of actions.

RESULTS AND DISCUSSION

Table 10.1 shows the results of the simulation compared with human data.

The most notable contrast between the simulation and the experimental results (detailed below) is that the actual subjects completed a greater number of trials, particularly in the widest spacing condition. Despite this, the optimization condition showed greater performance in both cases. The biggest problem for the model was the overprediction of performance. This may have been caused by somewhat inaccurate prior parameters, due to noise from the previous dataset, and the fact that three subjects were removed from Pavlik and Anderson's (2004) data during the parameter estimation because of extremely poor performance. However, while the quantitative predictions are a bit rough, the qualitative predictions were

TABLE 10.1. Simulation Compared With Free-Strategy Human Results

Session	Optimized Humans	Maximal Spacing Humans	Optimized Model	Maximal Spacing Model
Session 1: Mean Performance	0.73	0.29	0.82	0.44
Session 2: Trial 1 Performance	0.57	0.45	0.73	0.66
Session 1: Trials Completed	547	499	525	374
Items Introduced on Session 1	80	100	89	100

all in agreement with the data and in the correct directions. Considering the large individual differences observed in this between-subjects experiment, the similar pattern of results between model and data was encouraging despite the overall overprediction of performance by the simulation.

On the whole, the average percentage correct was 11.6% better for subjects in the optimized scheduling condition and 6.0% better for subjects in the mnemonic training strategy condition in Session 2. The performance across the three trials of Session 2 for each between-subjects condition is shown in Figures 10.2 and 10.3. The first analysis was an ANOVA to examine the effects of the between-subjects manipulations. This preliminary analysis revealed that only the optimization algorithm produced a significant effect ($F(1, 56) = 4.51$, $p < 0.05$).

As Figure 10.4 shows, almost the entire benefit (6.0%) for the mnemonic training occurred due to a 12% increase for subjects in the optimization condition. This indicated an interaction in which mnemonic training was effective only in the optimization condition. To perform a more sensitive analysis of this interaction and other relationships, an ANCOVA using a covariate to remove between-subject variability due to ability differences was also completed. The z-score of the Session 1 performance within each cell of the

design was used as a covariate. Because these z-scores were computed in each cell, the covariate used was not associated with the conditions. This more sensitive analysis revealed that the effects of mnemonic strategy and optimized condition were both significant ($F(1, 55) = 22.6$, $p < 0.001$ and $F(1, 55) = 6.08$, $p < 0.05$). Furthermore, the interaction discussed was significant ($F(1, 55) = 5.90$, $p < 0.05$).

Figure 10.4 shows that the mnemonic training strategy condition resulted in a benefit only for the optimized subjects. This finding may be related to work by Thomas and Wang (1996), which suggests that reinforcement testing may be necessary for mnemonically encoded items to be retained longer. Wang and Thomas (1999) have argued that mnemonics are effective only when they have testing reinforcement soon after learning. Based on this work one might speculate that the shorter initial spacing of practice produced in the optimized condition specifically benefited forming and retaining the mnemonic device.

Figure 10.5 shows the data for Session 1 performance across all of the conditions. These data again show results for the 2 × 2 (scheduling × strategy) design. The 77.3% average performance for the optimization condition subjects was less than the 95% level for the practice activation threshold. This discrepancy was

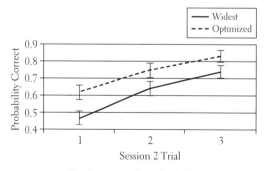

FIGURE 10.2. Performance for scheduling conditions in Session 2 (1 SE error bars).

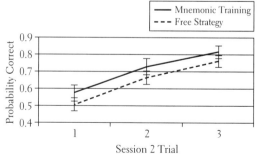

FIGURE 10.3. Performance for strategy conditions in Session 2 (1 SE error bars).

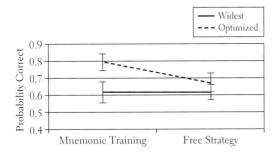

FIGURE 10.4. Average Session 2 performance with be-tween-subject conditions (1 SE error bars).

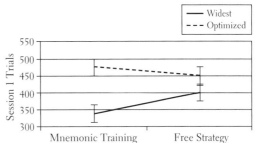

FIGURE 10.6. Total Session 1 trials with between-subject conditions (1 SE error bars).

caused by the fact that, with only one session of practice, there were not enough practices with each item to very accurately estimate the β_{si} parameter. Further, it is likely that the aggregate s was larger than the 0.253 value used to calculate the initial level of expected performance (78.0%). This graph also indicates that the benefit of mnemonics was about equal for both strategy conditions in Session 1; however, this benefit did not reach significance ($p < 0.08$). This suggests that whatever benefit there is to keyword training has some effect on the forgetting dependent on scheduling because, by Session 2, a large effect had developed in the optimized keyword cell. However, the three-way interaction of session × scheduling × strategy was not significant.

The number of Session 1 trials (where a trial is a study opportunity or a successful recall) in each condition depended on the speed with which subjects responded to tests and the amount of time they spent on study trials. On average, the subjects completed 17 more trials in the free-strategy versus mnemonic conditions and 92 more trials in the optimized compared to the widest scheduling conditions. Figure 10.6 shows

the number of Session 1 trials by condition. An analysis identical to the one performed for the Session 2 percent correct was completed. While only the effect of the optimization on increasing total trials completed was significant ($F(1, 56) = 13.8$, $p < 0.001$), in the analysis without covariate, when the covariate was used, the interaction was also found to be significant ($F(1, 55) = 4.22$, $p < 0.05$). The meaning of this interaction is unclear. Perhaps, if the spacing is narrow, the mnemonics are strong enough to produce a speed advantage but are easily forgotten so that, at wide spacing, they produce a speed disadvantage.

It is interesting to examine the practice schedules produced by the scheduling conditions. Figure 10.7 aggregates over the mnemonic conditions by subject. To facilitate a meaningful comparison, only items that had three tests in Session 1 were included. Thus, 10 subjects were excluded because they produced no sequences with only three Session 1 tests. Figure 10.7 shows that the optimization produces the expanding schedules described previously. It is striking how soon the first test occurs. Assuming this result is transferable to other domains, it implies that testing soon after first

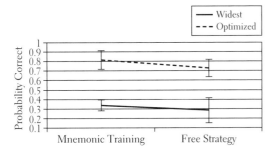

FIGURE 10.5. Average Session 1 performance with be-tween-subjects conditions (1 SE error bars).

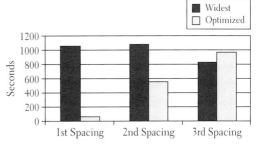

FIGURE 10.7. Average Session 1 spacing for items receiving three tests.

introducing information is the most efficient way to learn. This is also what the model predicts.

One outcome of the optimization was that it resulted in some of the subjects not having all of the items introduced during Session 1. There were averages of 8.2 and 19.7 items not introduced in the keyword and free-strategy optimization conditions, respectively. The fact that not all of the items are introduced is a natural outcome of the optimization algorithm since new items are introduced only when all other items are above the practice threshold. Thus, some items may not be introduced for subjects with poor performance. Regardless of how many items were introduced, all 100 items were tested during Session 2.

CONCLUSION

Several related implications of the model and experiment are important to consider. First, the model says that stability is a defining characteristic of any memory. While one might initially assume that what is learned is forgotten at a constant rate, this is not what the data show. Results such as those found by Pavlik and Anderson (2005) and Bahrick (1979) show that forgetting rates can differ, depending on the spacing of practice. Work by Whitten and Bjork (1977) and Cuddy and Jacoby (1982) similarly suggests that learning that is more difficult is more long lasting. It is interesting that even different theoretical approaches such as contextual fluctuation theory also result in differential forgetting as a function of spacing (e.g., Raaijmakers, 2003).

This suggests that any training experiment that does not consider the durability of learning has failed to thoroughly examine the outcomes of their procedures. Thankfully, data from the memory experiments we have run in our lab suggests that, given single-session training, differences in durability should become clear within a day or two after training (Pavlik & Anderson, 2005). In these results, the advantage from spaced practice was clearly revealed one day after a single learning session. However, this spacing advantage was significantly greater after a week as compared to performance after a single day. Both results indicate that spacing practice has strong effects on the rate of forgetting and show why immediate learning curves can be deceptive. Closely spaced practices might result in seemingly superior learning if tested immediately yet reveal their inadequacy after an interval.

The optimization of fact learning presented here provides useful suggestions for researchers studying the learning of more complex tasks. Because these complex tasks are likely to contain a memory component, to obtain efficient learning, we might usefully pay some attention to the model presented here. In general, the model moves beyond the simple claim that spacing should be maximal. By integrating efficiency considerations by incorporating the latency of each training instance, it predicts that an expanding schedule should be optimal. It seems likely that learning that is more complex would also be optimal given some version of this type of schedule. A carefully calibrated expanding schedule should result in each practice instance occurring before forgetting has been excessive and practice times increase prohibitively, yet still allow for enough forgetting so that newly acquired information is more stable.

PROJECTS AND OPEN PROBLEMS

Easy

1. Design a spreadsheet to confirm the conclusions in the Appendix.

2. Use the activation values and Equations 3 and 4 to compute the speed and percentage correct for each of the four tests in the Appendix example. Assume a fixed time cost of 0.6 s in Equation 4, $\tau = 0.7$, $s = 0.1$, and $F = 1.5$.

Hard

1. Using Equation 5 with a *fixed failure cost* = 13.6 s and a *fixed success cost* = 2.85 s, compute the gain score for the four tests in the Appendix at a retention interval of approximately 1 year (in seconds). This represents the efficiency of the practice depending on the retention interval (and approximates a more exact computation, which acknowledges the logarithm in Equation 1).

2. Generalize the efficiency computation across the range of activations from −0.7 to 0 with a retention interval of 1 day (given an h value of 0.017). Plot the gain score as a function of activation. Determine the activation level at which practice is maximally efficient.

APPENDIX

Because the math underlying the computation is recursive and a bit complex, the following is an example of the activation and decay computations for a condition with two tests and 14-item spacing in the first session and two retests in the second session. This is a sequence of five presentations; the first is the introductory study, and the remaining four are test trials. The long-term retention interval (1 day) is interposed between the third and fourth tests. This example does not use the β parameters, $c = 0.217$ and $a = 0.177$.

The actual average times of this sequence of practice are approximately 0; 126; 252; 83,855; and 84,888. This indicates that the first study occurs at time 0. The last two times include the 22.5 hours between the end of the first session and the beginning of the second, which is 81,000 seconds. To account for the reduced forgetting over this interval, we need to multiply the 81,000 seconds by the h factor (.025), resulting in a scaled value of 2,025. This means that the times after the long interval need to be reduced by 78,975 (the difference between the actual and psychological times) to convert them to a measure of psychological time. This results in the sequence: 0; 126; 252; 4,844; and 5,877.

Now the activation at each test time can be computed. At time 126 the first test occurs, according to Equations 1 and 2, $m_1 = \ln(126^{-0.177}) = -0.86$. Recall that the decay from the first study (d_1) is simply a.

To compute the activation of the second test, we need to use the activation at the time of the first test to compute the decay for that presentation. Using Equation 2, $d_2 = ce^{m_1} + a$, which equals 0.27. Since the age of the initial study is now 252 and the age of the first test is 126, from Equation 1 we get $m_2 = \ln(252^{-0.177} + 126^{-0.27}) = -0.43$.

To compute the activation of the third test, we now need to compute d_3, which is $ce^{m_2} + a = 0.32$. The age of the first presentation is now 4,844, the age of the second presentation is 4,717, and the age of the third presentation is 4,591. Therefore, activation m_3 is $\ln(4{,}844^{-0.177} + 4{,}717^{-0.27} + 4{,}591^{-0.32}) = -0.93$.

For the final test in this example sequence we need to compute the decay for the third test (fourth presentation), $d_4 = ce^{m_3} + a = 0.26$. The sequence of ages is 5,877, 5,750, 5,624, and 1,033. Activation m_4 is $\ln(5{,}877^{-0.177} + 5{,}750^{-0.27} + 5{,}624^{-0.32} + 1{,}033^{-0.26})$, which equals -0.62.

References

Anderson, J. R., Fincham, J. M., & Douglass, S. (1999). Practice and retention: A unifying analysis. *Journal of Experimental Psychology: Learning, Memory, and Cognition, 25,* 1120–1136.

Anderson, J. R., & Lebière, C. (1998). *The atomic components of thought.* Mahwah, NJ: Erlbaum.

Atkinson, R. C. (1972). Optimizing the learning of a second-language vocabulary. *Journal of Experimental Psychology, 96,* 124–129.

Atkinson, R. C. (1975). Mnemotechnics in Second-language Learning. *American Psychologist, 30,* 821–828.

Bahrick, H. P. (1979). Maintenance of knowledge: Questions about memory we forgot to ask. *Journal of Experimental Psychology: General, 108,* 296–308.

Crowder, R. G. (1976). *Principles of learning and memory.* Hillsdale, NJ: Erlbaum.

Cuddy, L. J., & Jacoby, L. L. (1982). When forgetting helps memory: An analysis of repetition effects. *Journal of Verbal Learning and Verbal Behavior, 21,* 451–467.

Estes, W. K, Hopkins, B. L., & Crothers, E. J. (1960). All-or-none and conservation effects in the learning and retention of paired associates. *Journal of Experimental Psychology, 60,* 329–339.

Glenberg, A. M. (1976). Monotonic and nonmonotonic lag effects in paired-associate and recognition memory paradigms. *Journal of Verbal Learning and Verbal Behavior, 15,* 1–16.

Langley, P. (1995). Order effects in incremental learning. In P. Reimann & H. Spada (Eds.), *Learning in humans and machines: Towards an interdisciplinary learning science* (pp. 154–167). Oxford: Elsevier.

Nesbitt, J. C., & Yamamoto, N. (1991). Sequencing confusable items in paired-associate drill. *Journal of Computer-Based Instruction, 18,* 7–13.

Pavlik Jr., P. I., & Anderson, J. R. (2004). An ACT-R model of memory applied to finding the optimal schedule of practice. In M. Lovett, C. Schunn, C. Lebière, & P. Munro (Eds.), *Proceedings of the Sixth International Conference of Cognitive Modeling* (pp. 376–377). Mahwah, NJ: Erlbaum.

Pavlik Jr., P. I., & Anderson, J. R. (2005). Practice and forgetting effects on vocabulary memory: An activation-based model of the spacing effect. *Cognitive Science, 29,* 559–586.

Peterson, L. R., Wampler, R., Kirkpatrick, M., & Saltzman, D. (1963). Effect of spacing presentations on retention of a paired associate over short intervals. *Journal of Experimental Psychology, 66,* 206–209.

Raaijmakers, J. G. W. (2003). Spacing and repetition effects in human memory: Application of the SAM model. *Cognitive Science, 27,* 431–452.

Rock, I. (1957). The role of repetition in associative learning. *American Journal of Psychology, 70,* 186–193.

Rohrer, D., Taylor, K., Pashler, H., Wixted, J., and Cepeda, N. J. (2005). The effect of overlearning on long-term retention. *Applied Cognitive Psychology, 19*(3), 361–374.

Smallwood, R. D. (1962). *A decision structure for computer-directed teaching machines.* Cambridge, MA: MIT Press.

Thomas, M. H., & Wang, A. Y. (1996). Learning by the keyword mnemonic: Looking for long-term benefits. *Journal of Experimental Psychology: Applied, 2,* 330–342.

Underwood, B. J. (1970). A breakdown of the total-time law in free-recall learning. *Journal of Verbal Learning and Verbal Behavior, 9,* 573–580.

Wang, A. Y., & Thomas, M. H. (1999). In defense of keyword experiments: A reply to Gruneberg's commentary. *Applied Cognitive Psychology, 13,* 283–287.

Whitten, W. B., & Bjork, R. A. (1977). Learning from tests: Effects of spacing. *Journal of Verbal Learning and Verbal Behavior, 16,* 465–478.

Williams, J. P. (1961). Supplementary report: A selection artifact in Rock's study of the role of repetition. *Journal of Experimental Psychology, 62*(2), 627–628.

Young, J. L. (1971). Reinforcement-test intervals in paired-associate learning. *Journal of Mathematical Psychology, 8,* 58–81.

Chapter 11

The Effects of Order: A Constraint-Based Explanation

Stellan Ohlsson

The theory of constraint-based specialization claims that strategies for cognitive tasks are learned by specializing overly general strategies on the basis of declarative knowledge that is expressed as constraints on correct solutions plus information about which constraints a given rule violates. This type of learning is shown to generate different outcomes depending on the order of the training tasks. A small family of related but different tasks—the counting task used by developmental psychologists to test children's understanding of number—is used to show that there are transfer effects as well as ordering effects among these tasks. The quantitative relations between transfer and ordering effects are summarized in a simple mathematical model.

The essence of learning is that the learner has more knowledge after learning than before. This change cannot come about in completely arbitrary ways because the person has to function even as he or she learns. Learning is like rebuilding an airplane while flying it: Each individual change must be such that it does not undermine the ability of the machine to stay aloft. Similarly, it is implausible that the mind will be able to wring just any kind of change on its knowledge structures, but it *is* plausible that the changes that occur during learning fall into specific types. It is also implausible that all instances of human learning can be explained by a single type of change, be it association, equilibration, restructuring, chunking, or analogy.

The balanced view holds that there is a small repertoire of primitive types of change. By "primitive" I mean that the changes are of such small scope that they cannot meaningfully be analyzed into yet smaller processes, at least not at the symbolic level of analysis. The next reduction would take us into their neural implementation. I refer to such primitive changes

as *learning mechanisms*, and I assume that to state a learning theory is to specify the set of learning mechanisms with which one proposes that the cognitive architecture is programmed, plus the mental conditions under which each of those mechanisms is triggered. Any one instance of learning is to be explained in terms of the operation of one or more of those mechanisms. Specific multimechanism learning theories of this sort have been proposed by Fitts (1964), Gagné (1965), Anderson (1983), Ritter and Bibby (2001), and others.

Because each learning mechanism produces only minimal change, the learning of something complex such as a new theory or strategy is accomplished by a long sequence of learning events, each one involving the application of a learning mechanism. The growth of a person's knowledge base follows a path through the space of all the revisions of his or her current knowledge that are possible given the repertoire of learning mechanisms. The immediate neighborhood around the current knowledge base, the part of the space that is reachable in a single learning event, is known in developmental psychology as *the zone of proximal development* (Vygotsky, 1978). Adjusting the term to broaden its usefulness, I refer to this concept as the *zone of proximal change.*

If a system moves forward toward the ever-receding horizon of proximal change by wringing successive changes on its current knowledge base, it matters in which order individual changes occur. By shaping the current knowledge base this way or that, a learning event might create or not create, as the case may be, the conditions that will trigger or enable a particular future change. Each step of each learning event helps set the stage and the conditions for future events. This is the ultimate cause of ordering effects in learning. In education, a particular type of ordering effect has long been recognized: A teacher presents easy problems before harder ones on the hypothesis that doing so facilitates learning if the pupils master the simple tasks first. A neural network simulation by Elman (1993) demonstrated a case in which the easy-before-hard sequence is not only helpful but necessary; unless the easy learning targets are mastered first, the model cannot learn the hard ones.

Although the easy-before-hard principle is well established, the existence of ordering effects in cognitive change poses more specific questions. Do different learning mechanisms make divergent predictions with respect to type and magnitude of ordering effects? If so, observations of such effects might turn out to be a hitherto underutilized source of empirical constraints on psychological learning theories. Is one combination of learning mechanism more or less robust than another with respect to the sequencing of learning experiences? A better understanding of the relative strengths and weaknesses of different combinations of mechanisms might inform the design of machine learning systems. Finally, a deeper theory of ordering effects than we currently possess might allow us to go beyond the easy-before-hard principle for the sequencing of instructional experiences.

The purpose of this chapter is to derive the ordering effects implied by a learning mechanism that was not originally designed to explain such effects. In the next three sections I specify the relevant type of learning, describe a formal model, and analyze the results of simulations in which the model learned to perform a small family of related but different tasks in different orders. I end with some reflections on what we learned from this theoretical exercise.

KNOWLEDGE AND ERROR IN SKILL PRACTICE

In the unsupervised practice of a cognitive skill, a learner attempts to perform the target task but does not yet know how to do it, so he or she does not succeed. The outcomes of his or her actions constitute feedback from the task environment. Reflecting on those outcomes, the learner comes to do the task correctly over a sequence of trials. The principle of a zone of proximal change applies: At each moment in time, during each practice trial, the learner can make only a small change in his or her current strategy for the target task.

Popular wisdom, such as it is, holds that learning is most efficient when learners are given positive rather than negative feedback, but this principle confounds motivation with information. It is probably true that praise and encouragement produce better learning than pain and punishment. But it is also true that errors and other types of undesirable outcomes constitute the main source of information for someone learning from unsupervised practice. A desired, positive, or expected outcome of a problem-solving step confirms what the learner must already know, namely that the step taken was the appropriate one at that point. An undesired, negative, or unexpected outcome, on the other hand, contains new information, and the extraction of that information is the main basis for improvements in the learner's current strategy. Interestingly, popular wisdom recognizes the power of learning from error, making such wisdom, taken in its entirety, a sure bet.

The fact that people can learn from their own errors is paradoxical. To learn from an error, the learner first has to detect it; that is, he or she has to recognize his or her action as erroneous or its outcome as different from the appropriate, correct, or expected one. But if the learner lacks the knowledge needed to avoid a particular error, then how does he or she detect that error? If knowledge of the correct action is missing, on what basis is the action recognized as erroneous? On the other hand, if a person has sufficient knowledge to recognize an action or its outcome as erroneous, then why did he or she make that error in the first place? Why not apply that knowledge so as to select a more appropriate action?

This paradox is resolved by the distinction between declarative and procedural knowledge; I prefer the term *practical knowledge* for the latter. *Declarative knowledge* about a task includes descriptions of what a good solution ought to look like, which features the relevant objects ought to exhibit at certain points in the solution, how long a solution is supposed to be in terms of steps or time, and so on. Knowledge of this sort can be used to judge the goodness of an ongoing solution attempt. *Practical knowledge* consists of knowledge about what to do—which action to take when pursuing which goal under which circumstances. The distinction between the two types of knowledge is necessary on logical grounds and is strongly supported by both behavioral data and neuroscientific evidence that show a dissociation between the ability to acquire declarative and practical knowledge in patients with localized brain damage (Squire, 1987).

Given this distinction, the ability to learn from one's own errors is not paradoxical: It is possible for a learner to possess incomplete or mistaken practical knowledge that inappropriately generates action A in situation S and at the same time possess declarative knowledge that allows him or her to judge A as an error.

Consider a case in which someone receives directions to an unfamiliar destination that includes the statement, "If you come to a bridge, you overshot your turn, and you've gone too far." When the hapless driver, no doubt already late for a dinner party, comes to the bridge, the error is easy enough to recognize. It is also obvious what to do: Stop, turn around, and search for the correct turn at the intersections already passed. Once the correct turn is identified, it becomes incorporated into the driver's procedure for getting to this particular location, and the error is unlikely to be repeated. The high probability of success for this learning event is a function of the specific nature of the learning target. What is learned is only how to get to a particular address, not a general strategy for how to get to dinner parties on time.

As a contrasting case, consider a chess player whose most valuable piece is unexpectedly zapped by the opponent's rook. The outcome is easy enough to recognize as undesirable, but what was the cause of the mishap? How should the player's strategy be revised to avoid such losses in future games? In this case, it is not useful to learn something about the specific actions taken because that particular game will never be played again. Instead, to learn means, in this case, to improve the learner's strategy for playing chess, a much more intricate mental computation. How can the learner infer exactly how his or her existing strategy should be revised to avoid similar disasters in the future? The model described in this chapter incorporates a general solution to this problem.

Although we are used to thinking about declarative knowledge as consisting of collections of *propositions*, I suggest that knowledge-based learning from error during unsupervised practice is most effective when the learner's declarative task knowledge takes the form of *constraints* on task solutions. Mathematics and the sciences abound in principles that serve as constraints: The algebraic laws of commutativity and associativity serve as constraints on the correctness of solutions to arithmetic problems; the law of conservation of mass serves as a check on the accuracy of chemical laboratory procedures; syntax rules (e. g., *a Lisp function should have as many right-hand parentheses as left-hand ones*) constrain the set of syntactically correct programs; and so on. Strong domain theories provide constraints that give the learner the power to recognize his or her errors and judge what is and what is not a correct or good task solution long before he or she has acquired sufficient practical knowledge to generate such solutions. The first contribution of the present project is a particular representation for declarative knowledge, the *state constraint*, specifically suited to support error detection.

The detection of an error is not in and of itself learning. To learn from an error is to change the underlying practical knowledge that generated the erroneous action. The question is how (by what process) the learner can translate an observation of a particular undesirable outcome into a revision of his or her practical knowledge that lowers the probability of similar outcomes in the future. How does the learner compute exactly which revision of his or her current strategy is implicated by an error he or she caught himself or herself committing? The second contribution of the present project is a domain-independent learning mechanism, *constraint-based rule specialization*, that constitutes a general and principled solution to this problem.

A MODEL OF CONSTRAINT-BASED LEARNING

The state constraint representation and the rule specialization mechanism were implemented in a computer model called HS. (The original meaning of the acronym is now only of archeological interest.) The core of the model is a standard production system architecture (Newell & Simon, 1972). To run the system, the user inputs a problem space—that is, an initial state, a set of operators, and a goal. The initial state is a description of the problem, each operator consists of an addition list and a deletion list, and the goal is a specification of a desired problem state. The second input is a set of initial production rules that include the applicability conditions for the operators but no heuristic conditions. The system solves problems by forward search through the problem space. Forward search is a weak method, but because HS searches adaptively, improving its rules even before it has found its first correct solution (Mostow & Bhatnagar, 1987), it need not search the problem space exhaustively.

To enable HS to learn, the basic production system architecture was augmented with the state constraint representation and the rule specialization mechanism. Given those two components, HS searches until it detects an error, learns from its error, backs up to the initial state, and tries anew to solve the problem. Eventually it performs the task correctly. The system was originally described in Ohlsson and Rees (1991b); see also Ohlsson (1993, 1996) for fuller conceptual expositions of the underlying principles than is possible here.

Representing Declarative Knowledge as Constraints

A piece of declarative knowledge C is represented in HS as a *state constraint,* a symbol structure that contains an ordered pair of patterns $\langle C_r, C_s \rangle$. C_r is the *relevance criterion,* and C_s is the *satisfaction criterion.* The relevance criterion specifies the set of situations in which the constraint is relevant, while the satisfaction criterion specifies in which situations the constraint is satisfied (given that it is relevant). A constraint consists of a pair of patterns because not all constraints are relevant for all problems or situations. For example, the law of commutativity of addition expressed as a state constraint becomes "if $x + y = p$ and $y + x = q$, then it ought to be the case that $p = q$." The principle of one-to-one mapping becomes "if object A has been assigned to object B, then there should not be some other object X that has also been assigned to B." The law of conservation of mass becomes "if M_1 is the mass of the ingredients in a chemical experiment, and M_2 is the mass of the products, then it ought to be the case that $M_1 = M_2$." The purpose of expressing domain knowledge in state constraints is to enable HS to identify search states that violate its knowledge of the relevant domain. This requires a matching process that can de-

cide whether a given pattern C matches a given search state S. The HS model was implemented with a RETE pattern matcher (Forgy, 1982), but the particular choice of a matching algorithm is a matter of convenience and carries no theoretical burden or implication.

Although it is convenient to express constraints in English by using the two-part if-then connective, constraints are neither inference rules nor production rules. They cannot be used to derive conclusions or to generate actions. Constraints do not specify what is true; instead, they make a conditional specification that if such and such a state of affairs holds, then such and such other assertions *ought* to be true as well; whether this is so is a matter of observation. A constraint base does not support deduction, prediction, or other classical operations over sets of propositions. Instead, it supports *judgment* (i.e., the evaluation of the current problem state as correct or incorrect, desirable or undesirable, likely or unlikely to be on a path to the goal).

Constraint-Based Error Detection

The first step in learning from an error is to detect it. The common term "error" is ambiguous. First, it can refer to the negative, undesirable, or incorrect outcome of an action taken vis-à-vis some task. Second, it can refer to the action that produced this outcome. Third, it can refer to the fault in the underlying practical knowledge that generated that action. For our present purposes, to detect an error is to evaluate an outcome as incorrect or undesirable.

In the HS system, a problem state is recognized as an error if it violates one or more constraints. When a production rule

$$P : R \Longrightarrow O$$

with condition R and action O is applied to a search state S_1, thereby generating a descendant state S_2, the relevance patterns of all of the constraints are matched against the new state S_2. If the relevance pattern C_r of constraint C does not match S_2, then C is irrelevant for that state, and no further action is taken with respect to that constraint. If C_r does match, then C is relevant, and the satisfaction pattern C_s is also matched against S_2. If C_s matches, the constraint is satisfied, and no further action is taken. However, if Cs does not match, then a constraint violation is recorded.

State constraints do not generate conclusions or trigger operators. A constraint functions as a classification device that sorts search states into those that are consistent with the principles of the domain—or the subset of the latter that are known to the learner—and those that are not. The constraints give HS the capability of detecting errors that it does not have enough practical knowledge to avoid making.

Constraint-Based Learning

The discovery of an error is not yet learning. Backing up and choosing an alternative path from a previous state in the problem space is not error correction in the sense in which that term is used in this chapter. Error correction is a revision of the underlying practical knowledge about the task—the production rules—such that the revised rules will generate fewer errors in the future than the unrevised rules would have produced. The mere detection of an error or an undesirable outcome does not in and of itself answer the question of how the relevant practical knowledge is to be revised. How can the learner's mind compute exactly which revision of a production rule is indicated by a particular error? The state constraint representation supports a precise answer to this question.

There are two types of constraint violations. Suppose that the rule

$$P : R \Longrightarrow O$$

were evoked in problem state S_1, leading to the generation of a new state, S_2. In a *Type A violation* the constraint C is irrelevant in S_1, and it is relevant but not satisfied in S_2. In a *Type B violation* C is both relevant and satisfied in S_1, and it remains relevant but is no longer satisfied in S_2. Each type of violation requires two distinct revisions of the rule P but not the same ones. The revised rules are computed in HS by regressing the constraint through the operator, but I will explain the mechanism with the help of a set-theoretic notation that shows why each type of violation gives rise to two new rules.

Revisions for Type A Violations

If the relevance pattern C_r does not match state S_1 but does match its immediate descendant, S_2, then the effect of operator O is to create working memory elements that enable C_r to match. But because, ex hypothesi, the constraint C is violated in S_2, O does not create the elements needed to complete the match for the satisfaction pattern C_s.

For example, the rule might be "if the goal is to store grocery items, item X remains to be stored, and there is a storage space S, then store X in S"; more colloquially, "put X anywhere." A relevant constraint might be "if item X is perishable and stored in location S, then it ought to be the case that S is the refrigerator." Grabbing the milk and shoving it into the pantry creates the situation: "The milk is perishable; the milk is stored in S; and S is the pantry," which violates the constraint.

This situation warrants two different revisions of the rule P that fired O. First, the condition of P should be revised so that the revised rule—call it P'—matches only in situations in which O does not complete the relevance pattern for C, thus ensuring that the constraint remains irrelevant. Second, the condition of P should be revised so that the revised rule—call it P''—fires only in those situations in which both the relevance and the satisfaction patterns of C are completed, thus ensuring that the constraint becomes satisfied.

(a) Revision 1: Ensuring that the constraint remains irrelevant. O will complete C_r when the parts of C_r that are not added by O are already present in S_1. Those parts are given by $(C_r - O_a)$, where O_a indicates the elements added to working memory by operator O and the symbol "−" signifies set difference. To limit the application of rule P to situations in which O will not complete C_r, we augment the condition of P with the *negation* of the expression $(C_r - O_a)$. The new rule is therefore

$$P' : R \ \& \ \mathbf{not}(C_r - O_a) \Longrightarrow O,$$

where "not" signifies negation and "&" signifies conjunction.

To continue the grocery example, if the action "store X in S" has the addition list, "X is stored and X is in S," and the deletion list, "X remains to be stored," then the expression $(C_r - O_a)$ turns out to be "X is perishable." Adding the negation of this expression to the condition side of the rule results in a new, more specialized rule that says, "if an item is not perishable, then store it anywhere." This rule is more specialized than the initial rule because it applies only to nonperishable items and to not items in general.

(b) Revision 2: Ensuring that the constraint becomes satisfied. To guarantee that C_r will become complete, we augment the condition R with the expression (C_r-O_a), without negating the latter. To guarantee that C_s will also become complete we augment R with those parts of C_s that are not added by O. They are given by (C_s-O_a). The desired effect is achieved by adding the entire expression $(C_r-O_a) \cup (C_s-O_a)$, where the symbol "$\cup$" signifies set union. The new rule is

$$P'' : R \cup (C_r - O_a) \cup (C_s - O_a) \Longrightarrow O$$

In the grocery example, we have already seen that (C_r-O_a) is "X is perishable." In addition, (C_s-O_a) turns out to be "S is the refrigerator." Adding these two conditions creates a revised rule that says that perishable items should be stored in the refrigerator. The learning mechanism has neatly split the space of possibilities into two subclasses, one in which it does not matter where the nonperishable item goes and one in which the perishable item must go into the refrigerator.

The two revised versions of the rule are added to the rule base, but the original rule is not deleted. At the end of this learning event, the system has three rules: P, P', and P''. Each rule may or may not be correct; if not, it will be further revised in the face of future constraint violations. For example, the first new rule might violate the constraint that nonperishable items *must not* go into the refrigerator and hence be further constrained when errors like putting the sugar in the refrigerator are detected. Repeated revisions of rules is common occurrence in runs with the HS system; see Ohlsson and Rees (1991b) for detailed examples.

Three technical points deserve mention. In order to add parts of a constraint to a rule condition, correspondences must be computed between the variables in the constraint and the variables in the rule. In HS those correspondences are computed by the standard goal regression algorithm used in many machine learning systems (Nilsson, 1980, pp. 288–289; Minton, 1988), but the choice of algorithm for this computation is a matter of convenience and carries no particular theoretical burden. A negated condition can cease to match as the result of the addition of elements to a search state. The implementation of the rule specialization algorithm in the HS system handles those cases as well. There are cases in which

one of the two revisions results in an empty list of new conditions. In those cases only one new rule is created.

Rule Revisions for Type B Violations

If the constraint C is both relevant and satisfied in state S_1 and relevant but not satisfied in S_2, the effect of operator O is to destroy the match for the satisfaction pattern C_s but not for the relevance pattern C_r. This situation also warrants two revisions of rule P.

(a) Revision 1: Ensuring that the constraint is irrelevant. Rule P is revised so that it will activate only in situations in which constraint C is not relevant and in which C will not become relevant. This is accomplished by adding the negation of the relevance pattern C_r to the condition R of the rule. The new rule is

$$P' : R \ \& \ \text{not} \ C_r \Longrightarrow O.$$

(b) Revision 2: Ensuring that the constraint remains satisfied. Rule P is revised into a rule P'' which fires only in situations in which the constraint remains satisfied. This is done in two steps. The first step is to constrain the rule to fire only in situations in which the constraint is relevant. This is accomplished by adding the relevance pattern C_r to the rule condition. The second step is to constrain the rule to situations in which the match of the satisfaction pattern is unaffected by the action of operator O. This is accomplished by adding the negation of the intersection between the satisfaction pattern and the deletion list, $\text{not}(C_s \cap O_d)$, to the rule condition, where the symbol "$\cap$" denotes set intersection. The desired effect is attained by adding the entire expression $C_r \cup \text{not}(C_s \cap O_d)$, so the new rule is

$$P'' : R \cup C_r \cup \text{not}(C_s \cap O_d) \Longrightarrow O.$$

Once again, at the end of this type of learning event, the system has three rules, the original but faulty rule P and its two descendants, P' and P''. These three rules are competing with each other during conflict resolution. Because P' and P'' are specializations of P, the condition of P is guaranteed to be satisfied in every problem state in which the conditions of P' and P'' are satisfied. However, the system keeps track of the genealogical relations, and the conflict resolution mechanism in HS prefers a descendant over the parent rule. The system applies the most specific knowledge it has available that fits. As learning progresses, the initial rules thus become roots of trees of descendants with varying levels of specificity. (For detailed displays of such rule genealogies, see Ohlsson and Rees, 1991b.) One way to visualize the action of the HS system is to imagine HS passing the description of the current search state through a rule tree, beginning with the leaves (the most specific rules) and moving toward the roots (the least specific rules) until it finds a match. The matching rule might generate the correct action, or it might produce novel errors that cause the tree to grow new branches.

Discussion

The first question regarding a model of learning is whether it passes the sufficiency test: Can it learn anything? The HS model has successfully learned correct rules for several well-known toy tasks, including the blocks world often used to test machine learning systems (Ohlsson & Rees, 1991a). Of more interest for our present purposes, it successfully learned three ecologically valid cognitive skills: to count a set of objects, a skill of much interest to researchers in cognitive development (Ohlsson & Rees, 1991b); to subtract multidigit numbers (Ohlsson, Ernst, & Rees, 1992); and to construct so-called Lewis structures, a standard ingredient in college courses in organic chemistry (Ohlsson, 1993). Constraint-based rule specialization passes the sufficiency test.

The next question is to what extent the model and its learning algorithm correspond to any process carried out by the human brain. There are supporting facts. First, the HS model produces humanlike, negatively accelerated learning curves. When combined with a strengthening mechanism for responding to positive feedback, the system reproduces the power law of learning (Ohlsson & Jewett, 1997). Second, the theory implies a particular philosophy for the design of intelligent tutoring systems, called constraint-based modeling (CBM; Ohlsson, 1992a). Multiple systems have been built according to the CBM blueprint, and the success of these systems supports the validity of the theory that underpins them (Mitrovic & Ohlsson, 1999; Mitrovic, Suraweera, Martin, & Weerasinghe, 2004). Third, the notion that declarative knowledge is encoded in constraints has turned out to be useful in explaining other cognitive phenomena, especially insight problem solving (Ohlsson, 1992b; Knoblich, Ohlsson, Haider, & Rhenius, 1999).

Finally, as I show in the next section, HS can reproduce a surprising numerical ability of young children, namely, to transfer their counting skill to nonstandard counting tasks.

The HS system is similar in basic conception to the FAILSAFE system described by Mostow and Bhatnagar (1987) and Bhatnagar and Mostow (1990). Both systems learn practical knowledge during forward search by using the information in failed solution attempts to revise the rules that generated those attempts. Both systems encode domain knowledge as constraints on correct solutions, and they both use regression to identify new rule conditions. However, there are also some differences. Where the HS system identifies a sufficient condition for failure and adds the negation of that condition to a rule, the FAILSAFE system identifies a necessary condition for failure and encodes it in a censor rule that rejects certain problem-solving steps. The major differences between HS and FAILSAFE concern the role of the domain theory. In the FAILSAFE system, as in Prodigy (Minton, 1988), the domain theory is used to construct an explanation for a detected failure. It is not used to recognize that a failure has occurred. In HS the constraints are used both to recognize a failure and to correct it, but HS does not construct an explicit explanation for the failure.

Psychological models of learning do not usually address the problem of the cognitive function of general declarative knowledge in skill acquisition. One exception is the ACT* theory proposed by Anderson (1983), the predecessor to the ACT-R theory (Anderson & Lebière, 1998). The former theory claimed that declarative knowledge structures are proceduralized during problem solving. The main difference between proceduralization and constraint-based specialization is that, in proceduralization, declarative knowledge participates only in the creation of initial rules; further improvement of those rules is handled by empirical learning mechanisms: generalization, discrimination, composition, and strengthening. In constraint-based specialization, declarative knowledge continues to influence rule revisions during the lifetime of the rule. The planning net model of counting competence proposed by Greeno, Riley, and Gelman (1984) and Smith, Greeno, and Vitolo (1989) addresses the same phenomenon as the HS system—children's flexibility in moving between different counting tasks—and their model also assumes that declarative knowledge of the counting principles is the source of this flexibility.

However, they characterize their model as a competence model, which makes it unclear how to compare it to a process model like HS.

ORDERING EFFECTS IN CONSTRAINT-BASED LEARNING

The HS model was designed as a vehicle for exploring the role of declarative knowledge in learning from error. The design was not guided by questions about ordering effects. Children's counting provides an opportunity to derive the ordering effects implied by its learning mechanism. Observations of children show that they understand the principles that underlie counting (Gelman & Gallistel, 1978; Gelman & Meck, 1986). Children learn to count collections of objects even without explicit instruction, and what they learn is a procedure for counting a collection of any size. Although counting is a simple task, it is worth noting that it involves an iterative loop, and the fact that it has to apply to collections of any size, containing objects of any type, implies that the procedure is abstract. Explaining the construction of an abstract, iterative procedure through unsupervised practice is a nontrivial theoretical challenge.

Modifying slightly the analysis by Gelman and Gallistel (1978), Ohlsson and Rees (1991b) identified three counting principles: (a) the *regular traversal* principle, which says that correct counting begins with unity and generates the natural numbers in numerical order; (b) the *one-one mapping* principle, which says that each object should be assigned exactly one number during counting; and (c) the *cardinality* principle, which says that the last number to be assigned to an object during counting represents the numerosity of the counted collection. These three principles form the conceptual basis of the procedure for standard counting, in which the objects are counted in any order. They are easily translated into state constraints (for the formal details, see Ohlsson and Rees, 1991b).

To probe children's understanding of numbers in general and counting in particular, Gelman and Gallistel (1978) invented two nonstandard counting tasks: *ordered counting*, in which the objects are counted in some predefined order (e.g., from left to right, or all blue objects before all yellow ones), and *targeted counting*, in which the objects are counted in such a way that a designated object is assigned a designated number. (Gelman and Gallistel referred to the latter as "constrained counting," but I use a different term here to avoid burdening the term "constrained" with too many meanings.) These three counting tasks require different procedures, but all three procedures are based on the three counting principles.

Simulation Experiments

HS can learn to count. The input to the system consists of a problem space for counting, state constraint representations of the counting principles, and an initial set of rules. The representation for the counting task used in the simulations reported below is fine grained. For example, the operations of setting and retracting goals are treated as search steps. In this fine-grained representation, counting three objects requires 48 steps through the problem space. Because the initial rules are minimal, containing only the applicability conditions for their actions but no heuristic conditions, the branching factor before learning is between two and four, giving a search space of more than 60×10^9 states. This search problem is too large to solve by brute force, but because HS searches adaptively, the system is nevertheless successful.

Table 11.1 shows three measures of the amount of work required to learn each counting procedure. The number of rule revisions reflects how much cognitive change had to happen for the system to master the task. This number is approximately the same (either 11 or 12) for each procedure when starting from scratch. The number of rule revisions is an order of magnitude lower than the number of production system cycles or the number of search states visited, so HS predicts that the density of learning events during skill practice is low, consistent with observations by VanLehn (1991).

The number of problem states visited is a measure of the selectivity of the system's search behavior.

TABLE 11.1. Three Measures of the Initial Learning Effort of HS for Three Counting Tasks

	Effort Measure		
Counting Task	Rule Revisions	Production System Cycles	Search States
Standard	12	854	979
Ordered	11	262	294
Targeted	12	451	507

During learning, this number is less than 10^3, so the system needs to visit only a small portion of the total problem space; 1/600 of 1%, to be exact. The ability to modify a procedure adaptively before the first correct answer has been found enables the system to focus.

The number of production system cycles is a measure of how much cognitive work is required to perform a task. This is the theoretical variable that we would estimate with solution times and subjective ratings of cognitive load. In terms of the number of production system cycles, standard counting requires more effort to learn than targeted counting, which in turn requires more effort than ordered counting. The differences in these numbers are large, up to three orders of magnitude. An agent who learns via rule specialization needs to do less cognitive work to master a more constrained task.

The question is what happens when a learner who has already mastered one of these counting tasks is asked to learn another one. First, what happens when the learner is a child? Observations of children show that they are able to switch from standard counting to either of the two nonstandard counting tasks (Gelman & Gallistel, 1978; Gelman & Meck, 1986). It requires no explicit teaching; once told what the new task is, children can work out how to do it, sometimes with very little cognitive work. This flexibility contrasts with many studies of transfer in adults in which researchers see less transfer than they expect (e.g., Cormier & Hagman, 1987; Detterman & Sternberg, 1993). A plausible explanation for children's flexibility in the case of counting is that children do indeed possess a mental representation of the counting principles and that they adapt their counting procedures to new task demands on the basis of that knowledge.

Second, what happens when the learner is HS? To answer this, we performed six simulation experiments. In each experiment, the system first mastered one of the three counting tasks from scratch. Once the system had mastered the initial task, we gave it counting problems of a different type. For example, having mastered standard counting, the system might be given targeted counting problems. There are three different pairs of tasks (standard vs. ordered, standard vs. targeted, ordered vs. targeted), and each pair can be tackled in two different orders (e.g., standard first, ordered second; or ordered first, standard second), so there are six possible task sequences. Table 11.1 shows that HS was capable of mastering each of the three counting tasks, but it does not follow that the system is

TABLE 11.2. Three Measures of the Effort Required by HS to Master the Second Task in Each of Six Different Pairs of Tasks in the Counting Domain as a Function of the Preceding Task

First Task	Second Task		
	Standard Counting	Ordered Counting	Targeted Counting
Standard			
Revisions	—	2	2
Cycles	—	110	127
States	—	119	141
Ordered			
Revisions	1	—	11
Cycles	184	—	297
States	209	—	334
Targeted			
Revisions	0	3	—
Cycles	162	154	—
States	180	190	—

able to handle each of the six sequences. The knowledge acquired in order to master the first task in a sequence might interfere with its mastery of the second one. Alternatively, learning the second task might cause the system to unlearn its ability to perform the first one.

This turned out not to be the case. HS successfully learned the second task in each sequence without losing the ability to perform the first one. Table 11.2 shows the amount of cognitive work required for each of the six sequences, quantified by the same three measures as in Table 11.1. The diagonal values are not filled in because they are all zeroes. The data in Tables 11.1 and 11.2 were previously reported in Ohlsson and Rees (1991a). In the following section, these raw data will be processed to answer questions about transfer and ordering effects that we did not originally consider.

Transfer Effects

The first question is whether mastery of one task affects the effort to master a subsequent task. In psychology, this is the classical question of whether prior practice on task A facilitates (or hinders, as the case might be) mastery of some other task B. This question is answered by comparing the effort to learn B from scratch and the effort to learn B after having mastered A. Such differences are traditionally called *transfer effects*, and in this context the first task in a sequence is called the *training task*, while the second one is called the *transfer task*.

Transfer effects are traditionally quantified in *savings measures*. For present purposes, I define the amount of transfer as the difference between the effort required to learn target task B from scratch and to learn B after first having mastered training task A, expressed as a percentage of the effort to learn B from scratch:

$$\text{Transfer}(A, B) = \frac{(B - B_A)}{B} \times 100,$$

where Transfer (A, B) is the amount of transfer from A to B, and B_A refers to the effort to master B, given that A has already been mastered. The amount of transfer exhibited by the HS system as computed by this formula is displayed in Table 11.3.

As Table 11.3 shows, there are transfer effects, they are positive, and they can be large. In the transfer from targeted to standard counting, no rule revisions were needed, saving 100% of the learning effort. (But not, of course, 100% of the performance effort; the task still has to be performed.) HS is able to apply what it has learned on the training task to the transfer task. Furthermore,

the transfer effect produced by one training task depends on the transfer task. For example, prior mastery of ordered counting saves 92% of the learning effort to master standard counting but only 8% of the effort to master targeted counting. In addition, the effort saved on the mastery of a given transfer task is a function of the training task. Learning standard counting instead of ordered counting first saves 83% (as compared to 8%) of the effort to learn targeted counting. In short, the knowledge of one of these tasks transfers to varying degrees to the other two tasks, and the amount of transfer to one of these tasks varies with the training task.

The transfer effects are usually but not necessarily asymmetrical; that is, the effort saved on task B by first learning A is not the same as the effort saved on A by first learning B. For example, the difference between the amount of transfer from standard to ordered counting as compared to the converse, when measured in terms of production system cycles, is 20%. The most spectacular asymmetry is between ordered versus targeted counting. When measured in terms of rule revisions, there is 8% transfer in one direction and 73% in the other. However, the transfer effects are not necessarily asymmetric; in terms of the number of problem states visited, the amount of transfer from ordered to targeted counting is very nearly the same as for the opposite direction.

The transfer effects differ depending on whether we focus on the performance measures (the number of cycles and problem states visited) or the learning measure (the number of rule revisions). The pronounced asymmetry between ordered and targeted counting is limited to the learning measure; the differences are much smaller when we look at the two performance measures. This is noteworthy because empirical measures of human behavior necessarily confound performance and learning.

Which factor determines the amount of asymmetry between the transfer in the two directions? The three counting procedures form a sequence, with the standard counting being the least constrained (it does not matter which number is assigned to which object), targeted counting somewhat more constrained (it matters only to which object the designated number is assigned), and ordered counting being the most constrained (the assignment matters for all of the numbers). Table 11.3 shows that there is less transfer between the two constrained counting procedures than between standard counting and either of the more constrained ones.

TABLE 11.3. Transfer Effects, Expressed as Percent Savings, for Three Measures

Training Task	Transfer Task		
	Standard Counting (percentage)	Ordered Counting (percentage)	Targeted Counting (percentage)
Standard			
Revisions	—	81	83
Cycles	—	58	72
States	—	60	72
Ordered			
Revisions	92	—	8
Cycles	78	—	34
States	79	—	34
Targeted			
Revisions	100	73	—
Cycles	81	41	—
States	81	35	—

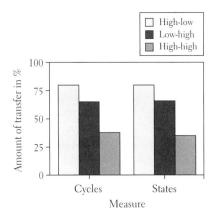

FIGURE 11.1. The average amount of transfer for pairs of tasks in which the training task is more constrained than the transfer task (high-low), the training task is less constrained than the transfer task (low-high), and pairs in which both tasks are highly constrained but in different ways (high-high).

Indeed, it turns out that a more specific regularity can be revealed by classifying each transfer into three categories: (a) from a more constrained to a less constrained task; (b) from a less constrained task to a more constrained one; and (c) from one highly constrained task to another, differently constrained task. Of the six transfer relations, two fall into each of these three categories. Averaging the amount of transfer over both instances of each category brings out the regularity; see Figure 11.1. Transfer from a less constrained to a more constrained task is large; transfer in the opposite direction is smaller; and transfer between two tasks constrained in qualitatively different ways is smaller still.

Ordering Effects

The second question we can answer on the basis of the raw data in Tables 11.1 and 11.2 is whether there

are *ordering effects*. That is, for any two tasks A and B, does it matter whether they are mastered in the order A-B or in the order B-A? To answer this question, we compared the total effort required to learn *both* tasks in either of the two different orders. We computed the total amount of cognitive effort needed to master both tasks in a pair by summing the effort needed to master the first task in the pair from scratch (Table 11.1) and the effort required to master the second task, when it is learned after the first (Table 11.2). Second, we display those amounts side by side for the two possible orders for each pair (see Table 11.4). The two possible orders for each pair are arbitrarily labeled Order 1 and Order 2. Order 1 is the order shown in the first column in the table; Order 2 is the opposite. The column labeled Ratio contains the ratios of the effort for Order 1 to the effort for Order 2. A ratio of 1.0 means that the effort was the same regardless of the order in which the two tasks in the pair were tackled (i.e., it indicates a lack of ordering effect). Values higher or lower than unity indicate that order did matter.

Table 11.4 shows that rule specialization produces large ordering effects in the counting domain. Focusing first on the two performance measures—cycles and states visited—and the first pair, standard versus ordered, it turns out that it requires more than twice as much effort to master standard plus ordered counting if standard is learned first than if ordered is learned first. The ordering effect for standard plus targeted counting is smaller but still substantial and similarly consistent across both measures. In contrast, the two nonstandard counting tasks, ordered and targeted counting, exhibit a small ordering effect on the performance measures; the relevant ratios are 0.90 and 0.92. If we recall that standard counting is the least constrained, targeted counting more so, and ordered counting the most constrained of the three, the trend in columns four and seven is that, when the two tasks

TABLE 11.4. Ordering Effects for Each of Six Different Two Task Sequences

Task Pair	Production Cycles			Problem States			Rule Revisions		
	Order			Order			Order		
	1	2	Ratio	1	2	Ratio	1	2	Ratio
Standard/ordered	964	446	2.23	1098	503	2.18	14	12	1.17
Standard/targeted	995	613	1.62	1120	687	1.63	14	12	1.17
Ordered/targeted	559	605	0.92	628	697	0.90	22	15	1.47

in a pair differ in how constrained they are (standard vs. ordered), then the ordering effects are large; when the difference is not so large (standard vs. targeted), the ordering effect is smaller; finally, when the two tasks in a pair are both constrained (ordered vs. targeted), it matters less which is learned first.

However, the learning measure—the number of rule revisions—does not exhibit this same progression. Instead, the first two pairs in the table exhibit a smaller ordering effect than the ordered versus targeted pair. Both of these pairs require more rule revisions than any order of the other two pairs, and it matters whether ordered or targeted is learned first.

The different outcomes for performance and learning measures is not paradoxical. Depending on the structure of the problem space, it may take more or fewer system cycles before the system has experienced enough errors to be able to construct the correct procedure. In a less constrained task, it may take longer before an error is discovered, while a strongly constrained task like ordered counting reveals errors very quickly. Because there are several constraints, unlearning the errors requires more learning events. The result is that there is less search but more learning, precisely the pattern we see in Table 11.4.

Relationship Between Transfer and Ordering Effects

The results of the counting simulations showed that there are transfer effects, that the transfer effects can be either symmetric or asymmetric, and that there are order effects. What is the relationship between these effects?

If $E(X)$ is the effort of acquiring strategy X from scratch, p_{XY} is the proportion of the effort to learn Y from scratch that is saved by transfer from X, then the magnitude of the ordering effect for the pair $\{X, Y\}$ is given by

$$
\begin{aligned}
\text{OrderEffect}(\{X,Y\}) &= E(\langle X,Y \rangle) - E(\langle Y,X \rangle) \\
&= [E(X) + (1 - p_{XY})E(Y)] \\
&\quad - [E(Y) + (1 - p_{YX})E(X)] \\
&= E(X) + E(Y) - p_{XY}E(Y) \\
&\quad - E(Y) - E(X) + p_{YX}E(X) \\
&= p_{YX}E(X) - p_{XY}E(Y), \qquad (1)
\end{aligned}
$$

where $\langle X, Y \rangle$ symbolizes a learning scenario in which X is learned before Y.

Equation 1 shows that the ordering effect is a function of both the amount of asymmetry of the transfer and also the effort required to solve each task from scratch. If the effort to learn X from scratch is equal to the effort to learn Y from scratch, $E(X) = E(Y)$, then there will be ordering effects if and only if the transfer effects are asymmetric. If the transfer effects are symmetric, $p_{YX} = p_{XY}$, then the magnitude of the ordering effect is only a function of the amount of effort required to learn each strategy from scratch. When neither equality holds, the magnitude of the ordering effect is a function of all four variables. Nonzero ordering effects do not necessarily result from unequal initial efforts and unequal transfer effects. For any given values of p_{XY} and p_{YX} there are values of $E(X)$ and $E(Y)$ such that the ordering effect for $\{X, Y\}$ is zero.

DISCUSSION

The theory of learning from error rests on two conceptual advances. The first is the idea of encoding declarative knowledge in terms of constraints rather than propositions. A constraint base supports the evaluation of the outcomes of the tentative actions a learner performs during practice. The second advance is the specification of a learning mechanism, constraint-based rule specialization, that translates an undesirable outcome or other type of negative feedback into a specific revision of the responsible strategy.

The transfer and ordering effects observed in the simulations arise in the interaction between the rule specialization mechanism and the differences between the relevant tasks. For any pair of tasks A and B, if A is the less constrained, then learning B before A will allow the learner to master the two tasks with less cognitive work than if he or she tackles them in the opposite order. The reason is as follows: A second task that is different but less constrained is one in which the production rules learned for the first task in the sequence do not apply, but the less specific rules that they were derived from might. It is crucial for this effect that old rules not be replaced during learning; instead, the entire genealogy of a rule stays in memory, with the earlier versions having less priority during conflict resolution than the later ones. This ensures the application of the most specific task knowledge that fits the task at hand. When that is not the latest (and therefore the most specific) version of the rule at hand, the system backs up in the genealogy to find the most specific rule that does fit. If that rule does not have to be modified (or modified only slightly) to suffice for the new task, then the prior learning of the more constrained task has in effect prepared for the mastery of the less constrained task. This shows up in transfer measures as large savings.

When the order is reversed, so that the less constrained task is learned first, then the rules learned in the course of mastering the first task might apply but be in need of further specialization to achieve correct solutions in the more constrained task. The magnitude of the transfer effect in this case depends on how much more they need to be specialized. In this case, too, the interaction between the two strategies shows up in transfer measures as a large amount of positive transfer, but the reason is quite different. In this case, the correct rules for the less constrained task can serve as starting points for the development of the more specialized rules needed for the more constrained task. The magnitude of the transfer effect will depend on exactly how much more specific the rules need to be to generate the correct performance.

It is noteworthy that the savings measures of the amount of transfer are uninformative about the contrast between these two underlying processes. Backing up in a rule genealogy to find a rule that applies and specializing previously learned rules are not the same process, but when viewed through the lens of savings measures, the differences between them are reduced to differences of degree, inviting the misconception that what goes on in one case is merely a greater or lesser version of what goes on in the other. It is not clear how to untangle these matters in empirical measures of human performance.

The alternative hypothesis about transfer effects that has received the most attention in the skill acquisition literature is the idea of identical elements. Singly and Anderson (1989) updated this idea by identifying the relevant elements with production rules. According to this hypothesis, the rules that were learned in the course of mastering task A either apply or do not apply to a transfer task B. If they do, they do not have to learned anew; if they do not, then they have no impact on the mastery of a second task. This hypothesis has two peculiar features. It predicts that there will be no negative transfer. However, this flies in the face of everyday experience: American drivers who rent a car in England are highly likely to turn on the windshield wipers when they intend to turn on the turn signal. That such capture errors slow down the

mastery of novel tasks is hardly to be doubted (Reason, 1990). Thus, the relationship between the mastery of task A and task B cannot be reduced to the mere reuse of existing rules.

The second peculiar feature of the identical rules theory is that it predicts symmetrical transfer: The magnitude of the transfer effect in switching from A to B should be exactly the same as the magnitude of the effect in switching from B to A because the set of identical rules is the same in both cases, so the number of rules that do not have to be learned because they are already known is the same in both cases. Because asymmetric transfer is a necessary prerequisite for ordering effects when the efforts of learning two strategies from scratch are equal, the identical rules theory and its parent, the identical elements hypothesis, cannot account for all of the ordering effects.

Like the identical elements hypothesis, the hypothesis that transfer effects are mediated by analogies predicts symmetrical transfer effects because the degree of analogical match between A and B is the same as the degree of analogical match between B and A. The constraint-based learning hypothesis, in contrast, predicts that transfer effects are asymmetrical when the tasks are related but one is more constrained than the other; in such cases, there will be ordering effects even when the initial efforts are equal. Empirical data are not available at this point to evaluate these contrasting predictions.

The constraint-based learning mechanism is more closely related to the idea that transfer effects happen because knowledge is, to some extent, abstract, and an abstraction can apply to some future task or situation that the learner has not encountered at the time of learning. The application of minimally specialized rules to a new task appears at first glance to be a process of the same kind because a minimally specialized rule seems analogous to an abstract concept or principle.

On closer inspection, the relation between specialization and abstraction is not simple. A rule with two elements E_1 and E_2 in its condition side is less specialized than a rule with the three elements E_1, E_2, and E_3, regardless of the level of abstraction at which those condition elements are expressed. If E_3 is expressed at the same level of abstraction as E_1 and E_2, then the abstraction levels of the two rules are equal, but the second rule is more specialized. The two dimensions are not entirely separate: If we reformulate E_1 and E_2 at a higher level of abstraction (without adding or removing any of the condition elements), then the rule is once again less specialized. Specialization is affected not only by the abstraction level of the rule conditions but also by the number of different conditions. Exactly how to test such subtle details of a learning mechanism against empirical data is an open question.

Continued exploration of constraint-based specialization might proceed along multiple tracks:

(a) We do not know how constraint-based specialization might interact with the special features of cognitive architectures less bland than HS. Reimplementation within ACT-R (Anderson & Lebière, 1998), Soar (Newell, 1990), or Icarus (Langley, McKusick, Allen, Iba, & Thompson, 1991) would throw light on this question.

(b) The generality of the learning mechanism needs to be investigated by verifying that it is sufficient for the acquisition of successful rule sets in additional domains.

(c) Order effects can be investigated by presenting tasks in different orders in those domains.

(d) Other types of ordering effects might appear if the system is given the constraints, as opposed to the tasks, in different orders rather than all at once.

(e) Comparisons between empirically observed order effects and model effects would be informative.

(f) The type of learning investigated in this chapter should be thought of as one learning mechanism in a repertoire of mechanisms. We should ask not only what kind of ordering effects are associated with this type of learning but also what ordering effects will emerge from the interactions of multiple mechanisms.

Opportunities abound for future explorations.

ACKNOWLEDGMENTS

This chapter builds on the raw simulation data previously reported in Ohlsson and Rees (1991a). Ernest Rees implemented the HS system and ran the simulations. He is not responsible for any errors in the additional data analysis and interpretations reported here. The implementation of the HS model was supported by ONR grant N00014-89-J-1681 and by the Xerox University Grant to the University of Pittsburgh. Preparation of this chapter was supported in part by ONR grant N00014-00-1-0640. The opinions expressed do not necessarily reflect the position of the sponsoring agencies, and no endorsement should be inferred.

References

Anderson, J. R. (1983). *The architecture of cognition.* Cambridge, MA: Harvard University Press.

Anderson, J. R., & Lebière, C. (1998). *The atomic components of thought.* Mahwah, NJ: Erlbaum.

Bhatnagar, N., & Mostow, J. (1990). Adaptive search by online explanation-based learning of approximate negative heuristics. In *Proceedings of the AAAI 90 Conference* (pp. 895–901). Menlo Park, CA: AAAI Press.

Cormier, S. M., & Hagman, J. D. (Eds.). (1987). *Transfer of learning.* San Diego: Academic Press.

Detterman, D. K., & Sternberg, R. J. (Eds.). (1993). *Transfer on trial.* Norwood, NJ: Ablex.

Elman, J. L. (1993). Learning and development in neural networks: The importance of starting small. *Cognition, 48,* 71–99.

Fitts, P. M. (1964). Perceptual-motor skill learning. In A. W. Melton (Ed.), *Categories of human learning* (pp. 243–285). New York: Academic Press.

Forgy, C. L. (1982). Rete: A fast algorithm for the many pattern/many object pattern match problem. *Artificial Intelligence, 19,* 17–37.

Gagné, R. M. (1965). *The conditions of learning.* New York: Holt, Rinehart, & Winston.

Gelman, R., & Gallistel, C. R. (1978). *The child's understanding of number.* Cambridge, MA: Harvard University Press.

Gelman, R., and Meck, E. (1986). The notion of principle: The case of counting. In J. H. Hiebert (Ed.), *Conceptual and procedural knowledge: The case of mathematics* (pp. 29–57). Hillsdale, NJ: Erlbaum.

Greeno, J. G., Riley, M. S., & Gelman, R. (1984). Conceptual competence and children's counting. *Cognitive Psychology, 16,* 94–143.

Knoblich, G., Ohlsson, S., Haider, H., & Rhenius, D. (1999). Constraint relaxation and chunk decomposition in insight problem solving. *Journal of Experimental Psychology: Learning, Memory, and Cognition, 25,* 1534–1555.

Langley, P., McKusick, K. B., Allen, J. A., Iba, W. F., & Thompson, K. (1991). A design for the Icarus architecture. *SIGART Bulletin, 2,* 104–109.

Minton, S. (1988). *Learning search control knowledge: An explanation-based approach.* Boston: Kluwer.

Mitrovic, A., & Ohlsson, S. (1999). Evaluation of a constraint-based tutor for a data-base language. *International Journal of Artificial Intelligence in Education, 10,* 238–256.

Mitrovic, A., Suraweera, P., Martin, B., & Weerasinghe, A. (2004). DB-Suite: Experiences with three intelligent, web-based database tutors. *Journal of Interactive Learning Research, 15,* 409–432.

Mostow, J., and Bhatnagar, N. (1987). Failsafe: A floor planner that uses EBG to learn from its failures. In *Proceedings of the International Joint Conference on Artificial Intelligence* (pp. 249–255), Milan, Italy, August.

Newell, A. (1990). *Unified theories of cognition.* Cambridge, MA: Harvard University Press.

Newell, A., & Simon, H. A. (1972). *Human problem solving.* Englewood Cliffs, NJ: Prentice-Hall.

Nilsson, N. J. (1980). *Principles of artificial intelligence.* Los Altos, CA: Morgan-Kaufmann.

Ohlsson, S. (1992a). Constraint-based student modeling. *International Journal of Artificial Intelligence in Education*, 3(4), 429–447.

Ohlsson, S. (1992b). Information processing explanations of insight and related phenomena. In M. Keane and K. Gilhooly, (Eds.), *Advances in the psychology of thinking* (Vol. 1, pp. 1–44). London: Harvester-Wheatsheaf.

Ohlsson, S. (1993). The interaction between knowledge and practice in the acquisition of cognitive skills. In A. Meyrowitz and S. Chipman (Eds.), *Foundations of knowledge acquisition: Cognitive models of complex learning* (pp. 147–208). Norwell, MA: Kluwer.

Ohlsson, S. (1996). Learning from performance errors. *Psychological Review*, 103, 241–262.

Ohlsson, S., Ernst, A. M., & Rees, E. (1992). The cognitive complexity of doing and learning arithmetic. *Journal for Research in Mathematics Education*, 23, 441–467.

Ohlsson, S., & Jewett, J. J. (1997). Ideal adaptive agents and the learning curve. In J. Brzezinski, B. Krause, & T. Maruszewski (Eds.), *Idealization VIII: Modelling in psychology* (pp. 139–176). Amsterdam: Rodopi.

Ohlsson, S., & Rees, E. (1991a). Adaptive search through constraint violations. *Journal of Experimental and Theoretical Artificial Intelligence*, 3, 33–42.

Ohlsson, S., & Rees, E. (1991b). The function of conceptual understanding in the learning of arithmetic procedures. *Cognition and Instruction*, 8, 103–179.

Reason, J. (1990). *Human error.* New York: Cambridge University Press.

Ritter, F. E., & Bibby, P. (2001). Modeling how and when learning happens in a simple fault-finding task. In *Proceedings of ICCM 2001: Fourth International Conference on Cognitive Modeling* (pp. 187–192). Mahwah, NJ: Erlbaum.

Singley, M. K., & Anderson, J. R. (1989). *The transfer of cognitive skill.* Cambridge, MA: Harvard University Press.

Smith, D. A., Greeno, J. G., & Vitolo, T. M. (1989). A model of competence for counting. *Cognitive Science*, 2, 183–211.

Squire, L. R. (1987). *Memory and brain.* New York: Oxford University Press.

VanLehn, K. (1991). Rule acquisition events in the discovery of problem-solving strategies. *Cognitive Science*, 15, 1–47.

Vygotsky, L. S. (1978). *Mind in society.* Cambridge, MA: Harvard University Press.

Part III

Getting In and Out of Order: Techniques and Examples From Education and Instructional Design

Chapter 12

Getting Out of Order: Avoiding Lesson Effects Through Instruction

Kurt VanLehn

Procedures, such as those used for solving arithmetic or algebra problems, often have subprocedures that are disjunctively related. That is, either one subprocedure or the other is applied at a given time, but not both. When textbooks teach such procedures, they often arrange the instruction so that disjunctively related subprocedures are taught in separate lessons. This suggests that instruction that obeys the one-disjunct-per-lesson constraint is more effective than instruction that teaches two or more disjunctively related subprocedures in the same lesson. This hypothesis was tested in two experiments. Young children were taught multiple-digit multiplication using a training sequence that either did or did not conform to the one-disjunct-per-lesson constraint. The expected effect did not appear, perhaps due to the use of tutoring instead of normal classroom instruction. Unexpectedly, it was found that on one measure, the students taught both subprocedures in the same lesson learned more than those taught the subprocedures in different lessons.

While constructing a model of arithmetic skill acquisition (VanLehn, 1987, 1990), I noticed that arithmetic textbooks obey a convention that I call *one disjunct per lesson*. If the procedure to be taught has two or more subprocedures that are disjunctively related (either one or the other is used but not both), then the textbooks introduce at most one of these subprocedures per lesson (see VanLehn, 1990, for a formal definition of disjunctively related subprocedures). For instance, the procedure for subtracting multidigit whole numbers has three disjunctively related subprocedures for processing a column:

1. If the column has just a single digit, write it in the answer.
2. If the column's top digit is smaller than the bottom digit, then borrow.
3. Otherwise, take the difference between the column's two digits and write the answer.

In the problem $371 - 29$, the second subprocedure is used on the units column, the third is used on the tens column, and the first is used on the hundreds column.

In order to illustrate the one-disjunct-per-lesson convention, suppose that students have mastered the third subprocedure but have not yet been introduced to the first two. They can correctly solve $56 - 23$ but not $56 - 3$, whose solution utilizes the first subprocedure; nor can they solve $56 - 29$, whose solution utilizes the second subprocedure; they also cannot solve $56 - 9$, whose solution utilizes both subprocedures. One could write a textbook that introduces both subprocedures 1 and 2 in the same lesson. It could, for instance, use the three problems just mentioned. Such a textbook would violate the one-disjunct-per-lesson convention.

I examined textbooks from Heath and Scotts Foreman (because their texts were used by the schools involved in the study) and from three other major publishers. In only one case was there any doubt about conformance with the convention. In the third-grade book of the 1975 Scotts Foresman series, there is a two-page lesson that introduces subprocedure 1 on one page and subprocedure 2 on the other. Whether this actually violates the one-disjunct-per-lesson convention depends on how "lesson" is defined, an issue that I discuss at length later. However, except for this one case, all of the other cases of subprocedure introduction took place in a lesson that introduced just one subprocedure.

Why would there be such conformance to the one-disjunct-per-lesson convention? Arithmetic textbooks have evolved over the past two centuries under the influence of many theories, experimental results, and practical experiences. Although the convention could simply be a fad among textbook designers, it is more likely that textbooks are written in conformance with conventions that facilitate learning. This would explain the ubiquity of the one-disjunct-per-lesson pattern.

Why would teaching at most one disjunct per lesson facilitate learning? Several possible explanations come to mind. Perhaps teaching two subprocedures makes the explanations more complex and presumably more difficult to understand. The text (and teacher) would have to say, "Today we're going to learn two things. The first is X, which you should use only when A. The second is Y, which you should use only when B." Further descriptions of the two subprocedures should always be prefaced by a remark indicating which subprocedure is being described. In order to avoid such complex explanations, textbook writers might obey the one-disjunct-per-lesson convention.

Another possibility is that having two subprocedures in the same lesson makes it hard to learn from examples. Students sometimes answer exercise problems by finding a similar exercise in the book that has already been solved, then mapping the solution over to their own problem (Anderson, Farrell, & Saurers, 1985; Chi, Bassok, Lewis, Reimann, & Glaser, 1989; Pirolli & Anderson, 1985; VanLehn, 1998). If this learning process is the one used for arithmetic, then a curriculum that puts two or more subprocedures in a lesson is going to make the students' task harder. They will have two types of solved exercises in the lesson, and they will have to decide which to use as the source for their analogical problem solving. If they decide incorrectly, they may develop misconceptions. On the other hand, if all of the lessons have just one subprocedure in them, then the students do not have to make a choice. They simply refer to any of the solved examples in the lesson. In short, regardless of whether students pay more attention to the examples or the

linguistic descriptions, it appears that introducing more than one disjunct in the same lesson harms the ability of the lesson to communicate the new material to the students.

Another possible explanation for the one-disjunct-per-lesson pattern is that instruction involves the communication of information, so the instruction should have conventions that govern it since other forms of communication between people seem to. The fact that the students and teachers do not have conscious access to the rules governing the communication between them is not an argument that such rules do not exist. In fact, it is circumstantial evidence that such rules *do* exist because the rules of human communication are often not available to introspection. In honor of some famous tacit conventions in natural language conversation, Austin's (1962) *felicity conditions*, the conjecture that there might be tacit conventions governing instruction is called the *felicity conditions conjecture* (VanLehn, 1987, 1990).

Finally, there are some formal results in learning theory that indicate the value of felicity conditions and the one-disjunct-per-lesson constraint in particular. Valiant's (1984) criterion is held to be an excellent definition of what it means to learn a concept from examples in a reasonable amount of time. Although the theory has not yet tackled concepts as complex as arithmetic procedures, simpler concepts have produced some negative results. Valiant (1984) presents strong evidence of the intractability of learning unconstrained Boolean functions (a Boolean function is a nested expression in propositional logic, containing just AND, OR, and NOT). The class of procedures subsumes the class of Boolean functions (because a sequence of actions is like an AND expression and a conditional branch is like an OR expression). So Valiant's evidence implies that procedure learning is also intractable.

However, Valiant concludes that, "If the class of learnable concepts is as severely limited as suggested by our results, then it would follow that the only way of teaching more complicated concepts is to build them up from some simple ones. Thus a good teacher would have to identify, name and sequence these intermediate concepts in the manner of a programmer" (Valiant 1984, p. 1135). Rivest and Sloan (1988) point out that having the teacher actually identify, name, and sequence the subconcepts makes learning easy, but it places a great burden on the teacher. They present an algorithm that eases the load on the teacher but still ensures successful learning. Their algorithm can learn any concept that can be represented as a Boolean function, with the help of a teacher who breaks the concept into subconcepts and teaches one subconcept per lesson, where a subconcept corresponds to a conjunction or disjunction in the Boolean expression. This is based, of course, on a type of felicity condition that is quite similar to the one-disjunct-per-lesson condition.

In short, there are at least three general perspectives that offer explanations for the one-disjunct-per-lesson convention:

- the cognitive perspective: The student's mental processes for comprehending lesson material must do more work in order to correctly understand a lesson with more than one disjunct. If this work is not done or is not done properly, misconceptions may develop.
- the social perspective: The classroom is a society that has persisted long enough to develop its own special conventions (called felicity conditions) for facilitating social discourse. One disjunct per lesson is a felicity condition.
- the computational perspective: Learning from examples is governed by the mathematical laws that determine the amount of computation necessary for success given the richness of the information accompanying the examples. A significant decrease in computation results from organizing a sequence of examples into lessons in such a way that only one disjunct is introduced per lesson.

Despite these motivations, regardless of whether the one-disjunct-per-lesson convention actually facilitates learning is an open empirical question. The simplest test would be a two-condition training experiment in which one condition's training material violates the one-disjunct-per-lesson convention and the other condition's training material obeys it. This chapter reports the results of two such experiments.

All three perspectives sanction the one-disjunct-per-lesson convention, but they give no explicit predictions about what students will do if forced to learn from material that violates the convention. Thus, the experiments were exploratory. The basic idea was simply to videotape the students as they learned and see

whether meaningful measures could be derived post hoc from transcripts of the training sessions. Protocol analysis has often been successfully used for exploratory studies of complex tasks.

Another design consideration was ecological validity. One of the strong points of the earlier study (VanLehn, 1990) is that it used real teachers teaching real students. In this experiment, an unusual curriculum was to be presented. Because it would not be ethical to use classroom teaching that is believed to be worse that normal classroom instruction, one-on-one tutoring was used. This would allow the tutor to correct, during the final session, any misconceptions that were acquired during the earlier sessions.

The need for verbal protocols suggested using older subjects than the second graders, who would be the natural choice if the subject matter were subtraction, which was the chief topic in the earlier study. Thus, multiplication was chosen as the subject matter, because it is taught in the third, fourth, and fifth grades.

The one-disjunct-per-lesson hypothesis depends crucially on what counts as a disjunct, which in turn depends on how the knowledge is represented. To find a plausible representation for multiplication, the simulation model developed for subtraction, Sierra, was run on a lesson sequence for multiplication. Due to technical difficulties, it could not complete the last lesson. (see VanLehn, 1987, for discussion). However, a fairly complete representation was obtained. Table 12.1 presents an informal, simplified rendition.

Disjunctively related subprocedures can be located in the table by finding conditional statements (the "if . . . then . . . else" statements; see VanLehn, 1990, for formal definitions). There are two conditional statements. The first one selects among the subprocedures Single-Digit-Multiply, ×N0, and ×NN. Subprocedure Single-Digit-Multiply is used for problems such as 123×6. Subprocedure ×N0 is used for problems like 123×50 and 123×500. Subprocedure ×NN is used for problems like 123×45, 123×456, 123×407, and 123×450. The second conditional statement is located inside the ×NN subprocedure. The first line of the conditional has a simple subprocedure that skips over zeros occurring in the multiplier. This would be used, for instance, in solving 123×406 and 123×450. For future reference, this subprocedure is called the skip-zero trick.

TABLE 12.1. The Multiplication Procedure Used in the Experiments

Main Procedure

If the multiplier (i.e., the bottom row) consists of a single digit, then call the subprocedure Single-Digit-Multiply (N), where N is the digit.
   Else if the multiplier contains just one nonzero digit, then call the subprocedure ×N0.
   Else call the subprocedure ×NN.

Subprocedure Single-Digit-Multiply (N)

For each digit M in the multiplicand (i.e., the top row):
   multiply M by N
   then add in the carry from the previous multiplication (if any)
   then write down the units digit of the result
   then set the carry to the tens digit (if any)

Subprocedure ×N0

For each zero in the multiplier, write down a zero in the answer.
Call the subprocedure Single-Digit-Multiply (N), where N is multiplier's nonzero digit.

Subprocedure ×NN

For each digit N in the multiplier, if N is zero, then skip it.
   Otherwise, write a zero for each digit in the multiplier to the right of N, then call the subprocedure Single-Digit-Multiply (N).
   Then add up the partial products just generated.

EXPERIMENT 1

The experiment had two main conditions, called 1D/L and 2D/L (i.e., one or two disjuncts per lesson). The training material in the 1D/L condition obeyed the one-disjunct-per-lesson convention, whereas the training material of the 2D/L condition violated it. The two disjuncts used for training were the ×N0 subprocedure and the ×NN subprocedure. In the 1D/L condition, they were taught in separate lessons. In the 2D/L condition, they were taught in the same lesson.

Logically, either the ×N0 or the ×NN subprocedure can be taught first. Thus, the presentation order (×NN/×N0 vs. ×N0/×NN) was crossed with the main manipulation, yielding four conditions. However, none of the dependent variables showed any effects for presentation order. For simplicity in the subsequent discussion of the design and results, the presentation order manipulation is ignored.

Materials

The training consisted of several lessons, each comprising the following four sections:

Review: The student reviews the preceding lesson's material by working a five-problem set.

Examples: The tutor works two examples out in detail, while the student watches and asks questions.

Samples: Two problems are worked with the tutor holding the pencil while the student tells the tutor what to write.

Practice: The student works about two pages of exercises at his or her own pace, asking questions as needed. The tutor watches carefully and interrupts whenever a nontrivial mistake is made.

There was no textbook. The tutor used only printed sheets of problems.

The training consisted of a four-lesson sequence. In both conditions, the first two lessons reviewed how to do single-digit multiplication, and the second two taught the new subprocedures, ×N0 and ×NN. In the 1D/L condition, Lesson 3 taught one subprocedure and Lesson 4 taught the other. In the 2D/L condition, Lessons 3 and 4 both taught both procedures using examples, samples, and practice exercises that alternated between ×N0 and ×NN problems.

To screen out subjects who already knew the target material, two trick problems were included in the review section of Lesson 3. One was an ×N0 problem, and the other was an ×NN problem. Subjects who correctly solved these problems were dropped from the experiment.

In Lesson 4, the second page of exercises for the practice section was actually (unbeknownst to the student) a page of transfer problems whose multipliers had a mixture of zeros and nonzero digits (e.g., ×N0N, ×NN0N, ×N00N). The purpose of these exercises was to see whether the students could invent the skip-zero trick on their own. The mathematical principles behind it had been presented as part of their instruction in the ×N0 and ×NN methods. If they really understood the two methods, they might be able to invent the skip-zero trick. Thus, the transfer section of Lesson 4 was designed to test their depth of understanding.

Subjects and Methods

Subject acquisition and retention were problematic. The experiment needed subjects who were at a particular point in their schooling and who would be willing to come to the university for four 1-hour sessions. Although the subjects were paid for their participation (one silver dollar per lesson), it was still difficult to find volunteers. The experiment ended with only 8 subjects in the 1D/L condition and 7 in the 2D/L condition. Four subjects, 1 in each condition, came from academic families whose children were in a university-run school. The rest of the subjects were recruited with newspaper advertisements.

The subjects were run individually. The sessions lasted between 45 minutes and an hour. When possible, the sessions were scheduled on 4 consecutive days. However, in some cases the last session did not occur until 2 weeks after the first. Most of the subjects were run during the summer in order to avoid intrusion from their normal mathematics classes into the experimental teaching. The subjects who were run during the school year were asked what they were learning in school; according to the subjects, multiplication was not taught in school during the course of the experiment.

Results

The experiment was designed with no specific predictions about how learning would differ among the conditions, so all of the sessions were videotaped, and Lessons 3 and 4 were transcribed.

Qualitatively, there was little apparent difference between conditions. All of the students found the learning task nontrivial, but some of them quickly assimilated the instruction and mastered the skill, whereas others never really understood the algorithm despite valiant efforts on their part and the tutor's. It did not look as though the differences in performance were caused by the conditions but rather by the individual differences among the subjects.

To quantify the degree of confusion engendered by the training, the subjects' errors were coded and counted using their worksheets and the protocol transcripts. Facts errors, (e.g., $3 \times 5 = 12$ or $7 + 9 = 13$) and errors in carrying were not counted since these skills were taught prior to the experiment. Table 12.2 lists the six error categories used. For each category,

TABLE 12.2. Protocol Coding Categories

X	Skipping a multiplier digit if it is zero Multiplying the multiplicand by zero, generating a row of zeros
S	Multiplying the multiplicand by a nonzero multiplier digit Skipping a nonzero multiplier digit
Z	Remembering to write the spacer zeros of a row Forgetting to write the spacer zeros
N	Writing the right number of spacer zeros Writing some spacer zeros but the wrong number of them
R	Moving to the next row before writing the next partial product Concatenating a partial product to the left end of the previous one
P	Remembering to add up the partial products Failing to add the partial products

the first line describes what the student should do, and the second line describes the modal error for that category. Thus, if the solution shown in following multiplication problem is generated by a student, then the count of opportunities for category X would be increased by one because the student had the opportunity to exercise the skip-over-the-zero subprocedure. However, the student did not use the skip-zero trick, so the error count for category X is also increased by one.

$$
\begin{array}{r}
123 \\
\times 201 \\
\hline
123 \\
0000 \\
+24600 \\
\hline
24723
\end{array}
$$

The term "spacer" in Table 12.2 refers to the zeros that are placed on the right end of a partial product's row. Although not all multiplication algorithms use spacers, the one taught in the experiment did.

Although these error counts could be used as the dependent measure, two aspects of the experiment suggested using a more complicated measure. Almost all of the errors were corrected, by either the tutor or the students themselves. However, some of the students tended to ask the tutor for help if they were unsure rather than make a mistake and have it corrected.

This suggests counting questions along with errors because both were probably caused by a lack of understanding.

Another consideration is that the students worked at different rates, mostly because their familiarity with the multiplication facts varied widely. Thus, it would not make sense to compare error/question counts across subjects, as the faster subjects have more opportunities to make errors and would encounter more transfer problems then slower subjects. Therefore, the number of errors and questions of each type were divided by the number of opportunities of that type. This calculation yields a rate that is similar to an error rate, except that it includes questions as well as errors. I call it a *confusion rate*. Confusion rate is the dependent measure.

If any difference between the 1D/L and 2D/L conditions is found, it could be attributed to the differences in the *amount* of teaching given to the subjects and not the organization of it into lessons. To test this, the words uttered by the tutor during the initial instruction on the algorithm were counted (the Examples sections of Lessons 3 and 4 for the 1D/L; the Examples section of Lesson 3 for 2D/L). The means (664 words for 1D/L and 520 words for 2D/L) were not significantly different.

Table 12.3 shows the main results, the confusion rates per category and section. The first two columns of figures show the confusion rates for the introductory sections of the lessons. For the 1D/L condition, the introductory sections were the Example and Sample

sections of Lesson 3. For the 2 D/L condition, the introductory sections were the Example and Sample sections of Lessons 3 and 4. The second two columns show the Practice sections of Lessons 3 and 4. The last two columns show the Transfer section of Lesson 4.

The mean confusion rates for single categories are shown in the top part of the table. The lower part shows combinations of related categories, which indicate what the results would have been if larger categories had been used. For instance, the combination of Z and N categories measures the rate of all confusions that involve spacers. The combination of S and X categories includes all confusions that mix up the ×NN method with the ×N0 method (on a narrow interpretation of "mix up"). The combination of the S, X, R, and P categories is a broader interpretation of the notion of mixing up the ×NN method with the ×N0 method. The combination confusion rates are calculated in the same way as a regular confusion rate—by dividing the number of confusions of that larger type by the number of opportunities for that type of confusion to occur. The difference between the means of the two conditions may be significant for a combination category even when the difference for the means of its constituent categories is never significant. This can occur when the category combines subjects who are high in one type of error with subjects who are high in another type; this reduces the variance, leading to significance.

In both the introductory and practice sections of the training, t-tests indicate that none of the mean

TABLE 12.3. Mean Confusion Rates During the Introductory, Practice, and Transfer Sections

Type		Intro 1D/L	Intro 2D/L	Practice 1D/L	Practice 2D/L	Transfer 1D/L	Transfer 2D/L
S	Skip nonzero digit	.276	.221	.085	.114	.426*	.063*
X	Omit skipping zero digit	.039	.142	.000	.119	.673	.300
Z	Omit spacers	.264	.148	.024?	.169?	.202	.262
N	Wrong number of spacers	.073	.033	.016?	.113?	.232	.336
R	Concatenate rows	.067	.040	.068	.146	.150	.032
P	Omit adding	.144	.071	.052	.074	.146*	.000*
Types S and X		.186	.194	.047	.116	.529**	.155**
Types Z and N		.147?	.079?	.019?	.135?	.223	.312
Types S, X, R, and P		.159	.152	.051	.118	.381**	.103**
All types		.154	.193	.037?	.113?	.309	.197

* = p < 0.05
** = p < 0.01
? = p < 0.10

confusion rates were significantly different, although there were a few marginally significant differences in the expected direction. The overall confusion rate, combining all categories in both sections, was 0.090 for the 1D/L and 0.112 for the 2D/L. This difference was not significant.

The transfer section (the last two columns of the table) exhibited an effect due to the experimental manipulation. Although the two conditions did not differ on the number of spacer errors (categories Z and N), they differed significantly on the other types (categories S, X, R, and P), which presumably are due to mixing up the ×NN and ×N0 methods. However, the trend was in the opposite direction from that predicted by the one-disjunct-per-lesson hypothesis. The 1D/L condition had a confusion rate that was three times larger than the 2D/L condition.

Discussion

The one-disjunct-per-lesson hypothesis predicts that the 1D/L students will be less confused by their training than the 2D/L students. The data did not confirm this prediction, although there was a mild trend in the expected direction.

A major effect, which was unexpected, is that the 2D/L students are better at solving transfer problems, which have multipliers of the form ×N0N, ×N0NN, ×N00N, and so on. The preponderance of errors of types S, X, R, and P indicates that 1D/L students are mixing up the ×NN and ×N0 methods. The S errors indicate that they are using the ×N0 method (or at least the skip-digit part of it) when the ×NN method is appropriate. The X errors indicate that they are using the ×NN method on zero-multiplier digits, which causes them to generate a row of zeros. If they had used a shifted-over version of the ×N0 method, they would have avoided this. In short, it seems that the 1D/L students have not learned to discriminate the conditions under which the two methods are appropriate, and this caused them to make three times as many errors during the transfer section as the 2D/L students.

One possible explanation of the main effect is that the 2D/L students were trained with a mixed drill (Quilici & Mayer, 1996), where different methods are used on different problems in the same lesson, whereas the 1D/L students were trained with a homogeneous drill, where the same method is used on every problem in a lesson. Thus, the 2D/L students had to learn *when* to apply the two methods, whereas the 1D/L students could simply use the same method they had used on the previous problem and never bother to induce the applicability conditions of the method. Thus, one would expect the mixed drill to facilitate performance on the transfer sections, where a choice between methods is necessary, and this is indeed the observed result.

EXPERIMENT 2

A possible explanation for the lack of an effect during training for the 2D/L condition is that the students understood a "lesson" to be a single example rather than a whole session/lesson. It is logically possible to define a lesson to be as small as a single example or even part of an example. In the subtraction studies of VanLehn (1990) and this study, a lesson was defined as the material taught in one class session. However, this might not be the definition that students use.[1] That is, if students had a felicity condition of one-disjunct-per-*example*, then neither the 1D/L nor the 2D/L curriculum of Experiment 1 would violate their felicity condition. This would explain why the confusion rates are not easily distinguished across conditions.

To explore this possibility, training material was constructed that attempted to teach two disjuncts in the same example and thus violate the felicity condition of students using a one-disjunct-per-example convention. This material cannot use the ×NN and ×N0 methods as its disjuncts because they require different types of problems. Thus, two new disjuncts had to be used. Unfortunately, this makes the performance on this training material incomparable with the performance of the 1D/L and 2D/L training material because it teaches a different subject matter. Although this training material was run at the same time as the other two, fewer subjects were run, and the analysis is different, so it is described as a separate experiment.

---

1. Indeed, older students would have to use smaller lessons in order to make sense of, say, high school algebra because algebra texts sometimes introduce several subprocedures (e.g., algebraic transformations) in material designed to be covered in one class period. Fortunately for the one-disjunct-per-lesson hypothesis, such material is often organized as a sequence of blocks of materials, with clearly evident boundaries between them.

Subjects and Methods

Four subjects were run, using the same subject selection procedures as in Experiment 1. The subjects were run in the same manner—in four sessions of tutorial instruction, with each session divided into four sections. As in the first experiment, the first two lessons reviewed single-digit multiplication. The new material was introduced in Lesson 3. The only difference in procedure between this experiment and Experiment 1 is the subject matter of Lessons 3 and 4.

Materials

The material in Lessons 3 and 4 was designed to teach the skip-zero trick (see Table 12.1). Except for the transfer section at the very end of the fourth session, students saw only problems whose multipliers had the form ×N0N, ×N00N, ×NN0N, and ×N0NN. On the initial example, which had the form ×N0N, the tutor verbally described the ×NN method as part of the explanation of multiplication of the multiplicand by the units digit. The rationale for the skip-zero step was explained during the multiplication by the tens digit, which is a zero. Thus, the students heard about two distinct methods for producing partial products during the initial example. They also saw instances of both disjuncts. However, the instance of the skip-zero disjunct occurred on a subproblem (i.e., the tens-digit multiply) that was different from the instances of the regular digit multiplication. Table 12.4 illustrates this with the relevant section of one of the protocols. Notice how the tutor combined the explanations for the ×NN method and the skip-zero trick.

As in Experiment 1, a transfer section was included at the end of Lesson 4. The transfer section used problems whose multipliers were of the form ×NN and ×N0.

Results

The protocols were transcribed and coded as before. Table 12.5 shows the resulting confusion rates for all three sections.

Discussion

Because this experiment taught material different from that in Experiment 1, it would not be mean-

TABLE 12.4. A Fragment of Protocol Showing the Initial Training on the xN0N Method

Tutor:	This is how you do these. [Displays worked example: 203×102.] What you were telling me first was pretty much right. First you look at the number in the ones column. [Points to the 2.] You pretend the other two aren't even there.
Subject:	Okay.
Tutor:	And then you multiply. You say, 2 times 3 is 6, 2 times 0 is 0, 2 times 2 is 4. Okay?
Subject:	Uh-huh.
Tutor:	That's the first step. Okay. Now, the way it works is this number gets its own row, which you just made, and how you move on to the next number, it gets its own row, too. You make another row. Okay? But in this case, since the tens number equals 0 [points to the zero in the multiplier], you get to skip this row. Because, see, if you multiplied the tens number, you'd say 0 times 3 is 0, 0 times 0 is 0, 0 times 2 is 0, and you'd have a whole bunch of zeros.
Subject.	Uh-huh.
Tutor:	Right. So you can skip that row. Okay. So you can move on to the hundreds number [points to the 1 in the hundreds place of the multiplier]. Okay, so now you're just looking at the hundreds number. And the only trick about this is that, when you do the ones number, you just do it like this. Okay, when you move on to the tens, what you'd do if we were going to work it out is you'd say, I have 0 ones. First, you'd put a 0 down.
Subject:	Yeah.
Tutor:	Okay. Then you'd multiply: 0 times 3 is 0, 0 times 0 is 0, 0 times 2 is 0. Now, when you move on to the hundreds, you have 0 ones and 0 tens. So you put down two zeros first. Okay? And then you multiply. You say 1 times 3 is 3, 1 times 0 is 0, 1 times 2 is 2. Okay?
Subject:	Uh-huh.
Tutor:	No.
Subject:	I don't understand.

TABLE 12.5. Mean Confusion Rates During the 2D/L Training

Type		Introductory	Practice	Transfer
S	Skip nonzero digit	.270	.093	.088
X	Omit skipping zero digit	.219	.099	.050
Z	Omit spacers	.333	.157	.192
N	Wrong number of spacers	.059	.061	.171
R	Concatenate rows	.119	.089	.083
P	Omit adding	.161	.031	.050
Types S and X		.245	.096	.069
Types Z and N		.196	.109	.182
Types S, X, R, and P		.192	.078	.068
All types		.271	.103	.124

ingful to compare their confusion rates statistically. However, it is clear that the overall confusion rates in the three sections of this experiment (Introductory: 0.271; Practice: 0.103; Transfer: 0.124) were of the same order of magnitude as the overall confusion rates for Experiment 1 (Introductory: 0.154 and 0.193; Practice: 0.037 and 0.113; Transfer: 0.309 and 0.197; for 1D/L and 2D/L, respectively). The expected aberrant behavior due to the violation of a felicity condition did not seem to occur. This confirms the subjective impression one has (on viewing the videotapes) that the students in this experiment acted just about the same as the students in Experiment 1.

GENERAL DISCUSSION

The results of Experiments 1 and 2 show that violating the one-disjunct-per-lesson (or one-disjunct-per-example) felicity condition does not lead to unusual or extraordinary learning behavior. The confusion rate data indicate that the differences between the conditions were at best marginally significant, except in the transfer section of Experiment 1. There, the 1D/L students made three times as many errors as the students in the 2D/L condition. This finding is partially consistent with a "mixed-drill" effect, which most frequently occurs when one is teaching two skills (e.g., multicolumn addition and subtraction) that have similar formats. If students are always given homogenous worksheets (e.g., either all addition or all subtraction), they will make many errors when given a test that has both addition and subtraction on it because they have not learned to pay attention to the single symbol that differentiates the two problem types. On the other hand, if students are also given training worksheets that

contain both types of problems (called "mixed drill"), they learn to differentiate the problems.

The 1D/L condition of Experiment 1 consisted of homogenous drill, and the 2D/L condition consisted of mixed drill. This predicts that students in the 2D/L condition will do better on tests that have both ×NN and ×N0 problems, just as the 2D/L condition had in its training sections. However, the transfer section of the experiment has problems that use the two different procedures within the very same problem because they have multipliers of the form ×N0N, ×N00N, ×NN0N, and ×N0NN. Although the mixed-drill effect would perhaps cause the students in the 2D/L condition to notice the zeros in the multiplier and know that different procedures should be applied, they would have to understand the procedures quite well in order to combine them appropriately. Thus, the mixed-drill effect can only partially explain the relative success of the 2D/L students in the transfer section of Experiment 1.

It may seem that the predicted effects of the felicity condition could exist but be hidden by the mixed-drill effect. However, this cannot be the case. The one-disjunct-per-lesson hypothesis predicts that the 2D/L students should be more confused by the introductory and practice sections than the 1D/L students. For the mixed-drill effect to hide the predicted effects, it would have to reduce confusion during those two sections. However, the mixed drill of the 2D/L condition should be, if anything, more confusing during the introductory and practice sections than the homogeneous drill of the 1D/L condition because the mixed-drill students need to learn more than the homogeneous drill students. The 2D/L students need to learn both *how* and *when* to do the ×NN and ×N0 methods, whereas the 1D/L students need only to learn *how* to do the methods. Thus, the mixed-drill effect should add to the confusion of the 2D/L students rather than subtracting from it. Because the 2D/L students were not significantly more confused than the 1D/L students during the introductory and practice sections, neither the felicity conditions nor the mixed-drill training seemed to have a profound effect in those sections.

A likely explanation for the lack of a felicity condition effect is that not enough subjects were run for the trend in the data to achieve statistical significance. The overall confusion rate in Experiment 1 (excluding the transfer section of Lesson 4, due to the mixed-drill effect) is 0.090 for the 1D/L condition versus 0.112 for 2D/L—a small trend that is rendered nonsignificant by the high variance among the subjects. However, my subjective impression on viewing the data tapes is that, if there is a felicity condition effect in this experiment, it is quite small in comparison to the vast individual differences among subjects. This is just what the statistics say, too.

The lack of a strong felicity condition effect is probably also due to the use of one-on-one tutoring instead of classroom instruction. It could be that students in the 2D/L condition were actually quite confused by the instruction, but the tutor was able to remedy their confusion so quickly that it did not show up in the confusion rates. Whenever a student made a serious mistake, the tutor would interrupt, correct the mistake, and explain the correction. This immediate, rich feedback means that most of the confusions introduced by the lesson material were quickly remedied.

The only kind of misconception that could escape this teaching method would be one in which an incorrect piece of knowledge happened to yield error-free performance on the training material. This may be what happened with the students in the 1D/L condition. They may have adopted the heuristic of always choosing the method that they used on the previous problem. During training, this buggy heuristic yielded correct solutions, so the tutor had no cause to interrupt and remediate. Consequently, the mistaken heuristic persisted into the transfer section, where it caused the 1D/L students to commit many errors.

On this view, the beneficial effects of one-on-one tutoring were so powerful (cf. Bloom, 1984) that they wiped out any confusion that the violation of felicity conditions might have caused but allowed the confusing effect of the mixed drill to come through unscathed.

If this explanation of the lack of a felicity condition effect is correct, then one-disjunct-per-lesson may still have a large effect in nontutorial situations, such as classroom teaching. If the lesson material introduces a confusion, students may harbor it for minutes, days, or years before it is detected and remedied. If so, then this would explain why curriculum designers tend to obey the one-disjunct-per-lesson convention. In the classroom context, it may make a difference how many disjuncts are packed into a lesson.

PROJECTS AND OPEN PROBLEMS

1. Examine university, high school, and grade school math and science textbooks. Does the single disjunct per lesson hold in these other educational materials?

2. Examine a foreign language or native language grammar textbook. Do these language textbooks follow the single disjunct per lesson as well?

3. Examine one of the computational models in this book or taken from elsewhere, and comment on how the model would work with one and two disjuncts per lesson.

ACKNOWLEDGMENTS

This research was supported by the Personnel and Training Research program, Psychology Sciences Division, Office of Naval Research, under contract N00014-86-K-0349. The author is grateful for the help of Micki Chi and Bill Clancey, whose close readings of early drafts were invaluable.

References

Anderson, J. R., Farrell, R., & Saurers, R. (1985). Learning to program in LISP. *Cognitive Science, 8,* 87–129.

Austin, J. L. (1962). *How to do things with words.* New York: Oxford University Press.

Bloom, B. S. (1984). The 2 sigma problem: The search for methods of group instruction as effective as one-to-one tutoring. *Educational Researcher, 13,* 4–16.

Chi, M. T. H., Bassok, M., Lewis, M. W., Reimann, P., & Glaser, R. (1989). Self-explanations: How students study and use examples in learning to solve problems. *Cognitive Science, 15,* 145–182.

Pirolli, P. L., & Anderson, J. R. (1985). The role of learning from examples in the acquisition of recursive programming skills. *Canadian Journal of Psychology, 39*, 240–272.

Quilici, J. L., & Mayer, R. E. (1996). Role of examples in how students learn to categorize statistics word problems. *Journal of Educational Psychology, 88*(1), 144–161.

Rivest, R., & Sloan, R. (1988). Learning complicated concepts reliably and usefully, *Proceedings of AAAI-88.* Menlo Park, CA: AAAI Press.

Valiant, L. G. (1984). A theory of the learnable. *Communications of the ACM, 27*(11), 1134–1142.

VanLehn, K. (1987). Learning one subprocedure per lesson. *Artificial Intelligence, 31*, 1–40.

VanLehn, K. (1990). *Mind bugs: The origins of procedural misconceptions.* Cambridge, MA: MIT Press.

VanLehn, K. (1998). Analogy events: How examples are used during problem solving. *Cognitive Science, 22*(3), 347–388.

Chapter 13

Order or No Order: System Versus Learner Control in Sequencing Simulation-Based Scientific Discovery Learning

Janine Swaak
Ton de Jong

What does sequencing have to do with scientific discovery or inquiry learning? Can principles of traditional instruction, such as sequencing, even coexist with ideas of self-regulated learning and constructivism? This chapter first shows that sequencing and scientific discovery can combine. Second, it illustrates that when sequencing and discovery are combined, the question of who is in control of the sequence must be addressed. The scientific discovery environment in the reported study, CIRCUIT, simulates the behavior of current and voltage sources in electrical circuits. It includes two main types of instructional support: (a) model progression and (b) assignments ordered according to different levels in the simulation learning environment. Two experimental conditions were created that were similar with respect to the support, but differed with respect to the amount of freedom given to the students. In the first group, students were free to choose their own sequence for going through the environment. In the second group, the sequence was largely controlled by the environment. The evaluation followed a pre-test post-test design. The results showed no gain in definitional knowledge but did reveal a gain in intuitive knowledge. No major differences between the experimental groups were detected in the post-test results, the interaction processes, or subjective ratings of feeling guided or constrained by the environments. We conclude that order does not always have to be 'built in' to instruction.

SEQUENCING AND SCIENTIFIC DISCOVERY LEARNING, REUNITED?

What does sequencing have to do with scientific discovery learning? Can principles of traditional instruction, such as sequencing (see Reigeluth, Chapter 2), even coexist with ideas of self-regulated learning and constructivism? This chapter first shows that sequencing and discovery can combine. Second, it illustrates that, when sequencing and scientific discovery are combined, the question of who is in control of the sequence must be addressed. We start by introducing

some ideas and findings regarding scientific discovery learning.

Discovery learning as an approach to learning and instruction already has a long tradition, with both advocates (Bruner, 1961) and opponents (Ausubel, 1968). The current trend toward learning and instruction (constructivism) favors scientific discovery learning. Because new environments (such as computer simulation environments) for scientific discovery learning are increasingly available, new theories of scientific discovery learning are emerging. Along with these theories, new issues also arise and old issues are revisited.

The central concept is that learning within scientific discovery environments is considered to be qualitatively different from learning that takes place within more expository instructional contexts. The latter environments typically involve a direct transfer of knowledge from teacher or textbook to student, emphasizing the formal aspects of the domain. In contrast, in scientific discovery environments the structure and contents of the subject matter are not given to learners directly. In other words, compared to expository instruction (e.g., textbooks) simulations have a relatively low transparency. As a consequence, mere verbal learning (i.e., reading) is not sufficient. Learners are expected to actively plan and perform experiments and to restructure and enlarge their knowledge base by means of inference processes based on their experiments within the scientific discovery environment.

Scientific discovery environments tend to invoke and require active involvement, ordering, and inference processes by learners. These processes are assumed to be substantially different from the learning processes required in traditional instructional settings. Many studies evaluating learning from simulations have indicated that, without instructional support added to simulations, learning gains were disappointing, unclear, or both (Klahr & Nigam, 2004; Leutner, 1993; Mayer, 2004; Rieber, 1990; Rieber, Boyce, & Assad, 1990; White, 1984, 1993). De Jong and van Joolingen (1998) have presented an overview of problems learners may encounter in discovery environments and also indicated how to support learners. This search for support and scaffolds is now a major part of the research in scientific discovery and inquiry learning (de Jong, 2006; de Jong & Pieters, 2006; Linn, Bell, & Davis, 2004; Quintana et al., 2004).

With regard to the problems learners may encounter, on the one hand, we feel we should support learners whenever possible in ordering their scientific discovery process. On the other hand, we believe we should emphasize their own responsibility (de Jong & van Joolingen, 1998). Learning should be more under the control of the learner, rather than directed by a technology-based system. At least three issues reappear frequently in research on learning with scientific discovery environments:

a. support for ordering scientific discovery learning

b. learning vs. system control in sequencing
c. measuring effects of scientific discovery learning

In this chapter we focus on the first and second issues, without forgetting about the third. We compare two simulations with the same instructional support for ordering but differing with respect to the amount of freedom given to the learners, and we also consider the measurement of the effects of learning from simulations. We first take a closer look at how to sequence learning with simulations and how much control to give to the learner or leave to the system and then focus on assessing the effects of learning from scientific discovery environments.

SUPPORT FOR ORDERING SCIENTIFIC DISCOVERY LEARNING

One approach to supporting scientific discovery learning involves guiding the process of ordering the learning events with the use of *assignments* and *model progression* (de Jong & van Joolingen, 1998). Assignments are well-defined exercises that support learners in planning their learning and also assist in discerning relevant variables, stating hypotheses, and interpreting the results of experiments (i.e., inferring knowledge from the discovery environment).

Model progression is more directly related to sequencing. In fact, model progression is itself a form of sequencing. It is limited to causal domains and entails starting with a simplified version of the model and gradually offering more and more complex versions of the model. White and Frederiksen (1990) introduced the idea of model progression, one of whose principles is to keep the simulation environment manageable by not introducing too many new ideas at a time. Quinn and Alessi (1994) used this idea in dividing a simulation with four input variables into sections of increasing complexity. Differences in overall performance were not seen in comparisons of groups starting with four, three, or two variables. However, at lower levels of complexity, subjects generated and test more hypotheses. Moreover, the simulated domain of Quinn and Alessi's (1994) study (a model of the spread of an influenza epidemic) was not highly complex in that there were relatively few input variables, which did not interact. In a follow-up study with a more complex domain, an electrician's multimeter, Alessi

(1995) found positive effects of gradually increasing complexity ("fidelity," as Alessi calls it) for both performance during the simulation and near transfer tasks. A study by Rieber and Parmley (1995) also indicated that model progression (which they call "structure") in a simulation on the laws of motion was more beneficial for the ability to apply rules than working with just the full complex model in the simulation.

Many studies outside the field of scientific discovery learning have examined order effects. In these sequencing studies, learning effects from ordered and scrambled material were compared. Among others, research by Tobias (1973) and Mayer (1977) indicated that for familiar material. scrambled and ordered conditions did not make a difference; however, for unfamiliar material scrambling had negative effects.

The general belief is that sequencing or model progression for more complex domains or domains unfamiliar to the students does indeed help learners to structure their learning processes in a profitable way. However, an important question remains. In the studies by Quinn and Alessi (1994), Alessi (1995), and Rieber and Parmley (1995), as well as in several other simulation environments (e.g., Smithtown [Shute & Glaser, 1990], QUEST [Ritter, 1987; White & Frederiksen, 1989, 1990], STEAMER [Hollan, Hutchins, & Weitzman, 1984], Newton [White, 1984], and ThinkerTools [White, 1993]), the system very much controls the pace and order for going through the environment. Recent environments such as Inquiry Island (White et al., 2002), GenScope (Hickey, Kindfield, Horwitz, & Christie, 2003; Hickey & Zuiker, 2003), BGuILE (Reiser et al., 2001), Bio-World (Lajoie, Lavigne, Guerrera, & Munsie, 2001), Model-It (Jackson, Stratford, Krajcik, & Soloway, 1996a, 1996b; Stratford, Krajcik, & Soloway, 1998), Co-Lab (van Joolingen, de Jong, Lazonder, Savelsbergh, & Manlove, 2005), and WISE (Linn, Davis, & Bell, 2004) allow learners more freedom, although here also, the sequencing of activities by the environment is often present, resulting in a kind of mixed initiative.

The questions therefore are, is system control in sequencing (i.e., superimposed sequencing) needed, and is it better than learner control in sequencing (i.e., self-imposed sequencing)? (In Chapter 12, by VanLehn, and Chapter 14, by Scheiter and Gerjets, these issues are addressed more broadly.)

LEARNER VERSUS SYSTEM CONTROL IN SEQUENCING

Though we feel we should support learners in sequencing their discovery processes, we would also like to emphasize learners' control of their own learning. The "locus of control" issue (that is, should the learner or the system be in control?) has been a central topic in the development of intelligent tutoring systems (ITSs). In addition, this issue has been subjected to sequencing studies. For example, work by Atkinson (1972) on second language learning showed that, although a sequence chosen by the subjects to learn the material (i.e., lists of words) was better than a random sequence, a sequence based on a decision-theoretical analysis of the task and taking into account the learners' state of learning during the task resulted in a far greater performance gain. Based on her review of sequencing studies, van der Hulst (1996) concluded that, for unfamiliar material, superimposed sequencing might be needed, while for familiar material a self-imposed sequencing could be more beneficial. Moreover, for familiar material, lack of autonomy in sequencing might even cause interference (van der Hulst, 1996, pp. 22–23).

The locus of control has also been central in several aptitude-treatment-interaction (ATI) studies. A general finding has been that, for learners who are anxious or less able and who report an external locus of control, system-controlled instruction is more effective. For more able, secure learners who report an internal locus of control, learner-controlled instruction is more profitable (e.g., Lohman, 1986). Lodewijks (1983) performed an ATI study specifically investigating the locus of control in sequence effects. This study (on learning physics concepts) showed an interaction between field dependence and the locus of control in sequencing, such that the field independent students profited more from the self-imposed sequence. Moreover, those same learners performed quite poorly in response to the superimposed sequence.

This debate is now reemerging, although with a somewhat different focus. Current conceptions of learning do not merely stress the learning of content but also favor the learners' own construction of knowledge, the development of learning skills, and the learners' own responsibility in the learning process (e.g., de Jong & van Joolingen, 1998).

We, as researchers, favor developing more responsible learners and believe that, if possible, learning should be more under the control of the learner, rather than being directed by a technology-based system. Also, we have learned from previous learner evaluation studies with university-level students (e.g., Swaak, van Joolingen, & de Jong, 1998) that the presence of assignments ordered according to the levels of model progression provided sufficient guidance for the students. There was no need to guide them by constraining the order in which they had to complete the assignments. However, the developers of the system—who were also teachers—believed it essential to have the students first complete a number of assignments before being allowed to proceed to subsequent levels in the model progression. They argued that the choice of either doing or skipping the assignments and, more importantly, the freedom to decide on the sequence for going through the environment should *not* be given to the students. The teachers reasoned that this freedom in ordering would demotivate and impede rather than motivate and support the learning processes of the middle vocational training students, the target group of the current study.

During the development of the simulation environment used in the present study the following question concerning learner versus system control in sequencing arose: Is a learning environment in which instructional support is present (i.e., assignments ordered according to the levels of model progression) sufficiently structured for the target learners? Or do middle vocational training students instead need to be guided through the order of the assignments and the sequence of the levels of model progression?

In the study reported in this chapter, we compared two simulation environments with the same model progression levels, the same assignments, and the same few explanations. The amount of learner control in sequencing, though, differed across the experimental conditions.

Strictly speaking, order effects are studied when learners see exactly the same material using different sequences (Langley, 1995). This paradigm was followed in the work comparing scrambled versus ordered material. By allowing students the freedom to choose the model progression levels and the assignments to carry out, we did not control the exact material they studied and therefore could not investigate order effects in this strict sense. We were, however, primarily interested in whether autonomy vs. system control in sequencing made a difference. As far as the

effects are concerned, we looked at differences in ways of working with the simulation environment and measured two forms of learning gains to find potential differences there.

ASSESSING THE EFFECTS OF SCIENTIFIC DISCOVERY LEARNING

In traditional instruction the goal is usually to assimilate and reproduce knowledge. The expected products are as explicit as the goal stated: What is expected from the learners at the end is what is given to them in the beginning. In contrast, goals for learning with simulations are different. The ways to achieve these goals are usually stated less explicitly. As a consequence, until recently the expected products were not easily defined. It is recognized that the products should, in one way or another, reflect the scientific discovery processes that have taken place. Jonassen (1991) mentions "learning outcomes that will reflect the intellectual processes of knowledge construction" (p. 30). It is speculated that, by means of the self-initiated extraction of knowledge, learners may acquire insight into the domain at hand. A number of studies have been conducted to evaluate the results of learning with simulations (Gijlers & de Jong, 2005; Leutner, 1993; Rieber, 1990; Rieber et al., 1990; Stark, Gruber, Renkl, & Mandl, 1998; van der Meij & de Jong, 2006; Veermans, de Jong, & van Joolingen, 2000; Veermans, van Joolingen, & de Jong, 2006; Vreman-de Olde & de Jong, 2004; White, 1993). An important finding from these studies is that learning from computer simulations may lead to a more intuitive, difficult-to-verbalize form of knowledge that might be measured more adequately by "functional knowledge" (Leutner, 1993) or "intuitive knowledge" tests (Swaak & de Jong, 1996; Swaak, de Jong, & van Joolingen, 2004; Swaak et al., 1998). This kind of knowledge allows the learner to predict what objects will do.

In line with the recent studies cited, literature on intuitive knowledge (e.g., Fischbein, 1987) tells us that this knowledge is hard to verbalize. In addition, intuitive knowledge is available immediately or not at all, visualizations play an important role, and intuitive knowledge can be acquired only after inferring knowledge in rich, dynamic situations (see Swaak & de Jong, 1996, for a detailed account of the features of intuitive knowledge). Simulations provide learners with those rich experiences and require them to actively infer knowledge because of their low transparency. Therefore, the results of learning from simulations may very well have an intuitive quality.

We compared the acquisition of intuitive knowledge with the mere reproduction of factual knowledge as measured by a definitional knowledge test. Apart from studying intuitive knowledge and factual knowledge, we looked at the learners' use of the support measures and their navigation through the system. In addition, a number of learners were queried on the extent to which they felt guided, constrained, lost, or free in their interaction with the simulation, and some informal observations were made.

CURRENT STUDY

This application simulated the behavior of current and voltage sources in electrical circuits. Circuits with one ideal current source, one resistor, and one or more voltage sources were covered in serial, parallel, and combined circuits. In addition, Ohm's law, Kirchhoff's current law, and Kirchhoff's voltage law were included in the domain presentation.

The Scientific Discovery Environment Circuit

The learning environment (created with the authoring environment SimQuest; see de Jong, van Joolingen, Veermans, & van der Meij, 2005; van Joolingen & de Jong, 2003) provided the possibility of visualizing changes in current and voltage in a straightforward way by means of simple animations. With the help of instructional support, the learners were assisted in their understanding of these animations and hence in their understanding of the behavior of electrical circuits. Three types of instructional supports were incorporated into the scientific discovery environment: model progression, assignments, and explanations.

Model Progression

The models implemented in the learning environment differed in complexity and/or perspective. Five levels of model progression were used. The first and second levels described an electrical circuit composed of one ideal source of current and one resistor. The resistor was fixed in the first level and changeable in

the second. At these levels Ohm's law was presented. The third level described circuits composed of two current sources and one resistor, while the fourth level presented circuits composed of three current sources and one resistor. The third and fourth levels highlighted Kirchhoff's current law, while the fifth level dealt with a circuit that emphasized the idea of voltage direction. One circuit at this level included an alternating voltage source and a resistor, while a second circuit at this same level included two alternating voltage sources and one resistor. The fifth level explored Kirchhoff's voltage law.

Assignments and Explanations

Seventeen assignments were implemented in the learning environment across all levels of the model progressions. An example of an assignment is the following: "Explain current flow 2: In this assignment you can explore the impact two different current sources have on a resistance. It is possible just to explore the impact of only current source 1, current source 2, or both at the same time. Pay attention to the direction of the current source. Also the values of the current source I1, I2, and IR should be taken into account." A total of six explanations were offered. In these, both text and graphical displays were used to explain the concepts to the learners. The learners were allowed to consult an explanation on their own initiative.

Figure 13.1 shows a simulation window of the scientific discovery environment Circuit. The simulation

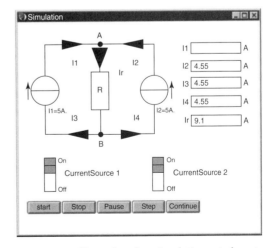

FIGURE 13.1. Example of a simulation window in Circuit.

window contained controls for manipulating the input variables of the simulation and tables (and optionally graphs) for presenting the output variables.

In separate windows the lists of assignments and explanations were available, and a dedicated window displayed the model progression. In the model progression window the learners could see the levels that they could go to (at that specific point in time).

Procedure

The study followed a pretest and posttest design with two groups of students. The design involved pretesting the entry knowledge of two groups of at least 20 students each. Then the students worked individually with either a "free" or a "constrained" application for a reasonable period of time. Finally, their resulting knowledge was posttested. All of the actions performed within the application were also tracked and recorded. An experimental session had a duration of approximately 2 hours. Of the 120 minutes, 70 were used for the interaction with the scientific discovery environment, Circuit, and pre- and posttesting took 40 minutes.

Subjects

Forty-one subjects participated in the study. They were first- and second-year students from middle vocational technical training and were from 16 to 18 years of age. The students had some basic knowledge of electrical circuits and an adequate level of computer experience. They were assigned to one of the two conditions such that 21 subjects participated in experimental Condition I (free) and 20 participated in Condition II (constrained). The subjects participated in the study on a voluntary basis and received a small fee for their participation.

Setup

Two versions of circuit were created. Both included model progression, assignments, and explanations. In the first "free" version, students could move freely through the environment; there were *no constraints* whatsoever on going from one model progression level to another. From the start of their session, the students could access *all* of the levels, and they were free to choose their own sequence of moving through the environment. Furthermore, they were completely free

either to do the assignments or to consult the explanations. *No navigation hints at all* were given to them. In the second "constrained" version, the students started with the first level and were allowed to proceed to the next one only after completing all of the assignments in their present level. The students were free to go back to simpler levels and to consult explanations.

Assessments

A series of two tests was used to assess the learners' knowledge. The *definitional knowledge tests* aimed at measuring their knowledge of concepts. The *intuitive knowledge tests*, called what-if tests, measured the students' difficult-to-verbalize, perception-driven knowledge of the topic. We used logfiles and some informal observations to assess the learning process. Finally, a questionnaire was used to gather subjective ratings by the students.

Definitional Tests

The definitional tests can best be compared with multiple-choice knowledge tests usually applied in instructional settings when the reproduction of facts is at stake. The definitional tests we created consisted of 20 items with three answer alternatives. The tests measure conceptual knowledge of facts, definitions, and principles of the simulated domain. The same definitional test was given as a both pre- and posttest.

What-If Tests

For measuring intuitive knowledge of the relationships between the variables of the domain, we created tests that we called what-if tests. In the what-if test, each test item consists of three parts: conditions, actions, and predictions. The conditions and predictions reflect possible states of the system. The conditions are displayed in a drawing of the system and some text. The action, or the change of a variable within the system, is presented in text. Finally, the predicted states are also presented in text.

The speeded what-if task requires the learner to decide as accurately and quickly as possible which of the predicted states follows from a given condition as a result of the action that is displayed. The items were kept as simple as the domain would permit. In order to prevent memorization effects, two parallel versions of the intuitive knowledge test were developed. Each version consisted of 27 three-choice questions. The versions were created so that a one-to-one mapping existed between the what-if pretest and the what-if posttest items (i.e., Item 1 of the pretest corresponded with Item 1 of the posttest; Item 2 of the pretest corresponded with Item 2 of the posttest, etc.). Parallel items covered the same content and were of similar difficulty but differed on the direction or size of the induced change. As mentioned, the subjects were instructed to answer as accurately and quickly as possible. Both correctness and answer time required were used to determine the level of intuitive knowledge. An example of a what-if item is depicted in Figure 13.2.

Logfiles

We kept a record of all of the actions the learners took while interacting with the simulation. This provided us with data on the use of the simulation and the supportive measures that were present. These data were used to compare how the two groups worked with the simulation.

Questionnaire

After working with the system, three of the students from each condition were asked to complete a questionnaire with one of the three supervisors present. Apart from asking the students their opinion of the

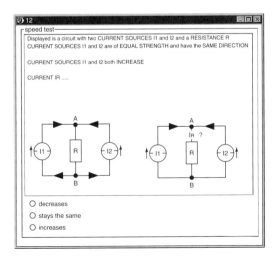

FIGURE 13.2. An example of a what-if test item used in the Circuit study (translated from Dutch).

salient parts of the application, we also queried them about the extent to which they felt guided, constrained, lost, or free during their experience interacting with the learning environment.

Results

In this section we first report the results for the different knowledge tests. Then we give an account of the interaction measures, the navigation measures, the questionnaire, and our informal observation of the sequencing behavior.

The Definitional Knowledge Test

The same form of the definitional knowledge test was given as a pre- and a posttest. It consisted of 20 multiple-choice items with three alternative answers each. Table 13.1 gives the average number of items correct for the definitional pre- and posttests for the two experimental conditions averaged over the subjects. The table shows that the average number of correctly answered items on the definitional posttest in Condition I is lower than that on the definitional pretest.

A repeated measures ANOVA on the definitional test scores showed no significant within-subject

TABLE 13.1. Means (Standard Deviations) for Knowledge Measures

Knowledge Measures	Condition I ($n = 21$) "free"	Condition II ($n = 20$) "constrained"	Overall
Definitional pretest (out of 20 items)	11.4 (2.4)	10.8 (2.1)	11.1 (2.2)
Definitional posttest (out of 20 items)	11.2 (2.4)	12.2 (2.5)	11.7 (2.5)
What-if pretest correctness (out of 27 items)	12.1 (4.2)	11.7 (3.3)	11.9 (3.8)
What-if posttest correctness (out of 27 items)	14.1 (5.1)	13.2 (4.1)	13.6 (4.6)
What-if pretest item response time (seconds)	16.6 (7.0)	20.1 (7.5)	18.3 (7.4)
What-if posttest item response time (seconds)	11.1 (3.0)	11.5 (3.4)	11.3 (3.1)

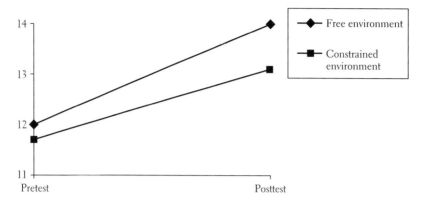

FIGURE 13.3. Average number of correctly answered items on the what-if pretest and posttest.

effect for number of items correct across conditions ($F_{1,36} < 1$). In addition, no interaction between the experimental condition and test scores was revealed in this analysis. Neither did a repeated measures analysis of the definitional test scores within Condition II show an effect at the $\alpha < 0.05$ level ($F_{1,17} = 4.17$, $p < 0.10$). In other words, with respect to the definitional test, no learning gain was found across or within the experimental conditions, and no differences between the free and constrained conditions were detected.

The Intuitive Knowledge Test

For the intuitive test, the items were scored on both the correctness of the answer and the time taken to answer. The average number of correctly answered items is given in Figure 13.3, and the average time to answer what-if items is given in Figure 13.4. These figures provide a graphical overview of the average number of correctly answered items and the average item response times for the what-if pre- and posttests, respectively.

A repeated measures ANOVA on the what-if test scores showed a significant within-subject effect for the number of correct items ($F_{1,39} = 6.98$, $p < 0.05$). No interaction between the experimental condition and the test scores was found ($F_{1,39} < 1$). The same picture emerged with respect to the observed latencies. A repeated measures ANOVA on the what-if test scores for speed showed a significant within-subject effect of a decrease in item response time ($F_{1,39} = 45.19$, $p < 0.001$). No interaction between the experimental condition and the item response times was found ($F_{1,39} = 2.26$, $p > 0.10$).

In summary, we see that, with respect to the what-if test, a learning gain was found across both experimental conditions, in terms of both an increase in correct an-

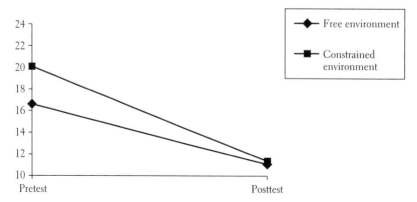

FIGURE 13.4. Average response times on the what-if pretest and what-if posttest items.

swers and a decrease in item completion time. Importantly, the what-if test scores showed *no* differences between the free and the constrained group. In other words, we conclude that the learning gains on the what-if test were identical for the two conditions.

Interaction Measures

We recorded all of the actions the students took while interacting with the simulation. This provided us with data on the use of the simulation and the supportive measures that were present.

Number of Runs

Students were rather active in the simulation. Table 13.2 displays the average number of runs in the two conditions. As the standard deviations show, the individual differences are considerable. An ANOVA on the number of runs across the two conditions showed no significant differences: $F_{1,37} = 1.96$, $p > 0.10$. Thus, the number of runs can also be considered to be similar for both the free and the constrained conditions.

Number of Assignments and Explanations Used

Most of the students made extensive use of assignments and explanations. For some, however, the assignments and explanations were less popular. One student in Condition I used only four assignments. It should be noted that in Condition I, the students were completely free to decide whether to use the assignments. In Condition II, the students needed to complete all of the assignments at one model progression level in order to proceed to another level. An ANOVA on the number of assignments indicated significant differences between the experimental conditions ($F_{1,37} = 5.22$, $p < 0.05$), such that the students in the

constrained condition tended to use more assignments than the students in the free condition. In contrast to the use of assignments, no constraints were implemented with respect to the use of explanations in either condition. Students in both groups consulted nearly the same number of explanations, on average. Table 13.2 displays the average number of assignments and explanations used.

Navigation Measures

Table 13.3 displays the average number of different model progression levels visited, the average number of model progression switches, the average number of switches in which the students spent at least 1 minute at a given level, and the average total time spent at each level.

An ANOVA on the number of model progression switches indicated significant differences between the experimental conditions ($F_{1,37} = 19.7$, $p < 0.001$). Likewise, an ANOVA on the number of model progression switches in which the students spent at least 1 minute at a certain level showed a significant difference between the experimental conditions ($F_{1,37} = 20.3$, $p < 0.001$). Both differences were in the same direction and indicated that students who were not constrained (by completing assignments) in switching between different levels indeed changed more frequently. However, if we look at the total time spent at each specific level, we do not find any differences between the free and the constrained conditions ($F_{1,37} < 1$ for all analyses).

Correlations Between Knowledge Measures and Navigation Measures

We have already seen that the experimental manipulations (i.e., the extent to which students could move freely through the simulation environment) had no

TABLE 13.2. Means (Standard Deviations) for Interaction Measures

Interaction Measures	Condition		
	I (n = 21) "free"	II (n = 20) "constrained"	Overall
Number of runs	48.5 (16.7)	38.2 (16.9)	42.0 (17.0)
Number of assignments completed (of 19)	13.6 (3.6)	17.4 (2.3)	15.5 (3.6)
Number of explanations accessed (of 5)	3.8 (1.8)	3.5 (1.9)	3.7 (1.9)

TABLE 13.3. Means (Standard Deviations) for Navigation Measures

Navigation Measures	Condition		
	I (n = 21) "free"	II (n = 20) "constrained"	Overall
Number of model progression levels visited (out of 5)	5 (-)	4.7 (.45)	4.9 (.34)
Number of model progression switches	18.6 (8.7)	8.6 (4.7)	13.6 (8.6)
Number of model progression switches longer than 1 minute	10.6 (3.6)	6.3 (2.1)	8.4 (3.6)
Total time (minutes) at MP 1	15.1 (9.5)	17.4 (5.5)	16.2 (7.7)
Total time (minutes) at MP 2	12.3 (7.1)	10.9 (15.5)	11.6 (5.7)
Total time (minutes) at MP 3	13.6 (7.1)	14.0 (5.1)	13.8 (6.1)
Total time (minutes) at MP 4	17.2 (11.4)	20.0 (5.2)	18.6 (8.8)
Total time (minutes) at MP 5	8.7 (6.3)	9.5 (8.1)	9.1 (7.2)

significant effect on the posttest scores. Here, we zoom in on possible relationships between the navigation measures and the posttest scores.

The correlations between the navigation measures and the posttest scores were calculated across the experimental conditions and are displayed in Table 13.4. Students who spent a longer time at the first level of model progression tended to perform worse on the definitional posttest. Spending a longer time at the second level appeared to relate to lower what-if posttest scores. Further, students who took more time for the last level tended to have higher scores on the what-if posttest. When computed within experimental conditions, the same pattern of correlations reappears in Condition I. For Condition II, no statistically significant correlations were found.

Questionnaire Ratings

Three students from each of the two conditions completed a questionnaire with one of the experimenters/supervisors. In this questionnaire, along with suggestions and remarks, the learners were asked to give ratings on 10-point scales. In one part, they were queried on their perceptions of the extent to which they felt constrained, guided, lost, or free. Here we contrast the ratings of the extent to which they felt free and the extent to which they felt constrained. The average rating for freedom experienced in the free condition was 7.7, and the average for the constrained condition was 6.8, where 1 means no freedom at all, and 10 means ample freedom. The average score for feeling con-

strained for both conditions was 6.8 (where 1 indicated too many constraints, and 10 indicated no constraints.)

Informal Observations on Sequencing

Though the logfiles we collected in principle contain sequential data (i.e., the exact sequences the learners followed to go through the simulation system), it is far from easy to extract this type of information from the log records. (The feasibility of using sequential records is discussed by Ritter, Nerb, & Lehtinen in Chapter 6 of this book.) Therefore, we report here some information based on informal observations of sequences used by the students. Because they had no other choice, all of the learners in the constrained condition started the session with the simulation in the first assignments of the first level of model progression, and, after completing all of them, continued with the second level. In comparison, the learners in the free condition, after 5 to 10 minutes of browsing through the system, also started with the first assignments in the first level. At this initial level, they completed nearly all of the assignments in the order listed in the simulation and then went to the second level. This learning behavior was very similar to that of the students in the constrained condition. The main difference was that, in the free condition, the students took more opportunities to browse (both forward and backward). Upon asking them about their systematic behavior, they answered that they would start a book given to them at the beginning as well and that they did not need to be told to do so.

TABLE 13.4. Correlations Between Posttest Scores and Navigation Measures Computed Across Experimental Conditions

Posttest Score	Navigation Measures						
	Number of Switches	Number of Switches > 1 min.	Time at MP1	Time at MP2	Time at MP3	Time at MP4	Time at MP5
Definitional test	.04	−.09	−.35*	−.11	.18	.07	.28
What-if correctness	.23	.13	−.30	−.44**	.07	.21	.33*
What-if time	−.05	−.16	.04	−.01	.03	.08	−.12

($n = 41$)

$^*p < 0.05$, $^{**}p < 0.01$

CONCLUSIONS

The first main finding from this study is that giving these students the freedom to choose their own sequence through the environment or forcing them to complete all of the assignments at one level of model progression before proceeding to another level did not make much difference. No major differences between the experimental groups were found either on the posttest scores or in the interaction data and navigation data as measured with the logfiles and in the questionnaires. If we consider the navigation measures, we see that the number of model progression switches differs for the two experimental groups but that the time spent at each of the levels does not show any significant differences The latter was corroborated by the informal observations of the students' sequencing behavior.

A second finding is that, as a whole, the subjects improved on the intuitive knowledge test. For definitional knowledge, there was no statistically significant gain between the pretest and the posttest, meaning that, on average, students acquired almost no definitional knowledge during the session of a little more than 1 hour. This is in line with our expectations that simulations have more of an effect on intuitive knowledge than on learning facts and definitions. On the basis of the results of this study and the work of other researchers (e.g., Leutner, 1993; Rieber, 1990; Stark et al., 1998; White, 1993), we conclude that, in the context of simulation-based scientific discovery learning, it makes sense to introduce new ways of measuring knowledge in addition to traditional definitional types of knowledge tests.

We now return to the title and subtitle of this chapter. First the title: Order or no order. After performing the experiment, we conclude that, in this study, we did not really have a "no order" experimental condition. Just the presence of levels of model progression and assignments seems sufficiently directive for students. This is also our main explanation for the absence of major differences between the conditions, which is in line with our experience from previous learner-evaluation studies with university-level students (e.g., Swaak et al., 1998). In addition, studies by Mayer (1977) and Tobias (1973) have indicated that, for familiar material, as the current domain is to the students in our experiment, sequencing does not matter.

PROJECTS AND OPEN PROBLEMS

Project 1. Take a simulation-based learning environment and design an experiment to actually study the differences between "order" and "no order." You are free to choose the type of learning environment supporting either scientific discovery learning (i.e., doing experiments) or other types of training. A prerequisite of your experiment is that both the "order" and "no order" variants should have instructional value. Which simulation-based learning environment would you choose? What domains? What types of participants? Which experimental design would you use? What measurements would you take?

The subtitle of this chapter, System versus learner control in sequencing simulation-based scientific discovery learning, has several dimensions. In the current study, the learners and system control did not actually differ, as the learners in the free condition did what the system directed in the constrained condition. A central question is why they did so. Does it relate to the limited complexity of the current system and the fact that the structure of the system is transparent for the learners? For more complex domains and systems and less transparent systems, increased system control has been shown to be beneficial (e.g., Alessi, 1995; Rieber & Parmley, 1995). Or can the results of this study be explained by the type of learners who participated?

In this study we did not control for students' learning styles and other characteristics. Different type of learners (e.g., university students, younger learners) might have utilized far more freedom in the free condition, compared to the middle vocational training students of this study. Alternatively, can the results of this study be explained by the amount of system feedback and system control? The learning gains in the present study were small, and we cannot exclude the possibility that more system feedback based on the learning state of the individual learner and more system control in pacing and sequencing the material could have increased learning.

> **Project 2:** Design a theoretical model describing the possible relations between the amount of system-imposed sequencing, system feedback, domain complexity, domain transparency, domain familiarity, and learner characteristics such as the internal versus external locus of control (see, e.g., Lodewijks, 1983), or field independency (see, e.g., van der Hulst, 1996)

> **Project 3:** Take a simulation-based scientific discovery environment and design an experiment to study the differences between system and learner control in sequencing. Which scientific discovery learning environments would you choose? What domains? What types of instructional support? How would you operationalize system control and learner control? What types of participants would you select? Which experimental design would you use? What measurements would you take?

It should be clear by now that sequencing and scientific discovery compose an interesting team. Together they show that there are multiple types of instruction and that order effects are subtle and depend on at least the type of instruction, the type of learners, and their familiarity with the instructed domain. For order to be present, the combination of sequencing and discovery learning also shows that order does not always have to be built in to the instruction.

ACKNOWLEDGMENTS

The work presented here was carried out under the DELTA program of the EC as project ET 1020. We gratefully acknowledge the contributions of all of our present and former colleagues from the SERVIVE project. Furthermore, we would especially like to express our gratitude to Wouter R. van Joolingen, Mark Gellevij, Renate Limbach (University of Twente, the Netherlands), Koen Veermans (University of Turku), and Vincent Blokhuis (ROC Oost-Nederland, the Netherlands) for their contributions in constructing the simulation environment and conducting the experiment described in this chapter.

References

Alessi, S. M. (1995, April). *Dynamic vs. static fidelity in a procedural simulation*. Paper presented at the American Educational Research Association, San Francisco.

Atkinson, R. C. (1972). Optimizing the learning of a second-language vocabulary. *Journal of Experimental Psychology, 96* 124–129.

Ausubel, D. P. (1968). *Educational psychology: A cognitive view*. New York: Holt, Rinehart, & Winston.

Bruner, J. S. (1961). The act of discovery. *Harvard Educational Review, 31*, 21–32.

de Jong, T. (2005). The guided discovery principle in multimedia learning. In R. E. Mayer (Ed.), *Cambridge handbook of multimedia learning* (pp. 215–229). New York: Cambridge University Press.

de Jong, T. (2006). Scaffolds for computer simulation–based scientific discovery learning. In J. Elen & R. E. Clark (Eds.), *Dealing with complexity in learning environments* (pp. 107–128). London: Elsevier Science.

de Jong, T., & Pieters, J. M. (2006). The design of powerful learning environments. In P. A. Alexander & P. H. Winne (Eds.), *Handbook of educational psychology* (2nd ed.; pp. 739–755). Mahwah, NJ: Erlbaum.

de Jong, T., & van Joolingen, W. R. (1998). Scientific discovery learning with computer simulations of conceptual domains. *Review of Educational Research, 68*, 179–202.

de Jong, T., van Joolingen, W. R., Veermans, K., & van der Meij, J. (2005). Authoring discovery learning environments: In search for reusable components. In J. M. Spector, C. Ohrazda, A. van Schaack, & D. A. Wiley (Eds.), *Innovations in instructional technology: Essays in honor of M. David Merrill* (pp. 11–29). Mahwah, NJ: Erlbaum.

Fischbein, E. (1987). *Intuition in science and mathematics*. Dordrecht, the Netherlands: Reidel.

Gijlers, H., & de Jong, T. (2005). The relation between prior knowledge and students' collaborative discovery learning processes. *Journal of Research in Science Teaching, 42,* 264–282.

Hickey, D. T., Kindfield, A. C. H., Horwitz, P., & Christie, M. A. (2003). Integrating curriculum, instruction, assessment, and evaluation in a technology-supported genetics environment. *American Educational Research Journal, 40,* 495–538.

Hickey, D. T., & Zuiker, S. (2003). A new perspective for evaluating innovative science learning environments. *Science Education, 87,* 539–563.

Hollan, J. D., Hutchins, E. L., & Weitzman, L. (1984). STEAMER: An interactive inspectable simulation-based training system. *AI Magazine, 5,* 15–27.

Jackson, S., Stratford, S. J., Krajcik, J., & Soloway, E. (1996a). A learner-centered tool for students building models. *Communications of the ACM, 39,* 48–49.

Jackson, S., Stratford, S., Krajcik, J., & Soloway, E. (1996b). Making dynamic modeling accessible to precollege science students. *Interactive Learning Environments, 4,* 233–257.

Jonassen, D. H. (1991). Evaluating constructivistic learning. *Educational Technology, 31,* 28–33.

Klahr, D., & Nigam, M. (2004). The equivalence of learning paths in early science instruction: Effects of direct instruction and discovery learning. *Psychological Science, 15,* 661–668.

Lajoie, S. P., Lavigne, N. C., Guerrera, C., & Munsie, S. D. (2001). Constructing knowledge in the context of BioWorld. *Instructional Science, 29,* 155–186.

Langley, P. (1995). Order effects in incremental learning. In P. Reimann & H. Spada (Eds.), *Learning in humans and machines: Towards an interdisciplinary learning science* (pp. 154–167). Oxford, UK: Elsevier Science.

Leutner, D. (1993). Guided discovery learning with computer-based simulation games: Effects of adaptive and non-adaptive instructional support. *Learning and Instruction, 3,* 113–132.

Linn, M. C., Bell, P., & Davis, E. A. (2004). Specific design principles: Elaborating the scaffolded knowledge integration framework. In M. Linn, E. A. Davis, & P. Bell (Eds.), *Internet environments for science education* (pp. 315–341). Mahwah, NJ: Erlbaum.

Linn, M. C., Davis, E. A., & Bell, P. (Eds.). (2004). *Internet environments for science education.* Mahwah. NJ: Erlbaum.

Lodewijks, H. (1983). *Leerstofsequenties: Van conceptueel netwerk naar cognitieve structuur.* [Subject matter sequences: From conceptual network to cognitive structure]. Lisse, the Netherlands: Swets & Zeitlinger.

Lohman, D. F. (1986). Predicting mathemathanic effects in the teaching of higher-order thinking skills. *Educational Psychology, 21,* 191–208.

Mayer, R. E. (1977). The sequencing of instruction and the concept of assimilation-to-schema. *Instructional Science, 6,* 369–388.

Mayer, R. E. (2004). Should there be a three-strikes rule against pure discovery learning? *American Psychologist, 59,* 14–19.

Quinn, J., & Alessi, S. (1994). The effects of simulation complexity and hypothesis generation strategy on learning. *Journal of Research on Computing in Education, 27,* 75–91.

Quintana, C., Reiser, B. J., Davis, E. A., Krajcik, J., Fretz, E., Duncan, R. G., et al. (2004). A scaffolding design framework for software to support science inquiry. *Journal of Learning Science, 13,* 337–387.

Reiser, B. J., Tabak, I., Sandoval, W. A., Smith, B., Steinmuller, F., & Leone, T. J. (2001). BGuILE: Strategic and conceptual scaffolds for scientific inquiry in biology classrooms. In S. M. Carver & D. Klahr (Eds.), *Cognition and instruction: Twenty-five years of progress* (pp. 263–305). Mahwah, NJ: Erlbaum.

Rieber, L. P. (1990). Using computer-animated graphics in science instruction with children. *Journal of Educational Psychology, 82,* 135–140.

Rieber, L. P., Boyce, M. J., & Assad, C. (1990). The effects of computer animations on adult learning and retrieval tasks. *Journal of Computer-Based Instruction, 17,* 46–52.

Rieber, L. P., & Parmley, M. W. (1995). To teach or not to teach? Comparing the use of computer-based simulations in deductive versus inductive approaches to learning with adults in science. *Journal of Educational Computing Research, 14,* 359–374.

Ritter, F. E. (1987). OREO: Orienting electrical circuits for qualitative reasoning [Tech. Report, #6560]. Cambridge, MA: BBN Labs.

Shute, V. J., & Glaser, R. (1990). A large-scale evaluation of an intelligent discovery world: Smithtown. *Interactive Learning Environments, 1,* 51–77.

Stark, R., Gruber, H., Renkl, A., & Mandl, H. (1998). Instructional effects in complex learning: Do objective and subjective learning outcomes converge? *Learning and Instruction, 8,* 117–129.

Stratford, S. J., Krajcik, J., & Soloway, E. (1998). Secondary students' dynamic modeling processes: Analyzing, reasoning about, synthesizing, and testing models of stream ecosystems. *Journal of Science Education and Technology, 7,* 215–234.

Swaak, J., & de Jong, T. (1996). Measuring intuitive knowledge in science: The development of the what-if test. *Studies in Educational Evaluation, 22,* 341–362.

Swaak, J., de Jong, T., & van Joolingen, W. R. (2004). The effects of discovery learning and expository instruction on the acquisition of definitional and intuitive knowledge. *Journal of Computer Assisted Learning, 20,* 225–234.

Swaak, J., van Joolingen, W. R., & de Jong, T. (1998). Supporting simulation-based learning: The effects of model progression and assignments on definitional and intuitive knowledge. *Learning and Instruction, 8,* 235–253.

Tobias, S. (1973). Sequence, familiarity, and attribute by treatment interactions in programmed instruction. *Journal of Educational Psychology, 64,* 133–141.

van der Hulst, A. (1996). *Cognitive tools: Two exercises in non-directive support for exploratory learning.* Unpublished PhD dissertation, University of Amsterdam, Amsterdam.

van der Meij, J., & de Jong, T. (2006). Supporting students' learning with multiple representations in a dynamic simulation-based learning environment. *Learning and Instruction, 16,* 199–212.

van Joolingen, W. R., & de Jong, T. (2003). SimQuest: Authoring educational simulations. In T. Murray, S. Blessing, & S. Ainsworth (Eds.), *Authoring tools for advanced technology educational software: Toward cost-effective production of adaptive, interactive, and intelligent educational software* (pp. 1–31). Dordrecht: Kluwer Academic.

van Joolingen, W. R., de Jong, T., Lazonder, A. W., Savelsbergh, E., & Manlove, S. (2005). Co-Lab: Research and development of an on-line learning environment for collaborative scientific discovery learning. *Computers in Human Behavior, 21,* 671–688.

Veermans, K. H., de Jong, T., & van Joolingen, W. R. (2000). Promoting self-directed learning in simulation-based discovery learning environments through intelligent support. *Interactive Learning Environments, 8,* 229–255.

Veermans, K. H., van Joolingen, W. R., & de Jong, T. (2006). Using heuristics to facilitate scientific discovery learning in a simulation learning environment in a physics domain. *International Journal of Science Education, 28,* 341–361.

Vreman-de Olde, C., & de Jong, T. (2004). Student-generated assignments about electrical circuits in a computer simulation. *International Journal of Science Education, 26,* 859–873.

White, B. Y. (1984). Designing computer games to help physics students understand Newton's laws of motion. *Cognition and Instruction, 1,* 69–108.

White, B. Y. (1993). ThinkerTools: Causal models, conceptual change, and science education. *Cognition and Instruction, 10,* 1–100.

White, B. Y., & Frederiksen, J. R. (1989). Causal models as intelligent learning environments for science and engineering education. *Applied Artificial Intelligence, 3,* 83–106.

White, B. Y., & Frederiksen, J. R. (1990). Causal model progressions as a foundation for intelligent learning environments. *Artificial Intelligence, 42,* 99–157.

White, B. Y., Frederiksen, J. R., Frederiksen, T., Eslinger, E., Loper, S., & Collins, A. (2002, October 23–26). *Inquiry island: Affordances of a multi-agent environment for scientific inquiry and reflective learning.* Paper presented at the Fifth International Conference of the Learning Sciences (ICLS).

Chapter 14

Making Your Own Order: Order Effects in System- and User-Controlled Settings for Learning and Problem Solving

Katharina Scheiter
Peter Gerjets

We present a model that explains order effects in problem solving as a result of learning during solving a problem and knowledge transfer across successive problems. Whenever problem orders differ in how they support these two processes, order effects may occur. In two experiments we tested the model's predictions by investigating the ambiguous influence of surface similarities on order effects among structurally dissimilar problems. Our findings confirmed the model's predictions by demonstrating that arranging problems according to their surface similarities may either foster performance by enabling learning during problem solving or by leading to negative transfer, depending on whether problem solvers have prior knowledge available. We also applied the model to user-controlled settings, where learners could determine the problem order by themselves. Findings from a questionnaire study and an experiment indicate that, when given the opportunity, students rearrange problems, particularly when the initial problem order is less suitable for problem solving. If problem solvers have a high level of prior knowledge, rearranging problems improves performance irrespective of the initial arrangement of problems, which suggests including structural variability in learning sequences for novice learners and giving more advanced learners the opportunity to rearrange material.

In this chapter we address the question of how tasks should be ordered to foster learning and the transfer of knowledge. Order effects are said to occur whenever performance varies as a function of the sequence in which multiple learning or problem-solving tasks are accomplished (cf. Langley, 1996; Ritter, Nerb, & Lehtinen, this volume). Order effects have been investigated mostly from an instructional perspective with the aim of identifying the sequences for the tasks that will maximize learning outcomes (cf. Langley, 1996; Posner & Strike, 1976; Reigeluth, Chapter 2; van Patten, Chao, & Reigeluth, 1986). Despite these efforts, the principles for designing optimal orders are still not fully known.

In this chapter we first review the existing findings on simple-to-complex sequencing and sequencing according to the structural variability of tasks. Second, for the explanation of order effects, we outline a model that supports deriving testable hypotheses for when and why instructional sequences should vary in performance. Third, we describe the results from two experiments that confirm these hypotheses. Fourth, the model of order effects is applied to user-controlled settings (i.e., those in which the students are allowed to determine the order of the problems). The role of rearranging problems is investigated by means of a questionnaire and an experiment. The chapter ends with a discussion of the instructional implications and some suggestions for future research in this area.

Many researchers have advocated the use of simple-to-complex training orders to maximize learning outcomes (e.g., see Gobet & Lane, this volume). Simplifying a training task at the beginning of an instructional sequence can be achieved in different ways: First, one may begin teaching lower-level subskills as prerequisites for more complex tasks later in the sequence (Gagné, 1962; Gagné & Paradise, 1961). Second, Reigeluth and van Merriënboer (Reigeluth & Stein, 1983; van Merriënboer, Clark, & de Croock, 2002; see also Swaak & de Jong, this volume) suggest teaching a simplified version of a whole task first, for instance, by illustrating a complex skill by a familiar and an easy-to-understand example and using more unfamiliar, vague, or difficult versions of the task later on. Third, the cognitive apprenticeship approach (Collins, Brown, & Newman, 1989) proposes to give learners who are handling complex tasks additional instructional support (scaffolding) that is faded out over the instructional sequence as the learners become more skilled (see also Renkl & Atkinson, this volume).

In addition to simple-to-complex sequencing, the design should deal with the question of how to account for structural similarity among the instructional tasks. Here, it has been discussed whether structurally similar contents should be taught successively with one topic at a time (i.e., one disjunct per lesson; VanLehn, this volume) or whether instruction should alternate with dissimilar contents (see Langley, 1995, for an overview). Exponents of the variability approach often claim that highly variable instructional sequences lead to more flexible knowledge and train the ability to recognize under which conditions a specific skill is applicable. Whereas Paas and van Merriënboer (1994) have confirmed the superiority of a highly variable sequence of examples in the domain of geometry, Clapper and Bower (1994) showed that learners achieved better outcomes if concepts were presented grouped according to their structural resemblances. VanLehn (this volume) did not find any differences between alternating and grouped instructional sequences for teaching mathematical procedures and concludes that there is no empirical support for the one-disjunct-per-lesson strategy found in textbooks. Langley (1996) offers a possible explanation for this apparent contradiction by alluding to the fact that the existing studies differ in whether they

investigated the acquisition of concepts (e.g., Clapper & Bower, 1994) or procedural skills (Paas & van Merriënboer, 1994; VanLehn, this volume). Moreover, Paas and van Merriënboer (1994) assume that the superiority of one training sequence over another may depend on whether a learner possesses the cognitive abilities to process highly variable instructional sequences. Accordingly, it has been proposed in the cognitive apprenticeship model (Collins et al., 1989), as well as in the 4C/ID-model (van Merriënboer et al., 2002), to have learners first practice a new skill repeatedly before greater variability in the instructional sequence is introduced.

When reviewing the literature on order effects in learning, it becomes evident that empirically founded design principles are often not available. Apparently, more theoretical explanations are needed for when and why instructional sequences should vary in learning outcomes. In particular, there are no assumptions concerning the underlying cognitive processes that could be used to derive testable hypotheses. To overcome this drawback, in the next section we outline a model that analyzes order effects in problem solving rather than learning. We do not think, though, that this restricts the model's applicability to problem solving.

A MODEL ON ORDER EFFECTS IN SYSTEM-CONTROLLED SETTINGS

Newell, Shaw, and Simon (1958) seem to have been convinced of the existence of order effects in solving complex problems when they commented on the marked resemblance between the Logic Theorist, a computer program for identifying logical proofs, and human problem solvers: "Its ability to solve a particular problem depends on the sequence in which problems are presented to it in much the same way that a human subject's behavior depends on this sequence" (1958, p. 162). Despite this strong conviction, order effects in problem solving have rarely been investigated in the psychological problem-solving literature. To better understand the emergence of order effects in problem solving, we developed our own model, one that informs us about the conditions under which order effects for so-called knowledge-rich problems occur.

Knowledge-lean as well as knowledge-rich problems consist of a set of structural features that determine the solution procedure for a given problem. The amount of computation necessary to solve a problem and thus the problem's complexity can vary greatly (Ohlsson, Ernst, & Rees, 1992). Knowledge-rich problems possess two additional characteristics that help to distinguish them from knowledge-lean problems: First, the former are often embedded in a semantically rich context (e.g., algebra word problems). These surface features are irrelevant to their solution but may nevertheless have a strong impact on problem-solving performance (Ross, 1987, 1989). Second, according to VanLehn (1989), solving knowledge-rich problems presupposes that a learner possesses a great deal of prior knowledge in the domain, which may be rather laborious to acquire.

Accordingly, in the model on order effects depicted in Figure 14.1, problems can be characterized by their complexity, as well as their structural and surface features. As Figure 14.1 shows, the distribution of these features across a sequence of problems (e.g., in a simple-to-complex sequence) is assumed to influence the emergence of order effects by either enabling or hindering learning during problem solving and knowledge transfer among successive problems (Scheiter & Gerjets, 2002, 2004; see also Nerb, Ritter, & Langley, this volume). That is, whenever problem orders differ in how they support these two processes, order effects may arise. Finally, we assume

that learning during problem solving, as well as transfer among successive problems, are moderated by a problem solver's prior knowledge.

Learning is seen as a change in the cognitive system of the problem solver that occurs due to solving a problem. Depending on the quantity of prior knowledge (e.g., the number and sophistication of problem schemas), as well as its quality (e.g., degree of activation and automaticity), learning during problem solving can range from simple automatization of already existing knowledge structures to the acquisition of rather sophisticated new symbolic knowledge structures. There is converging evidence that learning during problem solving is facilitated whenever problems are arranged in a simple-to-complex sequence (cf. Collins et al., 1989; Gagné, 1962; Gagné & Paradise, 1961; Reigeluth & Stein, 1983; van Merriënboer et al., 2002; Gobet & Lane, this volume).

Transfer, on the other hand, refers to the application of these knowledge structures to a subsequent problem. For making predictions concerning order effects in problem solving, the nature of this transfer process and what is seen as a prerequisite for successful transfer are considered crucial.

While simple-to-complex sequencing seems to affect learning, it has been less clear how the arrangement of structural features influences order effects in learning and problem solving. We suggest that the

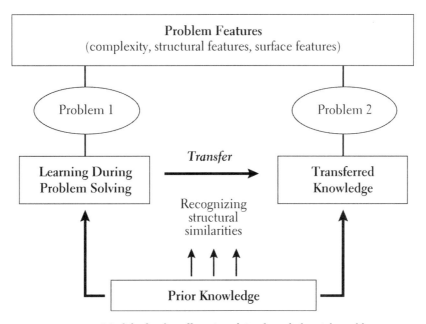

FIGURE 14.1. Model of order effects in solving knowledge-rich problems.

aforementioned variability of results is due to two things: First, we agree with Paas and van Merriënboer (1994) that prior knowledge serves as a moderating factor. Second, we suggest that it is not just the arrangement of structural features that affects order effects; rather, it is also the way a configuration of structural and surface features is distributed across a sequence of problems. In the following section we outline two different hypotheses that concern order effects that emerge from specific configurations of structural and surface features. Underlying these hypotheses are different assumptions concerning the nature of the transfer process. We illustrate our hypotheses by first giving an overview of the problem orders used for experimentation.

EXPERIMENTAL INVESTIGATION OF ORDER EFFECTS IN PROBLEM SOLVING

In two experiments we investigated the role of surface and structural similarities on the occurrence of order effects when solving knowledge-rich problems (cf. Scheiter & Gerjets, 2004; 2005a). The experiments were explicitly designed to assess order effects in problem solving by contrasting two different orders of the same materials (Langley, 1995).

Each of the two orders consisted of the same nine algebra word problems, whose surface and structural features were systematically varied. There were three algebra word problems for each of three problem categories, which shared the structural features and thus need to be solved by the same solution procedure (see Table 14.1). Moreover, as analyses of algebra textbooks have revealed, respective problems are often associated with a typical cover story that gives them their

name, for example, work-rate problems, motion problems, and (financial) interest problems (Mayer, 1981).

For the purpose of experimentally testing the impact of superficial and structural similarities on order effects, we cross-varied the surface and structural features of the problems (cf. Blessing & Ross, 1996). For each of the three problem categories (depicted in the columns of Table 14.1), there was always one problem embedded in the cover story that was typical for problems of that category (i.e., a so-called corresponding problem). Additionally, each problem category contained two so-called noncorresponding problems: These were couched in cover stories that did not correspond to the one that was typical for problems of their own category but rather were typical of one of the other problem categories. For instance, the noncorresponding problems shown in Table 14.2 belong to the problem category of work-rate problems; however, their cover stories are very similar to those that are typical of motion and interest problems. Irrespective of these differences in the cover stories, all three problems are solvable by the same solution procedure.

The corresponding problems of the two remaining problem categories were the following:

For the motion problem category (M – M): Bill and Sharon leave for Frankfurt at the same time. Bill starts out 135 km from Frankfurt, and Sharon starts out 200 km from that city. They reach Frankfurt at exactly the same time. Bill drove at a speed of 54 km/h. How fast did Sharon drive?

For the interest problem category (I – I): Bob wants to invest 8,000 Euros by buying shares. He decides to invest part of his money into debit.com shares with an annual rate of return of 6.5%. With the remaining money he buys different shares that

TABLE 14.1. Algebra Word Problems Used for Experimentation

| | | Problem Category | | |
		Work Rate	Motion	Interest
Cover Story	Work	Corresponding W – W	Noncorresponding M – W	Noncorresponding I – W
	Motion	Noncorresponding W – M	Corresponding M – M	Noncorresponding I – M
	Interest	Noncorresponding W – I	Noncorresponding M – I	Corresponding I – I

W stands for work rate, M for motion, and I for interest.

TABLE 14.2. Corresponding and Noncorresponding Problems for the Work-Rate Category

Problem Type	Problem Statement
Corresponding problem (W – W)	An electrician needs three hours to repair a lamp, while his apprentice needs six hours to perform the same job. How long would it take them to repair the lamp if they worked together?
Noncorresponding problem (W – M)	Jane needs six hours to drive to Tom by car, whereas Tom needs four hours for driving the reverse way. How long would they need to drive until they meet on the way if they started at the same time?
Noncorresponding problem (W – I)	At two different equity funds you buy a share certificate at a fixed price every month. For the first fund you will get 12% of a Mercedes share every year, whereas the second fund will result in 18% of a Mercedes share. How long do you have to invest to get one Mercedes share if buying share certificates from both funds in parallel?

The solution procedure common to all of the problems is $1 = (Rate_1 + Rate_2) * h$

together have an annual rate of return of 8%. At the end of the year he has had an increase of 557.50 Euros. What amount of money did he invest into the debit.com shares?

Although these problems, in terms of their surface features, seem similar to the second and third (noncorresponding) problem in Table 14.2, they both have to be solved by using different equations: $Average_2 = Total_2/(Average_1/Total_1)$ for the motion problem category and $Gain = Interest_1 * x + Interest_2 * (Sum - x)$ for the interest problem category.

Two different problem orders were constructed for the nine corresponding and noncorresponding test problems. In the *structure-blocked sequence*, the test problems were presented according to their category membership, resulting in three blocks of problems (work-rate, motion, interest category). Within each block, all of the problems could be solved in the same way. In the other condition, the *surface-blocked sequence*, the test problems were presented according to their cover stories, resulting in three blocks of superficially similar problems (work-rate, motion, interest cover story). Within every block, each of the three problems had to be solved by a different procedure. In both sequences, each block of problems began with a corresponding problem (i.e., a problem couched in its typical cover story), followed by two noncorresponding ones (i.e., problems couched in atypical cover stories).

Hypotheses

We investigated two contrasting hypotheses concerning performance differences between the two problem

orders, namely the transfer hypothesis and the near-miss hypothesis.

Transfer Hypothesis

The *transfer hypothesis* is based on the assumption that transfer depends simply on which knowledge structures are the most activated and are thus available when working on a succeeding task. According to this view, transfer occurs if (1) a problem's structural and surface features are encoded; (2) a knowledge representation in memory is activated that matches these features; and (3) this knowledge representation is applied to solve the problem, once the overall activation has exceeded a specific threshold. Positive transfer results if there is a match between the problem's structural features and the most activated knowledge representation, while negative transfer occurs if the activation process is dominated by its surface features (Holyoak & Koh, 1987; Novick, 1995; Ross, 1987, 1989). The transfer hypothesis postulates that problem order effects for the two sequences go back to their differences in making available adequate knowledge structures and thereby enabling transfer among succeeding problems.

According to the transfer hypothesis, the problem-solving performance in the structure-blocked sequence should be superior to that in the surface-blocked sequence. In line with the aforementioned mechanisms of activation summation (Holyoak & Koh, 1987), negative transfer among succeeding problems should occur in the case of a surface-blocked problem sequence, while there should be positive transfer in a structure-blocked sequence. There are no assumptions about differences among the two

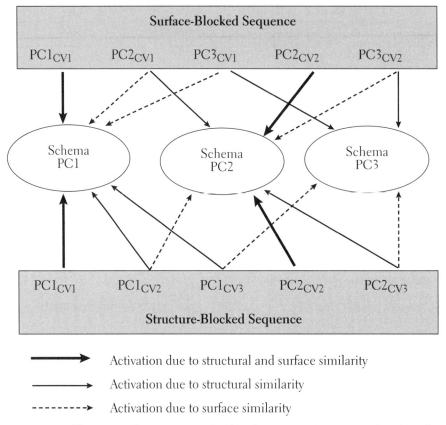

FIGURE 14.2. Negative and positive transfer based on activation summation (transfer hypothesis).

sequences regarding learning during problem solving. The predictions are illustrated in Figure 14.2.

The *surface-blocked sequence* (top of Figure 14.2) starts with a corresponding problem (indicated by identical indices for problem category PC and cover story CV) that may activate the correct problem schema. The second problem, $PC2_{CV1}$, is a non-corresponding problem from a problem category different from that of the first problem but embedded in a cover story typical for problems of problem category 1. Its structural features may activate the correct problem schema 2 (solid lines). However, its surface features activate problem schema 1 (dotted lines), which is already highly activated because it has been applied to solve the first problem. Therefore, problem schema 1 may be spuriously used to solve the second problem, resulting in negative transfer. A correct problem schema is applied again when the next cor-

responding problem, $PC2_{CV2}$, is encountered at the beginning of the second block.

On the other hand, in the *structure-blocked sequence* (lower part of Figure 14.2), the structural features of the second problem, $PC1_{CV2}$, cue the already highly activated problem schema 1, which has been used to solve the first (corresponding) problem and is also suited to solve the second problem. Additionally, there may be activation of the wrong problem schema 2 due to shared surface features. However, this should not be sufficient to dominate the selection process. In this problem sequence, non-corresponding problems within each block benefit from the previous activation of a problem schema by means of positive transfer. In the case of a surface-blocked sequence, performance for noncorresponding problems is impaired (i.e., negative transfer). According to the transfer hypothesis, order effects in favor of a structure-blocked sequence should thus be particularly observable for noncorresponding problems.

These hypothesized order effects in favor of a structure-blocked sequence are explainable by differences between the sequences with regard to *enabling transfer* among succeeding problems. According to this explanation, transfer among knowledge-rich problems occurs automatically as a function of the pattern of activation of knowledge structures helpful in solving a current problem.

Near-Miss Hypothesis

On the other hand, the near-miss hypothesis postulates that the transfer process among knowledge-rich problems is more complex and that successful transfer depends on whether the prerequisite processes have been terminated successfully. In particular, it takes into account that the encoding of a problem statement does not automatically lead to the recognition of structural features; rather, structural features are often not as salient as surface features and first have to be inferred from a problem statement by applying prior knowledge to construct a situation model of the problem (Nathan, Kintsch, & Young, 1992). Thus, transfer among knowledge-rich problems does not occur automatically; rather, it requires effort and metacognitive awareness (Novick, 1995; Salomon & Perkins, 1989; Weisberg, DiCamillo, & Phillips, 1978) for the recognition of structural features. In line with this assumption, problem solvers often fail to notice spontaneously that they have encountered structurally similar problems before and thus have knowledge available to solve a problem (Gick & Holyoak, 1980).

The near-miss hypothesis states that the two sequences differ in how they support the proper recognition of structural and surface features. According to this hypothesis, a surface-blocked sequence should be superior to a structure-blocked sequence because it highlights structural differences among succeeding problems. These problems share the same cover story and differ only with regard to a few—but crucial—structural features (Langley, 1995), which can then be more easily inferred from the problem statement (near-miss effect, Winston, 1975). On the other hand, in the structure-blocked sequence, in which superficially dissimilar problems of one category are presented in succession, attention may be directed toward these irrelevant differences and may thereby

even impede problem-solving performance. Again, order effects should be observable in particular for noncorresponding problems.

These order effects in favor of a surface-blocked condition can be explained by differences among the sequences with regard to enabling *learning during problem solving* (i.e., acquiring knowledge about structural features). Therefore, the near-miss hypothesis also allows predicting that the surface-blocked sequence should result in a better performance for solving subsequent transfer problems, which require an adaptation of known solution procedures. Transfer problems thus presuppose knowledge about structural features and their relation to solution steps, which can be more easily acquired in the surface-blocked condition. On the other hand, according to the transfer hypothesis, no differences between the two sequences for problems that are not part of this ordering can be expected.

The two contradicting hypotheses were tested in the two experiments described in the following sections. Further details are available in Scheiter (2003).

Experiment 1: The Impact of Surface and Structural Features on Order Effects

In this experiment, 40 students from Saarland University and the University of Göttingen, both in Germany, received a booklet in German that contained a worked-out example for each of the three problem categories. After the students had studied the examples for 12 minutes, the example booklet was exchanged for another booklet with the nine test problems that were isomorphic to the previously studied examples. The problems were arranged according to either the surface-blocked or the structure-blocked sequence. The participants were instructed to solve the problems in the given order. When they had finished working on the nine isomorphs, they had to solve three transfer problems. As dependent measures, participants' error rates for isomorphic and transfer problems were recorded and transformed into percentages.

Figure 14.3 shows that participants who were presented with the surface-blocked sequence made fewer errors than participants who worked in the structure-blocked condition with both isomorphic (left) and transfer problems (right). Among the isomorphic problems we further distinguished between corresponding and noncorresponding problems. This was done

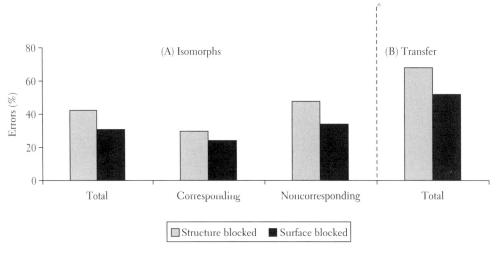

FIGURE 14.3. Problem-solving errors for (a) isomorphic problems (total, corresponding and non-corresponding) and (b) transfer problems as a function of problem order.

to see whether the superiority of a surface-blocked sequence was due mainly to a higher performance for noncorresponding problems, as had been predicted. As a comparison of the two intermediate groups of bars in Figure 14.3 shows, there were no performance differences between the two problem sequences for corresponding problems. However, participants in the structure-blocked condition clearly made more errors than those in the surface-blocked condition when working on noncorresponding problems. Overall, these results strongly support the near-miss hypothesis.

To conclude, presenting superficially similar problems successively emphasizes differences between these problems with regard to structural features. This fostered problem-solving performance especially for problems whose surface features are misleading in that they suggest a wrong solution procedure. Additionally, working on problems from different problem categories alternately seems to result in more knowledge about structural features, which helps to solve problems requiring an adaptation of known solution procedures. These results also confirm the findings of Paas and van Merriënboer (1994), who demonstrated the superiority of structural variability in learning from worked-out examples. It is important to note that the surface-blocked sequence is superior because it supports a process that seems to be the most crucial prerequisite for transfer, namely, recognizing structural features among problems. This explanation implies that the observed superiority of the surface-

blocked sequence should vanish if problem solvers are already sufficiently aware of the structural properties of the problems.

Experiment 2: Structural Awareness as a Moderator of Order Effects

In Experiment 2, we tested the assumption that structural awareness measured by means of a categorization task would moderate order effects. We expected that participants who are able to categorize the problems according to their structural features before solving them would no longer benefit from a surface-blocked sequence in which structural differences are highlighted. On the contrary, it might even be, in line with the transfer hypothesis, that, because good categorizers already know about the problems' structural similarities, they might benefit from the transfer opportunities in the structure-blocked sequence. However, for poor categorizers who experience difficulties in detecting the structural similarities among problems, the surface-blocked sequence might be another chance to recognize the structural properties of the problems. This superiority of the surface-blocked sequence may, however, be less pronounced compared to Experiment 1 because it might be partially overridden by the minor effects of prior problem categorization.

To test these assumptions, we used the same materials as in Experiment 1. Forty students from Saarland

University and the University of Göttingen first studied the booklet containing the three worked-out examples. In contrast to Experiment 1, they did not start working on the nine isomorphic test problems immediately after this learning phase. Rather, the participants received a sheet of paper that listed all nine problems, where the order of presentation depended on the experimental condition. They were instructed to categorize these problems according to their mathematical features. After having accomplished the categorization task, the participants were asked to solve the problems. The problem list and the category assignments were visible during the whole test. After having solved the nine problems, the participants received the three new transfer problems. The performance measures were the participants' errors in percentages for the isomorphic and transfer problems.

For the data analysis we distinguished between good and poor categorizers within each of the experimental conditions according to the students' ability to categorize problems by their structural similarities. The resulting categorization variable was used as a second factor in all of the analyses.

Neither problem order nor quality of categorization had an impact on solving isomorphic problems (left half of Figure 14.4). This lack of significant main effects was traced back to a significant cross-interaction between the two factors: As expected, the participants who performed poorly in detecting structural similarities in the categorization task did not show a reliable order effect, whereas the good cate-

gorizers performed better in the structure-blocked sequence compared to the surface-blocked sequence. Further analyses revealed that this pattern of results held only (and was even more pronounced) for non-corresponding problems, which is again in line with our predictions. For the transfer problems there was no main effect for problem order. However, good categorizers committed fewer errors in the transfer task than did poor categorizers. Finally, there was the same, but less accentuated, cross-interaction as for isomorphic problems.

To conclude, the quality of problem categorization moderated the effects of problem order. This is consistent with the model on order effects according to which order effects should be affected by prior knowledge. Not only did the order effect in favor of the surface-blocked sequence vanish for good categorizers, but participants who had been able to detect the problems' structural similarities in the categorization task even benefited from a structure-blocked sequence. For poor categorizers, we observed no sequence effect.

Summary

Order effects may arise whenever problem sequences differ in how they affect either learning during problem solving, knowledge transfer among successive problems, or both. These processes may either be hindered or supported, depending on the distribution of structure features, surface features, and the problems'

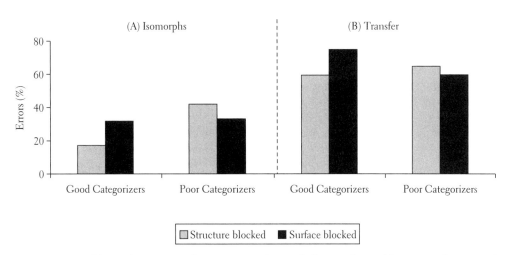

FIGURE 14.4. Problem-solving errors for (a) isomorphic and (b) transfer problems as a function of problem order and quality of categorization.

complexity across the sequence. Moreover, they are affected by the extent of prior knowledge a problem solver possesses.

We provided evidence from two experiments for some of the assumptions made in our order-effects model. Experiment 1 demonstrated that presenting superficially similar, but structurally dissimilar, problems successively can foster learning during problem solving by enabling the recognition of structural relations among problems. In addition, Experiment 2 demonstrated that structure-blocked sequences may foster the transfer process when structural relationships among problems have already been detected. Accordingly, we obtained support for the transfer hypothesis, as well as for the near-miss hypothesis, depending on whether or not the problem solvers were aware of structural features before problem solving. The latter finding supports the assumption that prior domain knowledge affects order effects.

Up to now, we have examined situations where problem solvers had to maintain a given order of problems when working on them. The order-effects model additionally allows one to predict whether problem solvers will make use of order effects in a strategic way by rearranging problems into a suitable sequence before solving them. Here it is of interest to know the conditions under which problem sequencing takes place, as well as whether problem-solving performance is affected by it.

ORDER EFFECTS IN USER-CONTROLLED SETTINGS: THE BENEFITS OF SEQUENCING

Deciding on an order in which to accomplish multiple tasks may be seen as a metacognitive problem-solving strategy in which a person incrementally develops a plan on how to approach a set of tasks with the aim of finding an order to optimize performance. Three questions guide our analysis of sequencing behavior: (1) Do problem solvers take the opportunity to arrange problems when given an opportunity, and, if so, how do they sequence them? (2) Which beliefs underlie problem solvers' sequencing activities? (3) What is the relationship between sequencing and problem-solving performance?

The first two questions were addressed in a questionnaire study in which we assessed students' beliefs and attitudes toward order effects and problem sequencing.

Questionnaire Study on Order Effects and Problem Sequencing

A self-developed questionnaire was administered to 127 students (98 female, 29 male) of Saarland University and the University of Göttingen. The students were told that they would have to answer several multiple-choice questions to provide information on their problem-solving behavior in mathematics. Here, only the most frequently chosen answers to the questions are presented (details are provided in Scheiter, 2003).

Beliefs in the Existence of Order Effects

When asked which predefined problem order would be best for solving multiple mathematical problems, 65% of the students stated that the best problem-solving performance would result if problems that have to be solved by a similar solution principle were presented in succession and if, within each block of similar problems, easy problems preceded more difficult ones. In addition, 16% of the students were convinced that problem-solving performance would be best if easy problems were presented before more difficult ones irrespective of structural similarity. On the other hand, 7% answered that performance would be best when structurally similar problems followed one another irrespective of problem difficulty. Only 7% were convinced that the order of solving mathematical problems had no effect on performance at all.

Sequencing Behavior

When asked how they would start working on a written examination, 47% of the students reported that they would first study all of the problems thoroughly before selecting one to start with. Twenty-six percent, however, would read all of the problems and then start working on the first one presented. Another 13% reported using a very deliberate scheduling strategy—they would first read all of the problems and then determine a working order for all of them before starting to solve the problems. Only 13% of the students would start with the first problem without even looking at the succeeding ones. Of the 77 students who reported any kind of sequencing strategy, 84% reported that they started with the seemingly easiest problem. When asked how they would proceed after having solved the first problem, 58% answered that they would continue working on the next easiest one. Far fewer students (23%) said that they would select the problem that seemed most structurally similar to the problem solved before. Of the whole sample of students, the vast majority (74%) reported that they would skip problems when experiencing difficulties with solving them, hoping that a solution would come to mind later on. Only 21% indicated that they would search for a similar problem that they had already solved and try to use its solution on the difficult problem.

The questionnaire study provides some initial insights that are relevant to investigating problem solvers' sequencing behavior. First, it demonstrates that the majority of problem solvers believe in the existence of order effects in mathematical problem solving—at least when being shown different problem sequences in a multiple-choice format. In particular, orders in which the problems are arranged according to their structural similarity and in increasing difficulty are judged more suitable. Second, most of the problem solvers reported that they would choose an order that sequenced the problems primarily according to their complexity. In addition, the selection of succeeding problems is oriented by difficulty; structural similarity is less important as a selection criterion. Overall, these findings suggest the experimental investigation of sequencing effects in problem solving as outlined in the next section.

Experiment 3: Effects of Problem Order and Sequencing in User-Controlled Settings

In this experiment (cf. Scheiter & Gerjets, 2002) we investigated the impact of problem order and sequencing on problem-solving performance using the hypertext-based learning and problem-solving environment HYPERCOMB (Gerjets, Scheiter, & Tack, 2000). It contained an introduction to the domain of combinatorics followed by a learning phase during which participants could study worked-out examples for six problem categories (i.e., permutations, variations, and combinations—each with and without the replacement of selected elements). Before starting, the participants were informed that they would have to solve six test problems listed on a single page. They were asked to study all of the problems carefully before selecting one to work on. They were further informed that they could solve the problems in any order they wanted. Whenever they had solved a problem, the initial list was presented again (including the

items already solved), and they were asked to select another problem.

The problems came from three of the six categories taught in the learning phase. For each category there was always one easy problem that required a single application of the respective solution principle to solve the problem. The second one was a difficult problem that required two applications of the solution principle (Table 14.3), thus demanding a larger number of cognitive operations (Ohlsson et al., 1992). Contrary to the two previous experiments in this chapter, the problems' surface features were not systematically varied.

Seventy-six participants from the University of Göttingen were provided with one of two different presentation orders for the problems. Based on a task analytical approach, the two orders were designed to differ with regard to enabling learning during problem solving and transfer: In the *suitable presentation order*, problems belonging to the same problem category were arranged in a simple-to-complex sequence, and the structurally similar categories were presented in succession. In the *unsuitable presentation order*, these principles were reversed. That is, the difficult problems were presented before the easier ones, and the structurally dissimilar problem categories were presented in succession.

TABLE 14.3. Easy and Difficult Test Problems of the Problem Type "Variation Without Replacement"

Easy Problem

A lighthouse can flash in six different colors (red, yellow, green, blue, orange, pink) from which colors are randomly chosen to form a signal. Each signal contains two colors in succession and none of the colors can appear twice in one signal. What is the probability that the lighthouse will send a red-orange signal, that is, it will first flash red and then flash orange?

Difficult Problem

At a soccer game there are two dressing rooms for the two teams. The players from Oxford wear T-shirts with odd numbers from 1 to 21 and Nottingham has even numbers from 2 to 22. As the aisle from the dressing rooms is very narrow only one player at a time can enter the field. The players of the two teams leave their rooms alternately with a player from Oxford going at first. What is the probability that the first five players who enter the field have the numbers five, two, thirteen, eight, and one (i.e., the first has the number five, the second has got the two and so on)?

The more suitable order was expected to result in differences that favored it. Additionally, we assumed that the students would rearrange the problems more often in the unsuitable order.

There were no clear predictions regarding the relationship between the students' reordering of the sequences and their problem-solving performance: On the one hand, their sequencing might result in performance improvements only if the problem solvers are able to identify an order that is more suitable for learning during problem solving and/or for knowledge transfer compared to the initial presentation order. Consistent with this reasoning, commentators on metacognition and problem-solving strategies (e.g., Pólya, 1945; Schoenfeld, 1985) teach problem solvers to make use of analogical transfer relations between problems as a general problem-solving strategy: "If you cannot solve the original problem, try first to solve an easier, related problem. Look for known solutions to related problems" (Schoenfeld, 1985, p. 86). The basic idea is that deviating from an initial problem order by first solving an easier problem that is structurally related to a more difficult problem in the set results in knowledge that can then be applied to the difficult problem. These assumptions fit well into the model on order effects, which predicts better performance for sequences that facilitate learning (i.e., simple-to-complex sequence) and transfer (i.e., structural similarity among successive problems).

On the other hand, sequencing problems may also enhance problem-solving performance irrespective of both the initial presentation order and the newly constructed one. According to this reasoning, the mere fact that problem solvers need to control their own problem-solving process by comparing different problems and deciding on an order to solve them may itself improve their performance. In instructional settings, similar effects have often been postulated for learning scenarios with a high degree of learner control (i.e., where the learner is allowed to select and sequence information; Merrill, 1980; Swaak & de Jong, this volume). However, it has been noted that not all learners benefit from learner-controlled instructional settings in the same way; rather, they have to possess specific cognitive prerequisites to regulate their information-processing behavior appropriately (Lawless & Brown, 1997; Niemiec, Sikorski, & Walberg, 1996).

Given this background, it is unclear whether the freedom to decide upon a problem order really has only specific effects (i.e., depending on the initial presentation order) or general benefits irrespective of both the initial presentation order and the order that they arrange on their own. Moreover, if there are positive effects of problem sequencing, we assume that these effects are likely to be moderated by a problem solver's prior knowledge—similar to the effects of learner control in instructional settings.

To test these assumptions, we used domain-specific prior knowledge as a second between-subjects variable beyond the presentation order. Moreover, the participants were classified into two groups based on whether they had rearranged the problems by deviating from the given presentation order. A participant was categorized as being a sequencer when at least one problem was solved in a new position. As performance measures, errors for easy and difficult test problems were registered and transformed into percentages.

There was an order effect in favor of the suitable presentation order for the overall problem-solving performance (Figure 14.5). This effect was caused mainly by participants with a suitable problem order outperforming participants in the unsuitable sequence condition on easy test problems, whereas there was no order effect for difficult test problems. Neither the effects for prior knowledge nor the interaction between presentation order and prior knowledge were significant. Thus, the superiority of the suitable presentation order could be demonstrated irrespective of participants' prior knowledge.

To determine whether participants would be more likely to rearrange problems when being confronted with an unsuitable presentation order and how this sequencing behavior would contribute to their problem-solving performance, we analyzed the percentage of those who deviated from the presentation order of problems (Figure 14.6). As we had predicted, the participants deviated more often from the unsuitable order. The sequencing behavior was unaffected by the participants' prior knowledge. Deviations from the given presentation order were caused mainly by the participants' preference for working on easy problems before approaching the more difficult ones—regardless of structural similarities among easy and difficult problems.

Figure 14.7 shows the impact of sequencing on problem-solving performance. There was no main effect of sequencing behavior for performance on easy test problems; however, sequencing behavior interacted with the participants' prior knowledge in that high prior-knowledge participants slightly improved

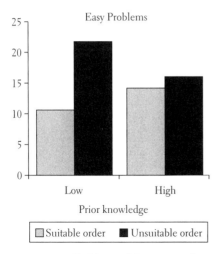

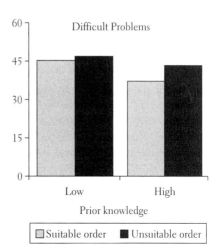

FIGURE 14.5. Problem-solving errors (in percentages) for easy problems (*left*) and difficult problems (*right*) as a function of presentation order and prior knowledge (Experiment 3).

their performance by rearranging the problems, whereas low prior-knowledge participants' performance even deteriorated. The performance of participants with high prior knowledge who reordered problems in the unsuitable-order condition was almost as good as that of those who had solved problems in the suitable-order condition. Although this effect seemed to interact with the presentation order, the triple interaction was not significant, nor was there an interaction between the presentation order and sequencing behavior. The impact of sequencing behavior on problem-solving performance for difficult test problems was different. Performance improved slightly by rearranging the problems, whereas there were no interactions with prior knowledge or presentation order.

To summarize, there were order effects that favored a sequence in which the problems were arranged according to their structural similarity and difficulty. Additionally, participants tried to make use of this effect by rearranging problems when they were presented in an unsuitable way. However, improvements due to problem sequencing were greater for participants with high prior knowledge, who were probably more likely to identify structural similarities among the problems. For low prior-knowledge participants, performance deteriorated when they deviated from a given unsuitable order of problems. Finally, we found that sequencing improved performance on difficult test problems irrespective of whether the participants deviated from a suitable or an unsuitable problem order. Possible explanations for these findings, as well as their instructional implications, are discussed in the next section.

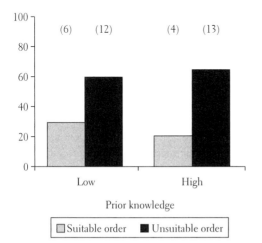

FIGURE 14.6. Percentage of participants deviating from the given order of problems as a function of presentation order and prior knowledge (Experiment 3). Absolute numbers of sequencers are in parentheses.

CONCLUSIONS AND INSTRUCTIONAL IMPLICATIONS

The experiments reported in this chapter have examined order and sequencing effects in problem solving,

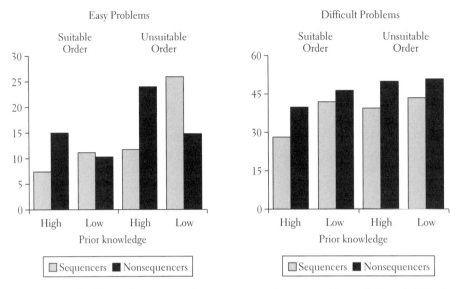

FIGURE 14. 7. Problem-solving errors (in percentages) for easy problems (*left*) and difficult problems (*right*) as a function of participants' sequencing behavior, presentation order, and prior knowledge (Experiment 3).

and the results can inspire the design of instructional materials. First, there are some hints as to which predefined problem-solving or training orders should be used for skill acquisition. Second, in particular the results of the third experiment help answer the question of whether learners should be allowed to decide upon an order for learning. We take these up in turn.

The first experiment reported here demonstrated the superiority of a problem order in which superficially similar, but structurally different, problems were solved in succession. Most importantly, a surface-blocked sequence also resulted in a better subsequent transfer performance. This effect was explained by assuming that a surface-blocked sequence highlights the structural differences among succeeding problems (Winston, 1975) and thus fosters learning during problem solving. There is some initial evidence that this near-miss effect can also inspire the design of example sequences by having instructional designers focus more on the sometimes helpful role of surface similarities (Park & Tennyson, 1980; Ross & Kilbane, 1997). In this vein, we were able to show in other experiments that surface similarities among examples that illustrate different problem categories may allow for profitable processes of example comparison by highlighting the structural differences between the

instances (Gerjets, Scheiter, & Tack, 2005; Scheiter & Gerjets, 2005b; Scheiter, Gerjets, & Schuh, 2004).

Overall, these findings suggest that it is necessary to refine the research question of whether instructional items (e.g., examples, training problems) should be presented blocked or alternating with regard to their structural features. This refinement may also help to explain why, up to now, empirical investigations dealing with that question have not come up with a satisfactory answer (Langley, 1995).

First of all, it is not just the arrangement of structural features that determines the suitability of a training order; rather, it is the way the structural and surface features are combined, as well as how this configuration of features is distributed across a sequence of problems. Thus, it is not sufficient to create example sequences that are highly variable with regard to their structural features. For learners to benefit from the near-miss effect, the surface features need to be kept constant while the structure changes.

Second, the moderating role of domain-specific prior knowledge has until now been neglected in empirical research on order effects. Our results demonstrate that, if problem solvers were sufficiently aware of the problems' structural features, then the aforementioned order effect would be reversed because now a structure-blocked sequence would be superior to the surface-blocked sequence. One might argue that a structure-blocked sequence thus cannot be recommended for instructional purposes because it presupposes that a learner already knows what is being taught, making further instruction unnecessary. However, there are at least two arguments against this position: First, even problem solvers with a high structural awareness (i.e., high prior knowledge) were far from a ceiling effect when solving problems. That is, even for them, further instruction may prove worthwhile. Second, structure-blocked sequences and surface-blocked sequences may serve different functions in instruction and help to acquire different kinds of knowledge. Similarly, Quilici and Mayer (1996) have argued that, in an example sequence in which problem categories are presented alternately, "students have the opportunity to notice which features differ between problem types, whereas in the blocked condition, students have the opportunity to notice which features are the same within a problem type" (p. 156).

Returning to the initial question of how prior knowledge moderates order effects, one might assume that in the initial stages of skill acquisition, orders that alternate surface features may help learners to identify structural differences, whereas in later stages students possess sufficient knowledge to be able to identify the structural commonalities of problems blocked according to their surface structure. This is contrary to the suggestion by Paas and van Merriën-boer (1994) that, because high prior knowledge is necessary to cope with a variable problem order, these sequences should be used only in the later stages of instruction. However, Paas and van Merriënboer did not discuss the role of surface features, which may support learning from variable problem orders and explain the contradictory conclusions regarding the use of structure-blocked and alternating problem orders. Further research is needed to provide evidence for the relative impact of prior knowledge as a moderator of order effects among successive problems that either do or do not share surface and structure features.

The second aim of this chapter was to take a closer look at the question of whether students make use of the opportunity of creating the sequences in which they want to work on problems and how this affects their problem-solving performance. The results of the questionnaire study, as well as of the experiment, show that students frequently make use of opportunities to rearrange problems. However, only very few

students appeared to use sophisticated sequencing strategies such as planning the order of all of the problems in advance. Rather, as had been proposed, the sequencing of problems most often seems to be opportunistic and is guided by on-line problem-solving experience. The questionnaire study led to the tentative conclusion that the selection of a problem order is based primarily on the problems' complexity because the students stated that they preferred to start with simple problems. Solving structurally similar problems in succession was seen as less important when sequencing problems. The experimental study confirmed this bias toward simple-to-complex problem orders. In this study it was also shown that problem sequencing was adapted to the quality of the initial presentation order. That is, the students tended to rearrange the problems more frequently when the presentation order was an unsuitable one.

On the basis of the model on order effects, one might have assumed that the value of sequencing problems becomes evident only if a problem solver is able to identify a problem order that is more suitable for problem solving and knowledge transfer than the presentation order. However, there was little support in favor of this position in our experimental data. Problem solvers who rearranged problems were superior to those who maintained the given order even when deviating from a suitable presentation order. To exaggerate, they thus benefited from "destroying" a problem order that had been rather optimal for supporting learning during problem solving and transfer. These findings, together with the results from another experiment (Experiment 6 in Scheiter, 2003), suggest that deciding upon a problem order has value in its own right as it supports an active processing in terms of studying these problems carefully and comparing them to one another. This may vary by individual. This effect of sequencing provides some support for the idea that learners should be allowed to take control of their learning processes. At first glance these results seem to contradict the findings of Swaak and de Jong (this volume), who found no differences between a system-controlled and a user-controlled sequencing condition in simulation-based learning. However, whereas in our study all of the students had to process the same materials, in the Swaak and de Jong study sequencing allowed the students to skip materials. Thus, potential sequencing effects may have been overridden by a learner's decision to not study helpful learning materials. This effect may also be due to problem solving with more knowledge, allowing the problem solver to be more active.

In our study, improvements due to problem sequencing were observable mainly for participants with high prior knowledge, who were probably more likely to identify structural similarities among problems. On the other hand, low prior-knowledge participants' performance deteriorated when they deviated from a given order of problems if these problems were unsuitably arranged. This confirms prior findings from research on learner control: Novice learners are ill equipped to manage their own instruction and often fail to make effective use of the control given them (Lawless & Brown, 1997; Niemiec, Sikorski, & Walberg 1996; Tennyson, 1980). Here, additional research is needed to determine either how to provide additional support to novice learners in regulating their learning processes or how to design adaptive instruction that provides guidance if a learner cannot cope with the additional requirements.

To conclude, the work reported in this chapter has provided insights into order and sequencing effects in problem solving, which can also be used to inform instructional design decisions. More research, however, needs to be done to obtain a more thorough understanding of these effects, which might address the following questions:

1. How can we foster the order effects that are caused by facilitating learning during problem solving? Which instructional strategies enhance the recognition of structural differences among superficially similar problems? To explore this area, create two orders and test them experimentally.

2. How does the number of problem categories affect order effects? That is, how many structural differences between problem categories can we possibly keep in mind when learning in a surface-blocked sequence—without first being excessively trained on each problem category in isolation? To explore this area, find some real-world instructional material, and count the number of problem types (e.g., mechanics problems in physics).

3. Why do students who rearrange problems sometimes perform better? That is, what are the underlying cognitive processes, and can they be stimulated by other instructional methods (e.g., those that also support novice learners)? Which features prompt students to rearrange problems in a specific way? Do students with high or low prior knowledge base their sequencing decisions on different features? Can we support students with low prior knowledge in their sequencing decisions? Examine this effect either by varying working memory (e.g., with a dual task) or by measuring working memory in subjects, and then examine their learning performance and the degree of reordering.

4. Which methods can be used to get a more detailed understanding of order and sequencing effects (e.g., think-aloud protocols)? What additional data do we need to model these effects? Gather pilot data from three subjects using a different methodology for each subject. Compare and contrast the data gathering and implications.

5. Can we observe similar effects in other domains? For instance, are there order effects in more ill-structured domains (e.g., history)? Use a theory from this book, such as EPAM (Gobet & Lane, this volume), to comment on this.

ACKNOWLEDGMENTS

This work was supported by a scholarship from the Deutsche Forschungsgemeinschaft awarded to the first author of the chapter as a member of the Graduate College for Cognitive Science at Saarland University, Germany. We thank Carina Kraemer, Frauke Lancker, Lisa Olbrich, Tina Schorr, and Julia Zimball for conducting the experiments, as well as Simon Albers for programming work.

References

Blessing, S. B., & Ross, B. H. (1996). Content effects in problem categorization and problem solving. *Journal of Experimental Psychology: Learning, Memory, and Cognition, 22,* 792–810.

Clapper, J. P., & Bower, G. H. (1994). Category invention in unsupervised learning. *Journal of Experimental Psychology: Learning, Memory, and Cognition, 20,* 443–460.

Collins, A., Brown, J. S., & Newman, S. E. (1989). Cognitive apprenticeship: Teaching the crafts of reading, writing, and mathematics. In L. B. Resnick (Ed.), *Knowing, learning, and instruction* (pp. 453–494). Hillsdale, NJ: Erlbaum.

Gagné, R. M. (1962). The acquisition of knowledge. *Psychological Review, 69*, 355–365.

Gagné, R. M., & Paradise, N. E. (1961). Abilities and learning sets in knowledge acquisition. *Psychological Monographs, 75*, 1–23.

Gerjets, P., Scheiter, K., & Tack, W. H. (2000). Resource-adaptive selection of strategies in learning from worked-out examples. In L. R. Gleitman & A. K. Joshi (Eds.), *Proceedings of the Twenty-second Annual Conference of the Cognitive Science Society* (pp. 166–171). Mahwah, NJ: Erlbaum.

Gerjets, P., Scheiter, K., & Tack, W. H. (2005). *Strategies of comparing instructional examples in hypertext environments: Are multiple examples really necessary for schema acquisition?* Manuscript submitted for publication.

Gick, M. L., & Holyoak, K. J. (1980). Analogical problem solving. *Cognitive Psychology, 12*, 306–355.

Holyoak, K. J., & Koh, K. (1987). Surface and structural similarity in analogical transfer. *Memory and Cognition, 15*, 332–340.

Langley, P. (1995). Order effects in incremental learning. In P. Reimann & H. Spada (Eds.), *Learning in humans and machines: Towards an interdisciplinary learning science* (pp. 154–167). Oxford: Pergamon.

Lawless, K. A., & Brown, S. W. (1997). Multimedia learning environments: Issues of learner control and navigation. *Instructional Science, 25*, 117–131.

Mayer, R. E. (1981). Frequency norms and structural analysis of algebra story problems into families, categories, and templates. *Instructional Science, 10*, 133–175.

Merrill, M. D. (1980). Learner control in computer-based learning. *Computers and Education, 4*, 77–95.

Nathan, M. J., Kintsch, W., & Young, E. (1992). A theory of algebra-word-problem comprehension and its implications for the design of learning environments. *Cognition and Instruction, 9*, 329–389.

Newell, A., Shaw, J. C., & Simon, H. A. (1958). Chess-playing programs and the problem of complexity. *IBM Journal of Research and Development, 2*, 320–335.

Niemiec, R. P., Sikorski, C., & Walberg, H. J. (1996). Learner-control effects: A review of reviews and a meta-analysis. *Journal of Educational Computing Research, 15*, 157–174.

Novick, L. R. (1995). Some determinants of successful analogical transfer in the solution of algebra word problems. *Thinking and Reasoning, 1*, 5–30.

Ohlsson, S., Ernst, A. M., & Rees, E. (1992). The cognitive complexity of learning and doing arithmetic. *Journal of Research in Mathematics Education, 23*, 441–467.

Paas, F. G., & van Merriënboer, J. J. G. (1994). Variability of worked examples and transfer of geometrical problem-solving skills: A cognitive-load approach. *Journal of Educational Psychology, 86*, 122–133.

Park, O., & Tennyson, R. D. (1980). Adaptive design strategies for selecting number and presentation order of examples in coordinate concept acquisition. *Journal of Educational Psychology, 73*, 745–753.

Pólya, G. (1945). *How to solve it: A new aspect of mathematical method.* Princeton, NJ: Princeton University Press.

Posner, G. J., & Strike, K. A. (1976). A categorization scheme for principles of sequencing content. *Review of Educational Research, 46*, 665–690.

Quilici, J. L., & Mayer, R. E. (1996). Role of examples in how students learn to categorize statistics word problems. *Journal of Educational Psychology, 88*, 144–161.

Reigeluth, C. M., & Stein, F. S. (1983). The Elaboration Theory of instruction. In C. M. Reigeluth (Ed.), *Instructional-design theories and models: An overview of their current status* (pp. 335–381). Hillsdale, NJ: Erlbaum.

Ross, B. H. (1987). This is like that: The use of earlier problems and the separation of similarity effects. *Journal of Experimental Psychology: Learning, Memory, and Cognition, 13*, 629–639.

Ross, B. H. (1989). Remindings in learning and instruction. In S. Vosniadou & A. Ortony (Eds.), *Similarity and analogical reasoning* (pp. 438–469). New York: Cambridge University Press.

Ross, B. H., & Kilbane, M. C. (1997). Effects of principal explanation and superficial similarity on analogical mapping in problem solving. *Journal of Experimental Psychology: Learning, Memory, and Cognition, 23*, 427–440.

Salomon, G., & Perkins, D. N. (1989). Rocky roads to transfer: Rethinking mechanisms of a neglected phenomenon. *Educational Psychologist, 24*, 113–142.

Scheiter, K. (2003). *Sequenz- und Sequenzierungseffekte bei der Bearbeitung voraussetzungsreicher Aufgaben* [Effects of problem sequence and sequencing in solving knowledge-rich problems]. Unpublished dissertation. Eberhard-Karls Universität, Tübingen.

Scheiter, K., & Gerjets, P. (2002). The impact of problem order: Sequencing problems as a strategy for improving one's performance. In W. D. Gray & C. D. Schunn (Eds.), *Proceedings of the Twenty-fourth Annual Conference of the Cognitive Science Society* (pp. 798–803). Mahwah, NJ: Erlbaum.

Scheiter, K., & Gerjets, P. (2004). Sequence effects in solving knowledge-rich problems: The ambiguous role of surface similarities. In R. Alterman & D. Kirsh (Eds.), *Proceedings of the Twenty-fifth Annual Conference of the Cognitive Science Society* (pp. 1035–1040). Mahwah, NJ: Erlbaum.

Scheiter, K., & Gerjets, P. (2005a). *The impact of surface and structure similarities on order effects in solving knowledge-rich problems: Near miss or spontaneous transfer?* Manuscript submitted for publication.

Scheiter, K., & Gerjets, P. (2005b). When less is sometimes more: Optimal learning conditions are required for schema acquisition from multiple examples. In B. G. Bara, L. Barsalou, & M. Bucciarelli (Eds.), *Proceedings of the Twenty-seventh Annual Conference of the Cognitive Science Society* (pp. 1943–1948). Mahwah, NJ: Erlbaum.

Scheiter, K., Gerjets, P., & Schuh, J. (2004). The impact of example comparisons on schema acquisition: Do learners really need multiple examples? In Y. B. Kafai, W. A. Sandoval, N. Enyedy, A. S. Nixon, & F. Herrera (Eds.), *Proceedings of the Sixth International Conference of the Learning Sciences* (pp. 457–464). Mahwah, NJ: Erlbaum.

Schoenfeld, A. H. (1985). *Mathematical problem solving.* San Diego: Academic Press.

Tennyson, R. D. (1980). Instructional control strategies and content structure as design variables in concept acquisition using computer-based instruction. *Journal of Educational Psychology, 72,* 525–532.

VanLehn, K. (1989). Problem solving and cognitive skill acquisition. In M. Posner (Ed.), *Foundations of cognitive science* (pp. 527–579). Mahwah, NJ: Erlbaum.

van Merriënboer, J. J. G., Clark, R. E., & de Croock, M. B. M. (2002). Blueprints for complex learning. *Educational Technology Research and Development, 50,* 39–64.

Van Patten, J., Chao, C.-I., & Reigeluth, C. M. (1986). A review of strategies for sequencing and synthesizing instruction. *Review of Educational Research, 56,* 437–471.

Weisberg, R., DiCamillo, M., & Phillips, D. (1978). Transferring old associations to new situations: A nonautomatic process. *Journal of Verbal Learning and Verbal Behavior, 17,* 219–228.

Winston, P. H. (1975). Learning structural descriptions from examples. In P. H. Winston (Ed.), *The psychology of computer vision* (pp. 157–209). New York: McGraw-Hill.

Part IV

Conclusions

Chapter 15

All Is in Order

John Sweller

Order effects are studied for a variety of reasons with instructional implications probably being pre-eminent. An understanding of instructional effects usually requires an understanding of human cognition and accordingly, the chapters of this book pay close attention to cognitive processes. In this chapter, I consider human cognition as a natural information processing system and use the resultant cognitive architecture as a base for cognitive load theory. That theory in turn, can be used to generate instructional procedures. The theoretical and empirical consequences of cognitive load theory are used as a framework in which to discuss the chapters of this book.

The chapters in this book provide an extensive survey of the viewpoints and methodologies that have been and can be used to study order effects in learning. Either implicitly or explicitly, each chapter includes assumptions about the structures and function of human cognition. This chapter similarly takes as its departure point a particular view of human cognition and the consequent instructional recommendations. That view derives from cognitive load theory, which is primarily an instructional theory. However, the instructional principles generated by its assumptions have provided further insights into human cognitive processes, which in turn have led to further instructional recommendations. The chapters of this book are here discussed in light of cognitive load theory. I begin by discussing the cognitive bases of the theory.

NATURAL INFORMATION-PROCESSING SYSTEMS

Human cognition is an example of a natural information-processing system. There are many such systems on earth, of which evolution by natural selection (that is, the system that gave rise to human cognition) is probably the most important. It can be hypothesized that all natural information-processing systems have a common base (Sweller, 2003; Sweller & Sweller, 2006). While there are many ways of representing that base, in this chapter I do so through five principles.

The Information Store Principle

In order to function in an inevitably complex environment, natural information-processing systems must have a massive information store that is central to their ability to process information. In the case of human cognition, long-term memory not only provides that store but is also critical to almost all human cognitive activities. It is the primary determinant of what we perceive and how we act. For example, the ability to read this text depends on immeasurable knowledge in long-term memory of individual letters, combinations of letters and words, and the relation of those symbols to the external world. Similarly, since de Groot's (1965) work on chess-playing skill, we have known that problem solving is also dependent on schematic knowledge held in long-term memory (see de Groot & Gobet, 1996, for an update of this classic work). Those schemas permit expert chess players to recognize huge numbers of board configurations and to visualize the appropriate moves associated with particular configurations.

A genome provides an equivalent information store for Darwinian evolution. Genomes govern biological activity in a manner similar to the way long-term memory governs cognitive activity.

The Borrowing and Reorganizing Principle

How do huge amounts of information enter a store? Almost entirely by being borrowed from other stores. The vast bulk of the information held in long-term memory has been borrowed from the long-term memories of other people by imitating what they do, listening to what they say, or reading what they write.

The process is constructive in the sense that the information obtained is rarely, if ever, precise. New information obtained from other people by imitating, listening, or reading must be reorganized and combined with previous information held in long-term memory. The new and old information must be combined to form new schemas that differ from both the new and the old information. Cognitive load theory is concerned primarily with techniques of presenting spoken, written, and diagrammatic information in a manner that assists in this process of borrowing information from others and storing it in long-term memory.

The borrowing and reorganizing principle is equally important in biological evolution. During asexual reproduction, an entire genome is copied in a manner that, as far as I am aware, has no equivalent in human cognition. In contrast, sexual reproduction appears to have evolved to gain the immense advantages of a constructive process. Each individual is a genetic construction of its immediate male and female ancestors, and the exact copying of individuals is precluded by the process. As a consequence, reorganization is a necessary concomitant of the process.

The borrowing and reorganizing principle has an inevitable random component as an element of reorganizing. The way in which information from one long-term memory combines with that from another long-term memory can no more be fully determined beforehand than the precise genetic structure that eventuates when male and female DNA combines during sexual reproduction. This random component has implications for other principles.

The Randomness as Genesis Principle

How does cognition proceed when information from another store is not available either because it has not yet been discovered or because we do not have access to the relevant information? While the constructive processes of the borrowing and reorganizing principle generate novelty, it is not the ultimate source of novelty. To be of any use, the information borrowed from someone else's long-term memory must be different from that in one's own. The randomness as genesis principle provides the ultimate source of this variation.

Consider a person solving a problem. Most of the information used to solve the problem comes from long-term memory, but occasionally, for a novel problem, the problem solver must choose between two or more possible moves with no information in long-term memory to assist. The only way forward under these circumstances is to randomly choose one move, either physically or mentally, and test it for effectiveness. Effective moves are retained, while ineffective moves are jettisoned. Failing information in long-term memory, the decision on whether a move is likely to be effective cannot be made prior to choosing it. Accordingly, it must be chosen randomly. I suggest this process is the ultimate source of all new knowledge held by humans, just as random mutation is the ultimate source of all genetic variation.

The Narrow Limits of Change Principle

The random aspects of both the borrowing and reorganizing and the randomness as genesis principles have structural implications. If randomness is an unavoidable feature of the accretion of knowledge to the information store, mechanisms must be available to ensure that the functionality of the store is not compromised by the addition of insufficiently tested information. A limited working memory when dealing with new information provides that mechanism. A large-capacity working memory that must determine how to combine elements using a random generate-and-test procedure will suffer from combinatorial explosions that render it ineffective. (There are 6 permutations of 3 elements but 3,628,800 permutations of 10 elements, for example.) For the same reason, substantial genomic changes due to mutations require a huge number of generations that can span millions of years. The epigenetic system controls the flow of information from the environment to the genome in the same way as working memory controls the flow of environmental information to long-term memory (Sweller & Sweller, 2006).

The Environment Organizing and Linking Principle

In contrast to new information, there are no limits to the amount of organized information from long-term memory that can be used by working memory to organize an environment. Ericsson and Kintsch (1995) have used the term "long-term working memory" as a label. When dealing with organized information from long-term memory, working memory can handle massive amounts of information. That information can impose order on immensely complex environments and generate very detailed cognitive activity. Similarly, using the biological analogy, there are no limits to the number of base pairs that constitute a gene that is structured to express particular polypeptides. Huge amounts of genetic material may be needed and are available to create protein. The processes are also under the control of the epigenetic system, which governs the flow of information from the genome to environmentally appropriate activity in the same way as working memory governs the flow of information from long-term memory to environmentally appropriate behavior (Sweller & Sweller, 2006).

COGNITIVE LOAD THEORY

Together, these five principles provide a base for natural information-processing systems and consequently provide a base for human cognition. That base, in turn, is integral to the instructional design principles of cognitive load theory, including ordering principles.

The borrowing and reorganizing principle and the randomness as genesis principle provide the learning mechanisms of natural information-processing systems. The random components of both systems lead to the narrow limits of change principle. Cognitive load the-

ory emphasizes that principle when learners are acquiring novel information. Working memory is narrow when dealing with novel information. The aim of acquiring novel information is to increase the organized information in long-term memory, which can be used to generate appropriate cognitive activity via the environment organizing and linking principle. Learning is defined as a positive change in long-term memory.

There are three categories of cognitive load. Intrinsic cognitive load is determined by the intrinsic complexity of the information being dealt with. Complexity is defined as the extent to which elements of information interact. If element interactivity is high, individual elements cannot be dealt with (i.e., understood) in isolation. They must be dealt with simultaneously, and that may impose a heavier working-memory load than dealing with elements individually. Extraneous cognitive load is the cognitive load imposed by instructional procedures. Some instructional procedures will impose a heavy cognitive load that interferes with schema acquisition. Germane cognitive load is the load imposed by instructional procedures that support schema acquisition. These three categories of cognitive load are cumulative. If they exceed working-memory capacity, learning will be compromised. The aim of instruction is to decrease extraneous cognitive load and increase germane cognitive load while not exceeding capacity.

ORDER EFFECTS

While the study of order effects was not the purpose of cognitive load theory, the theory has predicted many instructional effects. Three of these, which are based on order, are discussed.

Isolated and Interacting Elements Effect

To be understood, all relevant information must be able to be processed in working memory simultaneously. For very high element interactivity material that has not as yet been incorporated into schemas, it may be impossible to process all of the elements simultaneously. Learning may be enhanced if instead of presenting all of the elements simultaneously, they are presented and learned as individual elements first and only later presented with their interactions made explicit. The advantage of this procedure is that it artificially lowers the intrinsic cognitive load. The disadvantage is that the initial learning must occur in an environment where full understanding is virtually impossible. The assumption is that the initial failure to understand is irrelevant because, for very high element interactivity material, initial understanding is impossible anyway. Pollock, Chandler, and Sweller (2002) found that, if very high element interactivity material was initially presented as isolated elements followed by the same material presented in full interacting elements form, learning was enhanced compared to presenting the material in full interacting elements form twice. Thus the isolated and interacting elements effect suggests that the order in which high element interactivity material should be presented is as isolated elements first followed by interacting elements. The model introduced in Nerb and Ritter (this volume) and Ellman's model in Lane's chapter (this volume) both support this approach. Gobet and Lane's CHREST (this volume) generated slightly different results for recognition learning.

Expertise Reversal Effect

There are several versions of the expertise reversal effect (Kalyuga, Ayres, Chandler, & Sweller, 2003), and, like the isolated/interacting elements effect, all of them depend on changing levels of expertise. In general, the effect occurs when an instructional technique A is superior to technique B for novices, but, with increasing expertise, the difference first disappears and then reverses.

One version of the effect relies on interactions between levels of expertise and two simpler cognitive load effects: the worked-example effect and the redundancy effect. The worked-example effect occurs when novice learners who are given worked examples to study learn more than learners who are given the equivalent problems to solve. The effect occurs because worked examples rely more on the borrowing and reorganizing principle, which reduces extraneous cognitive load, whereas problem solving relies more on the randomness as genesis principle, which increases extraneous cognitive load.

In contrast, assume the same experiment is run using learners who are more expert. For these learners, studying worked examples may be a redundant activity. They have schemas or partial schemas for the problem solutions, and working through a worked example increases rather than decreases extraneous cognitive load. They may learn more by solving problems rather than by studying examples, providing an instance of the redundancy effect. The expertise reversal effect provides another example of an order effect. Learners should be presented with many worked examples first, followed by practice problems, a presentation order that leads to the guidance fading effect.

Guidance Fading Effect

The guidance fading effect is discussed by Renkl and Atkinson in this volume and below, and so little need be said here. Based on the example of the expertise reversal effect discussed earlier, an appropriate order of presentation as levels of expertise increase is full worked examples first, followed by partial worked examples in which learners must fill in the missing steps, followed by full problems.

LESSONS FROM THE CHAPTERS

In the remainder of this chapter, the contributions to this volume are discussed in light of the preceding theoretical and practical considerations.

Reigeluth's chapter is interesting because it provides a general view of instructional design that places its primary emphasis on knowledge structures rather than cognitive ones. He points out, for example, that whether the sequencing of information is important depends on the relationships between the elements of information. If the elements of the topic being taught are not interrelated, then the order in which they are taught should not matter. Order is important for material only where the elements are related. The bulk of Reigeluth's chapter describes the elaboration theory, which is concerned with the manner in which different tasks should be divided when they consist of related elements. Clearly, we need to place some emphasis on the characteristics of the information being taught, and that is the major lesson that I learned from Reigeluth's chapter.

Notwithstanding the importance of knowledge characteristics, there are limits to how far we may be able to go without considering cognitive characteristics. For example, Reigeluth suggests that even for related material, sequencing may not be very important if the teaching period is less than about 1 hour. Because working memory can hold only a limited number of elements of information for no more than about 20 seconds without rehearsal, sequencing may be important even for very short periods of instruction. The isolated/interacting elements effect, discussed earlier, refers to teaching material that is too high in element interactivity to be simultaneously processed in working memory and so must be initially taught as isolated (unrelated) elements before the relations between the elements are indicated. The isolated/interacting elements effect should be obtainable irrespective of the teaching times, provided the number of elements and their interactions exceed working-memory capacity. For high element interactivity material, having learners first learn elements in isolation before learning about the interactions should be beneficial even if the teaching period is short.

Cornuéjols discusses concepts developed using machine learning. This chapter is interesting for several reasons. It starkly illustrates some of the distinctions between natural information-processing systems (as discussed earlier) and machine learning. Machine learning has "virtually no notion of knowledge organization." A natural information store is not only very large compared to the knowledge stores of machine learning models, but organization is also one of its hallmarks. Learning, rather than being incremental as demanded by the narrow limits of change principle, is a "one-shot process." For these two reasons, machine learning theorists tend not to study order effects. Furthermore, the bulk of learning does not normally occur via the borrowing and reorganizing principle as it does in natural information-processing systems. Machine learning theorists are likely to term that type of learning "collusion." These distinctions, as indicated by Cornuéjols, are important and interesting. They can be used to provide a contrast with human learning and in the process tell us which characteristics of human learning are critical and why they may have evolved.

Nerb, Ritter, and Langley discuss the role of process models in learning. Historically, these models have played an important role in our understanding of human cognition, especially during the 1980s, when, arguably, they were central to research efforts to understand human cognition. In my mind, their most important, specific contribution was the role they played in demonstrating the significance of domain-specific knowledge in cognition, especially problem solving. It is a role that seems to be rarely acknowledged today, possibly because we all automatically accept the importance of domain-specific knowledge. It was not always so.

In the early 1970s, the concept of domain-specific knowledge and its influence was basically missing. Computational models of problem solving were largely based on a means-ends heuristics, and it was clear that the problem solving those models engaged in was quite different from most problem solving that humans engaged in. Why that difference occurred was not as clear at the time. Empirical evidence for the importance of domain-specific knowledge came from the game of chess. Evidence also came from the newer process models that emphasized domain-specific knowledge and so could solve more realistic problems in a manner that more closely modeled human problem solving.

I believe this work has provided us with one of the most important advances in our understanding of human cognition. This advance is mirrored in our current understanding of the centrality of knowledge held in long-term memory to all cognition, including problem solving. Accordingly, the evolution-based principles described earlier closely reflect our current understanding of the role of long-term memory. I see the use of process models to model order effects as a continuation of this advance.

Lane deals with neural networks and begins by discussing the ART network. He indicates that a major problem that any cognitive system must deal with is the tension between plasticity and stability. A system must be sufficiently stable to retain what has been learned previously but sufficiently plastic to acquire new information without destroying the old information. Indeed, that tension is present in all natural information-processing systems. I suggested earlier that human cognition handles the problem by having a very limited working memory to deal with new information (the narrow limits of change principle) but an unlimited working memory to deal with familiar information (the environment organizing and linking principle). Lane indicates that the ART system deals with the dilemma by allowing the system to learn very new information very quickly, while information that requires a modification of previous learning occurs slowly. It is understandable that such a system works, but it needs to be recognized that it probably differs substantially from natural information-processing systems, which may learn very new information more slowly than they adapt old information. It would be interesting to see these predictions compared in detail with empirical data on language learning.

Lane also discusses a simple recurrent network, especially with respect to order effects. He indicates that learning is facilitated by a simple-complex sequence, and empirical evidence supports this suggestion. From the point of view of competing models and systems, it is interesting that the production system model of Gobet and Lane (discussed below) predicts the superiority of the reverse, complex-simple order.

Ritter, Nerb, and Lehtinen provide a tutorial chapter on collecting and analyzing data that can be used to shed light on order effects. As it happens, their chapter could just as easily be used as a tutorial on data collection in the broader area of learning research. As someone who has spent much of his career running controlled experiments comparing the effects of various instructional procedures, I would like to say a little about the role of such experiments in learning theory research.

While controlled experiments can profitably be used at any stage during research into learning theory from the initial testing of theoretical points to providing evidence on whether a new instructional technique is effective in a classroom setting, they are essential when determining whether a new instructional technique should be introduced to a classroom. No instructional procedure should be introduced into an educational system until it has been properly compared with the prevailing procedures. Other research techniques such as the collection of verbal protocols, the construction of computational models, or even philosophical theorizing can be invaluable tools in determining cognitive processes and their instructional implications. They should never be used as a substitute for controlled experiments that indicate that a new instructional procedure results in more or better learning on a measure that is relevant to educational outcomes. For example, a process model can provide important insights into human cognition that can lead to equally important instructional hypotheses. Those hypotheses must be tested using controlled experiments. At the very least, the final step in recommending an instructional procedure to an education community should be positive results in at least one and preferably several controlled experiments. Until that point, we have research hypotheses for which there may or may not be evidence. We do not have procedures that we can recommend to an education community until after we have run appropriate, controlled experiments. Accordingly, I believe that no recommendations concerning order effects should be

passed on to an education community until after positive results from controlled experiments have been obtained. Once appropriate hypotheses have been successfully tested, the theories that gave rise to them can be used to design instruction and make instructional predictions. Currently, cognitive load theory is being used in this manner.

Renkl and Atkinson describe their work on the fading effect, an important finding in the instructional literature. The effect occurs when learning is enhanced by presenting learners with worked examples and gradually fading (i.e., decreasing) the guidance provided by the examples until the learners are able to solve problems on their own. Its importance derives from the fact that it was predicted from our knowledge of human cognitive architecture; it was tested and validated using randomized controlled experiments; and it has substantial practical implications. The fading effect derives from the worked-example effect. Since the time the worked-example effect was demonstrated in the 1980s, it has often been replicated by many researchers. As indicated previously, in recent years evidence has emerged that, as levels of expertise increase, differences between worked-example and problem-solving conditions first decrease and disappear and then reverse with problem solving proving superior to worked examples. This effect is an example of the expertise reversal effect. With increasing expertise, studying worked examples becomes redundant, while the generate-and-test procedures of the randomness as genesis principle are no longer needed because long-term memory contains sufficient information to provide learners with a problem solution. Practicing that problem solution imposes less of an extraneous cognitive load than assimilating and studying the information of a worked example.

The instructional consequences of this version of the expertise reversal effect can be found in the fading effect with most of the work on this effect over the last few years carried out by Renkl and Atkinson. Its most important practical implication is that it provides strong suggestions for presentation order: We should begin with an emphasis on worked examples and simultaneously encourage learners to self-explain. With increasing expertise, both the worked examples and self-explanation should be faded out until learners are solving problems with no guidance from worked examples. Renkl and Atkinson provide evidence from controlled experiments that this sequence is superior to simply emphasizing worked examples, a conclusion that would otherwise flow from the worked-example effect. The guidance-fading effect has important instructional ramifications with respect to instructional ordering. It can be derived directly from the cognitive architecture described earlier when discussing natural information-processing systems.

Gobet and Lane have used a new implementation of the well-known EPAM model to consider order effects. To investigate how the model was affected by the order in which it received data, they presented it with ordered sequences of random digits in which the number of digits in a "pattern" could vary from small to large. A small pattern could consist of a single random digit, while a larger pattern could comprise several random digits. There were three orders: small first, large first, and random.

The results indicated that performance in terms of exact matching was considerably worse for the small first order but better at subset matching when small patterns were presented first. In addition, the small first order required more tests to sort the test items.

According to these results, the order of presentation does matter to EPAM although, depending on the measure, more complex patterns followed by simpler ones may be preferable. I know of no data from humans supporting this suggestion. Nevertheless, predictions from EPAM indicate that under at least some circumstances, a complex first sequence is preferable. These data suggest that empirical work testing the complex first hypothesis may be worth pursuing. Of course, prior to embarking on such empirical work, the conditions under which a complex first hypothesis should hold would need to be identified using an appropriate and detailed model or theory. EPAM could provide that model, but detailed predictions would need to be in hand.

Morik and Mühlenbrock argue that scientific discovery is a slow evolutionary process and that computational models that "discover" major scientific principles in one step conflict with historical data. They go on to suggest that we can obtain information concerning the scientific discovery process by observing how children learn a scientific principle. The major part of their chapter provides information about a computational model designed to indicate the immense complexity of the information that must be assimilated by children who are learning why the earth rotating about its axis causes day and night.

Once we have learned and assimilated the concepts associated with the earth's rotation, it is easy to assume that these are simple concepts that children should be able to learn easily when they are pointed out. Historically, it has proved equally easy to assume that, because a single, expository lesson on the earth's rotation results in a minimal increase in relevant knowledge, the fault therefore lies in expository instructional techniques and that children can assimilate this information only by a discovery-based, constructivist teaching process. Nothing could be further from the truth.

The rotation of the earth and its relation to day and night is very high in element interactivity and extremely high in intrinsic cognitive load. Morik and Mühlenbrock's computational model does us a considerable service in demonstrating this point. Knowledge concerning the earth's rotation appears simple to us because of the environment organizing and linking principle. While it takes a very long time for learners to assimilate the required knowledge, once it is stored in long-term memory, it can easily be transferred from long-term to working memory and thus appears simple. It does not follow that the initial building of that knowledge in long-term memory was or is a simple process. Nor does it follow that the required knowledge is best built using the randomness as genesis principle rather than the borrowing and reorganizing principle. Quite the reverse applies. It may be difficult to assimilate the required knowledge via the borrowing and reorganizing principle, but it took millennia to discover the relevant principles via the randomness as genesis principle. Expecting learners to discover these principles, even with some guidance, is likely to be futile. Scientists have no choice but to engage in the discovery process because there is no one from whom they can borrow the information. In contrast, learners have instructional materials and teachers from whom to obtain the information via the borrowing and reorganizing principle (Kirschner, Sweller, & Clark, 2006).

Pavlik is concerned with massed versus distributed spacing effects in paired associate learning. He makes several points. We know that distributed practice is more effective than massed practice, but, of course, distributed practice requires more elapsed time. It is suggested that distributed practice is more effective because of forgetting effects. For any learning trial, poorly learned items, which tend to be difficult items, result in more durable learning for that particular trial because less is forgotten from it. The reason less is forgotten follows from the ACT-R model, which specifies that the amount of decay depends on the amount of activation. The greater the activation, the greater the decay, so if activation is high for better-learned items, the additional decay that occurs for them will result in the forgetting of more of what is learned during a particular trial. Spacing results in less activation of each item, and so less of what is learned on a particular trial is forgotten, resulting in more learning. Of course, the trade-off is more time. An alternative that eliminates this trade-off is to optimize training so that only the weaker items are trained. The positives of reduced forgetting due to training weaker items are thus obtained without the negatives of longer training times. An experiment supported this hypothesis, with optimized training proving superior to spaced training.

Pavlik is appropriately cautious in applying his theorizing and empirical results to more conceptual learning. My guess is that there is a good chance that his work will be applicable. All learning requires a positive change in long-term memory, and, without a positive change in long-term memory, no learning has occurred. This definition of learning applies irrespective of whether we are dealing with paired associates or more complex conceptual issues. It also applies irrespective of the method of learning, for example, via problem solving or a more direct procedure.

Ohlsson uses a computational model to suggest two general predictions. The first one is that learning from errors is important during skill acquisition: "Errors and other types of undesirable outcomes constitute the main source of information for someone learning from unsupervised practice." The second prediction concerns asymmetrical transfer. More constrained tasks are predicted to be easier than less constrained ones and should result in more transfer to less constrained (more difficult) tasks than the reverse sequence.

Both predictions require empirical testing, of course. There may be considerable evidence against the first one and some evidence in favor of part of the second prediction. Cognitive load theory shows that working-memory capacity is critical to learning and that including WM considerations could help provide better predictions.

With respect to the importance of making errors, the worked-examples effect suggests that, under at least some circumstances, making fewer or indeed no errors results in more learning than making more errors. Engaging in problem solving with its inevitable errors imposes a heavy cognitive load compared to studying worked examples with no errors. The reverse effect of more learning after problem solving seems to

occur only when using more expert learners in an area who are likely to make fewer errors (see Kalyuga, Tuovinen, Chandler, & Sweller, 2001).

With respect to asymmetrical transfer, many years ago I ran the following experiment (Sweller, 1976). A group of learners was given a paired-associate list consisting of consonant-vowel-consonant English words (e.g., bat-fig, van-mop) followed by another list of identical words, except that the last letter in each case was replaced by the letter q, resulting in the English words being turned into nonsense syllables. Another group was given the same two lists in reverse sequence. The English-nonsense group learned the English paired associates relatively quickly and the transfer task of nonsense syllables almost instantly. The nonsense-English group had considerable difficulty learning the nonsense syllables and showed much less transfer to the second task, in their case, the English words.

This asymmetric transfer with the easier task resulting in more transfer to the harder task than the reverse is in line with Ohlsson's second prediction. Nevertheless, although harder, there were more constraints in the construction of the nonsense syllables in that the last letter had to be q, whereas when using the easier English words, the last letter could be any letter, providing it resulted in an English word. Perhaps order effects are partially determined by the task difficulty of related tasks rather than constraints alone.

VanLehn's chapter is concerned with a version of an effect that has been described as the variability effect within a cognitive load theory framework (e.g., Paas & van Merriënboer, 1994). That effect suggests that, while initial learning may be inhibited by increasing variability, the transfer of learning may be facilitated. Whether the effect is obtained depends on cognitive load factors. Assume that total cognitive load (extraneous, intrinsic, and germane) is sufficiently low to permit an increase in the germane cognitive load. Increasing the variability of examples by increasing either the variability of cover stories or the number of distinct procedures taught simultaneously increases the germane cognitive load because, as Van-Lehn points out, learners must learn not only to implement a particular procedure but also to distinguish between procedures. The consequence is that learners who are given highly variable procedures are likely to perform relatively poorly on individual procedures during learning because of the increased cognitive load but better on transfer tests that require them to distinguish when to use particular procedures—which are basically the results VanLehn obtained.

In contrast, assume the material being taught is very complex and thus has a very high intrinsic cognitive load. The total cognitive load may be so high that increasing the germane cognitive load by increasing the variability may be counterproductive, with so little learned that all of the tests, including the transfer tests, indicate poorer performance under higher, rather than lower, variability conditions. Order effects can be hypothesized to be particularly relevant under these high intrinsic cognitive load conditions. Individual principles or procedures may need to be taught individually, followed by variable procedures to assist learners in distinguishing the critical conditions that should trigger a procedure.

Swaak and de Jong discuss the possibility of incorporating order effects into a discovery learning paradigm. As they indicate, on the surface at least, order effects and discovery learning are incompatible. By its very nature, discovery learning permits learners to follow any learning sequence that they wish. In its purer forms, learners should not have learning sequences imposed on them, apparently contradicting the concept of order effects. Of course, it is also possible to argue that learning is facilitated if learners discover appropriate learning sequences themselves rather than have appropriate sequences shown to them.

There may be both theoretical and empirical reasons to doubt the efficacy of a discovery learning paradigm when dealing with novices. Work on the paradigm was initiated about half a century ago prior to our more complete understanding of human cognitive architecture. Using the principles outlined at the beginning of this chapter, discovery learning places its emphasis on the inefficient randomness as genesis principle rather than the more effective borrowing and reorganizing principle. Failing knowledge, novice learners must randomly make decisions and test them for effectiveness rather than being presented with effective procedures such as the order in which to learn material. We might expect such procedures to result in less learning by novices, an outcome overwhelmingly supported by the empirical literature (Kirschner, Sweller, & Clark, 2006; Mayer, 2004).

Given these considerations, it is unlikely that Swaak and de Jong's free group would have outperformed the constrained group, but it is also appropriate to ask why there were no significant advantages for the constrained group. The answer is probably provided by Swaak and de Jong's informal observations on sequencing. Under the free condition, learners followed a sequence that was very similar to the ideal sequence forced on them in the constrained condition, eliminating the usual advantage of a constrained condition. Versions of the expertise reversal effect indicate that the disadvantages of discovery learning disappear as relevant knowledge increases. With further increases in knowledge, free conditions can be expected to be superior to constrained conditions (e.g., Kalyuga et al., 2001), with information in long-term memory providing a substitute for instructor-provided information. Increased expertise renders instructor-provided information redundant, and redundant instructor-provided information can have negative effects on learning (Kalyuga et al., 2001).

Scheiter and Gerjets describe three experiments, the second of which may have considerable, long-term influence. The first experiment demonstrated that, when structurally different but surface-similar problems are grouped, learning is enhanced, compared to a condition in which structurally similar but surface-dissimilar problems are grouped. Students must learn which features of a problem are relevant to the solution procedures. In contrast, learning which features of a problem are not relevant to the solution procedures is less important, presumably because they are potentially infinite in number—at the very least, a huge number of different cover stories are available.

More importantly, Experiment 2 indicates that, with increasing knowledge, this effect first disappears and then reverses. Learners with less knowledge of the appropriate problem categories benefited from surface-feature grouping in line with the results of Experiment 1. Learners with more knowledge of the problem categories benefited from structure grouping, possibly because instruction on how to distinguish between categories is redundant. Rather, these more expert learners need to practice solving particular categories of problems, an activity emphasized by the structure-grouping order.

I believe Experiment 2 provides a new example of the expertise reversal effect (Kalyuga et al., 2003). While, as always, additional research is needed, based on these preliminary results, learners should first be presented with surface-feature-grouped problems, followed by structure-grouped problems.

The third experiment presented learners with problems in either a suitable or an unsuitable order, but the learners were allowed to rearrange the order in which they dealt with the problems. Results indicated that high prior-knowledge learners benefited from resequencing the problems, whereas resequencing interfered with learning by low prior-knowledge learners. My interpretation is that high knowledge learners had sufficient working-memory resources to resequence and benefit from the resequencing, whereas similar resequencing attempts overloaded low prior-knowledge learners. This explanation is essentially identical to the one that can be used to explain VanLehn's results above. VanLehn varied task difficulty, while Scheiter and Gerjets varied learner knowledge and obtained essentially the same results. In both cases, variations in available working-memory capacity due to either variations in task difficulty or learner knowledge can be used to explain the results.

CONCLUSIONS

Our understanding of human cognition has advanced considerably in the last few years. A greater emphasis has been placed on the centrality of long-term memory to complex cognitive processes and there has been a greater willingness to relate human cognition to the rest of the natural world rather than to consider it as a completely unique system that can be considered in isolation. These changes in our understanding of cognition have had instructional consequences, including consequences for the order of presentation of information. The chapters of this book provide good examples of these rapidly evolving conceptualizations.

PROJECTS AND OPEN PROBLEMS

1. The natural information-processing system described at the beginning of this chapter has not been formalized as a computational model. What impediments might there be to the construction of such a model?

2. That natural information-processing system assumes that learning novel information occurs via the randomness as genesis principle and thus is slow, whereas learning to adapt previously learned information is more likely to occur via the more rapid borrowing and reorganizing principle. Is there any evidence for this view?

3. Should simpler material be presented to learners prior to more complex material, or would the reverse presentation order be more efficacious?

4. Should learners be presented with more or less guidance while learning?

References

de Groot, A. D., (1965). *Thought and choice in chess.* The Hague, Netherlands: Mouton. (Original work published 1946).

de Groot, A. D., & Gobet, F. (1996). *Perception and memory in chess: Heuristics of the professional eye.* Assen, the Netherlands: Van Gorcum.

Ericsson, K. A., & Kintsch, W. (1995). Long-term working memory. *Psychological Review, 102,* 211–245.

Kalyuga, S., Ayres, P., Chandler, P., & Sweller, J. (2003). Expertise reversal effect. *Educational Psychologist, 38,* 23–33.

Kalyuga, S., Chandler, P., Tuovinen, J., & Sweller, J. (2001). When problem solving is superior to studying worked examples. *Journal of Educational Psychology, 93,* 579–588.

Kirschner, P., Sweller, J. & Clark, R. (2006). Why minimal guidance during instruction does not work: An analysis of the failure of constructivist, discovery, problem-based, experiential and inquiry-based teaching. *Educational Psychologist, 41,* 75–86.

Mayer, R. (2004). Should there be a three-strikes rule against pure discovery learning? The case for guided methods of instruction. *American Psychologist, 59,* 14–19.

Paas, F., & van Merriënboer, J. J. G. (1994). Variability of worked examples and transfer of geometrical problem solving skills: A cognitive-load approach. *Journal of Educational Psychology, 86,* 122–33.

Pollock, E., Chandler, P., & Sweller, J. (2002). Assimilating complex information. *Learning and Instruction, 12,* 61–86.

Sweller, J. (1976). Asymmetrical transfer using a verbal learning paradigm. *Australian Journal of Psychology, 28,* 91–96.

Sweller, J. (2003). Evolution of human cognitive architecture. In B. Ross (Ed.), *The psychology of learning and motivation* (Vol. 43, pp. 215–266). San Diego: Academic Press.

Sweller, J., & Sweller, S. (2006). Natural information processing systems. *Evolutionary Psychology, 4,* 434–458.

Epilogue: Let's Educate

Oliver G. Selfridge

There is much we can learn about the education of people by studying learning in machines. Indeed, machine learning (ML) is an important major part of artificial intelligence (AI). Although we have a very long way to go, we have already learned some significant lessons about learning and education. Much of it is concerned with particular aspects of our living experiences. At present, ML seems to work on particular static problems of sophisticated applications, especially those requiring the use of advanced mathematics. Much of the ingenuity is to be admired, and some hard problems have been solved. But many difficulties remain.

The kinds of learning performed in ML studies seem to me to be very different from nearly all learning in people; look at the *Journal of Machine Learning*, and you will find it full of mathematical equations. Very few people think with equations. This is not to say that ML is not providing useful services but only that it is not doing its learning in the powerful ways that children and grown-ups do. Here I mention some of those ways.

For example, we all do learning *all the time*. That is not the learning that most people think of, which is what is done in schools. Yes, there is learning in schools, but there the education is directed at quite specific subjects, as this book describes so well. However, children learn to talk at home naturally enough; they learn to ride tricycles and bicycles, they learn to make friends (and probably enemies, too!), they learn to open and shut car doors, and so on. Grown-ups continue learning in their own ways, like understanding an unusual accent or how to handle etiquettes in different parts of the country or world, as well as various aspects of the jobs they hold.

It is clear that the sequences of lessons learned depend on the contexts and needs, both personally and socially. Most things that people learn rely on other things they have already learned. But the order need not always be the same. For example, in school it is not essential that geometry be studied before algebra or the other way around. However, it is clear that often the ordering of topics is essential: It is hard to learn how to follow a recipe from reading it in a cookbook if you do not know what a teaspoon is.

In computer software, however, most of the capabilities needed for ML have been programmed in— by programmers, that is—and not learned. Some of us would like to try to change that. We in ML need to look at the richness and varieties of learning and especially at how we *learn to learn*. For example, learning by rote (for example, the multiplication table) may not be much fun, but the rewards of doing it efficiently are clear. Moreover, the *understanding* of what multiplication consists of is essential to much of the rest of mathematics: That is a true ordering of learning. How many computer programs have any idea of what multiplication *means*?

Another distinction is that people learn through *experience*. That is, in people, learning is done with the whole person involved; yes, we may pay the most attention to a single factor, but we are nearly always aware of the surroundings, too. Many problems become apparent here, with very broad applications to general problems in education. A natural question is to ask how people learn to describe their experiences. For the most part, ML has not even faced that. What made somebody some 50,000 years ago notice that high tides were coupled with particular phases of the moon? Once that was noticed, the relationship was clear, although of course there was not the slightest hint of any mechanism or model. But from then on, the role of the heavens in the history of humankind must have become enormous—and it continues to be!

Nevertheless, that observation would have had no effect on civilization had not the social communication enabled and encouraged the sharing of it. By and large, people learn directly not merely from testing and trial themselves but also from sharing with other people—parents and teachers and friends! For the most part, ML has not faced that either. After all, that is what education is all about. Communication in a social environment is thus a key factor. It is encouraging that some facets of ML do use communication as a key: Robots (or agents) are being programmed to communicate with each other about what they may have found out.

Another key factor in learning is the motivations for it. Children and grown-ups all *care*, and that is obviously fundamental to learning and education.

Everybody is rewarded by learning—in many different ways. How do we reward our computer programs? I like to regard motivation as the expression of purposes at many, many different levels. Note that purposes in people change—and keep on changing, often as the result of learning. An especially interesting purpose is curiosity, and we must find out how to impart it to our software.

The basis for reward and punishment for people (and software, too) is often oversimplified. It is too easy (as is also true in some of the chapters in this book) to believe that education and learning are primarily concerned with making errors; one trouble with that point of view is that it implies an unchanging and constant world with constant standards of correctness and error. Learning to ride a bicycle is not merely learning to avoid falling off; rather, it is mostly discovering how to make the bike go where you want to go and in a comfortable way.

Is it an error to be checkmated when playing chess? Well, it depends. If you are teaching your six-year-old daughter to play chess, then almost the best thing to do is to sometimes let her checkmate you, and that may be hard to do if you do not play chess with some skill. Another even more important point is that the object of learning is not merely to learn how to avoid errors; rather it is to *make you better* at what you are trying to do, and of course that may change, depending on what you are trying to do and in what circumstances.

One of the difficulties in dealing with error is that it can be treated as a binary factor. No doubt that makes it far easier to handle mathematically—in equations, for example. But a great deal of learning is merely improving performance, balancing variable and changing constraints, understanding how to improve cognition, and on and on. None of these factors are easily quantifiable, even if they are unchanging.

My overall recommendation is that we should find out how to produce software that can be at least partly educated instead of having to be carefully programmed. The software must be able to learn not only how to accomplish the top-level desired tasks but also how to check and improve its performance on a continuing basis at many different levels.

Once we know how to better educate our software, we shall be in a much better position to understand how to educate not just our software but also our children—and indeed ourselves.

Author Index

Abrahamsen, A., 58
Agre, P. E., 87
Alessi, S., 182, 183, 192
Allen, J. A., 164
Amra, N. K., 61
Anderson, J. R., 31, 53, 59, 62, 67, 84, 96, 115,
    116, 137, 138, 139, 140, 141, 143, 144, 145, 148,
    149, 151, 157, 163, 164, 170
Angluin, D., 51
Arnold, M., 13
Asch, S. E., 85, 86
Ashcraft, M. H., 13
Assad, C., 182
Atkinson, R. C., 138, 139, 144, 149, 183
Atkinson, R. K., 6, 8, 63, 95, 96, 99, 100, 102, 103,
    115, 196, 218, 220
Atwood, M. E., 64
Austin, J. L., 170
Ausubel, D. P., 31, 35, 181
Ayres, P., 63, 97, 218

Baccino, T., 84
Bahrick, H. P., 138, 140, 148
Banathy, B. H., 23
Barto, A., 53

Bass, E. J., 63
Bassok, M., 96, 170
Baumann, M., 11
Baxter, G. D., 63
Baxter, J., 122
Bechtel, W., 58
Beilock, S. L., 13
Beissner, K. L., 32, 35
Belavkin, R. V., 84
Bell, P., 182, 183
Bhatnagar, N., 154, 157
Bibby, P., 53, 61, 151
Bielaczyc, K., 98
Bjork, R. A., 139, 148
Blessing, S. B., 198
Bloom, B. S., 178
Boshuizen, H. P., 86
Bothell, D., 84
Bovair, S., 12
Bower, G. H., 63, 196
Boyce, M. J., 182
Brewer, W. F., 121, 122, 123
Briggs, L. J., 24, 25, 26
Britt, M. A., 86
Brown, A. L., 98, 99

Brown, J. S., 7, 10, 89, 196
Brown, S. W., 206, 210
Bruner, J. S., 22, 31, 35, 181
Burges, C., 45
Burton, R. B., 10
Byrne, M. D., 84

Calfee, R. C., 85
Campbell, D. T., 85
Cañamero, L., 63
Carbonell, J., 119
Carpenter, G. A., 72, 75
Carr, T. H., 13
Carr-Chellman, A. A., 23
Cate, T. J., 86
Catrambone, R., 103
Cepeda, N. J., 142
Chandler, P., 63, 97, 98, 218, 222
Chao, C.-I, 195
Cheng, P. C. H., 111
Chi, M. T. H., 96, 97, 99, 100, 170
Chipman, S. F., 38
Christie, M. A., 183
Clapper, J. P., 196
Clarke, D. D., 82
Clark, R. E., 196, 221, 223
Cohen, P. R., 85, 90
Collins, A., 196, 197
Cook, C. R., 89
Cook, E. T., 29
Cooper, G. A., 96, 98
Cormier, S. M., 159
Cornuéjols, A., 6, 7, 10, 11, 41, 42, 57, 72, 85, 88,
    107, 219
Crossland, J., 82
Crothers, E. J., 141
Crowder, R. G., 141
Cuddy, L. J., 148

Daily, L. Z., 58
Darwazeh, A. N., 35
Davis, E. A., 182, 183
de Croock, M. B. M., 196
de Groot, A. D., 111, 216
Dehoney, J., 38
de Jong, T., 6, 9, 12, 13, 22, 23, 84, 86, 181, 182,
    183, 184, 185, 196, 206, 209, 223
Derry, S. J., 96
Detterman, D. K., 159
de Voogt, A. J., 111
DiCamillo, M., 201
Donchin, E., 63, 66, 83
Douglass, S., 84, 141
Drew, P., 87

Edwards, M. B., 87
Einhorn, H. J., 5, 11
Elman, J. L., 7, 62, 71, 75, 76, 77, 78, 152
Emde, W., 120, 121

Ericsson, K. A., 84, 87, 217
Ernst, A. M., 157, 197
Esposito, F., 120
Estes, W. K., 141, 142

Falkenhainer, B. C., 119
Farrell, R., 170
Feigenbaum, E. A., 108, 110, 111, 112
Feigenbaum, J. R., 58
Feurzeig, W., 87
Fincham, J. M., 141
Fischbein, E., 184
Fisher, C. A., 82, 87
Fitts, P. M., 151
Fleischman, E. S., 100
Ford, W. W., 28
Forgy, C. L., 154
Frederiksen, J. R., 182, 183
French, R., 47
Freudenthal, D., 111
Freund, Y., 45, 50
Frohlich, D., 87

Gagné, R. M., 24, 25, 26, 27, 28, 115, 151,
    196, 197
Gallistel, C. R., 158, 159
Gelman, R., 157, 158, 159
Gerjets, P., 6, 9, 11, 12, 22, 24, 31, 62, 84, 86, 87,
    183, 195, 197, 198, 205, 208, 223, 224
Gick, M. L., 62, 201
Gijlers, H., 184
Giles, C. L., 87
Gilmartin, K. J., 111
Glaser, R., 96, 170, 183
Glenberg, A. M., 138
Gluck, K., 67
Gobet, F., 6, 8, 10, 11, 53, 78, 88, 107,
    108, 110, 111, 116, 196, 197, 210, 216,
    218, 220, 221
Goldman, S., 52
Goleman, D., 39
Gottman, J. M., 83
Grant, D. A., 67, 87, 88
Gratch, J., 63
Greenberg, M. T., 39
Greeno, J. G., 7, 89, 157
Gregg, L. W., 112
Griffin, C. C., 86
Grossberg, S., 72, 75
Große, C. S., 8, 100
Gruber, H., 97, 98, 99, 103, 184
Guerrera, C., 183

Habel, C. U., 120
Hagman, J. D., 159
Haider, H., 157
Halverson, T., 84
Hammond, N., 5
Herbsleb, J. D., 83, 87

Hertwig, R., 64
Hickey, D. T., 183
Hinkofer, L., 99
Hogarth, R. M., 5, 11
Hollan, J. D., 183
Holyoak, K. J., 62, 199, 201
Hopkins, B. L., 141
Hornof, A. J., 84
Horwitz, P., 183
Howe, A., 121
Hudlicka, E., 63
Hunt, R. R., 111
Hutchins, E. L., 183

Iba, W. F., 164
Indiana Curriculum Advisory Council, 22
Ioannides, C., 120
Isen, A., 63

Jackson, S., 183
Jacoby, L. L., 148
Järvelä, S., 84
Jewett, J. J., 157
Johnson, T. R., 11, 61
Johnson, W. L., 88
Jonassen, D. H., 184
Jones, G., 58, 62, 111
Jones, R. M., 62, 100

Kalyuga, S., 63, 97, 218, 222, 223
Kane, M. J., 99
Kennedy, A., 84
Kibler, D., 85
Kieras, D. E., 88, 11, 12
Kietz, J.-U., 121
Kilbane, M. C., 208
Kim, Y., 23, 34
Kindfield, A. C. H., 183
Kintsch, W., 201, 217
Kirkpatrick, M., 138
Kirschner, P., 221, 223
Klahr, D., 58, 182
Klein, C. A., 122
Klein, L. C., 90
Knoblich, G., 157
Koh, K., 199
Kokar, M., 119
Kort, B., 63
Krajcik, J., 183
Krantz, D. H., 83
Krems, J. F., 11, 61, 64
Kuk, G., 13
Kukreja, U., 83, 86
Kusche, C. A., 39

Lajoie, S. P., 183
Lane, P. C. R., 6, 7, 8, 10, 11, 47, 53, 59, 71, 78, 88, 107, 108, 111, 196, 197, 210, 218, 219, 220, 221

Langley, P., 5, 6, 7, 10, 11, 25, 57, 58, 62, 64, 72, 85, 86, 97, 119, 120, 138, 164, 184, 195, 196, 197, 198, 201, 208, 219
Larkin, J. H., 84, 87
Lassaline, M., 53
Lavigne, N. C., 183
Lawless, K. A., 206, 210
Lazonder, A. W., 183
Lebière, C., 139, 157, 164
Lee, J. Y., 38
Lehtinen, E., 6, 7, 81, 84, 190, 195, 220
Lerche, T., 97
Lesgold, A., 22
Leshin, C. B., 21
Leutner, D., 182, 184, 191
Levine, D. S., 71, 72
Lewis, M. W., 96, 170
Lewis, R. L., 61
Linn, M. C., 182, 183
Lodewijks, H., 183, 192
Lohman, D. F., 183
Lord, F. M., 82
Louhenkilpi, T., 84
Lovett, M. C., 58
Luce, R. D., 83
Luchins, A. S., 62
Luchins, E. H., 62

Mahadevan, S., 53
Maier, U. H., 8, 99
Malerba, D., 120
Mali, G. B., 121
Mandl, H., 98, 99, 103, 184
Mane, A. M., 66
Manlove, S., 183
Manning, C. A., 87
Marsella, S., 63
Martin, B., 157
Mathias, D., 52
Mayer, R. E., 104, 175, 182, 183, 191, 198, 209, 223
McClelland, J. L., 64, 71
Machiels-Bongaerts, M., 86
McKendree, J., 5
McKusick, K. B., 164
McLeod, P., 71, 76
McNeese, M. O., 83
Mechner, F., 28
Meck, E., 158, 159
Merrill, M. D., 206
Merrill, M. M., 8, 100
Merrill, P. F., 28, 33
Meyer, D. E., 88
Michalski, R. S., 119
Miclet, L., 42
Miller, G. A., 109
Minsky, M., 42, 63
Minton, S., 156, 157
Mitchell, T., 42, 54, 76, 119
Mitrovic, A., 157

Monk, A., 87
Monty, R. A., 84
Morik, K., 6, 8, 10, 11, 12, 31, 119, 121, 125, 221
Mostow, J., 154, 157
Mühlenbrock, M., 6, 8, 10, 11, 12, 31, 119, 124, 125, 221
Munsie, S. D., 183
Murphy, G., 53

Nathan, M. J., 201
Neches, R., 58
Nerb, J., 3, 6, 7, 10, 11, 25, 57, 61, 63, 64, 72, 81, 88, 107, 190, 195, 197, 218, 219, 220
Neri, F., 120
Nesbitt, J. C., 138
Neuman, Y., 96
Neves, D. M., 62
Newell, A., 7, 58, 59, 60, 62, 64, 82, 87, 88, 153, 164, 196
Newman, S. E., 196
Niemiec, R. P., 206, 210
Nigam, M., 182
Nilsson, N. J., 156
Norman, D. A., 63
Norvig, P., 42
Novick, L. R., 199, 201
Novick, M. R., 82
Nussbaum, J., 121, 122

Ohlsson, S., 4, 6, 9, 10, 11, 54, 58, 64, 88, 151, 154, 156, 157, 158, 159, 164, 197, 205, 222
Olkinuora, E., 84
Olson, G. M., 83, 87
Oman, P. W., 89
Ortony, A., 63
O'Shea, T., 12
Osin, L., 22

Paas, F. G., 63, 96, 196, 198, 202, 209, 222
Papert, S., 42
Paradise, N. E., 196, 197
Park, O., 208
Parmley, M. W., 183, 192
Pashler, H., 142
Pavlik, Jr., P., 5, 6, 8, 9, 11, 48, 58, 62, 83, 84, 88, 103, 137, 138, 139, 140, 143, 144, 145, 148, 149, 221, 222
Perfetti, C. A., 86
Perkins, D. N., 201
Peterson, L. R., 138
Phillips, D., 201
Picard, R. W., 63
Pieters, J. M., 182
Pine, J. M., 111
Pirolli, P. L., 96, 98, 170
Plaut, D. C., 78
Plunkett, K., 71
Polanyi, M., 26
Pollock, E., 218
Pollock, J., 21

Polson, P. G., 12, 64
Pólya, G., 12, 206
Posner, G. J., 195
Pulos, S., 121

Quamma, J. P., 39
Quigley, K. S., 90
Quilici, J. L., 104, 175, 209
Quinlan, J., 48
Quinn, J., 182, 183
Quintana, C., 182

Raaijmakers, J. G. W., 148
Rauterberg, M., 87
Rayner, K., 84
Reader, W., 5
Reason, J., 163
Recker, M., 96
Reder, L. M., 58
Rees, E., 154, 156, 157, 158, 159, 164, 197
Reigeluth, C. M., 6, 7, 11, 12, 19, 21, 23, 24, 32, 33, 34, 35, 37, 38, 115, 181, 195, 196, 197, 218
Reilly, R., 63
Reimann, P., 96, 170
Reiser, B. J., 103, 183
Renkl, A., 6, 8, 63, 95, 96, 97, 98, 99, 100, 102, 103, 115, 184, 196, 218, 220
Resnick, L. B., 28
Retschizki, J., 111
Reynolds, J. H., 72, 75
Rhenius, D., 157
Richman, H. B., 64, 108, 110
Rieber, L. P., 182, 183, 184, 191, 192
Riley, M. S., 157
Ritter, F. E., 3, 6, 7, 10, 11, 13, 25, 53, 57, 58, 61, 62, 64, 67, 72, 81, 83, 84, 86, 87, 89, 90, 151, 183, 190, 195, 197, 218, 219, 220
Rivest, R., 53, 170
Rock, I., 141, 142
Rodgers, C. A., 33
Roediger, R., 90
Rohde, D. L. T., 78
Rohrer, D., 142, 149
Rollinger, C.-R., 120
Rolls, E. T., 71
Rose, D., 120
Rosenblatt, F., 42
Rosenbloom, P. S., 60, 64
Rosen, D. B., 72
Ross, B. H., 197, 198, 199, 208
Rouet, J. F., 86
Roy, A. K., 83
Rueter, H. H., 83, 87
Rumelhart, D. E., 64, 71
Russell, D. M., 63
Russell, S., 42

Sadler, P. M., 122
Salomon, G., 201

Salonen, P., 84
Saltzman, D., 138
Sanderson, P. M., 82, 83, 87
Saurers, R., 170
Savelsbergh, E., 183
Savoy, M. R., 23
Scandura, J. M., 33
Schapire, R., 45, 50
Scheiter, K., 6, 9, 11, 12, 22, 24, 31, 62, 84, 86, 87, 183, 195, 197, 198, 201, 204, 205, 208, 209, 223, 224
Schmidt, H. G., 86
Schoenfeld, A. H., 206
Schölkopf, B., 45
Schooler, L. J., 64, 87
Schraagen, J. M., 38
Schuh, J., 208
Schwarz, B., 96
Schweizer, K., 97
Schworm, S., 99
Seibel, R., 60, 64
Selfridge, O., 7, 10, 14, 225
Semeraro, G., 120
Senders, J. W., 84
Senge, P. M., 20
Shalin, V. L., 38
Shaw, J. C., 58, 196
Shrager, J., 87
Shute, V. J., 183
Siegler, R. S., 87, 121
Sikorski, C., 206, 210
Silverman, B. G., 63
Simon, H. A., 58, 64, 66, 82, 84, 87, 108, 109, 110, 111, 112, 116, 119, 153, 196
Singley, M. K., 53, 163
Sloan, R., 53, 170
Smallwood, R. D., 139, 142
Smith, D. A., 157
Smola, A., 45
Sneider, C., 121
Soloway, E., 183
Spada, H., 63
Squire, L. R., 153
Staley, R., 8, 99
Stanley, J. C., 85
Stark, R., 98, 99, 103, 184, 191
Staszewski, J., 108, 110
Stein, F. S., 196, 197
Sternberg, R. J., 159
Stevenson, W. E., 83, 86
Strack, F., 85
Stratford, S. J., 183
Strike, K. A., 195
Sun, R., 87
Suppes, P., 83
Suraweera, P., 157
Swaak, J., 6, 9, 12, 13, 22, 23, 84, 86, 181, 184, 191, 196, 206, 209, 223
Sweller, J., 6, 10, 11, 12, 13, 14, 20, 62, 63, 96, 97, 98, 143, 215, 217, 218, 221, 222, 223

Sweller, S., 217
Sykes, A. K., 111

Tack, W. H., 205, 208
Taylor, K., 142
Tennyson, R. D., 208, 210
Thagard, P., 63
Thomas, M. H., 146
Thompson, K., 164
Tindall-Ford, S., 98
Tobias, S., 183, 191
Trafton, J. G., 103
Tufte, E. R., 87
Tukey, J. W., 87
Tulbert, B. L., 86
Tuovinen, J., 97, 222
Tversky, A., 83

Underwood, B. J., 140
Utgoff, P., 47, 48

Valiant, L. G., 170
van der Hulst, A., 183, 192
van der Meij, J., 184, 185
van Joolingen, W. R., 182, 183, 184, 185
VanLehn, K., 6, 7, 9, 10, 11, 12, 13, 22, 23, 24, 82, 84, 87, 89, 96, 100, 143, 158, 169, 170, 171, 175, 183, 196, 197, 222–223, 224
van Merriënboer, J. J. G., 96, 196, 197, 198, 202, 209, 222
van Patten, J., 195
Vapnik, V., 45
Veermans, K. H., 184, 185
Velásquez, J. D., 63
Venekamp, R., 86
Viglietta, M. L., 122
Vitolo, T. M., 157
Vortac, O. U., 87
Vosniadou, S., 120, 121, 122, 123
Vreman-de Olde, C., 184
Vygotskii (also Vygotsky), L. S., 31, 152

Wager, W. W., 24, 25, 26
Walberg, H. J., 206, 210
Wampler, R., 138
Wang, A. Y., 146
Wang, H., 11
Wasserman, P. D., 72
Waters, A. J., 111
Weber, S., 97
Weerasinghe, A., 157
Weisberg, R., 201
Weiss, E. H., 9
Weitzman, L., 183
White, B. Y., 182, 183, 184, 191
Whitten, W. B., 139, 148
Williams, J. P., 141
Winston, P., 52
Winston, P. H., 52, 107, 201, 208
Wixted, J., 142

Wood, D. J., 58, 62, 116
Wood, S. D., 88
Wortham, D. W., 96
Wrobel, S., 120, 121

Yamamoto, N., 138
Young, E., 201

Young, J. L., 138
Young, R. M., 58, 64

Zaff, B. S., 83
Zhang, J., 11
Zuiker, S., 183
Zytkow, J., 119

Subject Index

ABACUS system, 119
abstract models, 64–65
activation,
   in ACT-R model, 140–144
   in ART networks, 73, 221–222
   in recurrent models, 58–59, 75–76
ACT-R architecture (Adaptive Character of
   Thought-Rational), 59, 62, 139–144
ACT theory, 157
Adaptive Character of Thought-Rational (ACT-R),
   59, 62, 139–144
adaptive resonance theory (ART), 7, 10, 72–75,
   78, 219
algebra skills. *See* problem solving, order effects
all-or-none theory, incremental learning, 141–142
analysis, in instructional systems design, 19–20
approach decisions, in instructional systems design, 21
ART (adaptive resonance theory), 7, 10, 72–75,
   78, 219
artificial intelligence, early perspectives, 107–108
artificial neural networks. *See* neural networks
ASEC cycle, in instructional systems design, 19–20
astronomy example, theory evolution, 120–121
attentional mechanisms, EPAM theory, 108–109,
   111–112, 116

back propagation of error, 76
BACON system, 119
bias input, in neural networks, 71, 72*f*
borrowing and reorganizing principle, 216, 218, 221,
   222–223
bridge, nailless, 3–4, 14–15

cardinality principle, in counting, 158
catastrophic forgetting, 47
category formation
   in ART networks, 72*f*, 73–75
   language learning, 77
change, in instructional systems design, 19–20
change measure, as data type, 83
change principle, in natural information-processing
   systems, 216–217, 219
   See also constraint-based learning
children's learning processes, counting tasks,
   158, 159
   See also day/night cycle, children's explanations
coded measures, as data type, 83–84
cognitive load theory
   and chapter contributions, 218–224
   order effects, 217–219
   principles of, 10, 12, 215–217

cognitive load theory (*continued*)
   See also specific topics, e.g., disjuncts per lesson;
     example-based approach; memory processes
cognitive models. *See* process models
cognitive skill acquistion
   early phase, 96–97, 99–100
   late phase, 96, 97
   See also example-based approach, cognitive skill
     acquisition
cognitive strategies, defined, 24
complexity
   in cognitive load theory, 217, 223
   definition challenges, 53
   in Elaboration Theory, 31–35
   See also disjuncts per lesson; problem solving, order
     effects
computational models. *See* process models
concepts
   in ART networks, 73–74
   in learning algorithms, 72
   in simple recurrent networks, 76–78
concept skills, in hierarchical task analysis, 25
concept task, in supervised learning, 43
conceptual elaboration sequence, 35, 36
conceptual expertise, in Elaboration Theory, 31–32
concrete concepts, in hierarchical task analysis, 25
confusion rates, in disjuncts per lesson experiments,
     174–175, 176–178
constraint-based learning
   in counting task experiments, 158–164
   electrical circuits simulation, 186–191, 223
   model of, 9, 153–158
   theoretical background, 151–153
context units, in simple recurrent networks, 75–76, 77–78
control parameter space, machine learning, 48–53
COPER system, 119
counting task experiments, 9, 10, 158–164
count system, 10

data collection, order effects studies
   overview, 7–8, 10, 81–82, 88
   analysis approaches, 87–88
   experimental designs, 85–87, 89–90
   importance, 220
   projects/problems, 88–89
   types of, 83–85
   See also chapters in Part III
day/night cycle, children's explanations
   overview, 120–122, 130–132, 221
   computational models, 123–128, 132–136
   instruction order experiments, 128–130
   projects/problems, 132
   verbal descriptions, 122–124
decay, in ACT-R model, 140, 142, 149
   See also forgetting
decision trees, learning algorithms, 47–48
declarative knowledge
   as constraint in HS model, 154, 157
   in error outcomes, 152–153

definitional knowledge, electrical circuits simulation, 186,
     187–188, 191
derived measures, as data type, 83
description approach, data analysis, 87
discipline-based models, in experimental design, 86
discovery learning. *See* scientific discovery learning
discrimination networks, EPAM theory
   overview, 108–110
   order effects, 111–115, 116*f*
   pseudocode, 117
discrimination skills, in hierarchical task analysis,
     24–25
disjuncts per lesson
   multiplication skill experiments, 9, 171–178
   traditional perspectives, 169–171
distributed spacing. *See* spacing effects, paired-associate
     learning
domain-dependent skills, defined, 24
domain expertise
   in Elaboration Theory, 29, 31–32, 35, 37
   order effects generally, 12
   and process models, 219
   reversal effect, 218, 223
   See also problem solving, order effects
domain-independent skills, defined, 24

Einstellung, 62
elaborating, in Simplifying Conditions Method, 33
Elaboration Theory of Instruction, 7, 29, 31–37
electrical circuits simulation, 9, 183, 185–191
emotion effects, information-processing, 63
empirical risk minimization principle, 44
EPAM theory
   overview, 8, 10, 108–111
   instruction relevance, 114–116
   order effects, 78, 111–116, 221
   projects/problems, 116
   pseudocode, 117
   training routines, 117
error outcomes
   complex nature, 226
   as data type, 83
   in HS model, 154–158
   knowledge effects, 152–153, 222
   models compared, 10–11
   in neural networks, 46–47, 59, 76
   in supervised learning, 43–44
evaluation, in instructional systems design,
     19–20, 21
evolution, as natural information-processing system,
     215, 216, 217
example-based approach, cognitive skill acquisition
   overview, 8, 95, 220–221
   instructional model for, 102–103
   learning processes, 96–99, 218, 222
   order effects, 99–102
   projects/problems, 103–104
   theoretical background, 95–96
expertise reversal effects, 218, 223

explanations
    in electrical circuits simulation, 185–186, 189
    in example-based approach, 97–99, 100, 102
extraneous cognitive load, 217–218, 223
eye-movement, as data type, 84

fading effect, in example-based approach, 95, 97, 100,
        102, 220–221
    See also reversal effect
FAILSAFE system, 157
familiarization process, in discrimination networks, 110
fatigue effects, information processing, 63
feature extraction process, EPAM theory, overview,
        108–109
features, in learning algorithms, 72
felicity conditions conjecture
    described, 9, 170, 171
    in disjuncts per lesson experiment, 175–178
flowchart, procedural task analysis, 30f
forgetting
    in ACT-R model, 140–141, 142, 143
    in all-or-none theory, 142
    in EPAM model, 111, 112
    in neural networks, 47
    in paired-associate learning, 138–139, 148
    prediction factors, 61–62
    See also memory processes
formal process models, advantages, 58

generality, in hypothesis search, 45
genesis principle, 216, 221
genomes in evolution comparison, 216, 217
germane cognitive load, 217, 223
gradient descent techniques, 45, 46–47
granularity of data, collection issues, 82
guidance fading effect, 218, 220, 223

heuristic rule skills, in hierarchical task analysis, 26
heuristic tasks, in Simplifying Conditions Method, 33–34,
        35f
hidden units, in simple recurrent networks, 75–76
hierarchical representations, in EPAM theory, 109, 115–116
hierarchical sequences
    analysis process, 24–27
    with elaboration sequences, 36
    with procedural sequences, 28–29
    relationship basis, 23
    selection considerations, 28
    Simplifying Conditions Method compared, 33–34, 34f
hierarchical task analysis
    defined concepts in, 25, 26
    identifying skills, 25
    use, 24
higher-order rules, in hierarchical task analysis, 26
high-level features, EPAM theory, 108–109
historical sequence, relationship basis, 23
HS computer model, constraint-based learning
    counting task experiments, 10, 154–164
    operations in, 153–158

hybrid measures, as data type, 83
hypertext, as experiment design, 86
hypothesis search, in machine learning, 44–46, 48,
        50–53

images, in EPAM theory, 109–110, 113
incremental learning
    ACT-R model, 139–141
    in all-or-none models, 141–142
    decision trees, 47–48
    neural networks, 46–47
    paired-associate memory tasks, 138
    See also machine learning
inductive concept learning, 44–46, 48
information storage, in natural information-processing
        systems, 215–216
input activation, in simple recurrent networks, 75–76
input layers, in ART networks, 72f, 73
input links, in neural networks, 46, 71, 72f
input matches, in ART networks, 73–75
instance-level order effects, in paired-associate learning,
        138–139
instances, in learning algorithms, 72
instructional explanations, in example-based
        approach, 98–99, 102
instructional procedures, in cognitive load theory, 217
instructional systems design (ISD)
    overview, 19–23, 37–38
    analysis in, 19–20
    and cognitive load theory framework, 218–219
    content decisions, 20, 21–23, 37–39
    Elaboration Theory approach, 29, 31–37
    hierarchical sequence strategy, 24–28
    procedural sequence strategy, 28–29, 30f
    projects/problems, 38–39
instrumented browsers, as experiment design, 86
interacting element effects, 217–218, 219
interaction patterns, as data type, 83
interest problems, in problem solving experiments, 198–199
intermediate phase, cognitive skill acquistion, 96, 97
intervention decisions, in instructional systems
        design, 19–20
intrinsic cognitive load, 217–218, 223
intuitive knowledge (what-if, prediction knowledge)
    electrical circuits simulation, 186–187, 188–191
    simulation program potentials, 184–185
ISD. See instructional systems design (ISD)
isolated element effects, 217–218, 219

keystroke loggers, for experiments, 86
Kibur's game, 41–42
knowledge-rich problems. See problem solving,
        order effects
KRT tool, 120

language learning, 76–77, 183
late phase, cognitive skill acquistion, 96, 97
learner control effects, problem-solving experiments, 204,
        205–207, 209–210

learning curves, as data type, 83
letter recognition, adaptive resonance theory, 73–74
lights-buttons task, as process model example, 60–61, 63–65
links
    in ART networks, 72f, 73
    between related models of day-night cycle, 126–128
    in EPAM theory, 109–110, 112
    in neural networks, 59, 62, 71, 75–76
Logic Theorist, 196
long-term memory
    EPAM theory, 108–109
    in natural information-processing systems, 215–216, 217
    in production systems framework, 58
loss function, in supervised learning, 44
low-level perception process, EPAM theory, 108–109

machine learning
    overview, 53–54, 219
    control parameter space, 48–53
    developments in, 42–43
    hypothesis space, 44–46, 48, 50–53
    projects/problems, 54–55
    sequencing effects, 48–53
    supervised type, 43–45
    theory limitations, 45–46, 225–226
machine learning algorithms, as data type, 85
massed spacing. See spacing effects, paired-associate
        learning
maximum likelihood principle, 44
means-ends-analysis strategy, 97
memory processes
    ACT-R model, 139–141
    and cognitive load theory framework, 218–224
    and cognitive overload, 62–63
    EPAM theory, 108–109
    in natural information-processing systems, 215–216,
        217–218
    in production systems framework, 58
    in recurrent neural networks, 58–59
    stress influences, 13
    See also forgetting
microgenetic approach, data analysis, 87
model progression
    in day/night cycle, 128–130
    electrical circuits simulation, 185–186, 189–191
    in scientific discovery learning, 182–184
mood effects, information processing, 63
motion problems, in problem solving experiments,
        198–199
motivation effects, 63, 226
mouse-movements, as data type, 84
multiple-strand sequencing
    in Elaboration Theory, 31–32, 35
    disjunctively related subprocedures, 171–178

natural information-processing systems, 215–219
    See also cognitive load theory
nearest neighbor technique, in hypothesis search, 45
near miss, in W system, 107

near-miss hypothesis, problem solving experiment,
        198–199, 201–204
neural networks
    overview, 46–47, 71–72, 219–220
    ACT-R model, 59, 62, 139–144
    adaptive resonance theory, 72–75
    recurrent types, 7, 58–59, 75–78, 220
nodes
    in discrimination networks, 109–110, 112, 113, 116f
    in recurrent neural networks, 58–59, 62

observation, as experiment design, 86
one-disjunct-per-lesson. See disjuncts per lesson
one-one mapping principle, in counting, 158
on-line learning, empirical findings, 46–48
optimization algorithm
    ACT-R model, 143–144, 144f
    and paired-word experiment, 145–148
    See also spacing effects entries
ordered counting tasks, in HS model experiments, 158
order effects, overview, 4–5, 10–14, 218–227
    suggestions for instructional design, 12, 13
    See also specific topics, e.g., EPAM theory; instructional
        systems design; scientific discovery learning
output activation, in simple recurrent networks, 76
output comparisons, in simple recurrent networks, 76
output links, in neural networks, 46, 71, 72f
outputs, in supervised learning, 43–44

paired-associate learning
    ACT-R model, 139–144, 221–222
    EPAM model, 111–112
    spacing effects experiment, 8–9, 137–139, 144–149,
        221–222
    transfer effects experiment, 222
partial systemic approach, intervention decisions, 19–20
part-task completion, as data type, 83
PATHS curriculum, 39n4
perception processes, EPAM theory, 108–109
performance differences, as data type, 83
performance relationships, in sequence decisions, 23
plasticity-stability dimension, adaptive resonance theory,
        72–75, 78
positive reinforcement, 152
practical knowledge effect, 152–153
practice spacing. See spacing effects, paired-associate
        learning
prerequisite skills
    in hierarchical task analysis, 24–27
    in procedural task analysis, 28–29
presentation order, in problem-solving experiment,
        205–207, 223–224
prior knowledge effects. See example-based approach,
        cognitive skill acquisition; problem solving, order
        effects
problem solving
    and domain expertise, 96–97, 219
    error effects, 222
    in hierarchical task analysis, 26

and *Einstellung* factor, 62
randomness principle, 218
problem solving, example-based approach
  and explanations, 97–99
  learning stages compared, 96–97
  order effects, 99–102, 220–221
problem solving, order effects
  overview, 9–10, 207–210, 223–224
  in example-based approach, 99–102, 220–221
  experiment designs, 198–199, 201, 202–203, 205
  hypotheses, 199–201
  learner control effects, 204, 205–207
  model of, 196–198
  participant beliefs, 204–205
  performance comparisons, 201–202, 203–204, 206–207
  projects, 210
  traditional perspectives, 195–196, 206
procedural rule skills, in hierarchical task analysis, 26
procedural sequences, analysis process, 23, 28–29, 30*f*, 36
procedural tasks, in Simplifying Conditions Method, 33,
  34–35
  See also disjuncts per lesson
process models
  overview, 7, 57–59, 219
  abstract approaches, 64–65
  development guidelines, 66–67
  as experimental design, 87–88
  lights/button example, 60–61
  prediction factors, 61–64
  projects/problems, 66
  See also, chapters in Part II
production systems, as process model, 58
protocol data, and theoretical frameworks, 84
psychological factors, and information processing, 63

qualitative measures, as data type, 83–84
quantitative measures, as data type, 83

randomness principle
  in natural information-processing systems, 216–217
  and problem solving, 218
  scientific discovery learning, 221, 222–223
reaction times, as data type, 83
recurrent neural networks, as process model, 7, 58–59, 62
redundancy effect, 218
regression task, in supervised learning, 43
regular traversal principle, in counting, 158
reinforcement learning, 51
relevance criterion, in HS model, 154–157
reorganizing principle, borrowing and, 216, 218, 221,
  222–223
resonance, in ART networks, 73–74
retrieval, in all-or-none theory, 142
reversal effect, 63, 97, 218, 220, 223
revision process
  in counting task experiments, 158–164
  in HS model operations, 155–157
rule skills, in hierarchical task analysis, 25–26
running models, guidelines, 89–90

same task-different order, as experimental design, 85–86
satisfaction criterion, in HS model, 154–157
scientific discovery learning
  overview, 8, 119–121, 181–182, 191, 221, 222–223
  knowledge test results, 187–190
  learner action measures, 189–190
  model progression approach, 182–183
  projects/problems, 191–192
  sequence control debate, 183–184
  simulation design, 185–187
  simulation program potentials, 184–185
  See also day/night cycle, children's explanations
SCM (Simplifying Conditions Method), 31, 33–35, 36–37
scope decisions, in instructional systems design, 20, 21–23,
  37–39
score results, as data type, 83
selection decisions, in instructional systems design, 20–21
self-explanation, in example-based approach, 97–98, 100, 102
sequence decisions, in instructional systems design
  overview, 20, 21, 22*f*, 23–24, 37–39
  elaboration types, 31–37
  hierarchical type, 24–28
  procedural type, 28–29, 30*f*
sequential data, collection issues, 82
seriality assumptions, EPAM theory, 108–109
serial position effect, EPAM model, 111–112
short-term memory
  EPAM theory, 108–109
  in production systems framework, 58
simple quantitative measures, as data type, 83
simple recurrent networks (SRN), 75–78, 220
simple-to-complex training
  in simple recurrent networks, 77
  traditional approaches, 196
Simplifying Conditions Method (SCM), 31, 33–35, 36–37
"simplifying conditions" sequence, relationship basis, 23
skill prerequisites, in hierarchical task analysis, 24–27
skill relationships, in sequence decisions, 23
skip-zero trick, in disjuncts per lesson experiments, 171–178
Soar, 59, 61, 62
spacing effects, in ACT-R model, 139–144
spacing effects, paired-associate learning
  overview, 8–9, 137–138, 148, 221–222
  experiment design and results, 144–149
  order effects, 138–139
  projects/problems, 148
specialization, in hypothesis search, 45
spiral sequencing, relationship basis, 23*f*, 24
SRNs (simple recurrent networks), 75–78, 220
STAHL system, 119
stimuli order, in EPAM theory, 111, 112–113, 114–116
strategy decisions, in instructional systems design, 21
stress effects, 13
structure-blocked sequence, in problem solving experiments
  overview, 208–209, 223
  design, 198–199
  hypotheses, 199–201
  performance comparisons, 201–204
  theoretical background, 196

subject-domain expertise, in Elaboration Theory, 29, 31
subprocedures, disjunctively related. *See* disjuncts per lesson
subtraction learning experiments, 10, 84, 171, 175, 177
suitable presentation order, in problem-solving experiment, 205–207, 223–224
supervised learning, 43–45, 76, 107–108
surface-blocked sequence, in problem solving experiments
    overview, 208, 223
    design, 198–199
    hypotheses, 199–201
    performance comparisons, 201–204
    theoretical background, 196
surveys, as experiment design, 86–87
synthesis, in instructional systems design, 19–20

tacit knowledge, defined, 26
tactical decisions, in instructional systems design, 21
targeted counting tasks, HS model experiments, 158–164
task completion, as data type, 83
task expertise, in Elaboration Theory, 29, 31–37
task order variation, as experimental design, 85–86
teachability, 52–53
teaching sequence, as experimental design, 86
theoretical elaboration sequence, 35–36, 37
theoretical expertise, in Elaboration Theory, 31, 32f
theoretical frameworks and protocol data, 84
theory evolution, in scientific discovery, 119–120
    See also day/night cycle, children's explanations
time, as data type, 83

time constraints, and information processing, 63–64
topical sequencing, relationship basis, 23–24
total systemic approach, intervention decisions, 20
transfer effects
    constraint-based learning theory, 159–161, 162–164, 222
    variability effects, 223
transfer hypothesis, problem solving experiment, 198–204
triangle examples, in hierarchical task analysis, 25
tutoring situations. *See* disjuncts per lesson

unsupervised learning, 47–48, 107, 108
    See also EPAM theory

Van Restorff effect, 111–112
variability effects, overview, 223–224
    See also disjuncts per lesson
verbal protocols, as data type, 84

water jug puzzles example, 62
what-if-tests, electrical circuit simulations, 186–187, 188–190
worked-out examples. *See* example-based approach, cognitive skill acquisition
working memory, and cognitive load theory, 218–219
    See also memory processes
work-rate problems, in problem solving experiments, 198–199
W system, 107

zone of proximal change, 152
zone of proximal development, 31, 152